Sporting News
BOOKS

presents

Pro Football's

HEROES
of the HALL

SportingNews
BOOKS

presents

Pro Football's

HEROES
of the HALL

PHOTO CREDITS

T = Top   B = Bottom   L = Left   R = Right   C = Center

CONTRIBUTING PHOTOGRAPHERS

The Sporting News Archives: Cover L (Joe Montana), Cover R (Jim Brown), Cover R (Joe Greene), 11, 12T, 12B, 18, 19, 21, 22-23, 26, 27, 28, 31, 32-33, 35, 38, 39, 40, 44, 45, 57, 66, 71, 72, 73, 74, 75, 80, 81, 86, 87, 88, 89, 94, 95, 96, 97, 99, 101, 102, 103, 104, 105, 107, 108, 112, 113, 115, 116, 117, 118, 119, 120, 122, 123, 130, 132BL, 132BR, 133BL, 133BR, 137, 145, 150, 154, 155, 156, 157, 158, 163, 165, 166, 167, 168, 174, 177, 180, 181, 182, 183, 188, 189, 192, 193, 195, 196, 197, 202, 203, 204, 205, 206, 207, 208, 209, 216, 217, 222, 226, 227, 229, 230, 231, 232, 233, 237, 238, 243, 248, 249, 250, 251, 260, 261, 265, 271, 278, 282, 286, 287, 288, 289, 291, 296, 299, 300, 302, 303, 308, 314, 319, 338, 339, 350, 351, 353, 354, 355, 357, 359, 364, 365, 367, 368, 369, 370, 371, 374, 375, 378, 379, 390, 391

Malcolm W. Emmons: Cover L (Ray Nitschke) Cover L (Johnny Unitas), Cover R (Roger Staubach), 20, 24, 25, 29, 36, 37, 42, 48, 49, 50, 58, 59, 62, 63, 64, 65, 78, 79, 82, 83, 84, 85, 92, 93, 110, 111, 124, 125, 128, 129, 134, 135, 140, 141, 162, 172, 173, 176, 178, 179, 184, 187, 190, 191, 198, 199, 210, 211, 221, 246, 262, 263, 268, 269, 274, 275, 276, 277, 279, 280, 284, 285, 294, 295, 304, 305, 316, 317, 318, 326, 327, 328-329, 330, 331, 333, 336, 340, 341, 344, 345, 346, 347, 348, 349, 360, 361, 362, 363, 372, 373, 376, 377, 380, 381, 396, 397

AP/Wide World Photos: 2-3, 8, 9, 10, 13, 14, 15B, 16-17, 30, 34, 41, 67, 76, 77, 100, 109, 114, 151, 152, 153, 186, 201, 224, 228, 234, 236, 239, 240, 241, 245, 253, 254-255, 264, 266, 267, 270, 272, 273, 281, 297, 298, 301, 306, 307, 311, 315, 332, 337, 352, 358, 385

Lew Portnoy: 60, 61, 90, 91, 212, 213, 225, 309, 312, 313, 322, 323, 334, 335, 342-343, 386, 387, 388, 389, 394, 395

Getty Images: 136, 200, 218, 219, 220, 257, 258, 259, 320, 321, 324, 325

Vernon Biever: 126, 127, 146, 147, 214, 215, 252, 310, 392, 393

NFL Photos: 70, 98, 131, 144, 148, 185, 223, 290, 356

Bettman/CORBIS: 15T, 159, 169, 194, 382, 383

Tony Tomsic: 43, 51, 52, 53, 139, 171, 283

Tony Tomsic/SportsChrome: 68, 69, 170, 292, 293

Stiller-Lefebvre Collection: 149, 160, 161, 242, 244

Bruce Bennett Studios: 55, 56, 164, 235, 366

Harry Frye: 46, 47

Icon Sports: 143, 256

Ron Wyatt/SportsChrome: 138

Diamond Images: 384

Robert Walker: 247

Chicago Tribune: 175

Cleveland Press Collection, Cleveland University: 121

John Cordes: Cover C (Walter Payton)

ISBN: 0-89204-712-7   10 9 8 7 6 5 4 3 2 1

ACKNOWLEDGEMENTS

The execution of a book is like the effort of any successful sports team — dedicated people working together in the never-ending pursuit of excellence. Much of the work on this volume — gathering hundreds of photographs, enhancing old images, designing pages, editing copy and reading proofs — was done behind the scenes by members of *The Sporting News* staff who quietly contributed their graphic and artistic magic in addition to performing their weekly obligations.

The book's concept, a natural extension of the baseball *Heroes of the Hall* volume published by TSN in 2002, came from editorial director Steve Meyerhoff, whose leadership keeps the book department on course. Special thanks to Dave Sloan, who jumped in to provide invaluable editing and proofreading help, and August Miller, who gathered the outstanding photographs that give personality to the 221 featured members of the Pro Football Hall of Fame.

The design strategy, which brings the pages to life, was coordinated by prepress director Bob Parajon and executed by Matt Kindt and Christen Sager. The job of making more than 400 photographs look great was a team effort by prepress specialists Dave Brickey, Steve Romer, Pamela Speh and Vern Kasal.

The statistical source for this project was *Total Football* and the display quotes were obtained from old issues of *The Sporting News* as well as newspapers, magazines and books from TSN's archives and massive clip files.

CONTENTS

FOREWORD
by Dan Dierdorf

The Pro Football Hall of Fame is a tremendous source of pride for everyone in Canton. I think that's true even to the casual observer. For someone who really loved the game of football, imagine how intoxicating it was to have this magic place and its incredible aura so close. I said in 1996 when I was inducted that I was joining a large group of people in that Hall of Fame, but there's nobody who could have appreciated the honor more than I.

Just in the sense that I grew up a mile from the Hall. I remember standing there with my father. We watched Pete Rozelle turn a spade full of dirt to start construction of the Hall of Fame and I went to every enshrinement, every Hall of Fame game until I went into the NFL. I would ride my bike down there and hang out while it was being built. I remember standing outside the locker rooms when the teams would come out to play the game.

I am the only member of the Hall of Fame that on the morning of the induction, if I would have chosen to do so, could have slept in my own bed and gotten up and walked to the Hall of Fame in about 15 minutes. The house where I grew up still sits right there. My mother still lives there.

I can still remember that first induction ceremony in 1963. I was 14 years old and the crowd seemed awfully big to me. I couldn't accurately guess how many were there, but it seemed like all of Canton. It was such a festive occasion. The Hall of Fame in Canton doesn't sit in a perfect, postcard location like Cooperstown, but for a love of the Hall, for a love of the men who are in it, no community anywhere could be more of a home than Canton is to the Pro Football Hall of Fame.

But making it there as a player was never in my thoughts. Some dreams are just too big. You have to understand that when I grew up, where I grew up in Ohio, high school football was just huge. And the Browns were my team. These were the late '50s and '60s and we held professional football players in a different light than we do today.

I view myself as really fortunate playing when I did. I was a rookie with the St. Louis Cardinals in 1971 and that meant that in my first couple of years I had the

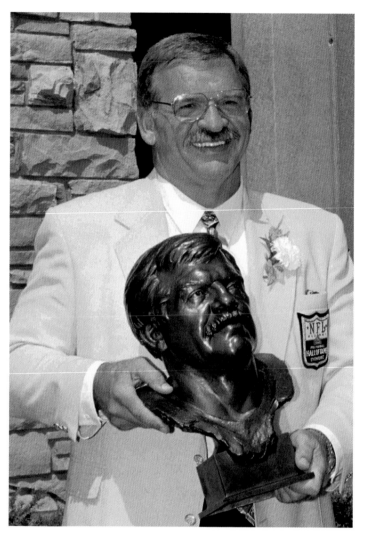

To finally join such an elite group was the culmination of a life's work. And there I was in 1996, in front of my friends and family in my home town. The high school band leading my car down the street during the Saturday morning parade was from my high school. And carrying the banner that stretched all the way across the street was my high school football team, including the sons of three or four of my best friends growing up.

I was sitting there with tears in my eyes, even before the parade started. There were so many people there for me. They had set up bleachers over on the side and there were several hundred people over there from my high school. And I looked out in the audience and there was my high school English teacher and my high school coach and all of my teammates. It was the first time I got to see what the view was from the steps — and it was mind-boggling.

I can't imagine any Hall of Famer who isn't — and you stretch for words like humble, appreciative, cognizant of what it really means. But the reality is, how many millions of young men in this country have ever walked on a football field, at any level, and you take that enormous base of millions and millions of young men over the last 80 years and put it into that funnel. Out of the bottom drops, what, 220?

And you say, 'How can anybody be so fortunate? How can anybody be that lucky?' I remember saying to myself, 'If I was ever elected to the Hall of Fame, I don't see how I could ever want or covet anything the rest of my life.' And you know what, that was the truth. It really was. It is such an affirmation of your achievements. Granted, it was a game. But being recognized at that level, there is nothing left to do.

"I have no more mountains to climb."

Dan Dierdorf

opportunity to play with and against the men who, in my mind, really built the game of pro football. I so admired the men who played in the '50s and '60s — especially the '60s, what I thought was the golden age of pro football — and I had a chance to compete against Dick Butkus, Deacon Jones, Bob Lilly and Merlin Olsen and I saw Sonny Jurgensen and Willie Lanier and Buck Buchanan and Ray Nitschke. I lined up and went toe to toe with these guys. And I'll be forever appreciative of that.

These men, to me, were larger than life. I was mesmerized by them. I still can't get over the thrill of lining up and looking across the ball and seeing Bob Lilly. I just wish I would have been a little less thrilled and a little more able to block him.

Among the 17 inductees in the first Hall of Fame class in 1963 were (front row, left to right) Dutch Clark, Curly Lambeau, Mel Hein, John McNally (Blood), Don Hutson; (back row) Sammy Baugh, Cal Hubbard, Bronko Nagurski, George Halas, Red Grange and Ernie Nevers. Former Buffalo quarterback Jim Kelly (opposite page) was a featured attraction 40 years later.

OVERVIEW

HEROES OF THE HALL

They are yesterday's icons, battered and bruised reminders of the National Football League's long, bumpy road to prosperity. Some are but grainy, leather-helmeted warriors from a distant time; others are locked firmly into memory, freeze-frame heroes of the heart. All are men who achieved distinction, athletes, coaches and game-shaping pioneers whose deeds have been passed with enthusiastic exaggeration from generation to generation.

Mention the words "Hall of Fame" and your mind is flooded with images of The Galloping Ghost, Bronko, Papa Bear, Slinging Sammy, Johnny U., the Fearsome Foursome, Juice, Bambi, Broadway Joe and L.T. Discussions of "immortality" begin with a Vince Lombardi roar, a Dick Butkus shot to the ribs or a Terry Bradshaw touchdown bomb.

It's a world where everybody has exceeded even the most lofty of expectations while molding and shaping a football sideshow into a fan-friendly, multi-million dollar spectacular. It's a place of the soul, occupied by dedicated and special people who dared to dream and backed up their vision with sweat and unyielding passion.

The Hall of Fame is equal parts concept and physical reality. The first exists in our hearts and memories; the second in a football-crazy midwest community where the professional game took root in 1920 and has been memorialized for four decades by a nostalgic and memory-sustaining Hall of Fame museum. But beyond the Canton, Ohio, busts, behind the highlight-reel reminders and memento-enhanced testimonials, are fascinating stories of everyday people, future farmers, coal miners, businessmen, bankers and teachers who were lured to loftier pursuits by their superior strength, incredible athletic abilities and intense will to succeed.

Off the field, Ray Nitschke was a balding, conservatively-

dressed businessman with horn-rimmed glasses; on the field he was a snarling, fire-breathing middle linebacker for Lombardi's Green Bay Packers. Tommy McDonald, a hyper 5-foot-9 jitterbug, was a pass-catching giant who won the everlasting affection of young Philadelphia fans. Raymond Berry more closely resembled a college professor than a wide receiver; stoop-shouldered Johnny Unitas looked anything but athletic; George Blanda was a limited-skill athlete who amazed critics and fans for an incredible 26 years.

Many went on to secondary fame in non-football-driven careers. Dan Fortmann, a Phi Beta Kappa from Colgate University, became a doctor after leaving the Chicago Bears. Former Viking Alan Page earned a law degree and

Induction ceremonies, staged for years outside the Hall's main building (below), were moved in 2002 to Fawcett Stadium (right). The Jim Thorpe statue (above) greets visitors to the Canton shrine.

became assistant Attorney General in Minnesota and an associate justice on the Minnesota Supreme Court. Nick Buoniconti went on to become an assistant district attorney, Steve Largent served as a U.S. Representative from Oklahoma and enigmatic, fun-loving Johnny "Blood" McNally settled down and taught economics and history at St. John's College in Minnesota.

These are stories of football builders and players who overcame wars, a depression, the technological revolution, civil rights battles, labor strife and other social barriers to challenge baseball for American affection. They are reminders of childhood and happy times, barometers for loyalty and success and living proof that wonderful things are sometimes wrapped in brown paper wrappers.

"Baseball is America's pastime," said longtime Raiders defensive end Howie Long in his 2000 Hall of Fame induction speech, "but football is America's passion."

That might not have been the case in 1961, when the still-struggling NFL designated Canton as the official Pro Football Hall of Fame site, and 16 months later, when

ground was broken on a wooded parkland area donated by the city. When the Hall's 17-member charter class was inducted at dedication ceremonies on September 7, 1963, the museum consisted of two buildings, one topped by a 52-foot, football-shaped dome that endures as the Hall's signature feature.

The original Hall of Fame weekend was a grand event focusing on such pro football heavyweights as George Halas, Jim Thorpe, Red Grange, Don Hutson, Curly Lambeau, Mel Hein and Bronko Nagurski. Festivities included a parade, luncheon, the induction ceremonies and the first Hall of Fame exhibition game, played across the street from the Hall at 23,000-seat Fawcett Stadium.

Four decades and more than 6 million visitors later, Hall of Fame weekend has blossomed into an 11-day, late-summer civic festival, complete with a queen pageant, a fashion show, a golf tournament, hot air balloons, road races, fireworks displays, an interactive theme park, dinners and a civic banquet honoring the enshrinees, a parade that draws 200,000 spectators and the AFC-NFC exhibition game.

Museum visitors enter a timeless world that showcases

Joe Namath (right), the man who put the American Football League on the map when he led the New York Jets to a startling Super Bowl III upset of Baltimore, was the center of attention in 1985, along with presenter Larry Bruno (left).

The Hall of Fame Selection Process

The Hall of Fame board of selectors, like the museum that houses the professional game's artifacts and memories, has grown significantly since the first election in 1963. The charter member group of 17 players, coaches and contributors was selected by a 14-man committee representing each city in the National Football League.

Today's 39-member board is made up of one media representative from each NFL city (two from New York), one representative of the Pro Football Writers Association of America and six at-large delegates, all of them writers or reporters from national publications, the Associated Press and major cities (Los Angeles) without an NFL team.

Nominations are made by fans who write to the Pro Football Hall of Fame, committee members and anyone else desiring input into the open process. The nominations are culled into a preliminary list of about 60 candidates and the board of selectors, through mail ballots, trims that list to a 15-man roster that will get final consideration at an election meeting during Super Bowl week.

From that final roster, which includes one pre-1978 nomination from a nine-man Seniors Committee, the new induction class is chosen. New electees must obtain at least 80 percent approval from board members at the meeting and current ground rules stipulate that at least four and no more than seven new Hall of Famers will be chosen in a given year.

Former players must be retired for at least five years before they are eligible for election. Coaches simply must be retired and other contributors can be elected any time.

professional football's past, now spread over a five-building complex that has more than quadrupled from its original 19,000 square feet to 83,000. It's safe to say the growth of the Hall of Fame has mirrored the sport it represents, a point driven home by its timeless displays — an exhibition rotunda that recounts the game's history, an art gallery, research library, the twin enshrinement halls, a mementos room, an NFL Films theater, a Super Bowl room and a turntable theater dubbed GameDay Stadium.

But the bottom-line focus for the annual festivities remains the Hall of Famers, old and new. Hundreds of thousands of fans descend on Canton to rub elbows with the stars, who in turn enjoy the opportunity to relive past glories while honoring the newest members of their elite fraternity. The rush of pride never wears thin. The accolades flow and exaggerations grow.

"The longer I'm away from the game, the better I get," said a smiling Hein before his 1963 induction. "It thrills me to think how good I'll be a hundred years from now."

Hall of Fame weekend is indeed a welcome spotlight for players whose talents and exploits are magnified by the passing of time. It also is a time for reflection and humility, both of which were displayed by former Vikings coach Bud Grant in his 1994 induction speech.

"My father," said Grant, "told me a long time ago, 'If you are ever asked to speak at such an auspicious occasion with so many great speakers, make sure you stand up good and tall so they all can see you and talk good and loud so they all can hear you, make a short speech so they all will listen to you, and then sit down so they all will like you.'"

Transcripts of the Hall of Fame's 221 induction speeches are filled with such humility, emotion, passion and intensity — the same qualities the inductees displayed routinely during their fabled careers. Enshrinement at Canton is the ultimate honor, an exclamation point for deeds well done. Nobody more elegantly expressed his sense of football closure than former Green Bay star Clarke Hinkle in his short-but-elequent three-line induction speech in 1964.

"Bronko, I am proud to sit in the Hall of Fame with you," Hinkle said. "Today I feel like the boy who has climbed the highest tree in the woods and conquered the forest. What else is there?"

Coaching great Paul Brown (right, bottom photo) was presented by fellow Hall of Famer and former protege Otto Graham in 1967. The 1979 Hall of Fame class included (left to right, top photo) Dick Butkus, Yale Lary, Ron Mix and Johnny Unitas.

HERB ADDERLEY

Born: 6-8-39, Philadelphia, Pa. **Ht/Wt:** 6-0/205 **College:** Michigan State **Drafted:** 1961, 1st round, Packers **Primary position:** DB
Career statistics: Interceptions, 48, 7 TDs; KO Returns, 120 att., 25.7 avg., 2 TDs **Teams:** Packers 1961-69; Cowboys 1970-72
Championship teams: NFL 1961, '62, '65, '66, '67 **Super Bowl champions:** 1966, '67, '71 seasons **Honors:** 1960s All-Decade Team

The longest route to the Green Bay end zone was through the left side of the defense. If big end Willie Davis didn't get you, cornerback Herb Adderley would. When offensive coordinators designed game plans against Vince Lombardi's Packers, it was pretty obvious where most of the plays would be headed. And it was a pretty good bet the team's top receiver would not be much of a factor.

The 6-foot, 205-pound Adderley had only himself to blame for his sometimes-diminished role. He was a former Michigan State running back who blossomed into the NFL's consummate one-on-one coverage corner, the guy who could take a big-play receiver out of the offense. Teams that tried to run around Adderley's end also were frustrated by an aggressive, physical tackler who seldom missed his target.

Adderley's style was not immediately embraced by his two professional coaches—Lombardi from 1961-69 and Dallas' Tom Landry from 1970-72. He liked to play off the receiver and use his speed to attack the ball. He was quick, instinctive and smart, a gambler who could go for the big play. Adderley seldom dropped a ball and was dangerous and creative on returns—both with interceptions and kickoffs.

> "When people leave the stadium, I want them to say they've just watched one of the best cornerbacks they've ever seen in their lives."
>
> —*Herb Adderley*

Seldom did he make a mistake, which only added to the luster of his 48 career interceptions and 21.8-yard return average on pick-offs. It's no coincidence the confident, easy-to-like Adderley was a starter for two of the premier defenses of his era. First he helped the Packers win five championships (and the first two Super Bowls) in a seven-year span. Then, working in a cornerback tandem with Mel Renfro, he helped the Cowboys reach two Super Bowls and claim one title in three years.

Adderley's signature moment came in Super Bowl II when he returned an interception 60 yards for a touchdown against the Oakland Raiders. The durable Philadelphian was a five-time Pro Bowl selection who missed only three games in his first 11 seasons.

GEORGE ALLEN

Born: 4-29-18, Detroit, Mich. **Died:** 12-31-90 **Teams coached (116-47-5 RS, 2-7 PS):** Rams 1966-70; Redskins 1971-77

George Allen was obsessed. His addiction was football, specifically the detail, creativity, intensity, psychology and "us against them" motivation that results in winning—his ultimate life ambition. It was a goal Allen achieved without fail over 12 NFL seasons as the always controversial, sometimes vilified coach of the Los Angeles Rams and Washington Redskins.

"The future is now," Allen liked to say and he backed up that philosophy by turning around two of the NFL's moribund franchises. He wheeled and dealed, trading draft picks for aging veterans, signing discarded free agents and motivating his Rams to consecutive records of 8-6, 11-1-2, 10-3-1, 11-3 and 9-4-1—after a 4-10 flop in 1965 under Harland Svare. When he took control of a Redskins franchise that had produced four winning seasons in 25 years, his 1971 debut ended 9-4-1 and his second team advanced to the Super Bowl (losing to Miami) after an 11-3 regular season.

Such was Allen's motivational ability that he made every game seem like the most important event in a player's life. And such was his

> ## "George Allen is an amazing man. This is an amazing team. I would do anything for either of them."
>
> — *Pat Fischer, Redskins cornerback, 1972*

innovative genius that he armed his "Over the Hill Gangs" with never-before-seen weapons—nickel and dime defensive coverages and dangerous special teams that were tutored by the NFL's first special teams coach.

Allen, who gained prominence as defensive coach for George Halas' Chicago Bears from 1958-65, was a paranoid motivator whose anything-for-an-edge tactics did not always sit well with employers. A five-year feud with Rams owner Dan Reeves ended with his firing in 1969. Redskins owner Edward Bennett Williams fired him in 1977. Rehired by new Rams owner Carroll Rosenbloom in 1978, Allen was sacked after two exhibition games and ended his NFL career with a 116-47-5 regular-season record.

The eccentric, workaholic ice cream lover did coach again—in the short-lived United States Football League and in 1990, when he resurfaced as the 72-year-old coach at Long Beach State. The longtime friend of U.S. presidents Richard Nixon and Ronald Reagan died later that year.

MARCUS ALLEN

Born: 3-26-60, San Diego, Calif. **Ht/Wt:** 6-2/210 **College:** USC **Drafted:** 1982, 1st round, Raiders **Primary position:** RB
Career statistics: Rushing, 3,022 att., 12,243 yds., 123 TDs; Receiving, 587 rec., 5,411 yds., 21 TDs; Passing, 12-of-27, 6 TDs **Rushing champion:** 1985 **Scoring champion:** 1982 **Teams:** Raiders 1982-92; Chiefs 1993-97 **Super Bowl champion:** 1983 season (MVP)

"Cerebral player with modest speed, ordinary body and intuitive moves"—the scouting report on Marcus Allen was enough to put any defender to sleep. Then the real Allen would go off like an alarm clock, a sound that exhilarated Los Angeles and Kansas City fans for 16 NFL seasons. He was the classic overachiever, the man who could make you scratch your head when final numbers were added up—numbers that supported his claim as one of the great running backs in football history.

The 6-foot-2, 210-pound former USC Heisman Trophy winner (1981) was a sometimes-elusive, sometimes-overpowering runner who seemed to flow through the line, slashing and angling his body through crevices that only he could see. His timing was impeccable, as was his ability to read blocks and make the perfect cut to daylight. Once through a hole, his great vision allowed him to avoid potential pursuit avenues.

The key was a football intelligence and understanding that allowed Allen to elevate his physical talents. He knew the job of every player on offense, he could consistently outthink opponents and he was consumed with the idea of getting

ALLEN

the maximum out of his abilities. He also was versatile, a first-rate runner, blocker, pass-catcher and master of the halfback pass.

Most of all, the quietly charismatic Allen was clutch, the man who could always deliver the first down and points in

> "When I reflect back on all the players I have seen play the game, both as a player and as a coach, I don't think I've ever seen a better football player than Marcus Allen. ... He is a guy who, down after down, game after game, runs, blocks, catches, subordinates his own self interest to the best interest of the team."
>
> —*Marty Schottenheimer, 2003, The Kansas City Star*

the red zone. Over 11 seasons with the Raiders and five with the Chiefs, he became football's first 10,000/5,000 man (12,243 rushing yards, 5,411 in the air) and scored 145 touchdowns, third behind Jerry Rice and Emmitt Smith on the all-time chart. His 1,759 yards led all NFL runners in an MVP 1985 campaign.

He also was named Super Bowl XVIII MVP after a 191-yard performance that included an electrifying 74-yard touchdown run in a Raiders' win over Washington. Allen, who helped the Chiefs reach the AFC title game in 1993, was a six-time Pro Bowl selection.

ALLEN

Player/Year elected: 1978

LANCE ALWORTH

Born: 8-3-40, Houston, Tex. **Ht/Wt:** 6-0/184 **College:** Arkansas **Drafted:** 1962, 2nd round, AFL Chargers; 1st round, NFL 49ers
Primary position: WR **Career statistics:** Receiving, 542 rec., 10,266 yds., 18.9 avg., 85 TDs **Receptions leader:** AFL 1966,
'68, '69 **Teams:** Chargers 1962-70; Cowboys 1971-72 **Championship team:** AFL 1963 **Super Bowl champion:** 1971 season
Honors: 75th Anniversary All-Time Team; All-Time AFL Team

He was Bambi, the bounding, graceful wide receiver who eluded defensive backs like a startled deer might flee from a hunter. His long, loping stride, dance-stepping footwork and high-flying style brought beauty to a sport filled with beasts. Lance

> ## "Lance was one of maybe three players in my lifetime who had what I would call 'it.' You could see right away that he was going to be a superstar." —Al Davis

Alworth was the ultimate pass-catcher of the 1960s, a crowd-pleasing showpiece for the American Football League in its battle to gain football respectability.

He joined the San Diego Chargers in 1962, a prize catch out of Arkansas, and quickly blossomed into the AFL's first true superstar. It was a perfect match: Sid Gillman's high-powered vertical passing game with John Hadl throwing to the speedy, fearless and acrobatic Alworth. He never met a defender he couldn't burn, and he never saw a pass he couldn't catch, thanks to his outstanding leaping ability and what Gillman called "the greatest hands I have ever seen."

Throw in those big brown eyes, a Prince Valiant haircut, Hollywood good looks and the stylish clothes that became his trademark and you have star quality. The 6-foot, 184-pound Alworth made it all work over a glitzy 11-year professional career that produced 542 receptions for 10,266 yards and 85 touchdowns.

The number that really jumps out is 18.9 — the remarkable yards per catch Alworth averaged over his career. But he also recorded seven straight 1,000-yard seasons, led the AFL in touchdowns three times and caught at least one pass in every AFL game he played. Alworth's showcase season was 1965, when he caught 69 passes for 1,602 yards and 14 touchdowns — averaging a whopping 23.2 yards per reception.

Alworth, who helped the Chargers win a 1963 AFL championship, spent his final two years in Dallas, where his free-wheeling style was restricted by Tom Landry's more conservative offense. Still, the seventime Pro Bowl selection and native Texan played a prominent role for the 1971 NFC champions, catching a TD pass in a Super Bowl win over Miami. In 1978, Alworth became the first AFL player to be named to the Pro Football Hall of Fame.

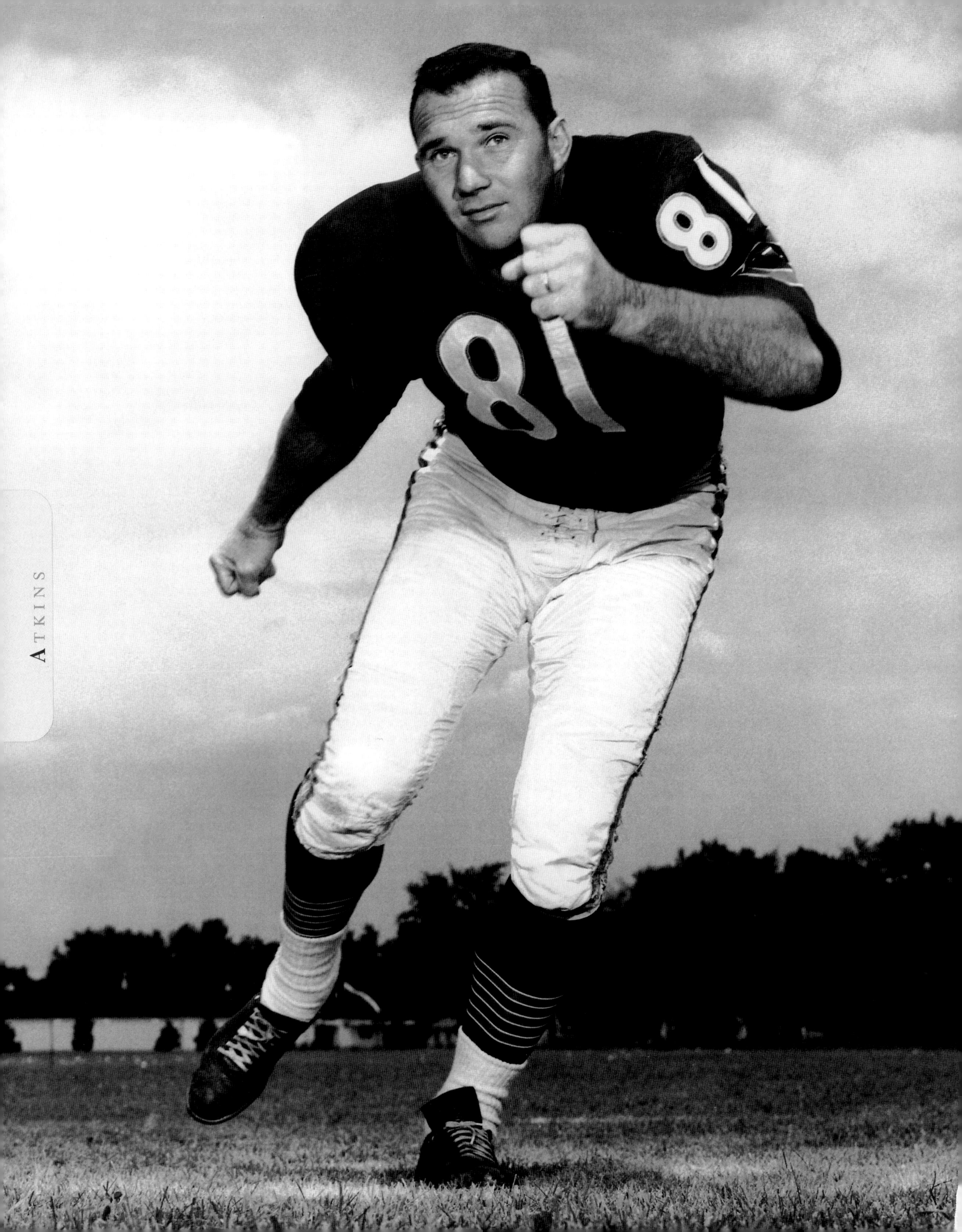

DOUG ATKINS

Born: 5-8-30, Humboldt, Tenn. **Ht/Wt:** 6-8/275 **College:** Tennessee **Drafted:** 1953, 1st round, Browns **Primary position:** DE
Teams: Browns 1953-54; Bears 1955-66; Saints 1967-69 **Championship teams:** NFL 1954, '63 **Honors:** 1960s All-Decade Team

Paul Brown and Weeb Ewbank marveled at his football-perfect 6-foot-8, 275-pound body. George Halas made him the centerpiece of his stifling Chicago defenses. For 17 NFL seasons, offensive linemen suffered the indignity of trying to block defensive end Doug Atkins, a pass-rushing giant with lumberjack arms and, by some accounts, the power of a runaway locomotive.

"One of his favorite tricks was to throw a blocker at the quarterback," former Baltimore star Johnny Unitas recalled. But the curly-haired Atkins could beat slower linemen with off-the-ball quickness as well as raw power. Preparation for a game against the Bears came with a warning: "Don't make Atkins mad." Those who did paid a stiff price for several excruciating hours.

If the former University of Tennessee three-sport star had a weakness, it was his laid-back personality—a nonchalant practice approach that frustrated coaches Brown and Halas. But players who dealt with Atkins on game day felt a different kind of frustration.

"I considered myself the best guard of this century and I played against some mean ones," former Colts Hall of Famer Jim Parker said. "But I never met anyone meaner than Atkins. After my first meeting with

> **"He is the strongest man in football and also the biggest. When he rushes the passer with those oak-tree arms of his way up in the air, he's 12 feet tall. And if he gets to you, the whole world suddenly starts spinning."**
>
> *— Fran Tarkenton*

him, I really wanted to quit pro football."

Atkins, an outstanding basketball player and high jumper at Tennessee, was signed by Cleveland assistant Ewbank and made an immediate impact for the 1953 Browns. But he battled injury problems in 1954 and was traded to Chicago, where he earned Pro Bowl invitations eight times in 12 years. He was a true Monster of the Midway, a key member of the Bears' 1963 championship team and leader of a prolific pass rush that pounded New York Giants quarterback Y.A. Tittle in the title game.

But differences of opinion with Halas eventually led Atkins to request a trade, which was granted after the 1966 season. Atkins played three more years with the expansion New Orleans Saints before retiring in 1969 at age 39.

RED BADGRO

Born: 12-1-02, Orillia, Wash. **Died:** 7-13-98 **Ht/Wt:** 6-0/190 **College:** USC **Primary positions:** OE, DE **Career statistics:** Receiving, 35 rec., 560 yds., 16.0 avg., 7 TDs **Receptions leader:** 1934 **Teams:** Yankees 1927-28; Giants 1930-35; Dodgers 1936 **Championship team:** NFL 1934

Morris "Red" Badgro was a football contradiction. The 6-foot, 190-pound two-way end was a pass-catching Giant for a grind-it-out, no-frills, smash-mouth New York team that seldom threw the ball. The athletically gifted Badgro could mix it up with anybody, but his most memorable moments were achieved as a receiver for a team that won one NFL championship and played in three straight title games from 1933-35.

It was Badgro who scored the first touchdown in an official NFL championship game in 1933 — a 29-yard reception from tailback Harry Newman that wiped out a 6-0 Chicago lead in the Giants' eventual 23-21 loss to the Bears. And he always seemed to make big catches with games on the line. Badgro's 16 receptions in 1934 (a high total for that period) tied for the NFL lead and he averaged 12.9 yards per catch.

But soft hands belied the toughness that allowed Badgro to compete against bigger players as an outstanding blocker and big-play defender. He was quick enough to outmaneuver opponents and bulldog enough to never give an inch. The versatile Badgro seldom left a game and consistently ranked among the top players at his position.

> **"I played with Red one year with the New York Yankees and against him five seasons he was with the Giants. Playing both offense and defense, he was one of the half-dozen best ends I ever saw."**
>
> *— Red Grange*

Badgro's talents were not limited to football. After playing in 1927 and '28 for the NFL's New York Yankees, he left football and tried his hand at major league baseball. Over two seasons with the St. Louis Browns, the swift outfielder batted .257 in 143 games and called it a career. Badgro signed with the Giants in 1930, rededicated himself to football and helped his team win the 1933, '34 and '35 Eastern Division titles and the '34 NFL championship.

Badgro, a native of Kent, Wash., is more recently remembered as the oldest person ever elected to the Pro Football Hall of Fame. When he was inducted in 1981 at age 78, it ended 45 years of waiting for the two-way star who played his final NFL game for the Brooklyn Dodgers in 1936.

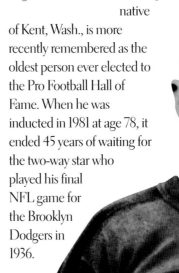

Player/Year elected: 1992

LEM BARNEY

Born: 9-8-45, Gulfport, Miss. **Ht/Wt:** 6-0/190 **College:** Jackson State **Drafted:** 1967, 2nd round, Lions **Primary position:** DB
Career statistics: Interceptions, 56, 7 TDs; Punt Returns, 143 att., 9.2 avg., 2 TDs; KO Returns, 50 att., 25.5 avg., 1 TD
Interceptions leader: 1967 **Team:** Lions 1967-77 **Honors:** 1960s All-Decade Team

The legs churned furiously, transporting a twisting, squirming body in its mad search for daylight. Watching a dazzling Lem Barney runback was worth

> **"Oh, there's no question that Lem can be considered a superstar. He draws people on his name alone. That's the test, I guess. Would I trade him? Yes, but only for Gale Sayers in perfect health. Nobody else would be worth it."**
>
> — *Russ Thomas, Lions G.M., 1969*

the price of admission. Then, when his sprinter's speed had separated him from the pack, he would slow down to cruise control, look back and wave to his pursuers, a theatrical maneuver that delighted Detroit fans and infuriated frustrated opponents.

It was clear from his first 1967 play that Barney was something special, a worthy successor at left cornerback to the just-retired Dick "Night Train" Lane. The former Jackson State star picked off a pass from Green Bay quarterback Bart Starr with a diving somersault, jumped to his feet and sprinted 24 yards for a touchdown. It was the first of 10 rookie interceptions and an auspicious beginning to an 11-year career that would

net 56, seven for TDs.

Packers wide receiver Carroll Dale once said "the only way to beat him is to be perfect," and sometimes that wasn't even enough. Barney was a physical, bump-and-run ballhawk who would lay back and use superior quickness to jump into the play. Like Lane, he was a confident gambler and big-play artist who also attacked the run with furious anticipation. The 6-foot, 190-pound Barney was so proficient at one-on-one coverage that the Lions were able to blitz a lot.

The always-smiling kid from Gulfport, Miss., seemed to be happiest when displaying his "sneaky and snaky" moves on punt returns and interceptions. It was like trying to catch a lightning bug as he darted in and out of traffic, a style that produced 11 touchdown runbacks. Four really enhanced his "offense on defense" reputation — a 98-yard kickoff return, 94-yard missed field goal return, 74-yard punt return and 71-yard interception runback.

Understandably, Barney became the fan favorite for weak Detroit teams that made only one brief playoff appearance before he retired in 1977. Never a champion, he did earn seven Pro Bowl selections.

CLIFF BATTLES

Born: 5-1-10, Akron, Ohio **Died:** 4-28-81 **Ht/Wt:** 6-1/195 **College:** West Virginia Wesleyan **Primary positions:** TB, DB
Career statistics: Rushing, 839 att., 3,511 yds., 4.2 avg., 23 TDs; Receiving, 38 rec., 4 TDs **Rushing champion:** 1932, '37
Teams: Redskins 1932-37 **Championship team:** 1937 **Honors:** 1930s All-Decade Team

Like a thief in the night, Cliff Battles slipped into Washington, stole the hearts of first-year football fans and then quietly disappeared, leaving only a tantalizing glimpse of what might have been. The NFL's leading rusher ... George Halas' choice as the greatest back of all time ... the perfect complement to rookie phenom quarterback Sammy Baugh simply retired at age 27 after helping the Redskins win the 1937 championship.

Battles' decision to leave over a $1,000 salary dispute with Redskins owner George Preston Marshall deprived the still-struggling game of a dynamic talent. Battles had already won two rushing titles, posted the NFL's first 200-yard game and played in two championship games—the first in his fifth season with the Boston Braves/Redskins. He was electrifying, a triple-option threat with the speed to go outside and the power to run between tackles.

It was not uncommon to see the 6-foot-1, 195-pound Ohioan rip off 70-yard runs, punt returns and kickoff returns—

> *"I often wonder how different it might have been for pro football in Washington, which became so spectacularly successful in its first year in the Capital, had it not been for Battles. ... Baugh without Battles, the Redskins without Battles, would not have captivated Washington as they did."*
>
> —*Shirley Povich, Washington Post columnist, 1955*

a big-play penchant that had earned him attention at little West Virginia Wesleyan College. Battles ran for an NFL-best 576 yards as a Braves rookie in 1932 and 3,511 over his six-year career. His 215 yards in an October 8, 1933, game against the Giants opened eyes, as did his then-impressive rushing total of 874 yards in 1937.

The pairing of Battles and the strong-armed Baugh was a gift from the football gods. The Redskins, playing their first season in Washington after moving from Boston, burned opponents over the top with an unparalleled passing attack and on the ground with the prolific Battles. In the final game of 1937, Battles scored three touchdowns in an Eastern Division-clinching win over the Giants. Baugh then threw for 335 yards and three touchdowns in the 28-21 championship game win over Chicago.

But Battles would never play again. The former Phi Beta Kappa student took a job as assistant coach at Columbia University and later coached Brooklyn for two seasons in the All-America Football Conference.

SAMMY BAUGH

Born: 3-17-14, Temple, Tex. **Ht/Wt:** 6-2/182 **College:** TCU **Drafted:** 1937, 1st round, Redskins **Primary positions:** QB, DB, P
Career statistics: Passing, 1,693-of-2,995, 21,886 yds., 187 TDs; Interceptions, 31; Punting, 338, 45.1 avg. **Teams:** Redskins 1937-52
Championship teams: NFL 1937, '42 **Honors:** 75th Anniversary All-Time Team, 1940s All-Decade Team

He blew through 1937 Washington like a twister off the West Texas plains. The tall, skinny, pin-legged kid with the shy drawl and powerful right arm ravaged conservative opponents while putting his new city on the NFL map. Teammates gasped, coaches shuddered and fans buzzed as Sammy Baugh raised offensive football to a new plateau and put the professional game on a fast track to prosperity and innovation.

The 6-foot-2, 182-pound All-American from Texas Christian University was everything he was cracked up to be. Slingin' Sammy, a poised and confident rookie, introduced his ball-control passing game and led the Redskins to the NFL championship in the franchise's first Washington season (after a move from Boston). He also touched off a remarkable 16-year career that would produce five division titles, another championship and 16 major records.

Baugh is remembered as the man who revolutionized the offensive game. He spent the first half of his career as a triple-threat halfback in the Redskins' single-wing offense and the second half as an All-Pro quarterback in the new T-formation. Opponents marveled at the whip-like motion Baugh used to deliver bullet passes in a pass-only-in-desperation era. Form meant nothing to the Redskins' quiet man, who delivered the ball underhanded, sidearm, off-balance, hard,

> "He was so automatic that he hardly ever looked at his receivers. He was the nearest thing to perfection."
>
> —*Sid Luckman*

soft or in any other manner that would get his team to the end zone.

But offense was only half the Baugh story. He doubled in his first seven seasons as an outstanding defensive back who once intercepted a record four passes in one game. He also was an outstanding quick-kicker and punter who still owns the records for career (45.1 yards per kick) and season average (51.4).

Baugh, who passed for 335 yards and three touchdowns in the 1937 championship game win over Chicago, retired in 1952 with a then-amazing 21,886 passing yards, a .565 completion percentage and a record 187 TD throws. The proud Texan also led the NFL in passing yardage four times.

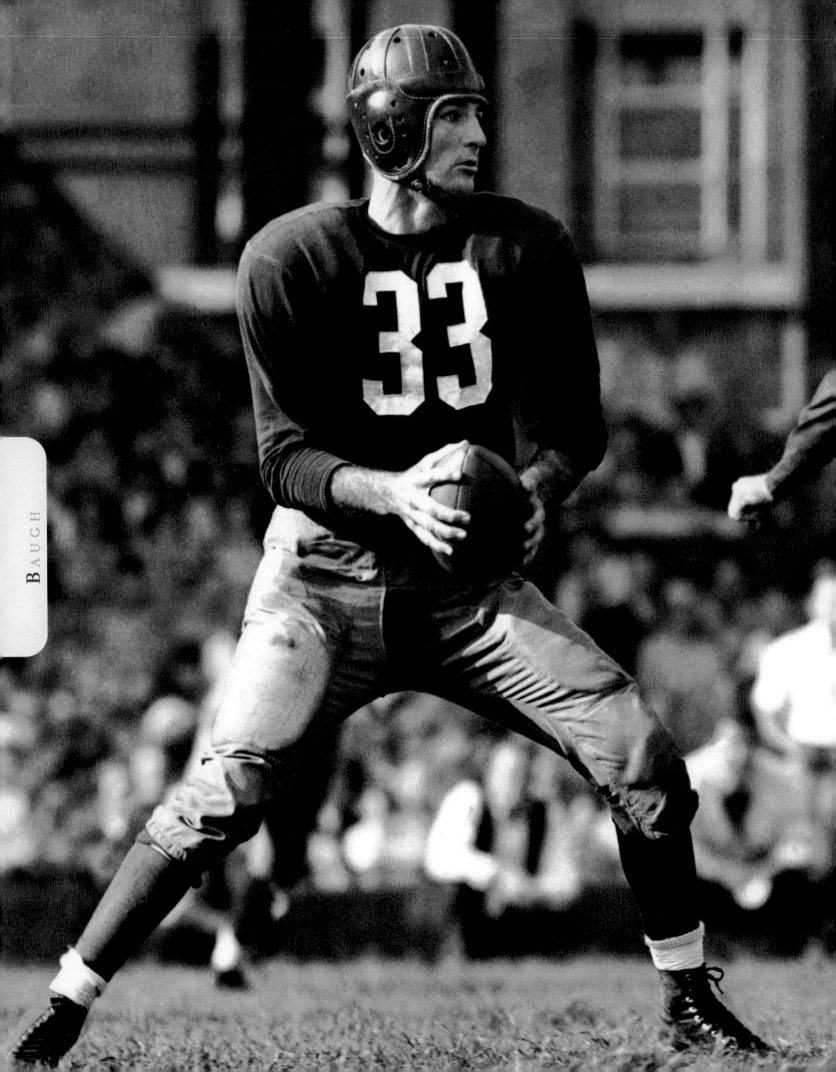

CHUCK BEDNARIK

Born: 5-1-25, Bethlehem, Pa. **Ht/Wt:** 6-3/233 **College:** Pennsylvania **Drafted:** 1949, bonus round, Eagles **Primary positions:** C, LB
Career statistics: Interceptions, 20, 1 TD **Teams:** Eagles 1949-62; **Championship teams:** NFL 1949, '60 **Honors:** 50th Anniversary Team, 1950s All-Decade Team

The No. 60 he wore on his Philadelphia jersey was prophetic, a harbinger of his now-enduring fame as professional football's last 60-minute player and hero of the Eagles' 1960 championship game. Chuck Bednarik was many things during his outstanding 14-year NFL career, but he'll always be remembered for the one magical season he celebrated at the not-so-tender football age of 35.

When the 1960 campaign opened, Bednarik was beginning his 12th NFL season and sixth straight at center, after a midcareer switch from linebacker. But an injury to linebacker Bob Pellegrini in the Eagles' fifth game prompted coach Buck Shaw to ask Bednarik to revive the long-discarded concept of two-way football. The former University of Pennsylvania star played both

> "I didn't feel any worse after 60 minutes than I used to after 30—because we were winning. If we'd lost, they'd have had to carry me off on a stretcher."
>
> —*Chuck Bednarik*

offense and defense the rest of the season and capped off his 58-minute championship game performance with a victory-saving, bear-hug tackle of Green Bay's Jim Taylor at the Eagles' 10-yard line.

Bednarik was as rugged as the Bethlehem, Pa., steel town he called home. He was an old-school competitor who threw his 6-foot-3, 233-pound body around with reckless abandon, whether creating holes as a relentless blocker or making punishing, sometimes vicious tackles. In an era of evolving offenses, he was the perfect linebacker: big, tall and agile with great mobility and the ability to cover short passes. He had a mean streak and played for keeps, prompting opponents to eye him with understandable trepidation.

Bednarik wasn't the fastest or strongest man to play linebacker, but he more than made up for that with a tunnel-vision dedication and great instinct for diagnosing plays. Wherever the ball was, Bednarik would be close by. And if the Eagles needed a big play, he would deliver.

The eight-time Pro Bowler finished his career in 1962 with a surprising 20 interceptions and a reputation for durability. Bednarik, who contributed as a rookie to the Eagles' 1949 championship run, missed only three of a possible 172 career games.

BERT BELL

Born: 2-25-1895, Philadelphia, Pa. **Died:** 10-11-59 **Executive career:** Founder and owner of Eagles 1933-40; co-owner of Steelers 1941-46; second commissioner of NFL 1946-59 **Teams coached (10-46-2):** Eagles 1936-40; Steelers 1941 (2 games)

He was a little man by pro football standards, a feisty and energetic bantam with a booming voice and oversized heart. But nobody ever doubted Bert Bell's 14-year status as the biggest force in the National Football League. The game's fiery, all-seeing second commissioner compensated for his lack of size with leadership abilities that helped lift the NFL into an era of growth and prosperity.

Bell became a commissioner of the people when he was elected in 1946, a former promoter, coach, press agent, team owner and ticket-seller in a long association with the profession he chose over the political and business pursuits of wealthy Philadelphia parents. Players and reporters appreciated his down-home style, forthright manner and media savvy; owners welcomed his experience, intimate football knowledge and quick, thoughtful decisions, even when they didn't go their way.

> ## "To me, being a diplomat is being a phony. Tell it to them the way it is. Nothing wrong with being honest."
> *— Bert Bell*

Under the dynamic guidance of Bell, the NFL took major steps upward in prestige. He helped the league overcome a major gambling scandal, weather the challenge of the All-America Football Conference and set a far-reaching standard for television and merchandising. It was Bell, during his days as owner of the Philadelphia Eagles, who proposed the idea for a college draft that was inaugurated in 1936.

Bell's business acumen was a product of his Ivy League education (Pennsylvania) and early ventures as a hotel executive and stockbroker. As longtime owner of the Eagles, he learned the game from the ground up—conniving, scheming and hustling to hold the franchise together during tough times—and he even served as the team's coach from 1936-40, a role that ended when he fired himself.

Bell, a Hall of Fame charter member, often is associated with former Pittsburgh owner Art Rooney, a 1930s contemporary with whom he combined forces during the lean war years as co-owner of the Steelers. It was, ironically, in 1959, while watching an Eagles-Steelers game, that Bell suffered a fatal heart attack at Philadelphia's Franklin Field, where he once played quarterback for Penn.

BELL

BOBBY BELL

Born: 6-17-40, Shelby, N.C. **Ht/Wt:** 6-4/228 **College:** Minnesota **Drafted:** 1963, 7th round, AFL Chiefs; 2nd round, NFL Vikings
Primary positions: LB, DE **Career statistics:** Interceptions, 26, 6 TDs **Teams:** Chiefs 1963-74 **Championship teams:** AFL 1966,
'69 **Super Bowl champion:** 1969 season **Honors:** 1970s All-Decade Team; All-Time AFL Team

He was a halfback and all-state quarterback in a dazzling high school career in Shelby, N.C. He started at the University of Minnesota as a quarterback and finished as an All-American offensive and defensive tackle. As a professional, Bobby Bell carved his Hall of Fame niche as a defensive end, outside linebacker and deep-snapper on punts and placekicks.

"Bobby is the most versatile athlete I ever coached," said former Kansas City Chiefs boss Hank Stram, who claimed the 6-foot-4, 228-pound Bell was big enough, strong enough and fast enough to play any of the 22 positions—and play them well. When Stram and the Chiefs landed Bell in the 1963 draft, the only question was how best to use the perfectly sculpted, ferocious defensive weapon they were about to unleash on unsuspecting opponents.

As a first-time defensive end, Bell quickly developed into one of the most feared pass rushers in

> "This guy is the best all-around football player I ever saw. He can throw a football 80 yards. He can center the ball back farther and more accurately than anyone in the business. He's the fastest runner you'll ever see. He can block. And he's the best defensive end, corner linebacker and anything else defensively in the whole universe." —*Buck Buchanan*

the AFL. In his second year, he earned all-league honors and began stepping back as a fourth linebacker in Stram's innovative third-down "stack defense." When Stram moved him to outside linebacker in 1966, Bell began a six-year run as either an All-AFL or All-NFL performer, cementing his legacy as the first outside linebacker to gain election to the Hall of Fame.

The do-everything Bell combined with linebacking mates Willie Lanier and Jim Lynch for a Kansas City team that won one of two Super Bowl appearances. He seemed to be everywhere, whether chasing down ballcarriers with cat-like quickness, thrusting aside double-team blockers with lineman-like strength or covering receivers with superior speed. He dealt out tremendous punishment and made big plays.

His 26 career interceptions resulted in runbacks totaling 479 yards and six touchdowns. His resume also is filled with touchdown-saving tackles, game-turning forced and recovered fumbles and well-timed sacks. Bell, who never missed a game in 12 seasons, was selected to play in nine Pro Bowls.

BELL

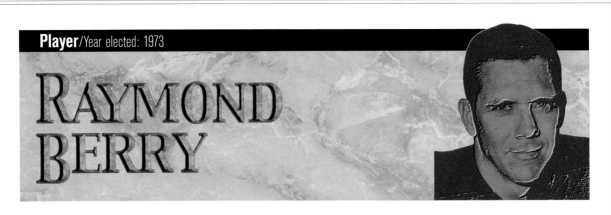

RAYMOND BERRY

Born: 2-27-33, Corpus Christi, Tex. **Ht/Wt:** 6-2/187 **College:** SMU **Drafted:** 1954, 20th round, Colts **Primary position:** WR **Career statistics:** Receiving, 631 rec., 9,275 yds., 14.7 avg., 68 TDs **Receptions leader:** 1958, '59, '60 **Teams:** Colts 1955-67 **Championship teams:** 1958, '59 **Honors:** 75th Anniversary All-Time Team; 1950s All-Decade Team

He looked out of place in a football locker room—a kitten in a room full of big, snarling dogs. The gangly build, the glasses and the shy, professorial look sentenced Raymond Berry to life as a football enigma. But what you saw was not what you got from the talented Texan, who teamed for 12 of his 13 seasons with Baltimore quarterback Johnny Unitas as one of the most prolific passing combinations in NFL history.

The shy, reticent Berry was not blessed with NFL-like athleticism. He wore a corset for his bad back, he was nearsighted and he had above-average, but not spectacular, speed. What he did have was a determination, work ethic and creativity that constantly amazed coaches and teammates. His practices started early and ended well after the locker room had cleared. He studied film at home, caught backyard passes from his wife and invented sun goggles, wrist bands and other gimmicks that became a part of the Berry mystique.

Attention to detail is what gave Berry his edge—and it showed with every move, every precise pass route that confounded NFL defensive backs. He figured out ways to beat them and then

executed, a winning formula that made him one of the greatest possession receivers of all time. Lack of speed kept him from going deep, but his big, soft hands caught everything within reach and outstanding leaping ability allowed him to make impossible catches seem routine.

Berry, who retired after the 1967 season with a then-record 631 receptions for 9,275 yards and 68 touchdowns, led the NFL in receptions three times and never caught fewer than 43 passes from 1957-66. He also helped the Colts win consecutive NFL championships in 1958 and '59. The five-time Pro Bowler's defining moment came in the classic 1958 title game against the New York Giants when he caught 12 passes for 178 yards and a touchdown—three receptions for 62 yards on the Colts' dramatic game-tying drive in the final two minutes of regulation.

"In all my years in coaching, almost 30 years in high school, college and the pros, I have never seen a more serious athlete. Why, I have to drive him to the shower room at practice or he would stay out until it got dark." — *Weeb Ewbank*

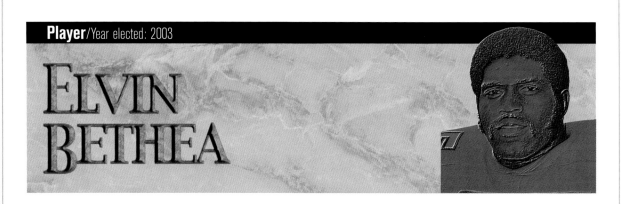

ELVIN BETHEA

Born: 3-1-46, Trenton, N.J. **Ht/Wt:** 6-2/260 **College:** North Carolina A&T **Drafted:** 1968, 3rd round, Oilers
Primary position: DE **Team:** Oilers 1968-83

He was a quiet warrior, the immovable rock that anchored Houston defensive teams for 16 NFL seasons. Determined, hard-working Elvin Bethea operated on the fringe of football's spotlight, much as his Oilers played in the shadow of the powerful Pittsburgh Steelers in the late 1970s. A day in the trenches with big No. 65 was like 60 minutes of combat with a quarterback-hunting Grizzly bear.

"Elvin was one of the quickest guys I've ever been around," said former Raiders offensive tackle Art Shell, who waged annual battles against Houston's 260-pound defensive end from 1968, the rookie season for both players, through 1982, Bethea's second-to-last campaign. The blue-collar Bethea combined that quickness with outstanding lateral speed and near-legendary strength as a premier combination pass rusher/run stuffer in the 1970s.

Preparing for Bethea was a difficult proposition. Blockers never knew whether he would zip past them off the snap or deliver a pride-sapping blow with his forearm. He had an instinctive sense of

> **"When people ask me who was the best guy I ever played against, I always tell them Elvin Bethea and Lyle Alzado. These two guys were complete ballplayers."**
>
> —*Art Shell, 2003,*
> *The Houston Chronicle*

when to stay home and when to pursue, something he did with Alan Page-like proficiency. Former teammates and coaches have called the former North Carolina A&T All-American the best defensive player in Tennessee/Houston history.

It wasn't always easy sustaining that high performance level for Bethea, who played for Oilers teams that posted consecutive 1-13 records in 1972 and '73 and seven straight .500-or-lower seasons from 1968-74. When the Bum Phillips-coached Oilers rose to prominence in the late 1970s, they could not get past the formidable Steelers in the AFC Central Division or consecutive AFC championship games. Bethea never played in a Super Bowl.

But the numbers he posted are impressive. When Bethea retired after a 1983 season he played as a favor

for Houston management, he owned team records for seasons played (16), regular-season games (210), consecutive games (135) and sacks (105). The eight-time Pro Bowl selection led the Oilers six times in sacks, an unofficial statistic when he played.

CHARLES BIDWILL

Born: 9-16-1895, Chicago, Ill. **Died:** 4-19-47 **Executive career:** Owner of Cardinals 1933-47

He was a strong-willed, blue-shirted contradiction. On one hand, Charles W. Bidwill was the spendthrift owner of a Chicago Cardinals franchise that ranked among the most inept in NFL history. On the other, he claimed membership in the pioneering inner circle of eight owners who decided the course pro football would follow in search of growth and popularity.

Bidwill's contributions far exceeded any indignities he might have suffered as owner of a team that compiled a 38-107-8 record from 1933, when he plunked down $50,000 for the franchise, through his death in 1947. The biggest deterrent to success was his long love for the Chicago Bears and his support, both financially and spiritually, for good friend George Halas.

Bidwill, who built his fortune as a prominent Chicago lawyer, regarded his Cardinals as little more than a toy and his teams, in direct competition with the Bears, never turned a profit. He sat quietly on game days in his owner's box, never interfered with coaching decisions and seldom visited the locker room. When a Cardinals game conflicted with a big Bears

> **"Charley always knew the NFL would reach its present status. He had a standard answer for anyone critical of the league. He'd look at the guy and snap, 'You don't know what you're talking about.'"**
>
> *— George Halas*

game, Bidwill, wearing his trademark dark blue shirt, could usually be found rooting his Chicago rivals to victory.

Bidwill enjoyed his greatest influence as a member of the eight-man group—Joe Carr, Halas, Curly Lambeau, Tim Mara, George Preston Marshall, Art Rooney, Bert Bell, Bidwill—that literally ruled the game. He helped decide league policy, rules and direction. He was front and center in 1946 when the new All-America Football Conference challenged the NFL, boldly placing a franchise in Chicago. Suddenly aroused, Bidwill built the best team in Cardinals history around the "Dream Backfield" of Paul Christman, Pat Harder, Elmer Angsman and Marshall Goldberg. He dealt a crippling blow to the AAFC by signing Georgia star Charley Trippi for an unprecedented $100,000 and the 1947 Cardinals rose to a 9-3 record and won an NFL championship.

It was an ultimate victory Bidwill did not see. He died in April 1947 of pneumonia at age 51.

BIDWILL

FRED BILETNIKOFF

Born: 2-23-43, Erie, Pa. **Ht/Wt:** 6-1/190 **College:** Florida State **Drafted:** 1965, 2nd round, Raiders **Primary position:** WR
Career statistics: Receiving, 589 rec., 8,974 yds., 76 TDs **Receptions leader:** 1971 **Team:** Raiders 1965-78
Super Bowl champion: 1976 season (MVP)

Discussions about Fred Biletnikoff inevitably start with the hands—big, soft, supple and covered with the green, gooey substance he called "stickum." They were amazing hands, ball-attracting magnets that pulled in any pass within the time zone of his pattern. If Biletnikoff could touch a ball, he could catch it—a fact he proved over and over during a 14-year AFL/NFL journey that started in Oakland and ended in the Hall of Fame.

> "We've been together so long we know exactly what to expect from each other. I know where he's going before he gets there and he knows where I'll be throwing almost before I do. Like a great pianist, he is tops in his field. I look at him sometimes and wonder how he does the things he does."
>
> —*Ken Stabler, 1977*

Pennsylvania kid who studied reels of film before every game and spent hours catching practice passes. The work habits were born from chronic worry, which was responsible for the ulcer he developed during college. He agonized, paced and threw up before every game, and it took hours for him to calm down afterward. He was enraged, absolutely mortified, by every dropped pass.

The former Florida State star wasn't fast and his narrow-shouldered, 190-pound frame should by all rights have disintegrated with the heavy pounding it absorbed from 1965-78, when Biletnikoff turned sideline and over-the-middle pass catching into an art form. He couldn't beat the faster defensive backs physically, but he could outwork and outthink them. Biletnikoff's precise, perfectly-timed, sleight-of-foot patterns became legendary, as did his ability to make the difficult catch at the crucial point of a game.

Nothing came easy for the bony-kneed

With quarterbacks Daryle Lamonica and Ken Stabler throwing to him, Biletnikoff thrived as the clutch, big-game possession receiver for Raiders teams that never had a losing season. He played in three AFL championship games, six AFC title games and two Super Bowls, winning MVP honors in a Super Bowl XI victory over Minnesota.

Biletnikoff was a picture of consistency, topping 40 catches for 10 straight seasons and 100 yards in a game 21 times. When he retired after the 1978 campaign, he had caught 589 passes for 8,974 yards and 76 touchdowns and owned two postseason records—70 receptions and 1,167 yards in 19 games. He also earned six Pro Bowl selections.

GEORGE BLANDA

Born: 9-17-27, Youngwood, Pa. **Ht/Wt:** 6-2/215 **College:** Kentucky **Drafted:** 1949, 12th round, Bears **Primary positions:** QB, K
Career statistics: Passing, 26,920 yds., 236 TDs; Scoring, 335 FG, 943 PAT, 2,002 pts. **Scoring champion:** 1967 **Teams:** Bears
1949, 1950-58; Colts 1950; Oilers 1960-66; Raiders 1967-75 **Championship teams:** AFL 1960, '61, '67 **Honors:** All-Time AFL Team

We will always remember the long, gray hair and the lined, craggy face. George Blanda never got old, he just got better. Over 26 incredible NFL seasons, he posted a record 2,002 points and an impressive 236 touchdown passes as a placekicker

and quarterback. But the real legacy of George Blanda is the magic he created as an American folk hero who continued to deliver clutch performances in his fourth football decade, until the amazing age of 48.

Through much of his career, Blanda was a backup quarterback and full-time kicker with a straight-on, confident and accurate stroke. That confidence carried over to his quarterback duties, which he executed with a veteran savvy that overcame limited arm strength and lack of speed. Blanda was a scoring machine for 10 years as a Chicago Bears kicker, an icy competitor when he finally got his first call as a starting quarterback and led Houston to championships in the AFL's first two seasons. He threw for 3,330 yards and fired 36 touchdown passes in 1961, seven in one memorable game.

But nothing could

match the dramatic impact Blanda brought to the Oakland Raiders from 1967 until his 1975 retirement as the oldest player in football history. In a magic 1970 season, at age 43, the Old Man came off the bench in five straight games and delivered a dramatic kick or touchdown pass that produced a win or tie. The heroics continued in subsequent seasons as the blazing blue eyes, protruding jaw and craggy face of No. 16 became a highlight-film regular.

The former Kentucky star was a popular, sometimes-testy leader who played in a record 340 games.

"He is one of the all-time great pros. George is a born winner."

—Al Davis

He was the epitome of the grizzled veteran, the definitive clutch performer and symbol of everlasting youth. It's no coincidence the determined, unflappable Blanda played in one Super Bowl and 11 AFL/NFL championship games in a career that produced 335 field goals, 943 extra points and 1,911 pass completions for 26,920 yards.

MEL BLOUNT

Born: 4-10-48, Vidalia, Ga. **Ht/Wt:** 6-3/205 **College:** Southern **Drafted:** 1970, 3rd round, Steelers **Primary position:** DB **Career statistics:** Interceptions, 57, 2 TDs; KO Returns, 36 att., 25.3 avg. **Interceptions leader:** 1975 **Teams:** Steelers 1970-83 **Super Bowl champions:** 1974, '75, '78, '79 seasons **Honors:** 75th Anniversary All-Time Team; 1980s All-Decade Team; All-Time NFL Team

Love him, hate him. The choice was simple for Pittsburgh fans, who enjoyed 14 glorious seasons with one of the great cornerbacks in NFL history. For everybody else, the tall, almost sinister figure of Mel Blount—the Darth Vaderish man in black—symbolized the evil intentions of a Steel Curtain defense that shrouded the league through much of the 1970s.

The 6-foot-3, 205-pound Georgian was the best athlete on the Steelers' talent-filled roster, maybe even in the league. He was tall for a corner, but he matched his contemporaries in quickness and speed and he had the power and toughness of a linebacker. Blount was the prototype cornerback of his era, maybe the best bump-and-run pass defender ever. He ran with the speedy wideouts stride for stride and his aggressive pounding of receivers only added to his intimidating persona.

Blount, a tireless worker who refined his skills while frustrating Steelers stars Lynn Swann and John Stallworth in practice, was cocky enough to believe nobody could beat him one-on-one. He also was a punishing run-support tackler and a durable performer who missed only one regular-season game because of injury. The physical style perfected by the Steelers secondary prompted NFL officials to legislate against the bump-and-run, but Blount adjusted and continued to thrive.

Quarterbacks had to be wary of the former Southern University star, who, apparently beaten, would swoop out of nowhere to knock away or pick off a pass with his long arms. Once beaten, Blount seldom fell for the same move again as he shut down most of the best receivers in the game. In an amazing 1972 season, nobody beat Blount for a touchdown.

The five-time Pro Bowl selection made 57 career interceptions, including a league-leading 11 in 1975. But his greatest legacy was membership on powerful Steelers teams that played in five AFC championship games and won four Super Bowls in a six-year span from 1974-79.

> "Size, speed, quickness, toughness—that's what Mel had. If you gave Blount free rein to hit you, you were in trouble because, if he missed, he had the speed to catch up. A lot of receivers got short arms when they were in Mel's territory."
>
> —*Terry Hanratty, former Steelers quarterback*

BLOUNT

Player/Year elected: 1989

TERRY BRADSHAW

Born: 9-2-48, Shreveport, La. **Ht/Wt:** 6-3/215 **College:** Louisiana Tech **Drafted:** 1970, 1st round, Steelers **Primary position:** QB
Career statistics: Passing, 2,025-of-3,901, 27,989 yds., 212 TDs; Rushing, 444 att., 2,257 yds., 32 TDs **Team:** Steelers 1970-83
Super Bowl champions: 1974, '75, '78 (MVP), '79 (MVP) seasons **Honors:** 1970s All-Decade Team

They called him buffoon, rube and country bumpkin. They cracked jokes about his rural naivete and suggested he was dumb. But Terry Bradshaw had everyone fooled. The big blond quarterback with the sparkling blue eyes, sly smile and dimpled chin was dumb like a fox. And naive enough to lead the Pittsburgh Steelers to four Super Bowl championships over a fascinating 14-year career.

It all seemed so simple in 1970 when the lowly Steelers grabbed Bradshaw out of tiny Louisiana Tech with the No. 1 overall pick. Everyone predicted the 6-foot-3, 215-pound phenom with the rifle arm, quick release and running back speed would lead the franchise to long-awaited respectability. But Bradshaw was a diamond in the rough, a small-town boy unprepared for the more-sophisticated professional game. His first

few seasons were a struggle, both on the field and off.

And then, like magic, he blossomed into a big-play machine. Bradshaw's incredible deep touch began producing long touchdown passes to Lynn Swann and John Stallworth. His short passing game and scrambling ability confused defenses. His play-calling became clever and efficient. And his reputation grew as one of the great postseason performers in football history.

Bradshaw's Super Bowl ledger is remarkable: 932 passing yards and nine touchdowns. He earned consecutive MVP awards in Super Bowls XIII and XIV with a combined 624 yards and six touchdowns, including TD throws of 28, 75, 47 and 73 yards. In six AFC title games, he threw seven touchdown passes and he totaled 3,833 passing yards and 30 touchdowns in 19 postseason games.

Throughout his career, Bradshaw was exciting and unpredictable. He could throw an 80-yard touchdown pass on one play, a 10-yard interception into triple coverage on the next. He also was unpredictable in his personal life, a free-spirited, fun-loving celebrity who dabbled in everything from business to country singing and acting. When he retired in 1983 with 27,989 passing yards and 212 TD passes, longtime Steelers owner Art Rooney called him the greatest quarterback of all time.

> ## "You've got to hand it to Bradshaw, he's bursting with talent. My God, his arm is like a rifle."
>
> — *Terry Hanratty, former Steelers quarterback,* 1972

BRADSHAW

JIM BROWN

Born: 2-17-36, St. Simons Island, Ga. **Ht/Wt:** 6-2/230 **College:** Syracuse **Drafted:** 1957, 1st round, Browns **Primary position:** FB
Career statistics: Rushing, 2,359 att., 12,312 yds., 5.2 avg., 106 TDs; Receiving, 262 rec., 2,499 yds., 20 TDs **Rushing champion:**
1957, '58, '59, '60, '61, '63, '64, '65 **Teams:** Browns 1957-65 **Championship team:** NFL 1964 **Honors:** 75th Anniversary All-Time
Team; 50th Anniversary Team; 1960s All-Decade Team; All-Time NFL Team

He came, he saw, he conquered. And then, like a thief in the night, he disappeared from professional football with every rushing record known to man. Many have been reclaimed, but the legend of Jim Brown remains as powerful as the body-scattering runs that lifted him to prominence as the Cleveland Browns' ultimate weapon from 1957-65—and the greatest pure runner in NFL history.

Brown was a physical masterpiece, a gift from the

> "He told me, 'Make sure when anyone tackles you he remembers how much it hurts.' He lived by that philosophy and I always followed that advice."
>
> —*John Mackey, 1999*

football Gods. His 18-inch neck, wide shoulders and 45-inch chest tapered down to a 32-inch waist and massive thighs that carried him around the field with animal grace. Brown ran with head high, nostrils flaring, legs pumping and powerful arms swatting away tacklers like flies. He was an amazing combination of power and speed, a big cat who could juke past slower defenders or run over linebackers and defensive backs.

The former Syracuse multi-sport star stormed through the NFL as a 1957 rookie, running for 942 yards and posting the first of eight rushing championships he would claim over a nine-year career. His yearly rushing totals would become the standard at which future runners would aspire: 1,527, 1,329, 1,257, 1,408, 1,863, 1,446 and 1,544.

The beauty of Brown was that everybody knew he was going to get the ball, but nobody could stop him. He topped the 100-yard mark in 58 of his 118 games and his 126 touchdowns stood as an NFL record for many years. Brown took extreme punishment, played hurt and posted at least 200 carries in every season, but he never missed a game.

The nine-time Pro Bowler was equally intimidating off the field, where his menacing glares, in-your-face attitude and outspoken views often were interpreted as resentful and rebellious. He played without emotion, the same way he delivered the shocking 1966 news that he would retire, at age 29, while filming a movie in London. He left at the top of his game, the owner of one championship ring (1964) and 20 NFL records that included rushing yards (12,312) and yards per carry (5.2).

PAUL BROWN

Born: 9-7-08, Norwalk, Ohio **Died:** 8-5-91 **Teams coached AAFC (47-4-3 RS, 5-0 PS):** Browns 1946-49 **Teams coached NFL (166-100-6 RS, 4-8 PS):** Browns 1950-62; Bengals 1968-75 **Championship teams:** AAFC 1946, '47, '48, '49; NFL 1950, '54, '55

He was the first coach for two NFL franchises and an innovator who affected the course of pro football's evolution. Paul Brown is best remembered as a ground-breaking pro football pioneer. But the proud, no-nonsense Ohioan also was an astute judge of talent who guided the Cleveland franchise named after him to seven league championships and 11 appearances in league title games.

More than anything else, the resolute Brown changed the game through his innovations. He introduced player intelligence testing and film evaluation. He made scouting a full-time, year-round profession. He was the first to keep extra players on "taxi squads," the first to shuttle plays to quarterbacks and the first to run scrimmage-free practices. The 2-minute drill was a Brown brainstorm, as were the draw play, sideline and screen passes and the facemask. He turned the kicking game, previously an afterthought, into an important offensive weapon.

> "We don't want any butchers on this team. Don't eat with your elbows on the table and don't make noise when you eat. Don't wear T-shirts to the dining room. ... If you are a drinker or a chaser, you weaken the team and we don't want you. We're here for just one thing—to win."
>
> —*Paul Brown, 1950 training camp speech*

Often perceived as aloof, intimidating and unforgiving, Brown could motivate players with a stern look or soft-spoken challenge. But he didn't need psychological ploys to inspire the talent-filled Cleveland teams he formed to play in the All-America Football Conference. Led by quarterback Otto Graham and tailored to run a sophisticated passing attack, the Browns carved out a 47-4-3 regular-season record from 1946-49 and won all four AAFC championships before taking their act to the NFL.

Brown's "basketball team in cleats" shocked skeptics by winning an NFL championship in 1950 and reached the title game in six of the next seven years, winning twice. After leaving the Browns in 1962, he returned to the game in 1968 as owner and coach of the Cincinnati Bengals, an AFL expansion team. The Bengals won two AFC Central Division titles before Brown retired in 1975.

Brown's legendary status in Ohio preceded his 1946 pro football debut. He became coach at famed Massillon High School at age 24 and took over at Ohio State at 33, directing the Buckeyes to the 1942 national championship.

ROOSEVELT BROWN

Born: 10-20-32, Charlottesville, Va. **Ht/Wt:** 6-3/255 **College:** Morgan State **Drafted:** 1953, 27th round, Giants
Primary position: OT **Team:** Giants 1953-65 **Championship teams:** NFL 1956 **Honors:** 75th Anniversary All-Time Team;
1950s All-Decade Team; All-Time NFL Team

The path Roosevelt Brown followed from the 27th round of the 1953 NFL draft to pro football stardom was straight and narrow, unlike the paths he cleared for New York Giants ball-carriers. He was known around football circles as a quick hitter, someone who could knock a defender off the line before he knew what was happening. Brown was Mr. Reliable over a 13-year career that started in the trenches and ended in the Hall of Fame.

Brown, an afterthought draft pick out of Morgan State, gained instant attention when he arrived at the Giants camp and began throwing his 6-foot-3, 255-pound body around. He was tall with wide shoulders and a powerful upper body that could deliver punishment. But unlike most other offensive linemen of the era, he had excellent straightaway speed and superior quickness.

Brown was quickly inserted into the tackle slot, a job he would hold for the rest of his career. He was too quick for the stronger defensive linemen and too

> "Rosey never did the same things twice. He was incredible. He was my favorite, my idol. Everything I learned, I picked up from him. I wanted to be just like him."
>
> *— Jim Parker, 1998*

persistent for anybody who tried to get past him on a pass play. He was so fast the Giants installed special plays to use him as a pulling blocker—one of the first tackles to be used in that manner. The Giants also utilized Brown's speed and agility on kick-coverage teams.

But Brown was valuable beyond his obvious skills and physical assets. He was very popular among teammates and inspired them with his never-give-an-inch desire and relentless determination. The Giants also liked to use him on goal-line stands, a move that always seemed to give the defense an emotional lift.

Brown, a nine-time Pro Bowl selection, was an important member of Giants teams that carved out an 86-35-5 record over a successful 10-year stretch from 1954-63. He played for six conference title winners and on the 1956 NFL championship team that included such players as Rosey Grier, Frank Gifford, Emlen Tunnell, Charley Conerly and Sam Huff.

WILLIE BROWN

Born: 12-2-40, Yazoo City, Miss. **Ht/Wt:** 6-1/200 **College:** Grambling State **Drafted:** Undrafted **Primary position:** DB
Career statistics: Interceptions, 54, 2 TDs **Teams:** Broncos 1963-66; Raiders 1967-78 **Championship team:** AFL 1967
Super Bowl champion: 1976 season **Honors:** 1970s All-Decade Team; All-Time AFL Team

The week leading up to Willie Brown was never a pleasant one. Good receivers fretted and worried; great receivers studied film, looking for weaknesses they knew didn't exist. Facing Brown, one of the game's outstanding coverage cornerbacks, was like a trip to the dentist or an IRS audit. He was a bad dream that lasted for 16 AFL/NFL seasons — four with the Denver Broncos and 12 as the unquestioned leader of a superior Oakland Raiders secondary.

The first thing you noticed was the boyish enthusiasm Brown brought to every play, a trait he complemented with size (6-foot-1, 200), mobility and uncanny instincts. The second was the way he took charge with a subtle swagger that intimidated receivers and impressed teammates who looked up to him as a defensive leader and guru. Brown's flamboyant, gambling style provided a stark contrast to his quiet modesty and soft, friendly off-field manner.

He will always be remembered as the man who invented the bump-and-run style that intimidated some receivers and

> "He gives you nothing. He tries to take away the short patterns so you can get a half step on the deep patterns. But if it is not a perfect pass, you can't complete it. He's the best."
>
> — *Joe Namath, 1964*

disrupted the pass patterns of others. But he also could intimidate with his ability to shadow pass-catchers, who marveled at how he always seemed to know where they were going. A lot of it was instinct and quickness, but the hard-hitting former Grambling star also viewed hours of film and studied the moves and tendencies of every receiver he would face.

The incredible instinct resulted in 54 regular-season interceptions, four in a record-tying 1964 performance against the New York Jets. Brown also added seven post-season interceptions and returned three of those for touchdowns. His signature career moment was a 75-yard interception return that provided the clinching TD for the Raiders in a Super Bowl XI win over Minnesota.

It's no coincidence that in Brown's 12 Oakland seasons, the Raiders were 128-35-7 with nine AFC/AFL championship game appearances and two Super Bowls, one a winner. The talented Mississippian also played in nine Pro Bowls.

BUCK BUCHANAN

Born: 9-10-40, Gainesville, Ala. **Died:** 7-16-92 **Ht/Wt:** 6-7/280 **College:** Grambling State **Drafted:** 1963, 1st round, AFL Texans; 19th round, NFL Giants **Primary position:** DT **Teams:** Chiefs 1963-75 **Championship teams:** AFL 1966, '69 **Super Bowl champion:** 1969 season

The sight was unnerving, like a Volkswagen going nose-to-nose with a bulldozer. There was 6-foot-7 Buck Buchanan, his 280 pounds tucked into a three-point stance, exploding into an offensive guard and crunching him to the ground before bouncing away in

> ## "Buck had it all—size, speed, quickness and great, great attitude. He gave us the big player and the big personality we needed."
>
> *—Hank Stram*

hot pursuit of the football. The size and power were bad enough. The speed, quickness and agility with which the Kansas City Chiefs huge defensive tackle terrorized opponents for 13 seasons were another matter altogether.

Nobody had ever seen such a complete package of physical abilities in a tall frame, much less tried to defend against them. So Chiefs coach Hank Stram changed the course of defensive line play by unleashing his monster on the suddenly undersized offensive lines of 1963. Not only did the Chiefs have a potent run-stuffer and speedy sideline-to-sideline pursuer in the interior of their defense, they had one of the game's best pass rushers, all 6-7 of him, crashing right up the middle.

The emergence of the hard-working, always-friendly

Buchanan, who evolved from a raw-power tackle into a smart, technically-advanced defender, forced other teams to take quick action. Raiders boss Al Davis drafted 6-5, 255-pound guard Gene Upshaw with the express purpose of neutralizing Buchanan, but even the future Hall of Famer had trouble dealing with his quickness. "I'd go at him and it was like hitting a ghost," Upshaw said. Once through the line, Buchanan could either bat down passes with his long arms or drop the quarterback.

Not coincidentally, Buchanan's career mirrored the 1960s rise of the Chiefs into a championship contender and their 1970s decline into an AFC also-ran. He was the anchor and co-captain for an outstanding defense that lost in the first Super Bowl but came back three years later to upset Minnesota in Super Bowl IV. The eight-time Pro Bowl selection, who was credited with the first Super Bowl sack, missed only one game before retiring in 1975.

Player/Year elected: 2001

NICK BUONICONTI

Born: 12-15-40, Springfield, Mass. **Ht/Wt:** 5-11, 220 **College:** Notre Dame **Drafted:** 1962, 13th round, AFL Patriots; Not selected NFL
Primary position: LB **Career statistics:** Interceptions, 32 **Teams:** Patriots 1962-68; Dolphins 1969-74, 1976 **Super Bowl**
champions: 1972, '73 seasons **Honors:** All-Time AFL Team

The fire in his eyes reflected the intensity and passion that infected players around him. Nick Buoniconti might have looked like an undersized middle linebacker, but he acted and played like the defensive leader of the NFL's most revered winning machine. Fire, pride, motivation, determination ... Buoniconti provided powerful fuel for Miami's consecutive Super Bowl championships of 1972 and '73.

That the former Notre Dame star would one day gain esteem as captain of the Dolphins' "No-Name Defense" seemed unlikely in 1962, when he went undrafted by NFL teams and wasn't picked until the 13th round of the AFL draft by the Boston Patriots. Seven seasons in Boston resulted in five AFL Pro Bowl selections, but he still was viewed as an overachiever when the Dolphins, a fourth-year expansion team, acquired him in a 1969 trade.

It didn't take Don Shula long to recognize Buoniconti's value when he took Miami's coaching reins in 1970. What the 5-foot-11, 220-pound veteran lacked in size, he more than made up for with intelligence and tunnel-vision intensity. He could quickly recognize formations and make defensive switches. He outsmarted blockers, pounded ballcarriers and dropped back in coverage, an ability that produced 32 career interceptions.

But former teammates remember the intangibles. Buoniconti worked himself into a frenzy before games and that passion was infectious. He was a field general in the huddle, where he called defensive schemes and kept everybody focused. Buoniconti was an extension of Shula and the Dolphins reached three straight Super Bowls, winning in an incredible 1972 season that produced an unprecedented 17-0 record and again in '73.

Buoniconti, who went on to a post-football life as an assistant district attorney, sports agent and chief executive, played through 1974 and "unretired" in 1976 as a one-year favor to Shula. The man who "played bigger than his size" retired again after his 14th season with three NFL Pro Bowl selections and a spot on the All-Time AFL Team.

> "Every play is like life or death. I can't think of anything except the play that is taking place at the moment." —*Nick Buoniconti*

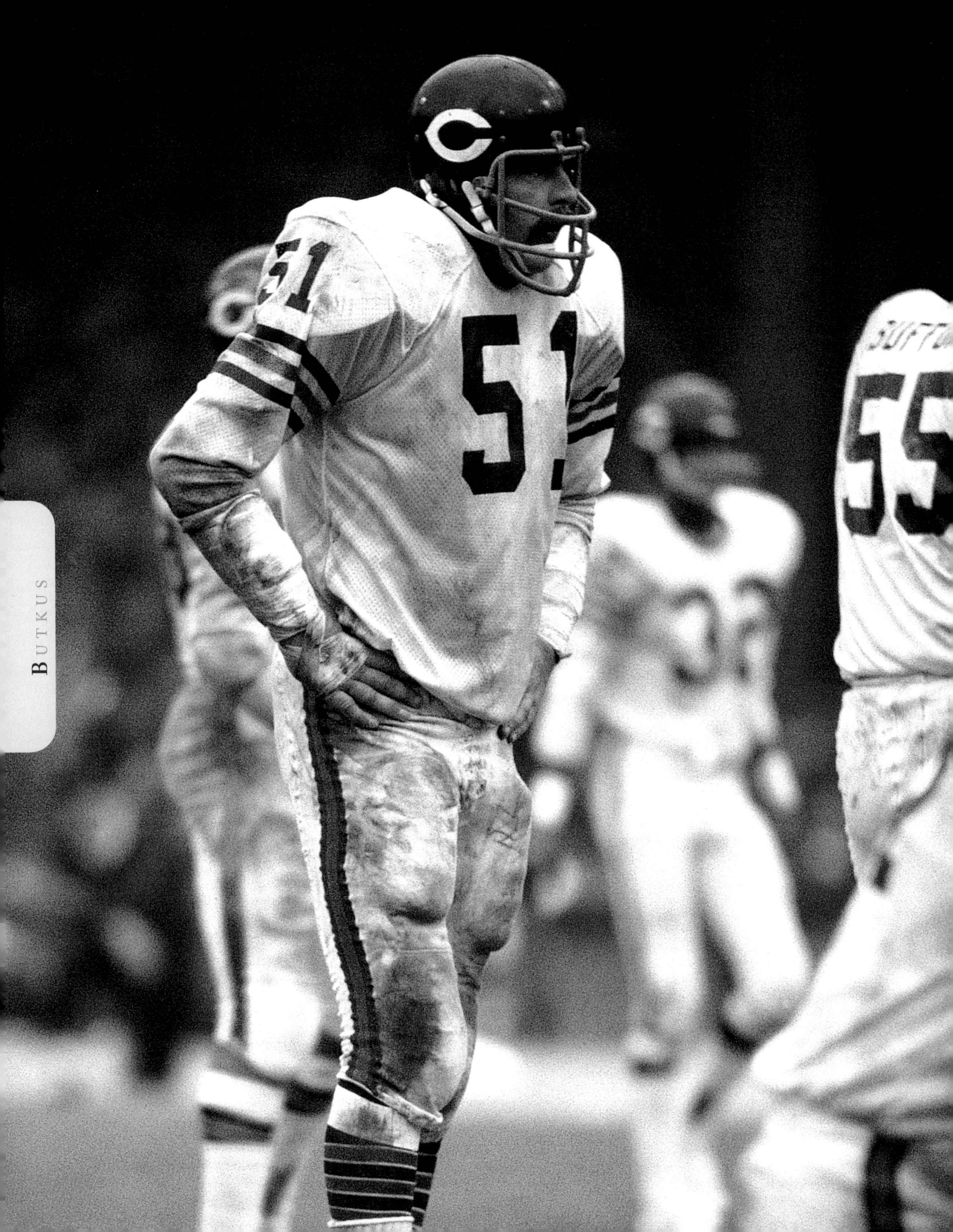
51
51
55

DICK BUTKUS

Born: 12-9-42, Chicago, Ill. **Ht/Wt:** 6-3/245 **College:** Illinois **Drafted:** 1965, 1st round, NFL Bears; 2nd round, AFL Broncos
Primary position: LB **Career statistics:** Interceptions, 22 **Teams:** Bears 1965-73 **Honors:** 75th Anniversary All-Time Team;
1960s All-Decade Team; 1970s All-Decade Team; All-Time NFL Team

He was a grunting, snarling, snorting defensive machine, dedicated to the creation of football mayhem and the destruction of offensive game plans. Dick Butkus' road to the Hall of Fame was paved with

> ### "The minute that guy walked into camp, I started packing my gear. There was no way he wasn't going to be great."
>
> —*Bill George, former Bears middle linebacker*

blood, sweat, pain—and the intense anger that coursed through the veins of the most celebrated middle linebacker in the history of the professional game.

The 6-foot-3, 245-pound Butkus served as the Chicago Bears' defensive leader and enforcer from 1965-73, when the almost-constant physical pounding finally took its toll on a body that had been pushed to full throttle on every play. The former University of Illinois All-American was both loved and despised for the mean, take-no-prisoners style he brought to the field, but his success was fueled by a consuming drive to be the best and a tunnel-vision dedication to his profession. "When they say All-Pro middle linebacker," he once told a writer, "I want them to mean Butkus."

The burly, blue-collar Butkus combined surprising speed with a fearsome strength that he used to fight off powerful blockers and make tackles. A ballcarrier who fell into the grasp of his long, thick arms could expect to be squeezed into helpless submission. Other runners and offensive linemen were constantly amazed by the ferocity of his hits. Butkus could run down ballcarriers from sideline to sideline, cover receivers out of the backfield and make the right calls for coach George Halas' complicated defense. Once burned, he never made the same mistake again.

Butkus' misfortune was that he played for weak Chicago teams that never challenged for an NFL championship. But still he played in eight Pro Bowls and the acclaim—the notoriety—he gained beyond his hometown of Chicago reached almost legendary status. Butkus' incredible instinct for the ball can be documented by the 25 opponent fumbles he recovered and the 22 interceptions he recorded in 119 professional games.

Player/Year elected: 1991

EARL CAMPBELL

Born: 3-29-55, Tyler, Tex. **Ht/Wt:** 5-11/232 **College:** Texas **Drafted:** 1978, 1st round, Oilers **Primary position:** RB **Career statistics:** Rushing, 2,187 att., 9,407 yds., 4.3 avg., 74 TDs **Rushing champion:** 1978, '79, '80 **Teams:** Oilers 1978-84; Saints 1984-85 **Honors:** 1970s All-Decade Team

You could always tell when the Earl Campbell Express was coming. The ground rumbled, bodies tumbled and fearless hearts crumbled. He was equal parts freight train, thoroughbred and warrior, all blended into a heavily-muscled, bowling ball-like 232-pound

> "Earl hits you; you don't hit Earl. Did you ever see two cars get into a wreck? Usually, the sonufagun goin' the fastest comes out of it with the least amount of damage. Well, that one's Earl."
>
> — *Bum Phillips, 1983*

body. Campbell was raw power, a yard-eating machine that terrorized NFL defenders from 1978 through 1985.

To say that Campbell was not your normal, everyday running back was something of an understatement. His 5-foot-11 frame featured tree-trunk thighs that measured 36 inches, only two less than his waist, and a big, battering-ram head. He ran with a forward lean, providing a low center of gravity and a small margin of error for tacklers. He was a sincere, no-nonsense East Texas Southern Baptist whose heart was as big as his massive thighs. He refused to give up on any run, taking great pride in dealing out punishment while gaining every possible inch.

Campbell, the No. 1 overall draft pick in 1978, literally exploded onto the NFL scene after a Heisman Trophy-winning senior season at the University of Texas. Playing for his homestate Houston Oilers, the Tyler Rose rumbled for an NFL-leading 1,450 yards in a spectacular rookie season and followed that with league-leading seasons of 1,697 and 1,934.

Campbell, generally considered the league's best power back since Jim Brown, topped the 100-yard barrier 11 times in 1979 and posted a record four 200-yard performances during his 1980 showcase. Through his first six seasons as the centerpiece of Houston's offense, he averaged 1,383 yards and helped the Oilers reach two AFC championship games.

The pride that prodded Campbell to stretch out every run over eight grueling seasons for the Oilers and New Orleans Saints also might have been responsible for his relatively short career. All the pounding he absorbed, all the bone-jarring blows from second, third and fourth tacklers wore down his body and prompted a premature dropoff in performance. When Campbell retired after the 1985 season, he had 9,407 yards (1,176 per season), 74 touchdowns and five Pro Bowl appearances.

TONY CANADEO

Born: 5-5-19, Chicago, Ill. **Ht/Wt:** 5-11/190 **College:** Gonzaga **Drafted:** 1941, 7th round, Packers **Primary positions:** HB, DB, P
Career statistics: Rushing, 1,025 att., 4,197 yds., 26 TDs; Receiving, 69 rec., 579 yds., 5 TDs; Passing, 1,642 yds., 16 TDs; KO Returns, 75 att., 23.1 avg. **Teams:** Packers 1941-44, 1946-52 **Championship team:** NFL 1944 **Honors:** 1940s All-Decade Team

At first glance, his compact 5-foot-11, 190-pound body was a football anomaly. The deception was only heightened by Tony Canadeo's friendly demeanor and prematurely gray hair. But hidden beneath this atypical athletic facade was the heart of a warrior and a dogged determination that fueled one of the most gifted two-way stars of the professional game's formative era.

Canadeo was a high-voltage machine from 1941-52 for the Green Bay Packers. Not blessed with outstanding speed, he used football savvy and instincts to pile up 8,667 yards—1,642 as a passer, 4,197 as a runner, 579 as a receiver and 2,249 as a return man. When not churning out yards, Canadeo was playing defensive back (nine career interceptions) and punting.

A seventh-round draft pick out of Gonzaga University in 1941, Canadeo joined a high-flying Packers team that had won two NFL championships and appeared in another title game over the last five years. This was an offensive powerhouse featuring Cecil Isbell in a triple-option backfield throwing to the great Don Hutson. The "Gray Ghost of Gonzaga" was another weapon at Curly Lambeau's disposal and the coach used him well.

> "The man loves football. He never complains. ... His teammates love him, especially the younger ones. They kid him a lot about his frosty thatch. In a hotel lobby, you'd think he was our traveling secretary—or one of the owners."
>
> —*Gene Ronzani, Packers coach, 1952*

over his final seven seasons.

In 1949, Canadeo ran for 1,052 yards and became the third back in NFL history to top the 1,000 barrier. He also enjoyed prominence as one of the most popular players in Packers history, a favorite among both teammates and fans because of his upbeat personality—and, of course, his tenacious, never-give-an-inch style of play.

When Canadeo retired after the 1952 season, he had averaged 75 all-purpose yards over 116 NFL games.

The Packers were 10-1, 8-2-1 and 7-2-1 in his first three seasons and they won another championship in 1944, a campaign in which Canadeo was limited to three games because of military duty during World War II. When he returned in 1946, Hutson and Isbell were gone and Canadeo became the focus of a more-grounded Packers team that compiled a 29-53-1 record

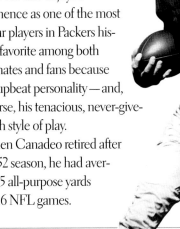

JOE CARR

Born: 10-22-1880, Columbus, Ohio **Died:** 5-20-39 **Executive career:** Co-founder of NFL 1920; President of NFL 1921-39

He was a bespectacled, mild-mannered gentleman who brought structure and order to the infant National Football League. In the chaotic, brawling 1920s era of professional football, Joe Carr stood resolute among the giants and slowly, methodically helped his sport earn respect and credibility. From 1921 to his death in 1939, the NFL's second president provided a voice of reason and set the league on a course to prosperity.

Carr, a member of the group that formed the American Professional Football Association (later the NFL) in 1920, established the league's constitution and by-laws, restricted player movement with standard contracts, gave teams territorial rights and directed league growth toward bigger cities with larger fan bases. He insisted the game should always strive for honesty and integrity.

Convincing such league heavyweights as George Halas, Curly Lambeau, Tim Mara and George Preston Marshall to sacrifice profit for high standards was not always easy. Carr pushed through and doggedly enforced rules that outlawed contact with players already under contract, the signing of under-class college players and the use of collegians under assumed names, a subterfuge that almost cost Lambeau his Packers franchise. It was Carr who recruited Mara to form the New York Giants in 1925.

Carr, who replaced figurehead first president Jim Thorpe in 1921, was a former newspaperman who had dabbled in semipro baseball and football. He later served as first president of the American Basketball Association (1925-28) and director of the National Association's promotional department (1933-39), helping major league baseball expand its minor league system from 14 leagues to 41. But Carr's workaholic moonlighting never interfered with his NFL priorities.

It was Carr, a charter member of the Hall of Fame, who introduced official standings in 1921 and settled early championship disputes by league vote. Under his guidance, the NFL introduced its official league title game in 1933, matching Eastern and Western division champions. When the proud Ohioan died in 1939, the league he helped form with 14 teams in such places as Decatur, Rock Island, Dayton and Canton was operating smoothly with 10 franchises in nine major cities.

> "We believe that there is a public demand for professional football ... and to the end that this league may not jeopardize the amateur standing of any college player, it is the unanimous decision that every member of the NFL be positively prohibited from inducing ... a college player to engage in professional football until his class at college shall have graduated." — *Joe Carr, NFL president*

Player/Year elected: 2002

DAVE CASPER

Born: 9-26-51, Bemidji, Min. **Ht/Wt:** 6-4/240 **College:** Notre Dame **Drafted:** 1974, 2nd round, Raiders **Primary position:** TE
Career statistics: Receiving, 378 rec., 5,216 yds., 13.8 avg., 52 TDs **Teams:** Raiders 1974-80, 1984; Oilers 1980-83; Vikings 1983
Super Bowl champion: 1976 season **Honors:** 1970s All-Decade Team

Opponents yanked, pushed and grabbed Dave Casper, using every trick imaginable to keep the 240-pound wide body from his appointed rounds. Coaches marveled at his skill, questioned his commitment and shuddered at the off-center views he eagerly shared with anybody who would listen. High maintenance, exasperating and unstoppable were adjectives that defined the prototypical tight end over his colorful 11-year NFL career.

The 6-foot-4 Casper is best remembered as a defense-shredding pass catcher and steamrolling run blocker for John Madden's powerful Oakland Raiders from 1974-80. With Ken Stabler throwing to Cliff Branch and Fred Biletnikoff on the outside, Casper was especially dangerous over the middle, a sure-handed target who could outleap defensive backs and outmuscle linebackers. He was a runaway bull when allowed to catch and run or he could trade blows with big linemen.

The former Notre Dame star averaged 55 catches for 739 yards from 1976-80 and enjoyed several signature moments. It was Casper's

> "I think he's the best tight end in the league. I can't think of anyone I'd rather have. He's not as fast as guys like Rich Caster or Raymond Chester, but he's an intelligent player and he knows how to get open."
>
> *— Ken Stabler, 1976*

42-yard touchdown catch that forced overtime and his 10-yard TD reception in the second extra period that gave the Raiders a memorable 37-31 win over Baltimore in a 1977 AFC playoff game. It was Casper who recovered the infamous multi-kicked and batted "touchdown fumble" that beat San Diego in a 1978 regular-season game. "The Ghost" also caught a touchdown pass in the Raiders' Super Bowl XI win over Minnesota.

The flip side was Casper's quirky personality that raised eyebrows with such comments as "football has never been fun for me" and "I can't understand why people come out and pay their money to watch the game." He railed against training camp and practice and entertained reporters with his thoughts about "weird coaches" and having to wear shoes.

The eccentric Casper was selected for five straight Pro Bowls through 1980, a season he split between Oakland and Houston. He never again was a dominant player over a career-ending run that included one season with Minnesota and a 1984 cameo with the Raiders in Los Angeles.

GUY CHAMBERLIN

Born: 1-16-1894, Blue Springs, Neb. **Died:** 4-4-67 **Ht/Wt:** 6-2/196 **College:** Nebraska **Primary positions:** OE, DE **Teams played:** Staleys 1920-21; Canton Bulldogs 1922-23; Cleveland Bulldogs 1924; Yellowjackets 1925-26; Cardinals 1927 **Teams coached (58-16-6):** Bulldogs 1922-24; Yellowjackets 1925-26; Cardinals 1927 **Championship teams:** 1922, '23, '24, '26 **Honors:** 1920s All-Decade Team

As a two-way player, Guy Chamberlin helped the 1921 Chicago Staleys win the future National Football League's second championship. As a player, coach and team organizer from 1922-26, he delivered four of the NFL's next five title winners. To say Chamberlin was a good man to have on your side in professional football's formative years was something of an understatement.

The former Nebraska star, a speedy 6-foot-2 offensive and defensive end, was a classic 60-minute performer known for his big-play ability. Chicagoans fondly remembered Chamberlin's 65-yard interception return that resulted in a key 1921 victory over Buffalo and he was one of the game's most proficient receivers when teams were still experimenting with the forward pass.

Chamberlin was one of pro football's first stars, a prime recruit when George Halas organized his Staleys — the future Chicago Bears. But Chamberlin's greatest acclaim was to come as a coach — first with the Canton and Cleveland Bulldogs and later with the Frankford Yellowjackets. His 58-16-6 overall record and .763 winning percentage is amazing by any standards and few coaches can match his greatest legacy: four championships in five seasons.

The first two came in 1922 and '23 when the Canton teams he organized, featuring future Hall of Famers Wilbur "Pete" Henry and Link Lyman, compiled a 21-0-3 two-year record and won consecutive titles. When the franchise was moved to Cleveland in 1924, Chamberlin reorganized his team, posted a 7-1-1

> ## "(Chamberlin) was a tall boy and very fast. He was the greatest two-way end of all time."
>
> *— George Halas*

record and won his third straight championship.

Chamberlin's Yellowjackets finished 13-7 in 1925, but he returned to the winner's circle the next year with a 14-1-1 masterpiece. The championship was decided when Chamberlin blocked an extra-point attempt by Chicago in a 7-6 win over Halas' Bears. Chamberlin's only losing season (3-7-1) as a coach or player came with the Chicago Cardinals in 1927 and he promptly ended his 92-game NFL career.

When asked some years later about the man he recruited to the NFL wars, Halas called Chamberlin "the greatest two-way end of all time." The coaching legacy speaks for itself.

JACK CHRISTIANSEN

Born: 12-20-28, Sublette, Kan. **Died:** 6-29-86 **Ht/Wt:** 6-1/185 **College:** Colorado State **Drafted:** 1951, 6th round, Lions **Primary position:** DB **Career statistics:** Interceptions, 46, 3 TDs; Punt Returns, 85 att., 12.8 avg., 8 TDs; KO Returns, 59 att., 22.5 avg. **Interceptions leader:** 1953, '57 **Teams:** Lions 1951-58 **Championship teams:** NFL 1952, '53, '57 **Honors:** 1950s All-Decade Team

The calm, clean, crew-cut look and disarming smile masked a Mr. Hyde scowl that unnerved receivers and quarterbacks when he stepped onto the field. Jack Christiansen, defensive back, was nobody's Mr. Nice Guy, especially when his pride was at stake. He was fearless, mean and sneaky, not above throwing a little dirt in a pass catcher's eyes or resorting

> "I remember Chris baiting receivers and passers out there. He'd let them think they could throw his way, then he'd snuff them out. You had to be honest with him."
>
> — *Jim David, former Lions defensive back, 1967*

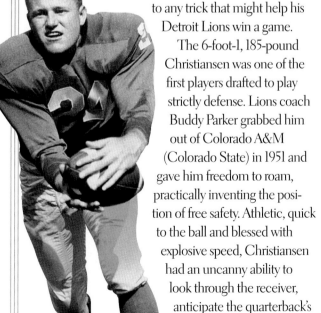

to any trick that might help his Detroit Lions win a game.

The 6-foot-1, 185-pound Christiansen was one of the first players drafted to play strictly defense. Lions coach Buddy Parker grabbed him out of Colorado A&M (Colorado State) in 1951 and gave him freedom to roam, practically inventing the position of free safety. Athletic, quick to the ball and blessed with explosive speed, Christiansen had an uncanny ability to look through the receiver, anticipate the quarterback's throw and swoop to the ball.

It didn't take long for him to show another talent as well. In a spectacular rookie season, Christiansen returned four punts for touchdowns—two in one game against Los Angeles, two in another against Green Bay. He was instant offense for Detroit, potential disaster for opponents who started using spread punt formations to defend against his rampages. When the long-striding, quick-cutting Christiansen got to full speed, few could catch him.

Former Cleveland star Mac Speedie said the Browns operated by two basic rules when they played the Lions: "Don't throw in his area and don't kick to him on punts." Detroit's defense, known affectionately as Chris' Crew, became the scourge of the NFL. Christiansen teamed with fellow Hall of Famer Yale Lary to key the Lions' run to four conference titles and championships in 1952, '53 and '57.

The man who brought awareness to the defensive secondary retired in 1958, after his eighth professional season, with 46 interceptions and averages of 12.8 yards per punt return and 22.5 per kickoff return. The two-time NFL leader in interceptions scored eight of his 13 career TDs while returning punts.

DUTCH CLARK

Born: 10-11-06, Fowler, Colo. **Died:** 8-5-78 **Ht/Wt:** 6-0/185 **College:** Colorado College **Primary positions:** TB, DB, K **Career statistics:** Rushing, 2,772 yds., 36 TDs; Receiving, 341 yds., 6 TDs; Passing, 1,507 yds., 11 TDs; Points, 369 **Scoring champion:** 1932, '35, '36 **Teams:** Portsmouth Spartans 1931-32; Lions 1934-38 **Championship team:** 1935 **Honors:** 1930s All-Decade Team

He was a quarterback before the position even existed, a quick-minded surgeon who cut a wide swath through helpless defenses. Everybody marveled at the triple-threat versatility of Earl "Dutch" Clark, but it was his instinctive genius that fueled the Portsmouth/Detroit teams he played for in the 1930s. "If Clark stepped on the field with Grange, Thorpe and Gipp," former college coaching great Clark Shaughnessy once said, "he would be the general."

Nearly blind in one eye and uncomfortable in the spotlight, the 6-foot, 185-pound Clark nevertheless masterminded the so-called "infantry attack" the Lions used to steamroll opponents from 1934-38. Teaming with fellow halfbacks Ace Gutowsky, Ernie Caddel and Frank Christensen, the cat-quick Clark called signals, handled passing duties and darted around and through overmatched defenders.

A talented defensive back when not running the offense, Clark posted then-huge season rushing totals of 763 yards, 427, 628 and 468 for a well-grounded attack that set a long-standing team rushing record in 1936.

> "Dutch is like a rabbit in a brush heap when he gets into the secondary. He has no plan but only instinct to cut, pivot, slant and run in any direction equally well."
>
> — *Potsy Clark, former Lions coach*

As a passer that season, Clark completed an astonishing 53.5 percent (38-of-71) of his throws and his offensive legacy includes three NFL scoring titles — the result of 42 career touchdowns and his accuracy as a drop-kicker.

With the former Colorado College star accounting for 1,218 rushing, passing and receiving yards and scoring eight touchdowns, the Lions finished 10-3 in 1934, but were beaten out by undefeated Chicago in the Western Division. Clark's numbers dipped in 1935, but he led the Lions to a division-best 7-3-2 record and scored on an electrifying 40-yard run in a 26-7 NFL championship game win over the New York Giants.

The Lions thought so much of Clark's leadership skills they promoted him to player/coach when Potsy Clark stepped down after the 1936 season. Dutch ended his seven-year playing career after the 1938 campaign to become coach of the Cleveland Rams, a job he held for four years. Clark was honored as a charter member of the Pro Football Hall of Fame in 1963.

CLARK

GEORGE CONNOR

Born: 1-21-25, Chicago, Ill. **Died:** 3-31-2003 **Ht/Wt:** 6-3/240 **College:** Holy Cross, Notre Dame **Drafted:** 1946, 1st round, Giants
Primary position: OT, DT, LB **Teams:** Bears 1948-55 **Honors:** 1940s All-Decade Team

Some opposing coaches worried about George Connor's ability to open holes as an explosive offensive tackle for the Chicago Bears. Others cursed the way he controlled the line of scrimmage as a defensive lineman. But nobody understood the full impact of the 6-foot-3, 240-pound "Moose" until George Halas turned him loose as one of the most devastating linebackers of his era.

The smart, fast, ruggedly handsome Connor, who was considered briefly for the screen role of Tarzan, earned All-Pro honors at all three positions during an eight-year NFL career (1948-55) with his hometown Bears. Such acclaim was not unusual for Connor, who had earned two All-American citations at Notre Dame while helping the Irish win national championships in 1946 and '47. He arrived in 1948 and made his mark in Chicago's trenches, but his future really was decided in an eye-opening fourth game of the 1949 campaign.

Preparing for the powerful Philadelphia Eagles and agonizing over how to stop their devastating end sweep with Steve Van Buren following a wall of blockers, Halas got creative. He moved Connor to outside linebacker, asked him to take out as many blockers as he could and then watched in amazement as he consistently broke through and dropped the powerful Van Buren. The Bears pulled off a 38-21 upset and Connor's fate was sealed.

While he continued to see time on the offensive line, Connor became an outstanding linebacker — at his best when allowed to roam and track down ballcarriers with his remarkable radar. He was especially astute at recognizing keys, a concept that wouldn't become popular for several years, and he seldom was caught out of position. When he was, Connor simply used his speed to compensate.

After a knee injury-shortened 1954 season, the four-time Pro Bowl selection returned for one final hurrah. The 1955 Bears finished 8-4 and Connor was outstanding, even scoring a memorable touchdown on a 48-yard fumble return in a 21-20 comeback win over Detroit.

> "George Connor parlayed leadership and intelligence and fine ability into one of the great careers of our time. We set high standards for him as a player. He exceeded them."
>
> *—George Halas*

JIMMY CONZELMAN

Born: 3-6-1898, St. Louis, Mo. **Died:** 7-31-70 **Ht/Wt:** 6-0/175 **Positions:** HB, DB **Teams played:** Staleys 1920; Rock Island 1921-22; Milwaukee 1922-24; Detroit 1925-26; Providence 1927-29 **Teams coached (87-63-17 RS, 1-1 PS):** Rock Island 1921-22; Milwaukee 1922-23; Detroit 1925-26; Providence 1927-30; Cardinals 1940-42, 1946-48 **Championship teams:** NFL 1928, '47 **Honors:** 1920s All-Decade Team

He was an author, actor, boxer, piano player, baseball executive, sportswriter, newspaper publisher, playwright, orator, advertising executive, song writer and minor league baseball player. In his spare time, the ever-versatile and talented Jimmy Conzelman also played in 102 NFL games and coached 167, a skill that procured two championships and earned the popular St. Louisan Hall of Fame distinction.

A close friend of former Great Lakes Naval Training Station teammate George Halas, the 6-foot, 175-pounder played for Papa Bear's Chicago Staleys in the NFL's inaugural 1920 season and spent the next 10 years as a player, coach and short-term owner. On the field for teams in Chicago, Rock Island, Milwaukee, Detroit and Providence, the talented halfback scored 26 touchdowns and 169 points, but it was as a magnetic leader and popular strategist that he gained his greatest recognition.

"The Gray Fox" won his first NFL championship in 1928 when he led Providence to an 8-1-2 record. The second came two decades later in Chicago, after he had spent most of the Depression era coaching

> ## "I've done almost anything and everything I wanted to do. It's been a rewarding life."
>
> — *Jimmy Conzelman*

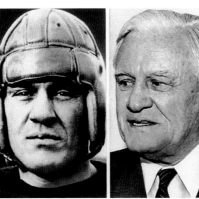

Washington University football and pursuing other interests. The "golden era" of Cardinals history occurred under Conzelman, who took the coaching reins in 1940, left in 1943 to work for baseball's St. Louis Browns and returned to Chicago for a glorious encore in 1946.

His first post-War team, featuring backs Paul Christman, Elmer Angsman and Pat Harder, finished 6-5. In 1947, when newcomer Charley Trippi was teamed with Angsman in Chicago's "Dream Backfield," the Cardinals posted a 9-3 record and won their first championship since 1925 with a 28-21 win over Philadelphia. After going 11-1 in 1948, the Cardinals barely missed another when they suffered a 7-0 title-game loss to the Eagles in a blinding snowstorm. And Conzelman retired—from football.

Never lacking for another talent to explore or a name to drop, Conzelman raised eyebrows in 1964 when he asked longtime friend William O. Douglas to introduce him at his Pro Football Hall of Fame induction. The U.S. Supreme Court Justice agreed.

LOU CREEKMUR

Born: 1-22-27, Hopelawn, N.J. **Ht/Wt:** 6-4/255 **College:** William & Mary **Drafted:** 1948, 24th round, Eagles; 1950, 2nd round of special draft, Lions **Primary positions:** OT, OG, DT **Teams:** Lions 1950-59 **Championship teams:** NFL 1952, '53, '57

Quarterback Bobby Layne was a huge fan of Lou Creekmur. So was Doak Walker, who ran in the NFL fast lanes because of the 6-foot-4, 255-pound tackle from Hopelawn, N.J. Big Lou was an iron-man enforcer in the 1950s, a trench warrior who helped the Detroit Lions win three championships while serving as chief protector for two Hall of Fame-bound teammates.

Creekmur was a sometimes-flamboyant, always-reliable power blocker who could operate either from the guard or tackle positions. He began his professional career in 1950 at guard and earned All-Pro status in 1951 and '52. But Creekmur is best remembered as a talented left tackle, Layne's impenetrable shield, and a quietly efficient centerpiece for Lions teams that defeated the Cleveland Browns in the 1952, '53 and '57 championship games while losing to

> "We didn't know anything about plastic helmets or face masks. That leather was our security blanket. By the mid-1950s, after suffering over a dozen broken noses, I decided to start wearing a mask."
>
> — *Lou Creekmur, 1996, The Associated Press*

them in '54.

Creekmur dominated opponents with surprising quickness and strength. Walker thrived while running through holes created by his big tackle; Layne free-lanced with complete confidence that his blind side was protected. Creekmur also was used as an anchor for Detroit's defensive line in short-yardage situations and he willingly played middle guard when Lions coach Buddy Parker needed defensive help in 1955.

Creekmur, who went to William & Mary as a 6-foot, 200-pound freshman, served two years in the military and returned as a 250-pound giant. The Lions grabbed him on the second round of a special 1950 draft and plugged him into their offensive line, where he played 165 straight games over a 10-year career that generated eight Pro Bowl invitations. No matter what position Creekmur played, he was a focus in Detroit's high-powered game plans.

He also was an NFL trendsetter. Creekmur, who suffered numerous broken noses over the course of a career that started with players wearing leather helmets, became one of the first to use a face mask. He played through the 1958 season, retired and returned for eight games in 1959 at the request of coach George Wilson.

LARRY CSONKA

Born: 12-25-46, Stow, Ohio **Ht/Wt:** 6-3/235 **College:** Syracuse **Drafted:** 1968, 1st round, Dolphins **Primary position:** FB
Career statistics: Rushing, 1,891 att., 8,081 yds., 4.3 avg., 64 TDs **Teams:** Dolphins 1968-74, 1979; Giants 1976-78
Super Bowl champions: 1972, '73 (MVP) seasons

He was a defense's worst nightmare, a courage-deflating bull who stomped, snorted and trampled any obstacle in his path. Pity the poor tackler who got first shot at Larry Csonka, the ultimate power fullback of the 1970s and the driving force for three Miami Super Bowl teams. Zonk's road to success traveled through defenders, not around them, and the relentless punishment he delivered over 11 NFL seasons is still being felt.

Dubbed "the Bronko Nagurski of the 1970s," the 6-foot-3, 235-pound former Syracuse star simply dared tacklers to give him their best shot. There was nothing fancy about his style, which produced 8,081 rushing yards, a 4.3-yard average and 64 rushing touchdowns over eight seasons with the Dolphins (1968-74, 1979) and three with the New York Giants (1976-78). Csonka simply pounded the middle and created room for one of the best ground attacks in history.

With Csonka controlling the middle, Mercury Morris providing an outside threat and Jim Kiick running and catching passes, Don Shula's Dolphins led the NFL in rushing in 1971 (2,429 yards) and 1972 (2,960), both Super Bowl seasons. The '72 Dolphins capped a perfect 17-0 effort with a 14-7 Super Bowl win over Washington as Csonka ran for 112 yards. The 1973 season concluded with Csonka running for a then-Super Bowl record 145 yards in a 24-7 win over Minnesota.

A five-time Pro Bowl selection and three-time 1,000-yard rusher, Zonk simply wore defenders down.

"The longer the day gets, the better he is, the more he hurts you," lamented former Oakland coach John Madden, a sentiment shared throughout the NFL.

> **"My job is no big deal. I'm a fullback, a power back whose assignment is to establish an inside running game. That's my work."** —*Larry Csonka*

And the proud Csonka never took a play off, whether delivering devastating blocks or running out the clock. Amazingly, the durable workhorse fumbled only 21 times on 1,997 career runs and receptions.

Miami's glory years ended when Csonka jumped with teammates Kiick and Paul Warfield to the Memphis Southmen of the newly formed World Football League in 1975. When the WFL folded, big No. 39 played three seasons in New York before making a one-year return to the Dolphins.

Contributor/Year elected: 1992

AL DAVIS

Born: 7-4-29, Brockton, Mass. **Teams coached (23-16-3):** Raiders 1963-65 **Executive career:** Coach of Raiders 1963-65; AFL commissioner 1966; owner of Raiders 1967-present

Call him the Darth Vader of football, the clever and belligerent dark lord of the NFL's most controversial franchise. Call him brash, self-serving and stubborn; call him a maverick, a rebel, a troublemaker. Go ahead, call Al Davis whatever you want, as long as everybody understands what he really is and wants more than anything else to be—a winner.

Davis, of course, has been so much more—innovator, coach, owner and power broker—during his four-decade association with the Raiders. He was a coach who embraced the "vertical passing game," an American Football League general manager who outbid NFL teams for prime talent, an owner who built one of the game's outstanding franchises and the

> "I used to be bored when other coaches talked offense. But this fellow Davis really knows pass offense. I doubt if anyone else has as much football knowledge as Al. In addition, he has a way of handling players that makes them feel like giants."
>
> —*Art Powell, wide receiver, 1966*

short-term AFL commissioner who helped affect the historic NFL merger.

Few have had more impact than the NFL's man in black. Fans know Davis as creator of the "Raiders Mystique," the man who built the Silver and Black into the league's most consistently successful franchise. He was coach and general manager from 1963-65, AFL commissioner in 1966 and the managing general partner whose astute drafts and trades produced one AFL champion and three Super Bowl winners from 1967 to the present.

Davis revels in his image as an NFL renegade. He outfitted his teams in black, signed players branded as troublemakers by other organizations, encouraged edgy play and dirty tricks, demanded rugged defense and passionately exhorted his troops to "Just win, baby." His Raiders have, posting the game's best winning percentage from 1963-2002.

Davis, once described by commissioner Pete Rozelle as a "charming rogue," is known for his contrary postures. He won a long, expensive legal battle against the NFL over his right to move the Raiders from Oakland to Los Angeles in 1982 — and then moved them back in 1995. In 1986, he testified on behalf of the United States Football League in its antitrust suit against the NFL. A more positive contribution was his 1989 hiring of Art Shell as the modern era's first black head coach.

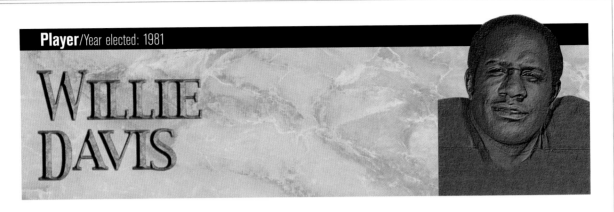

WILLIE DAVIS

Born: 7-24-34, Lisbon, La. **Ht/Wt:** 6-3/245 **College:** Grambling State **Drafted:** 1956, 15th round, Browns **Primary position:** DE
Career statistics: 21 fumble recoveries **Teams:** Browns 1958-59; Packers 1960-69 **Championship teams:** NFL 1961, '62, '65,
'66, '67 **Super Bowl champions:** 1966, '67 seasons **Honors:** 1960s All-Decade Team

It was impossible not to notice Willie Davis. He had a special knack for being in the wrong place at the right time—wrong for opponents, right for Vince Lombardi's Green Bay Packers. In an era when defensive ends were seldom seen and heard, Big Willie grabbed the spotlight with a big-play flair that contributed to the most prolific championship run in NFL history.

Davis was unusually fast for a man 6-foot-3, 245 pounds, and he could beat offensive tackles with a bull rush, explode past them off the snap or throw them aside with quick, powerful hands. He was a rock on the Packers' impenetrable front wall and the worst nightmare for overly patient quarterbacks. Davis also was a focused, durable competitor who never missed a game or took a play off over his 12-year career.

Lombardi loved the consistency his former Grambling star provided game after game, play after play, but he also loved the intelligence that allowed Davis to diagnose game situations and make quick decisions that often resulted in sacks or fumbles. He was relentless, whether fighting through a pass block or pursuing a speedy ballcarrier. "Davis is a great pass rusher," said Hall of Fame quarterback Y.A. Tittle. "He's always towering over you, coming, coming, all the time."

The gregarious, affable Davis chased down quarterbacks on Sundays and a master's degree in business administration in his spare time. He was outspoken and civic minded, a player who was respected off the field as well as on. As the Packers rolled to five NFL championships and wins in the first two Super Bowls over a seven-year stretch in the 1960s, Davis became a symbol of their success—classy and unstoppable.

It was an impressive plateau for Davis, who started his career in Cleveland as a 15th-round draft pick. When he retired after the 1969 season with five Pro Bowl selections, he had recovered 21 opponents' fumbles—a team record that still stands.

> **"Willie is the quickest defensive end in the business. He's not the strongest or the biggest, but he's always in there, always managing to get at least his arm in the way."**
>
> —*Billy Wade, former NFL quarterback*

LEN DAWSON

Born: 6-20-35, Alliance, Ohio **Ht/Wt:** 6-0/190 **College:** Purdue **Drafted:** 1957, 1st round, Steelers **Primary position:** QB
Career statistics: Passing, 2,136-of-3,741, 28,711 yds., 239 TDs; Rushing, 1,293 yds., 9 TDs **Teams:** Steelers 1957-59; Browns 1960-61; Texans/Chiefs 1962-75 **Championship teams:** AFL 1962, '66, '69 **Super Bowl champion:** 1969 (MVP) season

Hank Stram called him "the most accurate passer in pro football." Teammates marveled at the calm, quiet leadership that defined the 19-year career of Len Dawson, the architect of three AFL championships and one of the game's biggest Super Bowl upsets. What Lenny the Cool might have lacked in pure athleticism he made up for in more cerebral ways.

Dawson spent his first five professional seasons on the bench with the Pittsburgh Steelers and Cleveland Browns. But when he was signed by the AFL's Dallas Texans in 1962, he took the reins as Stram's starting quarterback, led the team to a championship and claimed Player of the Year honors. The former Purdue star completed 61 percent of his 310 passes for 2,759 yards and 29 touchdowns — numbers that would become typical over the next decade.

The handsome, articulate 6-footer, who won four AFL passing titles, was a coach's dream. Using Stram's innovative "moving pocket," he ran game plans to perfection, called most of his own plays and seldom made a mistake, cleverly using the talent at his disposal. Dawson, blessed with only average arm strength, was a thinking man's quarterback and a quiet enforcer who could deliver reprimands with a laser-like glare.

The Texans moved to Kansas City in 1963 and Dawson led the Chiefs to Super Bowl berths after the 1966 and '69 seasons. Super Bowl I against Green Bay ended in a 35-10 loss but Super Bowl IV was a different story. Burdened by gambling allegations in the week leading up to the game, Dawson shook off the unfounded charges and led the Chiefs to a stunning 23-7 win over powerful Minnesota. His MVP performance included a 46-yard clinching touchdown pass to Otis Taylor.

Dawson had one more big season, leading the Chiefs to a 10-3-1 record and AFC West title in 1971, but he remained a competent field general through 1975 before retiring at age 40. He left the game with 2,136 completions for 28,711 yards and 239 touchdowns. The proud Ohioan was named to six AFL All-Star Games and one Pro Bowl.

> "I think he was a lot like Bart Starr: a quiet, cool leader. He wasn't flamboyant. ... he very quietly controlled the offense, moved it deliberately and tried not to make mistakes. Few guys I ever saw did that as well."
>
> — *Jerry Mays, former Chiefs teammate*

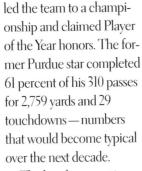

DAWSON

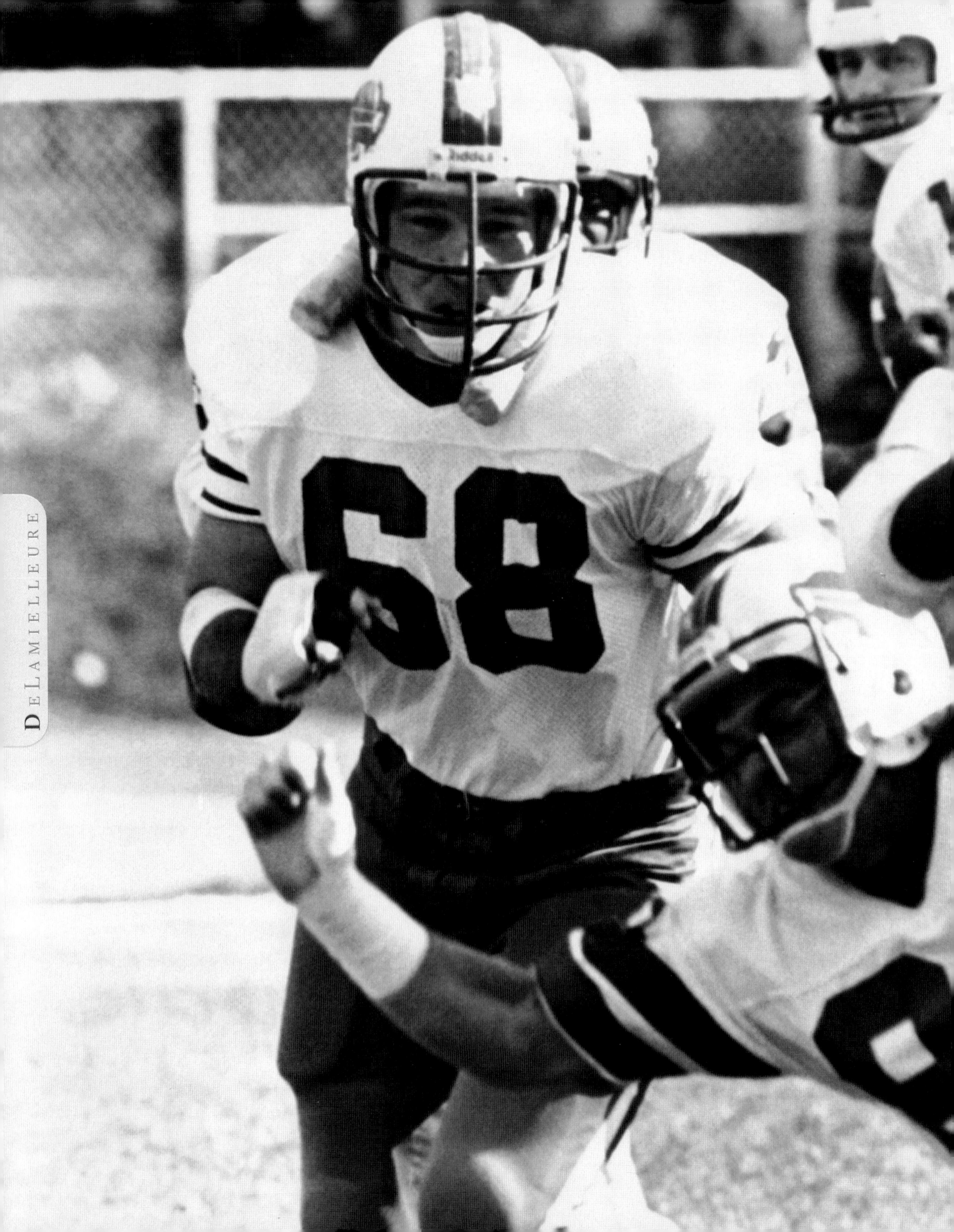
68

JOE DELAMIELLEURE

Born: 3-16-51, Detroit, Mich. **Ht/Wt:** 6-3/254 **College:** Michigan State **Drafted:** 1973, 1st round, Bills **Primary position:** OG
Teams: Bills 1973-79, 1985; Browns 1980-84 **Honors:** 1970s All-Decade Team

Buffalo fans remember Joe DeLamielleure as the pathfinder right guard for the "Electric Company" offensive line that helped O.J. Simpson make history in 1973. Cleveland fans revered the unyielding pass blocker who protected high-powered quarterback Brian Sipe from 1980-83. By any measure, Joe D. was a 13-year NFL heavyweight, from the 254 pounds he carried on his muscled body to his 13-letter last name.

Off the field, DeLamielleure was an articulate, quick-witted charmer with a receding blond hairline and a smile that could light up a locker room. That smile was absent on Sunday afternoons when defenders encountered a 6-foot-3 grinder with massive forearms and an obsessive desire to pound them into submission. DeLamielleure's Popeye-like strength came from a fanatic workout routine that never varied, in season or out.

Few players made a bigger rookie impact than the former Michigan State All-American, a first-round draft pick who stepped in as an immediate starter on a line that

> **"I had difficulty with him. I always thought Joe was a tough offensive lineman. I'd put Joe in the same class with Larry Little and Jim Langer."**
>
> *—Mean Joe Greene, 2003, The Buffalo News*

included guard Reggie McKenzie, tackles Dave Foley and Donnie Green and center Bruce Jarvis. Behind the "Electric Company," Simpson (The Juice) pounded out a record 2,003 yards in 1973 and followed with seasons of 1,125, 1,817 and 1,503. From 1973-78, the Bills gained more rushing yards than any other team.

Playing for the Browns in 1980, DeLamielleure was a member of the AFC Central-champion "Kardiac Kids," who suffered a devastating playoff loss to Oakland. Many questioned his ability to adjust from Buffalo's run-oriented attack to the high-powered passing offense of Cleveland, but he performed admirably for five years. When he returned to Buffalo in 1985 for a final season, he was one of the game's most well-rounded and honored offensive linemen.

Joe D., who claimed he would have played football for "a cap and a T-shirt," was a six-time All-AFC performer and six-time Pro Bowler. He played in 185 straight games from the beginning of his career, sitting out for the first time in his final season.

DELAMIELLEURE

ERIC DICKERSON

Born: 9-2-60, Sealy, Tex. **Ht/Wt:** 6-3/220 **College:** SMU **Drafted:** 1983, 1st round, Rams **Primary position:** RB **Career statistics:** Rushing, 2996 att., 13,259 yds., 4.4 avg., 90 TDs; Receiving, 281 rec., 2,137 yds., 6 TDs **Rushing champion:** 1983, '84, '86, '88 **Teams:** Rams 1983-87; Colts 1987-91; Raiders 1992; Falcons 1993 **Honors:** 1980s All-Decade Team

You couldn't help but notice the glide, the way his feet seemed to hydroplane over a football surface like a speedboat barely touching water. Or the incredible acceleration that shot Eric Dickerson through the slightest crack in an opponent's line. He was instant offense, a touchdown waiting to happen. And he was one of the game's spectacular running backs over a sometimes-phenomenal, always-controversial 11-year NFL career.

The muscular 6-foot-3, 220-pound former SMU star was easy to spot. Off the field, he was charismatic, the man you would notice in a crowded room. On the field, he looked like something out of Star Wars—clear goggles, a facemask with four horizontal bars, a protective neck collar, extra reinforced shoulder pads, a flak jacket, elbow pads and tape covering his shoes. The colorful yellow-and-blue Los Angeles Rams uniform and his explosive, upright running style were exclamation points.

Dickerson became an NFL prodigy in 1983 when he posted rookie numbers of 390 carries, 1,808 yards, 51 receptions and 20 touchdowns for the suddenly respectable Rams. It was the first of seven straight 1,000-yard seasons and a fitting appetizer for the

> **"Every time Dickerson gets the ball, you don't breathe until he's tackled. And considering the number of times he gets the ball, that kind of wears on an opposing coach during the course of the afternoon."**
>
> *— Raymond Berry, Patriots coach, 1986*

spectacular 1984 performance that netted a single-season rushing record of 2,105 yards. Another explosion, 1,821 yards in 1986, earned Dickerson his third rushing title in four years.

Los Angeles fans marveled at the long-striding explosiveness, which allowed Dickerson to run around tacklers and avoid the Jim Brown-like punishment he openly disdained. But they cringed in 1987 when a bitter contract dispute cut short his Rams career and triggered a spectacular three-team, 10-player trade that landed

him in Indianapolis. He continued to churn out big yardage for the lowly Colts, but he also battled management for five years before ending his career with one-year stops in Los Angeles (the Raiders) and Atlanta.

Dickerson never played on a championship team, but his impressive ledger included 13,259 rushing yards (second all-time when he retired in 1993), 2,137 receiving yards on 281 catches and six Pro Bowls.

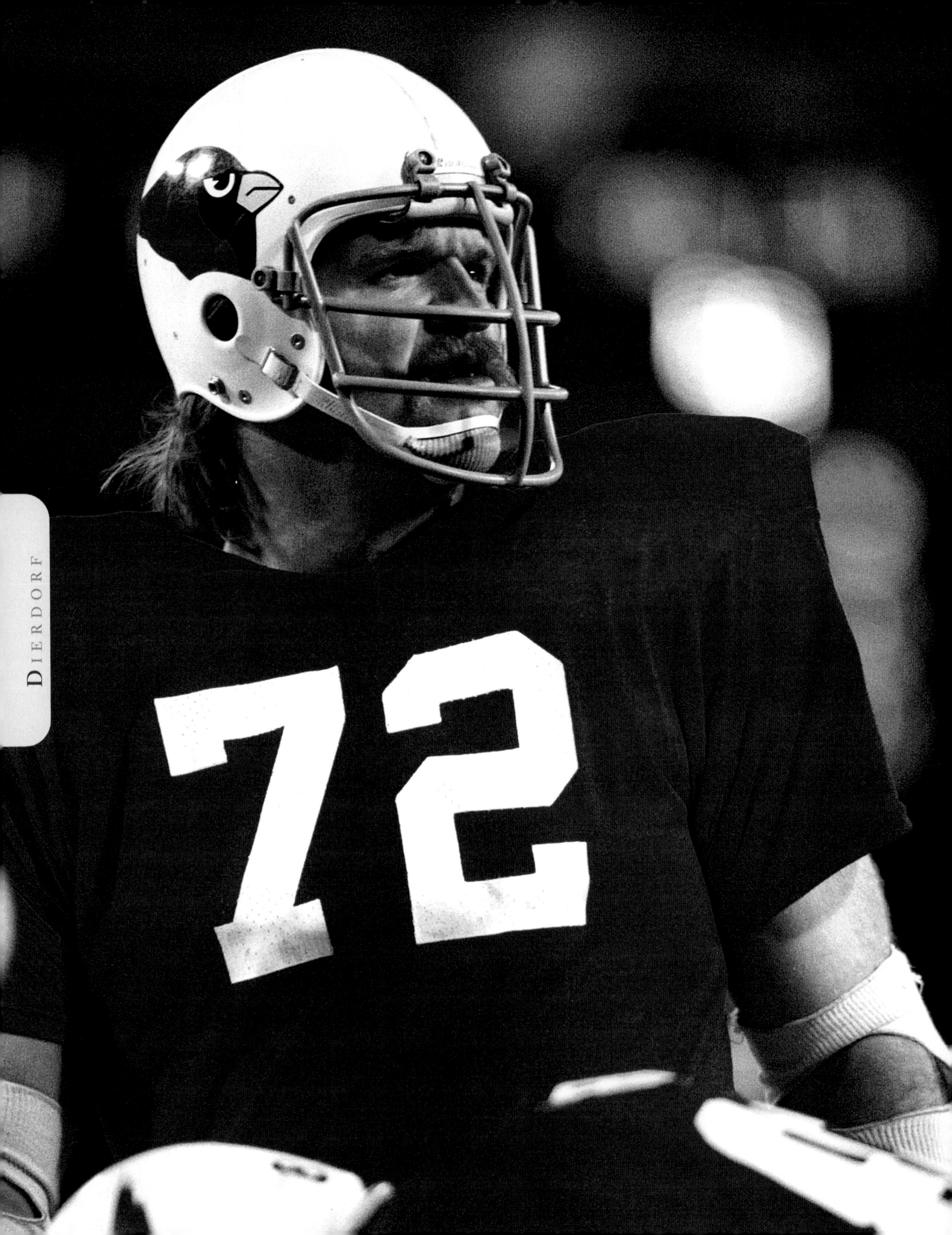

DAN DIERDORF

Born: 6-29-49, Canton, Ohio **Ht/Wt:** 6-3/290 **College:** Michigan **Drafted:** 1971, 2nd round, Cardinals **Primary position:** OT
Team: Cardinals 1971-83 **Honors:** 1970s All-Decade Team

P ity the poor defensive ends and tackles who had
to deal with Dan Dierdorf for 60 minutes. On
one play he
would run over
them like a Mack
truck; on the next
he would guard
the St. Louis
backfield like an
impenetrable
wall. Often hailed as the best offensive lineman of the
1970s, the Cardinals' big right tackle firmly believed it
was better to give punishment than to receive it.

> "Dan Dierdorf was the greatest offensive
> lineman of his time. ... How could such
> an intelligent, sensitive man be imparted
> in that huge, imposing body?"
>
> — *Bill Walsh*

"It was a thing of beauty," said former linemate
Conrad Dobler, referring to Dierdorf's one-on-one
blocking proficiency. At 6-foot-3 and 290 pounds,
Dierdorf was rock-solid, strong as an ox and surprisingly quick. He had amazing leverage, the product of
tremendous lower-body strength, and near-perfect
technique, a result of his passion to be best. The driv-
en and durable Dierdorf never took a play off, either in
practice or games.

He did not go unnoticed, even though he played 13
seasons (1971-83) for weak Cardinals teams that
reached the playoffs only three times and never won a
postseason game. He was a six-time Pro Bowl participant, a consistent All-Pro, the leader of a line that
allowed a record-low eight sacks in the 14-game 1975
season and a three-time choice (1976-78) by the NFL
Players Association as the league's best blocker.

Dierdorf remained the standard for blocking excellence until he suffered a dislocated knee in 1979 and
never regained
top form.

The man with
the big voice and
droopy mustache
also was affable,
intelligent,
humorous and
outspoken, an offensive lineman who provided post-
game analysis and a visible restaura-
teur in the St. Louis community. After his retirement,
Dierdorf started another
career as a radio personality
and television broadcaster —
most notably on ABC's
Monday Night Football.

The former Michigan
All-American, who began
his pro career in 1971 as
an offensive guard
and finished in
1983 as a cen-
ter, traveled
full circle
in 1996
when he was inducted into the Pro Football Hall of
Fame — in his hometown of Canton, Ohio.

DIERDORF

MIKE DITKA

Born: 10-18-39, Carnegie, Pa. **Ht/Wt:** 6-3/228 **College:** Pittsburgh **Drafted:** 1961, 1st round, Bears **Primary position:** TE
Career statistics: Receiving, 427 rec., 5,812 yds., 13.6 avg., 43 TDs **Teams played:** Bears 1961-66; Eagles 1967-68; Cowboys 1969-72 **Teams coached (121-95 RS, 6-6 PS):** Bears 1982-92; Saints 1997-99 **Championship team:** NFL 1963
Super Bowl champion: 1971 season **Honors:** 75th Anniversary All-Time Team

The bristly crew-cut topped a small, round, chubby face with a small mouth, flaring nostrils and narrow, deep-set eyes. If you looked closely at the eyes, you could see the blazing fire that burned within Mike Ditka. It raged every time he took the field for 12 NFL seasons in a career that redefined the tight end position. And it stoked the imagination of Chicago fans, who embraced him as one of the most popular players in the Bears' long history.

> "I just try to hit the other guy before he hits me and if I hit hard enough, maybe he won't want to hit me back." —*Mike Ditka*

Before Ditka was drafted out of Pittsburgh in 1961, tight ends were hard-nosed blockers who occasionally caught a pass over the middle. Iron Mike fit the blocking profile, but Bears coach George Halas had much more in mind. Big (6-foot-3, 228 pounds), fast and agile, Ditka became an offensive weapon, a pass-catching force over the middle and outside—and he could go long if crowded by a defender.

His rookie season produced amazing numbers—56 catches, 1,076 yards, 12 touchdowns—and sent defensive coordinators scurrying to

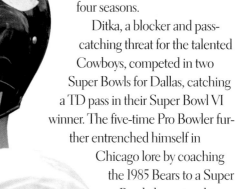

find a solution. Not only was the bull-necked, broad-shouldered Ditka hard to tackle when he caught the ball, he defiantly stiff-armed his way past tacklers and had the speed to outrun many defensive backs. He consistently flashed that Irish temper and every-play intensity that gave him an intimidating edge.

Ditka's first four seasons produced reception totals of 56, 58, 59 and 75 and he was a big part of the Bears' run to a 1963 championship—the team's first in 17 years. But the continual pounding took a toll and his pass-catching numbers declined. A trade to Philadelphia was followed by mediocre 1967 and 1968 seasons and another trade to Dallas, where he spent his final four seasons.

Ditka, a blocker and pass-catching threat for the talented Cowboys, competed in two Super Bowls for Dallas, catching a TD pass in their Super Bowl VI winner. The five-time Pro Bowler further entrenched himself in Chicago lore by coaching the 1985 Bears to a Super Bowl championship.

DITKA

ART DONOVAN

Born: 6-5-25, Bronx, N.Y. **Ht/Wt:** 6-3/270 **College:** Boston College **Drafted:** 1950, 3rd round, Colts **Primary position:** DT **Teams:** Original Colts 1950; Yanks 1951; Texans 1952; Colts 1953-61 **Championship teams:** 1958, '59 **Honors:** 1950s All-Decade Team

He was Baltimore's happy warrior, a feared combat expert and lovable prankster who knew how to mix business with pleasure. Burly defensive tackle Art Donovan would destroy opponents with a sweep of his powerful arms, then make them laugh with a self-deprecating one-liner. His ferocious play helped the Colts win consecutive NFL championships in 1958 and '59; his infectious personality helped them win the heart of an entire city.

As a locker room jester and unofficial ambassador for one of the game's great teams, Donovan kept teammates laughing and enthralled fans with his storytelling genius. On the field, when push came to shove, the round, almost angelic face of the 6-foot-3, 270-pound giant would suddenly turn serious and opponents would brace for the devastation to come.

Donovan could split double-teams, clog up the middle and shut down running games. Working in tandem, defensive end Gino Marchetti and Donovan formed one of the best pass-rush combinations in football history. Big Art was adept at reading keys and surprisingly quick, attributes that helped him win five straight Pro Bowl selections (1954-58).

The son of Art Donovan Sr., a famous boxing referee, the former Boston College star played for the original Baltimore Colts team of 1950, a franchise that folded, and the Baltimore Colts that began play in 1953. Donovan and Marchetti soon were joined by coach Weeb Ewbank and such players as Johnny Unitas, Lenny Moore, Raymond Berry and Big Daddy Lipscomb. As the Colts edged toward championship form, Donovan provided valuable chemistry.

The beer-loving New Yorker had problems controlling his weight and the annual preseason weigh-in became a much-anticipated Baltimore event. Gruff and outspoken, Donovan spared no one and saved the most-pointed barbs for himself. His infectious humor carried over to the field, but never got in the way. When the popular Donovan retired in 1961, he was honored before a 1962 game at Memorial Stadium—one of the most touching sports tributes in Baltimore history.

> ### "Art is a pro's pro. He's always trying to improve. He's got that one thing every great athlete must have—pride."
>
> —*Weeb Ewbank*

Player/Year elected: 1994

TONY DORSETT

Born: 4-7-54, Rochester, Pa. **Ht/Wt:** 5-11/192 **College:** Pittsburgh **Drafted:** 1977, 1st round, Cowboys **Primary position:** RB
Career statistics: Rushing, 2,936 att., 12,739 yds., 4.3 avg., 77 TDs; Receiving, 398 rec., 3,554 yds., 13 TDs **Teams:** Cowboys 1977-87; Broncos 1988 **Super Bowl champion:** 1977 season

At first glance, Tony Dorsett appeared grossly overmatched in the land of the giants. But then he tucked the ball into his muscular 5-foot-11, 192-pound body and destroyed that myth, much like he would destroy game plans with exciting consistency over a memorable 12-year career. Touchdown Tony was a yardage-eating machine for the Dallas Cowboys, living proof that good things do come in small packages.

Dorsett, the 1976 Heisman Trophy-winning back who set an NCAA career rushing record at Pittsburgh, was blessed with amazing balance and acceleration, qualities that allowed him to stop and start, dart and slash while searching for a hole. Woe to the defense that allowed him to wander along the line of scrimmage looking for daylight. Nobody could rev up to top speed faster and nobody could cut against the grain with such spectacular results.

Of Dorsett's 77 rushing touchdowns, five came on runs of 75 yards or longer — one on a record 99-yard burst against Minnesota in

> "His ability, his speed and quickness, put a new dimension in our offense. Here we had a guy that every time he touched the ball, anything could happen. He just blended with Roger (Staubach) very well."
>
> —*Tom Landry, 1994, Pittsburgh Post-Gazette*

1983. He consistently defied skeptics, who marveled at his durability and the eight 1,000-yard efforts he turned in over his first nine professional seasons. In his 46 100-yard games for the Cowboys, they were 42-4.

Dorsett's running style matched his off-field personality. He was quiet and shy when he leaned forward, looking, looking, looking for the hole. He was articulate and expressive when his big brown eyes lit up and he suddenly exploded into action. Dorsett expressed himself to the tune of 12,739 yards in regular-season play — second all-time when he retired — and 1,383 more as one of the top postseason rushers in history.

Dorsett, a four-time Pro Bowl selection, also was a competent pass-catcher, a willing blocker and good team player who helped the Cowboys reach five NFC championship games and two Super Bowls, one of which produced a victory over Denver. He later would play one season with those same Broncos, posting 703 yards in that 1988 swan song before retiring.

DORSETT

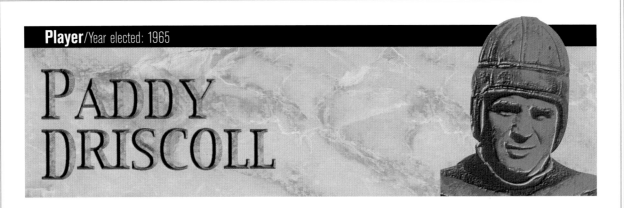

PADDY DRISCOLL

Born: 1-11-1896, Evanston, Ill. **Died:** 6-29-68 **Ht/Wt:** 5-11/160 **College:** Northwestern **Primary positions:** TB, QB, DB, K, P
Career statistics: Rushing, 25 TDs; Receiving, 4 TDs; Passing, 16 TDs; Scoring, 51 FGs, 63 PAT, 402 pts. **Scoring champion:** 1923, '26 **Teams:** Staleys 1920; Cardinals 1920-25; Bears 1926-29 **Championship team:** 1925 **Honors:** 1920s All-Decade Team

He was a cleverly disguised football hero, a 160-pound balding, mild-mannered Irishman who transformed magically into an athletic superman. Nobody could beat you in more ways than Paddy

Driscoll and no one could do it more impressively. Field general, runner, passer, receiver, defensive back, return man, kicker—from 1920-29, Driscoll was the professional game's ultimate weapon.

> "Paddy was the guy who actually started to put pro football in the big-league bracket. His debut preceded George Halas' by about two years and Paddy was a big gate attraction before Red Grange finished his career at Illinois in 1925."
>
> —*Bill Whalen, former Cardinals teammate, 1956, Chicago American*

Opponents who underestimated the 5-foot-11 "mighty mite" spent much of their game day chasing his elusive shadow. Driscoll was a triple-threat halfback and elusive return man for the Chicago Cardinals from 1920-25 and a four-year star from 1926-29 for the cross-town Bears, coached by old friend and teammate George Halas. A member of the Cardinals' 1925 championship team, Driscoll's more enduring legacy was achieved as the game's first great kicker.

He could dictate field position with his precision punts and decide outcomes with his accurate dropkicks. When 36,000-plus fans showed up to watch the great Red Grange make his professional debut for the Bears in 1925, Driscoll frustrated them by punting away from the Galloping Ghost. He scored all of his team's points in 6-0 and 9-0 wins over the Bears in 1922 and once dropkicked four field goals in a game. He amazed fans by kicking two 50-yard field goals.

Driscoll's celebrated athleticism earned him early distinction on the football field at Northwestern and the baseball field in Chicago—he played 13 major league games for the 1917 Cubs. He also was a member of the celebrated Great Lakes Naval Training Station team (joining stars Halas and Jimmy Conzelman) that won the 1919 Rose Bowl. Driscoll, a respected strategist, doubled as Cardinals coach in his first three professional seasons.

After ending his career with the Bears in 1929, Driscoll coached at the high school and college levels before rejoining Halas as an assistant. When the Papa Bear retired in 1955, Driscoll guided the 1956 Bears to the NFL title game, where they lost to the New York Giants. After a 5-7 followup campaign, he retired.

DRISCOLL

BILL DUDLEY

Born: 12-24-19, Bluefield, Va. **Ht/Wt:** 5-10/180 **College:** Virginia **Drafted:** 1942, 1st round, Steelers **Primary positions:** HB, QB, DB, K, P **Career statistics:** Rushing, 3,057 yds., 19 TDs; Receiving, 1,383 yds., 18 TDs; Passing, 985 yds., 6 TDs; Punt returns, 124 att., 12.2 avg., 3 TDs; KO Returns, 78 att., 22.3 avg.; Interceptions, 23, 2 TDs; Scoring, 484 pts. **Rushing champion:** 1942, '46 **Interceptions leader:** 1946 **Teams:** Steelers 1942, 1945-46; Lions 1947-49; Redskins 1950-51, 1953 **Honors:** 1940s All-Decade Team

He ran like a slow-footed duck, threw with a herky-jerky sidearm delivery and kicked with an unorthodox, no-step motion. Bill Dudley also was brash, outspoken and preachy, personality traits that did not always endear him to coaches, teammates and fans. But cloaked beneath these imperfections, hidden deep within a 5-foot-10, 180-pound body, were the heart, soul and unexplainable instincts of a football superstar.

In a career that stretched from 1942-53 minus two years of military duty during World War II, Dudley carved out his legacy while serving three-year hitches with three teams—Pittsburgh, Detroit and Washington. Small, slow and awkward, he still led the NFL in rushing and punt return yardage twice, interceptions once and field goal percentage (.769, 10-of-13) in 1951. To illustrate his versatility, Dudley passed for six career touchdowns and scored 44 on runs (19), receptions (18), punt returns (3), kickoff returns (1), interceptions (2) and fumble recoveries (1).

"Bullet Bill," who once finished last in a 15-man exhibition sprint, was a football contradiction. He was quick and instinctive, able to dart, juke and cut to daylight; he was a ballhawk and ferocious tackler,

drawing praise from Steelers coach Jock Sutherland as a better defender than runner. Pittsburgh officials who drafted Dudley No. 1 in 1942 watched him sprint 55 yards for a touchdown in his first game and score on a kickoff return in his second.

It wasn't long before Dudley was handling the ball on virtually every play—as a runner, passer, receiver, defender, return man, punter and kicker. But success couldn't camouflage his sometimes grating personality. Dudley complained about strategy, which didn't sit well with coaches, and teammates endured his religious preaching and sideline criticism. When he swept the NFL's rushing, punt return and interception titles in 1946, he was rewarded with a trade to the Lions.

The high-strung Dudley produced wherever he played, but he never competed in a postseason game. He did play in the first two modern-era Pro Bowls after the 1950 and '51 seasons.

> "He doesn't seem to be able to do anything real well, but he's a helluva football player. I'd say Bill was a real specialist—specializing in everything." —*Sammy Baugh*

TURK EDWARDS

Born: 9-28-07, Mold, Wash. **Died:** 1-12-73 **Ht/Wt:** 6-2/260 **College:** Washington State **Primary positions:** OT, DT
Teams: Braves/Redskins 1932-40 **Championship team:** NFL 1937 **Honors:** 1930s All-Decade Team

If Turk Edwards wasn't the heavyweight champion of 1930s-era professional football, he was at least a top contender. Few players could match the 260 pounds he carried on his 6-foot-2 frame and few could neutralize the steamrolling, smothering havoc he wreaked as a bulldozing two-way tackle. What Edwards lacked in speed and finesse he made up for with raw power and intimidation.

By 1930s standards, Edwards was a hulking enforcer for eight-plus seasons with the Redskins franchise, first in Boston, later in Washington. His sleepy, hound-dog face belied a machine-like determination to clear a path as a blocker for Cliff Battles and to protect quarterback Sammy Baugh. Slow afoot and not overly agile on defense, Edwards clogged up the middle like an immovable rock.

The former Washington State University star, who teamed with New York Giants great Mel Hein on a Cougars team that played in the 1931 Rose Bowl, was the foundation around which the Redskins' first championship

> **Slow afoot and not overly agile on defense, Edwards clogged up the middle like an immovable rock.**

team was built. He and Battles were rookie stars for the first-year Boston Braves in 1932 and both played for the renamed "Redskins" when they advanced to the NFL championship game in 1936. When the Redskins moved to Washington the next season, rookie quarterback Baugh led them to a 28-21 title game win over the Chicago Bears.

The always durable Edwards was still going strong when a strange accident ended his career early in the 1940 season. After participating in a coin toss with Hein before a game against the Giants, big Turk pivoted toward his bench, caught his cleats in the turf and stumbled—an unfortunate weight shift that devastated his already battered knee. He never played another game.

He did, however, continue his association with the Redskins, first as an assistant coach for five seasons and then as head coach for three. Edwards' teams compiled a 16-18-1 record from 1946-48 before he retired, ending 17 straight years of service under Washington owner George Preston Marshall.

WEEB EWBANK

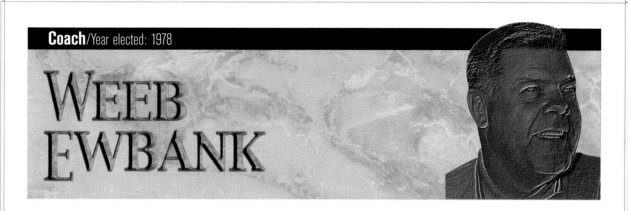

Born: 5-6-07, Richmond, Ind. **Died:** 11-17-98 **Teams coached (130-129-7 RS, 4-1 PS):** NFL Colts 1954-62; AFL Jets 1963-69; NFL Jets 1970-73 **Championship teams:** NFL 1958, '59; AFL 1968 **Super Bowl champion:** 1968 season

He was the winning coach in two games that altered the course of pro football history, the mentor for two Hall of Fame quarterbacks and the man who lifted two franchises to championship glory. Weeb Ewbank was equal parts builder, strategist and teacher, a roly-poly little Paul Brown disciple whose 20-year career must be measured more by impact than wins and losses.

Ewbank's record of 130-129-7 belies his contribution to the Baltimore Colts, New York Jets and pro football in general. After five years on Brown's Cleveland staff, Ewbank became coach and general manager of a struggling Colts team in 1954, molded it into a winner and then guided it to consecutive championships in 1958 and '59. He took over the Jets in 1963 and guided them to the 1968 AFL championship and victory in Super Bowl III.

The Colts' 1958 title game win over New York and the Jets' Super Bowl victory over the Colts were classics — and important milestones in the game's growth and popularity. The 1958 contest, still remembered as "the greatest game ever played," was an emotional, dramatic and nail-biting battle witnessed by millions of network television viewers who were treated to foot-

> "(Football is) a great game because there's always a chance. There are two halves to every ballgame. You can be beaten silly in the first half and win in the second. And if you win in the first half you still have to keep winning in the second."
>
> — *Weeb Ewbank, 1973*

ball's first sudden-death overtime. The 1969 Super Bowl was a shocking upset, an AFL right of passage that brought instant credibility to the league and stoked interest in the AFL-NFL title game extravaganza.

The patient and player-friendly Ewbank built both of his champions around great quarterbacks with remarkably different personalities — Baltimore's stoic and unflappable Johnny Unitas and New York's flamboyant Joe Namath. An astute judge of talent, the Indiana-born Ewbank pulled Unitas off a Pittsburgh amateur team in 1956 and boldly outbid the NFL for No. 1 draft pick Namath in 1965.

Ewbank, who paid his coaching dues at the high school and college levels, eventually spawned his own school of proteges in Bud Grant, Don Shula, Chuck Noll and Chuck Knox. When he retired in 1973, he stood as the only coach in history to win championships in both the AFL and NFL.

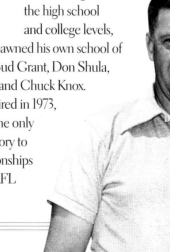

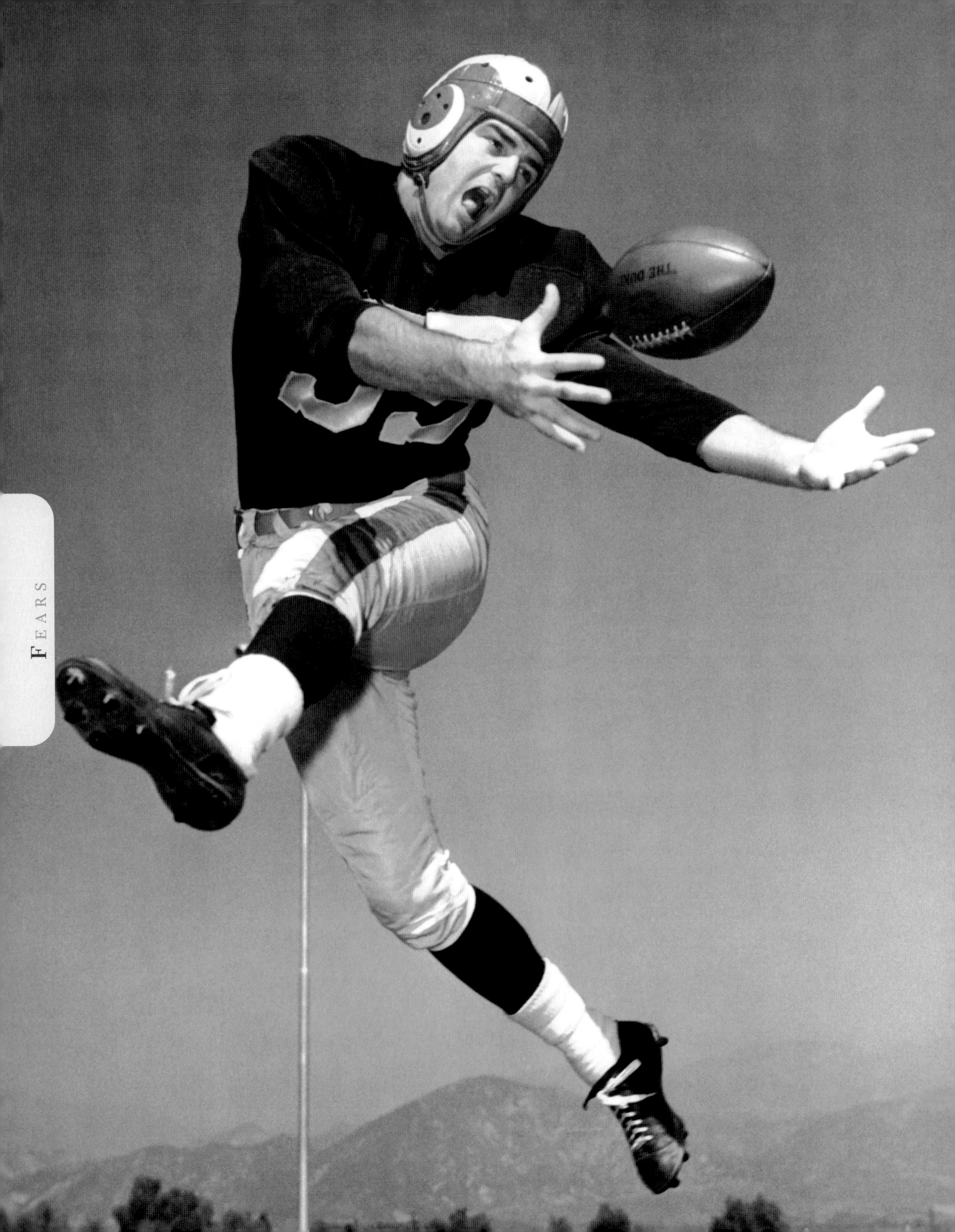

TOM FEARS

Born: 12-3-23, Los Angeles, Calif. **Died:** 1-4-2000 **Ht/Wt:** 6-3/216 **College:** UCLA **Drafted:** 1945, 11th round, Rams **Primary position:** E **Career statistics:** Receiving, 400 rec., 5,397 yds., 13.5 avg., 38 TDs **Receptions leader:** 1948, '49, '50 **Team:** Rams 1948-56 **Championship team:** NFL 1951 **Honors:** 1950s All-Decade Team

He was a trend-setting ballhawk in Rams clothing, a favorite target for future Hall of Famers Bob Waterfield and Norm Van Brocklin. Tom Fears turned "getting open" into an artform while helping redefine the end position in the post-World War II professional game. The 6-foot-3 Los Angeles star juked, deked, hooked and slanted his way through nine outstanding NFL seasons as the go-to man in the Rams' innovative multiple-receiver offense.

Whereas predecessor Don Hutson had used great speed to set receiving records at Green Bay, the 216-pound Fears relied on precise patterns, an innate ability to find a secondary's weakness and his fearless knack for working the middle of the field. Not blessed with Hutson-like speed, he was elusive, smart and intense. And he rarely dropped a pass.

Not bad for a former UCLA star who signed as a defensive back in 1948. Rams coach Clark Shaughnessy watched Fears intercept two passes in his first NFL game and immediately switched him to end. Split out like a wide receiver in Shaughnessy's innovative offense, the Los Angeles-born rookie went on to lead the league with 51 catches.

He caught an NFL-record 77 passes for 1,013 yards and nine touchdowns in 1949 and upped his mark to 84 catches for 1,116 yards in 1950. Highlighting that 1950 performance was an 18-catch record in a December victory over the Packers — a mark that stood for a half century. While Fears never led the NFL in catches again, he was front and center for Rams teams that won an NFL championship in 1951 and reached the title game three other years.

It was Fears who broke the heart of Cleveland fans in 1951 when he caught a spectacular 73-yard TD pass that gave the Rams a 24-17 championship game win. In a 1950 Western Division title showdown with Chicago, he pulled in TD passes of 43, 68 and 27 yards in a 24-14 win. When Fears retired after the 1956 season, he had caught 400 passes for 5,397 yards and 38 touchdowns.

> "Fears is as quick as a cat despite his size, and he has a great pair of hands. But there's something else about Tom that makes him really great. It is his insane desire to win."
>
> *—Red Hickey, Rams assistant coach, 1950*

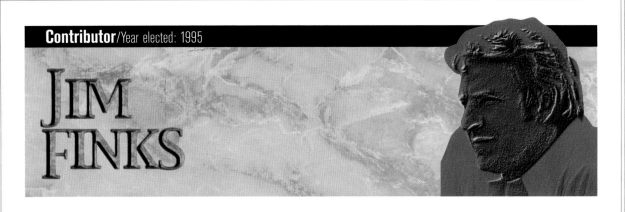

JIM FINKS

Born: 8-31-27, St. Louis, Mo. **Died:** 5-8-94 **Ht/Wt:** 5-11/180 **College:** Tulsa **Drafted:** 1949, 12th round, Steelers **Primary position:** QB **Career statistics:** Passing, 661-of-1,382, 8,622 yds., 55 TDs **Team:** Steelers 1949-55 **Executive career:** General manager, vice president/G.M. of Vikings 1964-73; executive vice president/G.M. of Bears 1974-82; president/G.M. of Saints 1986-93

As a franchise builder and contributing architect for the modern NFL, Jim Finks had few peers. He turned three struggling franchises into Super Bowl contenders, crafted league policy, evaluated important changes, negotiated with the players' union and even came within three votes of succeeding Pete Rozelle as NFL commissioner. Finks was the ultimate football craftsman, a four-decade go-to executive for a league on the rise.

> **"What I remember is how knowledgeable he was about football. Everybody was crazy about Jim Finks. He had great integrity. It was unusual for a G.M. to be so respected."**
>
> —*Chuck Foreman, former Vikings running back, 1995, The Times-Picayune*

He also was a defensive back and Pro Bowl quarterback for Pittsburgh from 1949-55 before embarking on his path as a front-office decision-maker. After spending eight years in the Canadian Football League as coach, scout and general manager, he returned to the states and changed the course of pro football in Minnesota, Chicago and New Orleans.

When Finks became Vikings general manager in 1964, the 3-year-old expansion team had a 10-30-2 record; six years later, the Vikes played in the first of four Super Bowls with Finks-built teams. When he took over the Bears in 1974, they had not reached the playoffs in 10 years; they did in 1977 and won a Super

Bowl in 1985 using 19 starters acquired by Finks before his 1982 departure. The Saints had never posted a winning record in their 20-year existence; in 1987, Finks' second year, they finished 12-3 and made their first playoff appearance.

In every case, he displayed uncanny instincts, superb player evaluation skills and patience, cloaked by his downhome charm and wry sense of humor. Writers enjoyed his colorful sayings and he gave everybody a personalized nickname. A chain smoker with a quick, winning smile, the wavy-haired Missourian was consistent, fair and even-handed.

When Rozelle stepped down in 1989, Finks received unanimous endorsement from the nominating committee but failed to become commissioner when a bloc of younger owners revolted. Paul Tagliabue was selected on the sixth ballot and Finks became chairman of the powerful competition committee. Finks, who even spent one season (1984) as president of baseball's Chicago Cubs, was president and minority owner of the Saints when he died in 1994.

FINKS

Coach/Year elected: 1976

RAY FLAHERTY

Born: 9-1-04, Spokane, Wash. **Died:** 7-19-94 **Ht/Wt:** 6-0/190 **College:** Washington State, Gonzaga **Positions:** OE, DE **Teams played:** Yankees 1927-28; Giants 1928-35 **Championship team:** NFL 1934 **Team coached NFL (54-21-3 RS, 2-2 PS):** Redskins 1936-42 **Teams coached AAFC (26-16-2 RS, 0-2 PS):** Yankees 1946-48; Hornets 1949 **Championship teams:** NFL 1937, '42

His florid complexion and quiet manner disguised a fierce, no-nonsense intensity. When Ray Flaherty did speak, everybody listened to words that were chosen with care and delivered with heartfelt conviction. Nobody played professional football with more passion or coached it with more dedication than Flaherty, who earned championship acclaim three times with the New York Giants and Washington Redskins over a two-decade career.

The soft-spoken redhead could wilt huge players or meddling owners with his icy glare and inspire players with a few pointed comments or a terse challenge. He also could prepare his teams, organize a game plan and strategize with George Halas-like efficiency. Those qualities came in handy over an eight-year playing career (1927-35) and 11-year coaching run that often produced intense confrontations with Halas' Chicago Bears.

It was Flaherty, a 6-foot All-Pro end with the Giants, who suggested to coach Steve Owen that his team use sneakers for better traction on the icy surface of New York's Polo Grounds in the 1934 NFL champi-

> "Up in Boston, you fellows complained all last season that we didn't have a passer. But now we've gone out and hired Sammy Baugh, the best damn passer in the world, for you. ... And I want you to give Sammy protection every minute. The man who misses a block and lets him get hurt is going to be fined. ..."
>
> —*Ray Flaherty, addressing his team before its first game as the 'Washington' Redskins in 1937*

onship game. The Giants changed shoes at intermission, outscored the slip-sliding Bears 27-3 in the second half and claimed a 30-13 victory. Three years later, second-year coach Flaherty led his Redskins to a 28-21 title game win over the Bears, thanks in large part to an innovative screen pass designed for rookie quarterback Sammy Baugh.

Flaherty's Redskins were 54-21-3 from 1936-42 and won a second championship, beating Chicago in the 1942 title game. But they also lost to the Bears in 1940—a humiliating 73-0 disaster that remains the most lopsided defeat in NFL history. After serving in the Navy during World War II, Flaherty coached the New York Yankees of the All-America Football Conference from 1946-48 and the AAFC's Chicago Hornets in '49.

The man from Spokane, Wash., also pioneered platoon football in the NFL. He utilized an air squad and ground team—one platoon filled with speedy receivers and pass-blockers for Baugh; another featuring ball-control backs and run-blockers.

LEN FORD

Born: 2-18-26, Washington, D.C. **Died:** 3-14-72 **Ht/Wt:** 6-5/260 **College:** Morgan State, Michigan **Drafted:** Undrafted **Primary position:** OE, DE **Career statistics:** Receiving, 67 rec., 1,175 yds., 17.5 avg., 8 TDs; 20 fumble recoveries **Teams:** AAFC Dons 1948-49; NFL Browns 1950-57; Packers 1958 **Championship teams:** NFL 1950, '54, '55 **Honors:** 1950s All-Decade Team

Wind him up and watch him destroy an offense. Len Ford was a big, powerful, athletic toy, a defensive monster empowered and manipulated by pro football's ultimate magician. When Cleveland coach Paul Brown got his hands on this 1950s prototype, he secured an important piece of his championship puzzle and unleashed a new kind of devastation on the NFL.

The new-age defensive end made enemies and influenced the game with incredible athleticism and full-throttle intensity that only success and mayhem could appease. At 6-foot-5 and 260 pounds, Ford had linebacker speed, running back quickness and an ability to leap high and bat down passes. But blockers were most intimidated by the blacksmith arms and hammer-like elbows he used to batter them during a mad race to the quarterback.

The former Michigan star played his first two seasons with Los Angeles in the All-America Football Conference, catching 67 passes for 1,175 yards and eight touchdowns as a two-way end. Dons coach Jimmy Phelan was so impressed he predicted Ford could "become the greatest

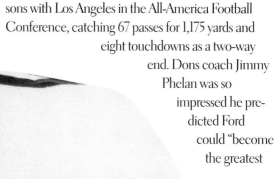

all-around end in history," but the AAFC and L.A. franchise folded after the 1949 season and Brown signed the free agent—a fortuitous addition before his team's 1950 entry into the NFL.

Ford's offensive days were over. Brown restructured his defense to fit Ford's talents and began using a four-man front with three linebackers—an innovative 4-3 alignment. Ford played havoc with his outside rush and used his speed from sideline to sideline. From 1950-57, only Baltimore's Gino Marchetti could challenge his defensive end prowess and the Browns won three championships, reached four more title games and allowed the fewest points in the NFL six times.

Ford, as affable off the field as he was intense on it, recovered 20 fumbles over a nine-year NFL run that ended in 1958 with a final season in Green Bay. The four-time Pro Bowl participant intercepted two passes in a 56-10 championship game win over Detroit in 1954.

> "I tell my brother I wouldn't give him a break on the field. I tell him I would be coming through if I could. I wouldn't give him a break or anybody else. If they can't take it, they shouldn't be out there. I'm going to do my job."
>
> —Len Ford

DAN FORTMANN

Born: 4-11-16, Pearl River, N.Y. **Died:** 5-23-95 **Ht/Wt:** 6-0/210 **College:** Colgate **Drafted:** 1936, 9th round, Bears **Primary positions:** OG, LB **Teams:** Bears 1936-43 **Championship teams:** NFL 1940, '41, '43 **Honors:** 1930s All-Decade Team

They called him a "Monster of the Midway," but 6-foot, 210-pound Dan Fortmann was a physical misfit. He was an offensive lineman in a defensive back's body, a punishing blocker without the beef and muscle of those intimidating Chicago Bears who surrounded him. Never has an athlete earned more respect or garnered more accolades on pure grit and determination than the Phi Beta Kappa from Colgate University.

What Fortmann lacked in brawn he made up for with brains and full-throttle intensity. He was a battering-ram blocker who shot off the line, hitting bigger opponents low and hard, inflicting pain with every snap. Coach George Halas thought so much of his brainy guard that he had him call signals for a Hall of Fame line that included Bulldog Turner, Joe Stydahar and George Musso. When the team needed short yardage, Fortmann and tackle Stydahar typically were the go-to blockers.

On defense, Halas lined Fortmann up at middle linebacker

> "I was impressed with George Halas. It was so typical of him that when he heard I was interested in becoming a doctor, he went all out to see that my ambition was fulfilled. He was intent on helping me. ..."
>
> —*Dan Fortmann, 1980*

inaugural NFL draft in 1936—a selection Halas made because he "liked his name." But he did a double take when the undersized Fortmann showed for preseason camp and quickly wrote him off as a mistake. Some mistake! The determined 20-year-old was starting by the regular-season opener and remained in the lineup for eight years, seldom missing a game.

It was no coincidence the Bears, featuring quarterback Sid Luckman and operating from the T-formation, won three NFL championships and appeared in two other title games during his stay. The proud New Yorker, a perennial All-Pro, retired after the 1943 season to begin a new career as a doctor.

and watched him diagnose and disrupt enemy plays. He was instinctive, fast and a ferocious tackler, an extension of Halas on the field. Fortmann was a favorite of the proud Papa Bear, who rewarded his protege by arranging time away from summer practice to attend medical school.

Fortmann was the Bears' ninth-round pick in the

FORTMANN

DAN FOUTS

Born: 6-10-51, San Francisco, Calif. **Ht/Wt:** 6-3/204 **College:** Oregon **Drafted:** 1973, 3rd round, Chargers **Primary position:** QB
Career statistics: Passing, 3,297-of-5,604, 43,040 yds., 254 TDs **Team:** Chargers 1973-87 **Honors:** 1980s All-Decade Team

He was ringmaster of the aerial circus known as "Air Coryell," the passing fancy in a prolific offense that threw the ball first and asked questions later. Defenses braced for the inevitable onslaught and fans gasped in anticipation when Dan Fouts took the field. He might not have fit the classic quarterback mold, but there's no denying the 43,040 yards and 254 touchdown passes Fouts delivered over a 15-year career with the San Diego Chargers.

At first glance, Fouts fell short of the job description. His 6-foot-3, 204-pound body did not look athletic, his arm was ordinary and he was painfully slow. But closer inspection revealed a super-quick release and a feathery touch that dropped passes between the seams in a zone. Fouts was a master at the quick-hitting pattern, but he also had extraordinary peripheral vision and stood fearlessly in the pocket, waiting for someone to get open as the world collapsed around him.

Teammates marveled at the presence Fouts brought to the huddle. All was quiet when he barked orders in an I'm-in-charge tone that commanded respect. His intense personality sometimes grated on teammates, but nobody doubted his competitive fire and desire to succeed—a desire that would not be fulfilled until Don Coryell brought his wide-open offense to San Diego in 1978.

That's when the former Oregon star began piling up yards—and points—in bunches. Throwing to Charlie Joiner, John Jefferson and Kellen Winslow in 1979, Fouts passed for a single-season-record 4,082 yards. He followed that with seasons of 4,715 and

4,802 and never fell below the 2,500-yard level over the rest of a career that ended in 1987.

Fouts, a six-time Pro Bowl selection, never led his team to the championship he craved, but he did guide the Chargers to three AFC West titles and championship game appearances in 1980 and '81. Fouts topped 300 passing yards in a game 51 times, a mark topped only by former Miami star Dan Marino.

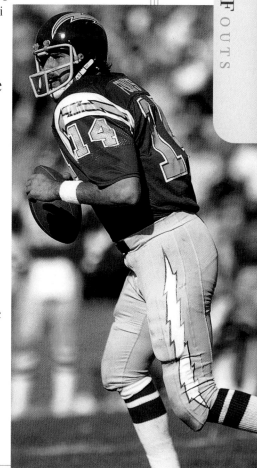

> "He has such a flexible mind. He doesn't have all the qualities you'd want in an ideal quarterback. He's not a runner. He's a fine athlete, but he doesn't have the speed. But he is very intelligent and extremely competitive and tough mentally."
>
> —*Don Coryell, 1980*

FRANK GATSKI

Born: 3-18-22, Farmington, W. Va. **Ht/Wt:** 6-3/240 **College:** Marshall, Auburn **Drafted:** Undrafted **Primary position:** C, LB
Teams: Browns AAFC 1946-49; NFL 1950-56; Lions 1957 **Championship teams:** AAFC 1946, '47, '48, '49; NFL 1950, '54, '55, '57

Silent, resolute and unyielding, Frank Gatski was the immovable force at the heart of Cleveland's championship legacy. The 6-foot-3, 240-pound center seldom spoke for 12 professional seasons and he never missed a practice or game, always delivering the ball on cue. From 1946 through 1957, Gatski snapped, blocked and protected for quarterbacks who also delivered—an amazing 118-24-4 record, eight championships and 11 conference titles.

A product of the West Virginia coal mines, Gatski was a blond, muscular giant with enormous shoulders and an unwavering work ethic. "In 10 years of taking the ball from Frank, I don't remember him saying a word on the field," Browns quarterback Otto Graham once said. But Graham did recall the rhythmic quality of his snaps, the way Gatski plugged the middle, cutting down would-be quarterback assassins, and his durability.

"Gunner," a nickname Gatski acquired in his pre-World War II days at Marshall College, was the strongest man on a talent-filled Cleveland roster that included such bulls as Len Ford, Marion Motley and Lou Groza. His legs were so long Graham could stand erect to take snaps, allowing him better vision of defensive alignments. After the snap, Gatski simply

> ## "He was the best and the toughest I ever played against. As a linebacker, I sometimes had to go over the center, but Gatski was an immovable object."
>
> *—Chuck Bednarik*

stood up and invited any defender to try and get past.

Few did. And, according to offensive tackle Groza, Gatski was the only center he ever saw pull on a trap play. Gatski began his career during Cleveland's All-America Football Conference dominance as a linebacker and center backup to Mo Scarry. But he replaced the veteran midway through the 1947 season, giving up his defensive duties, and started every game through the rest of his career.

The only season the Browns failed to reach a league championship game during Gatski's stay was 1956, the year after Graham retired. Written off by coach Paul Brown, Gatski moved to Detroit in 1957, started all 12 regular-season games and finished his career by helping the Lions post a 59-14 win over his old team in the NFL championship game.

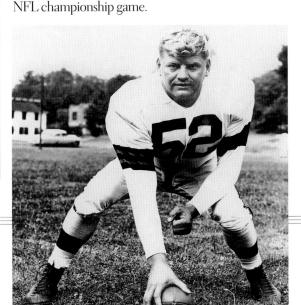

GATSKI

BILL GEORGE

Born: 10-27-30, Waynesburg, Pa. **Died:** 9-30-82 **Ht/Wt:** 6-2/237 **College:** Wake Forest **Drafted:** 1951, 2nd round, Bears
Primary position: LB **Career statistics:** Interceptions, 18 **Teams:** Bears 1952-65; Rams 1966 **Championship team:** NFL 1963
Honors: 1950s All-Decade Team

He didn't hit with Chuck Bednarik savagery or dominate with Dick Butkus intensity, but nobody can deny Bill George his distinction as one of the great middle linebackers in football history. He was the first to play the position and the man who defined the way it would be played for generations to come. His innovative standup routine changed the course of defensive football.

> "Guys like Sam Huff and Joe Schmidt, although they were fine players, got most of the attention because they played with teams that were always in contention. But George was the tops as far as I was concerned. He brought all the present romance and charisma to the position."
>
> —*Abe Gibron, former Bears teammate and coach*

career that started in 1952, George served as Halas' defensive captain and signal-caller. The former Wake Forest kid with the closely-cropped black hair and thick eyebrows diligently studied film, filled notebooks with opponent tendencies and prepared meticulously for each game. Not only was he totally prepared to perform his job, he understood the nuances of every position in every possible situation.

George was a 6-foot-2, 237-pound middle guard operating in the Chicago Bears' basic 5-2 defense when he first stood up, took a step back and began operating as a third linebacker. He had the quickness and speed to rush the passer, chase down a ballcarrier or defend against short passes in the new 4-3 scheme. But more exciting to coach George Halas was the way George grasped the Bears' complicated defensive schemes — and his ability to smell out plays before they happened.

Through most of a 15-year

His intelligence and uncanny ability to call for the perfect defensive formation just before every snap unnerved many quarterbacks. It was futile to run plays right at George, frustrating to watch him diagnose and react to plays that went away from him. George, who had explosive quickness off the snap, also was a dangerous inside blitzer and a pass defender who made 18 career interceptions.

Thanks in large part to a defense designed around George, the 1963 Bears rolled to an 11-1-2 record, the Western Conference title and their first NFL championship in 17 years. The eight-time Pro Bowl selection played through 1965 with the Bears and retired after one season with the Los Angeles Rams.

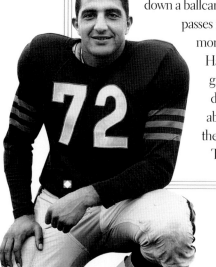

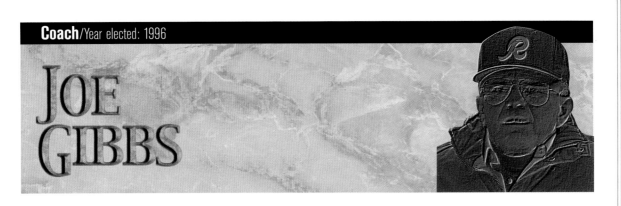

JOE GIBBS

Born: 11-25-40, Mocksville, N.C. **Teams coached (124-60 RS, 16-5 PS):** Redskins 1981-92 **Super Bowl champions:** 1982, '87, '91 seasons

He was a wolf in sheep's clothing, an intense, over-worked, hot-tempered coach buried beneath a calm, collected exterior. Looks could be deceiving with Joe Gibbs, who dramatically changed the course of Washington football with a hands-on, no-nonsense, Jekyll-Hyde passion. The genius of this quiet and poised, fiery and driven football contradiction could be measured by the 124 wins and three Super Bowl titles he delivered over 12 memorable seasons from 1981-92.

It was not uncommon for Gibbs to work 20-hour days, skip meals and sleep overnight in his office while searching for the perfect game plan. He was a tireless and dedicated teacher, a poised and detail-oriented leader who could get the most out of players supplied by general manager Bobby Beathard, one of the game's top talent gurus. He spoke softly and seldom yelled at players, but momentary tantrums revealed the fire that burned inside.

Nobody knew what the Redskins were getting in 1981 when they signed Gibbs, a longtime college and pro assistant who had worked under passing guru Don Coryell. He quickly established a system of power football backed by disciplined, intelligent teams that were motivated to peak late in the schedule. Gibbs' 16-5 record in postseason play was no fluke. Eight of his 12 Redskins teams won 10 or more games, eight reached the playoffs and four played in Super Bowls.

Gibbs had a knack for building around his changing talent. Big John Riggins provided the inspiration for his effective one-back offense. His three Super Bowl victories, after the 1982, '87 and '91 seasons, were directed by different quarterbacks — Joe Theismann, Doug Williams and Mark Rypien. Gibbs won with Hogs, the Smurfs and even teams that were not overloaded with talent. Two of his squads (1983 and '91) finished 14-2 in the regular season.

When the proud North Carolinian retired with a 124-60 record after the 1992 season, he was keeping select company. His combined (regular and postseason) winning percentage of .683 ranked only below Vince Lombardi (.740) and John Madden (.731) on the all-time list.

> "I never thought it was a gamble to hire Joe. Everyone I talked to who knew him said he was an ideal head coach. There is something about him that makes him a winner. He is a fierce competitor, he's intelligent, he has a way with players."
>
> —*Bobby Beathard, 1983*

GIBBS

GIBBS

FRANK GIFFORD

Born: 8-16-30, Santa Monica, Calif. **Ht/Wt:** 6-1/197 **College:** USC **Drafted:** 1952, 1st round, Giants **Primary positions:** RB, WR, DB
Career statistics: Rushing, 840 att., 3,609 yds., 34 TDs; Receiving, 367 rec., 5,434 yds., 43 TDs; Passing, 823 yds., 14 TDs; Punt Returns 25 att., 4.8 avg. **Teams:** Giants 1952-60, 1962-64 **Championship team:** NFL 1956 **Honors:** 1950s All-Decade Team

Even by New York standards, Frank Gifford had star power. He could light up a football field with his electrifying athleticism and do-everything versatility; he could energize a franchise with his matinee idol looks and down-home charm. "Frank lent a certain dignity and tone to an entire organization," said Jack Mara, who also watched the USC All-American carry his Giants to championship heights.

On the field, Gifford was a halfback, flanker, kick returner and defensive back who occasionally threw passes and kicked field goals and extra points. Off the field, he was a movie actor, model and broadcaster who occasionally wrote sports columns for his hometown newspaper in Bakersfield, Calif. The 6-foot-1, 197-pound Gifford was one of New York's most glamorous athletes in the 1950s, a Joe DiMaggio/Joe Namath-caliber icon.

Gifford arrived in 1952 amid great expectations and became a two-way performer for the struggling Giants — a gifted halfback who could run, catch and pass; a ballhawk defender with game-breaking instincts. By 1954, he was concentrating his efforts on offense and

> "He is one of the most versatile halfbacks I've seen in years. He has hard-running ability, is an accurate passer, a strong blocker, a superior defensive halfback—and I believe he could be a consistent placekicker with practice."
>
> *—Steve Owen, Giants coach, 1952*

by 1956 he was the big weapon for an 8-3-1 team that delivered the first Giants championship since 1938. Gifford rushed for 819 yards, caught 51 passes for 603, threw two touchdown passes and scored nine more. He was voted league MVP by his peers.

Former Giants assistant Vince Lombardi marveled at how quickly he could burst through a hole and his ability to spot and exploit enemy weaknesses. Not surprisingly, the Giants won four more conference championships with Gifford — two (1958 and '59) before a serious head injury on a celebrated tackle by Philadelphia linebacker Chuck Bednarik temporarily ended his career in 1960; two after his 1962 return as a game-affecting wideout.

Gifford, a seven-time Pro Bowl selection at three different positions (defensive back, halfback, flanker), retired after the 1964 season with 9,043 combined rushing/receiving yards and 78 touchdowns. He began a second career as a CBS broadcaster and later became a longtime member of ABC's *Monday Night Football* team.

Coach/Year elected: 1983

SID GILLMAN

Born: 10-26-11, Minneapolis, Min. **Died:** 1-3-2003 **Teams coached (122-99-7 RS; 1-5 PS):** NFL Rams 1955-59; AFL Chargers 1960-69; NFL Chargers 1971; NFL Oilers 1973-74 **Championship team:** AFL 1963

He was father of the modern passing game, the man whose quick-strike concepts redefined how football is played. Sid Gillman spent 18 seasons in his "attack, attack, attack" mode as a professional head coach, 11 as the offensive genius who helped bring success to the American Football League. When soft-spoken Sid preached his "vertical" gospel as coach, consultant and guru, everybody was well-advised to listen and learn.

Nobody was more responsible for the credibility of the AFL than Gillman, whose imaginative passing style forced other teams to play a faster, more wide-open game that generated instant fan appeal. His high-scoring Los Angeles/San Diego offenses, featuring quarterback John Hadl, receiver Lance Alworth and backs Paul Lowe and Keith Lincoln, could strike from

> "The big play comes from the pass. God bless those runners because they get you the first down, give you ball control and keep your defense off the field. But if you want to ring the cash register, you have to pass."
>
> *—Sid Gillman*

anywhere, like the lightning bolt on the helmet of the Chargers teams he coached.

Opponents marveled at Gillman's advanced schemes, multiple-receiver formations, gambling game plans and precise patterns, but it was all an extension of his organizational skills. As Chargers general manager, he relied on a prototype scouting department, an innovative taxi squad and advanced film study. Gillman enjoyed a great rapport with players and tapped the brain power of such visionary assistants as Al Davis, Chuck Noll and Bum Phillips.

Gillman, a tunnel-vision workaholic, spent 21 years as a college assistant and head coach before taking his first professional job with the Los Angeles Rams in 1955. His first Rams team lost in the NFL championship game, but he really hit stride after taking control of the infant Chargers in 1960. Gillman's AFL teams reached the league championship game in five of their first six years and won the title in 1963.

The bow-tied, pipe-smoking Minnesota native finished his head coaching career in 1973 and '74 with Houston but remained a visible sideline coach and consultant for more than a decade. Many of today's sophisticated passing schemes are mere reflections of concepts advanced by the man who fashioned a 122-99-7 regular-season coaching record.

OTTO GRAHAM

Born: 12-6-21, Waukegan, Ill. **Ht/Wt:** 6-1/195 **College:** Northwestern **Drafted:** 1944, 1st round, Lions **Primary positions:** QB, DB
Career statistics: Passing AAFC, 10,085 yds., 86 TDs; Passing NFL, 13,499 yds., 88 TDs; Rushing AAFC, 99 att., 200 yds., 11 TDs; Rushing NFL, 306 att., 682 yds., 33 TDs **Teams:** AAFC Browns 1946-49; NFL Browns 1950-55 **Championship teams:** AAFC 1946, '47, '48, '49; NFL 1950, '54, '55 **Honors:** 75th Anniversary All-Time Team; 1950s All-Decade Team

He was the perfect quarterback for the near-perfect franchise. What Otto Graham lacked in arm and physical strength, he more than made up for with uncanny throwing accuracy, poise and leadership. He was a winning machine—the generator that powered the newborn Cleveland Browns through their incredible first decade as a professional football team.

Automatic Otto was just that from 1946 through 1949 when he led the Browns to a 47-4-3 record and four straight championships in the All-America Football Conference, and from 1950 through 1955 when his Browns captured three NFL titles and lost three other times in the title game. Ten straight championship-game appearances and a 105-17-4 10-year record are legacies unmatched by any other quarterback.

Graham, a former basketball and football star at Northwestern and a one-year professional in the old National Basketball League, was a clever ballhandler who was hand-picked by franchise architect Paul Brown as the centerpiece for his innovative T-formation offense. The athletic 6-foot-1, 195-pounder with wavy black hair became a master tactician who always seemed to make the right decision. Game after game, he would scramble for the unexpected yards, drop soft, easy-to-catch passes over the shoulders of receivers and make the big play at just the right moment.

Everything about Graham was precision and confi-

dence—and never was his poise more evident than when the Browns, undisputed champions of the outlaw AAFC, made the difficult 1950 move to the stronger NFL. Graham threw three touchdown passes to lead the "inferior Browns" to a humbling 35-10 victory over defending NFL-champion Philadelphia in the season opener, four more TD passes in a 30-28 victory over the Los Angeles Rams in the season-ending championship game.

And, blessed with an outstanding corps of running backs and receivers, the outspoken kid from Waukegan, Ill., went on to post career totals of 23,584 passing yards (AAFC and NFL combined) and 174 touchdown passes in an era still dominated by power running attacks.

> ## "He was great, one of the great football players of all time. He could have played today for any team out there. He was one of the greatest quarterbacks ever."
>
> —*Tony Adamle, former Browns fullback*

RED GRANGE

Born: 6-13-03, Forksville, Pa. **Died:** 1-28-91 **Ht/Wt:** 6-0/185 **College:** Illinois **Primary positions:** HB, DB **Career statistics:** Rushing, 21 TDs; Receiving, 10 TDs; Passing, 10 TDs **Teams:** NFL Bears 1925, 1929-34; AFL Yankees 1927 **Championship teams:** 1932, '33 **Honors:** 1920s All-Decade Team

He was an honest-to-God hero, a bigger-than-life superstar in the class of 1920s contemporaries Babe Ruth, Jack Dempsey, Bill Tilden and Bobby Jones. Red Grange was the Galloping Ghost from the University of Illinois, the legend upon which the NFL was constructed. When No. 77 ran with the football, fans flocked to watch, the media took notice and professional football was the center of the sports universe.

Grange's contributions should be measured in status and fan appeal rather than yardage or years.

Today's professional game took root when Grange signed an incredible share-the-gate contract with the Chicago Bears after his final 1925 college game and played an exhibition before a packed house of 36,000 at Wrigley Field. Hundreds of thousands would stream through the turnstiles over the next three months during a wild 19-game barnstorming tour that featured an incredible eight games over one 11-day stretch.

What they saw was the same effortless glide, ghost-like weave, explosive speed and nimble elusiveness that had carried Grange to legendary fame at Illinois. He was equally dangerous on running plays or kick returns and Bears coach George Halas conceived the man-in-motion maneuver to free him for pass receptions. Grange's willingness to block and his humble manner made him popular among both teammates and opponents, who appreciated his trailblazing efforts.

The whirlwind 1925 exhibition tour brought Grange fortune, but it also wore him down. He left the Bears in 1926 to help form the rival American Football League, playing with the New York Yankees. When the AFL folded after one season, he returned with the Yankees to the NFL and suffered a knee injury that kept him on the sideline through 1928.

Grange returned to Halas and the Bears in 1929, an association that would last six more seasons. But the knee, protected by a brace, limited him to mere mortal status. He played his final few years on defense before retiring in 1934 at age 31.

"He is three or four men rolled into one. He is Jack Dempsey, Babe Ruth, Al Jolson, Paavo Nurmi and Man o' War."

—Damon Runyon

Coach/Year elected: 1994

BUD GRANT

Born: 5-20-27, Superior, Wis. **Team coached (158-96-5 RS, 10-12 PS):** Vikings 1967-83, 1985 **Championship team:** NFL 1969

The Iceman. Old Stoneface. The Abominable Snowman. Bud Grant, by any name, was the icy, unsmiling and stoic patriarch of Minnesota Vikings football for 18 seasons. The image of the glowering, unemotional king of cool remains frozen in time, not unlike the tough-minded and coldly efficient teams he led to one NFL championship, four Super Bowls and 12 playoff appearances from 1967-85.

Friends described another side of Grant—a friendly practical joker who lived with six children and 43 assorted pets at his Bloomington, Minn., home. But his football persona was serious and no-nonsense. He was a strict disciplinarian who banned smoking and profanity from the locker room; a conservative strategist who made quick, bold decisions in the heat of battle.

Players who had tasted the bombastic tantrums of predecessor Norm Van Brocklin were amazed at Grant's low-key approach. He was soft-spoken, blunt and fair; reprimands were delivered with a pride-sapping glare. His convictions were solid, like the frozen turf at Metropolitan Stadium.

> "He's a great leader, a very consistent man, very solid, fully capable in any situation that comes up and very fair."
>
> —*Fran Tarkenton, 1973*

One was that cold is a state of mind—and he banned heaters from the sideline during frequent sub-zero games. Grant built his bruising defenses and ground-oriented offenses around players who were suited to the wintry ways of the upper midwest. While other teams worried about staying warm, the Vikings dissected them with cold indifference.

A three-sport star at the University of Minnesota, Grant played one season with the 1949-50 NBA-champion Minneapolis Lakers and two as an outstanding NFL receiver with Philadelphia. After playing four years in the Canadian Football League, he coached Winnipeg to four Grey Cup titles in 10 years before returning to Minnesota, where his third Vikings team finished 12-2, won the NFL championship and was upset by Kansas City in Super Bowl IV.

Three more of Grant's teams lost in the Super Bowl, giving him distinction as the first coach to lose the classic four times. But that didn't diminish the 158-96-5 record compiled by one of the most interesting coaches in NFL history.

JOE GREENE

Born: 9-24-46, Temple, Tex.. **Ht/Wt:** 6-4/275 **College:** North Texas State **Drafted:** 1969, 1st round, Steelers **Primary position:** DT
Team: Steelers 1969-81 **Super Bowl champions:** 1974, '75, '78, '79 seasons **Honors:** 75th Anniversary All-Time Team;
1970s All-Decade Team; All-Time NFL Team

If the bear-paw hands couldn't twist a blocker into submission, the club-like forearms might finish the job. The heads of many NFL giants were sent into a throbbing spin by bell-ringing blows from Joe Greene. He was the meanest, nastiest, most ornery member of Pittsburgh's Steel Curtain defense and the cornerstone upon which a four-time Super Bowl champion was built.

The 6-foot-4, 275-pound Greene could single-handedly dominate a game. He was strong, mobile and hostile — a grizzly bear looking for a quarterback snack. Mean Joe didn't just overpower blockers, he brutalized them. He was cocky enough to believe he could do anything he wanted at any time — and he usually did, double- and triple-team blockers notwithstanding.

Like in the December 10, 1972, game against Houston when Greene recorded five sacks,

blocked a field goal, forced a fumble and recovered a fumble in a 9-3 victory that helped the Steelers secure the first of their seven AFC Central titles in the 1970s. Off the field, Greene was articulate, outspoken, thoughtful and quick to smile. On the field, he was on a mission of destruction, the anchor for a run-stuffing

wall that included L.C. Greenwood, Ernie Holmes and Dwight White.

Times were tough in Pittsburgh when Greene, out of North Texas State, was drafted fourth overall in 1969—the first pick in the Chuck Noll coaching era. More top-flight talent would quickly follow. But nobody would better epitomize the rise of the Steelers to NFL prominence than big No. 75, the acknowledged leader for one of the greatest winning

> "He's the best I've seen. He set the standard for us. Physically, he had all the necessary attributes but he also set the standard for attitude. There will never be another Joe Greene. Joe will always be something special."
>
> —*Chuck Noll*

machines ever assembled.

With Greene leading the charge, Pittsburgh ended almost four decades of frustration by reaching the AFC championship game in 1972. In a six-year span from 1974-79, the Steelers won four Super Bowls and lost in another AFC title game. Greene, a 10-time Pro Bowl selection, remained a force through 1981, when he ended his 13-year career as one of the most revered sports figures in Pittsburgh history.

FORREST GREGG

G R E G G

Born: 10-18-33, Birthright, Tex. **Ht/Wt:** 6-4/249 **College:** SMU **Drafted:** 1956, 2nd round, Packers **Primary position:** OT, OG
Teams: Packers 1956-70; Cowboys 1971 **Championship teams:** NFL 1961, '62, '65, '66, '67 **Super Bowl champions:** 1966, '67,
'71 seasons **Honors:** 75th Anniversary All-Time Team; 1960s All-Decade Team

Admirers called him the best dancer since Fred Astaire. Green Bay opponents called him masterful and frustrating. For Forrest Gregg, playing offensive tackle was all a matter of footwork and superior technique. Size was overrated. So was strength and power. Quickness was the name of his game and success was measured by his ability to do-si-do a bigger defensive end at the point of attack.

Nature dictated that finesse would play a major role in the life of the gruff, no-nonsense, straight-talking Texan, who at 6-foot-4 and 249 pounds was undersized and not as strong as the players he had to block. So he became a great technician. Gregg studied film on Jim Parker and Roosevelt Brown, two of the greatest linemen in football history. He worked hard on his footwork, learned about leverage and balance, studied film on opponents and mastered the sophisticated system of coach Vince Lombardi. He became the offensive anchor for one of the best teams ever assembled.

The feet would move up and down like well-oiled pistons as his powerful upper body maneuvered the defender away from the ball. Nobody beat the determined Gregg when he was protecting quarterback Bart Starr and he seldom made a mistake on run-blocking assignments. He was tireless and intelligent, the ultimate team leader whom Lombardi called "the finest player I ever coached."

With the durable Gregg (he never missed a game in 15 Green Bay seasons) clearing the way for such runners as Paul Hornung and Jim Taylor, the Packers won five NFL championships (and the first two Super Bowls) from 1961-67. He, literally, was the beacon in Lombardi's "run to daylight" offensive philosophy.

The nine-time Pro Bowl selection also was indispensable. Gregg was lured out of retirement three times, twice to serve as a player/coach for the Packers and finally to finish his career with a Dallas Cowboys team that won Super Bowl VI after the 1971 season.

> "Excellent technique and excellent footwork. Forrest always kept himself perfectly centered. He and Rosey Brown were the best technicians of all the offensive linemen. As a run-blocker, he was outstanding."
>
> —*Lenny Moore, 1999*

BOB GRIESE

Born: 2-3-45, Evansville, Ind. **Ht/Wt:** 6-1/190 **College:** Purdue **Drafted:** 1967, 1st round, Dolphins **Primary position:** QB
Career statistics: Passing, 1,926-of-3,429, 25,092 yds., 192 TDs; Rushing, 261 att., 994 yds., 7 TDs **Teams:** Dolphins 1967-80
Super Bowl champions: 1972, '73 seasons

Go ahead, call him boring. But don't expect Bob Griese to apologize for the patient, unspectacular, sleep-inducing way he carved up defenses and choreographed Miami victories over 14 professional seasons. There was no gunslinger recklessness in Griese, a two-time Super Bowl-winning quarterback who was happy in his role as the cool, confident, super-efficient extension of Dolphins coach Don Shula.

It wasn't that the former Purdue All-American couldn't throw with Johnny Unitas-like fervor. He completed 56.2 percent of his 3,429 passes for 25,092 yards and 192 touchdowns over a career that started in 1967 for the AFL Dolphins and ended in 1980. But he took pride in his role as leader of the game's most powerful rushing offense and willingly sacrificed numbers for success—spectacular bombs to Paul Warfield for more efficient handoffs to Larry Csonka and Jim Kiick.

"He's probably the most unselfish guy I've ever been around," Shula once said. The 6-foot-1, 190-pound Indiana native also was smart and quick to exploit defensive weakness. Griese, who was legally blind in his right eye and wore glasses during games, had an accurate arm, quick feet that allowed him to scramble and run quarterback draws and, contrary to popular opinion, the ability to go deep. He once threw 122 straight passes without an interception.

Reserved, withdrawn and soft-spoken in the locker room, "straight arrow" Griese was the no-nonsense leader in the huddle. It's no coincidence the Dolphins posted a 124-75-3 record during his Miami years and reached the playoffs seven times. From 1971 through '73, Miami was 36-5-1 and played in three straight Super Bowls, winning two. Griese completed 14-of-18 passes for 161 yards in Super Bowls VII and VIII — combined.

Griese, who played in two AFL All-Star Games and six Pro Bowls, enjoyed his signature performance in 1972. After missing nine weeks with a broken leg, he came off the bench to rally the Dolphins past Pittsburgh in the AFC championship game and then directed a 14-7 Super Bowl win over Washington, completing Miami's historic 17-0 season.

> "Bob has the perfect mental approach. He is the master of the position of quarterback. Bob knows the people and how to use them. He knows the defenses inside and out."
>
> *— Don Shula*

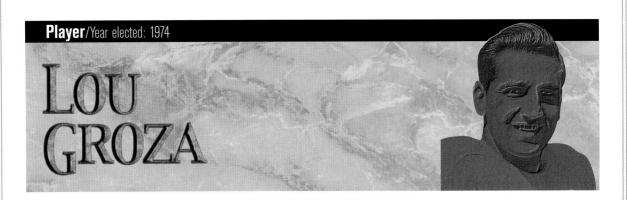

LOU GROZA

GROZA

Born: 1-25-24, Martins Ferry, Ohio **Died:** 11-29-2000 **Ht/Wt:** 6-3/240 **College:** Ohio State **Drafted:** Undrafted **Primary positions:** OT, DT, K **Career statistics:** Scoring AAFC, 30 FG, 169 PAT, 259 pts.; Scoring NFL, 234 FG, 641 PAT, 1,349 pts. **Scoring champion:** 1957 **Teams:** AAFC Browns 1946-49; NFL Browns 1950-59, 1961-67 **Championship teams:** AAFC 1946, '47, '48, '49; NFL 1950, '54, '55, '64 **Honors:** 50th Anniversary Team; 1950s All-Decade Team

He was known as The Toe, a nickname he lived up to every day for 21 professional seasons. Lou Groza was a placekicking pioneer who just happened to double as an All-Pro-caliber offensive tackle. He could open up holes for the Cleveland Browns' machine-like offense and then cap a drive with a 40-yard field goal. He was a point-producing luxury in the era of 33-man rosters.

The thick-shouldered, friendly giant from Martins Ferry, Ohio, was pro football's first great kicker. He was automatic on extra points and everybody marveled at his accuracy from as far away as midfield. He approached his craft scientifically, working constantly on technique while measuring off precise steps and distances. He became so proficient that Cleveland coach Paul Brown began using him as a fourth-down field-goal option, a huge advantage in the Browns' rise to prominence.

Groza, who played only three freshman games at Ohio State because of military service during World War II,

> "I remember when the goal posts were on the goal line. One day Groza lined up to kick a 53-yard field goal. I said, 'What's happening here? Do they have a trick play?' He made the kick, absolutely made it. I was seeing a new game."
>
> —*Ara Parseghian, former Browns teammate*

was part of Brown's master plan when he constructed the Cleveland franchise that would dominate the new All-America Football Conference from 1946-49 and the NFL through much of the 1950s.

Not only did the 6-foot-3, 240-pounder give the Browns a point-producing dimension, he contributed as a solid run-blocking tackle for 14 seasons before back problems forced him to concentrate strictly on kicking.

The personable, always-popular Groza succeeded in the trenches without the warrior mentality of the normal lineman. His secret was technique and coolness under pressure, which was front and center in 1946 when he kicked 50- and 51-yard field goals, and 1950 when he kicked a 16-yarder with 28 seconds remaining to give the Browns a 30-28 victory over the Los Angeles Rams and their first NFL championship.

By the time he retired after the 1967 season, Groza held virtually every NFL kicking record and had totaled 1,608 professional points. He also held records for games played, extra points, field goals and consecutive games scoring (107).

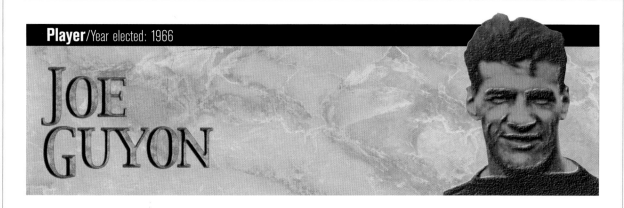

JOE GUYON

Born: 11-26-1892, White Earth Indian Reservation, Min. **Died:** 11-27-71 **Ht/Wt:** 6-1/180 **Primary positions:** TB, DT, P **Teams:** Canton Bulldogs 1920; Washington Senators 1921; Cleveland Indians 1921; Oorang Indians 1922-23; Rock Island Independents 1924; Kansas City Cowboys 1925; New York Giants 1927 **Championship team:** NFL 1927 **Honors:** 1920s All-Decade Team

As an infant on Minnesota's White Earth Indian Reservation, he was O-Gee-Chidaha, full-blooded Chippewa. In the outside world where he was educated and admired for his athleticism and fun-loving personality, he was Joseph Napoleon Guyon, sensational football player. By any name or nationality, he was a warrior and pioneer who brought prestige to his culture and respect to the fledgling National Football League.

The 6-foot-1, 180-pound Guyon played most of his career in the shadow of Jim Thorpe, a fellow Native American and longtime friend who is revered by many as the greatest athlete in the first half of the 20th century. But Guyon made his own impression on opponents, who remembered his instinctive triple-threat offensive talents, fierce competitiveness and devilish smile—a fixture on his ruggedly handsome face.

Many former teammates considered the consistent, always-ready-to-play Guyon superior to Thorpe, who was more spectacular but sometimes lacking in effort. The effervescent, fast-quipping Guyon, like his friend, was a capable passer, runner, punter, tackler and blocker who played a leading role for seven NFL teams over a seven-year professional career.

Guyon gained early acclaim as Thorpe's teammate on the famed Carlisle Indian School team in 1912 and later performed as a star tackle for John Heisman's 1917 Georgia Tech national championship team. When

the NFL began operation as the American Professional Football Association, Guyon and Thorpe shared backfields with the 1920 Canton Bulldogs, 1921 Cleveland Indians, 1922 and '23 Oorang Indians and 1924 Rock Island Independents.

But Guyon's most memorable season was his last—a 1927 championship finale with the 11-1-1 New York Giants. He was a key member of a defense that allowed only 20 points as well as a triple-threat runner, passer and punter. It was his late-season touchdown pass that beat the Chicago Bears, 13-7, and ended their title hopes in what Hall of Fame tackle Steve Owen called "the toughest, roughest football game I ever played."

"Tackling Guyon was like grabbing an airplane propeller."

—Bill Fincher, former Georgia Tech line coach, from Myron Cope's book, The Game That Was

Contributor, Player, Coach/Year elected: 1963, charter member

GEORGE HALAS

Born: 2-2-1895, Chicago, Ill. **Died:** 10-31-83 **Ht/Wt:** 6-0/182 **College:** Illinois **Primary position:** E **Teams played:** Staleys/Bears 1920-28 **Teams coached (318-148-32 RS, 6-3 PS):** Staleys/Bears 1920-29; 1933-42; 1946-55; 1958-67 **Championship teams:** NFL 1921, '33, '40, '41, '46, '63 **Honors:** 1920s All-Decade Team **Executive career:** Founder and owner of Staleys/Bears, 1920-83

He was player, coach, general manager and owner — all at the same time. He was a founder, pioneer, innovator, strategist and legend, the grand and crotchety Papa Bear who breathed life into the professional game and its most revered franchise. What George Halas might have lacked in tact and polish he made up for as the passionate and visionary patriarch of the NFL.

Halas' career spanned an incredible 64 years, nine as a crafty, hard-nosed end for the Decatur Staleys-turned-Chicago Bears team he founded in 1920 and 40 as the franchise's innovative coach. Halas guided

the team through four separate 10-year periods, always with an eye toward growing and popularizing the NFL while delivering six championships.

The Chicago-born Halas, who briefly played baseball with the 1919 New York Yankees, was synonymous with professional football through its first half century. He was there at the 1920 organizational meeting in Canton, Ohio, and he paid legendary Illinois star Red Grange $100,000 in 1925 to play on a 19-game, three-month barnstorming tour that gave the league nationwide exposure. It was Halas, the masterful talent appraiser and tactician, who opened up NFL offenses by introducing the T-formation and man in motion.

Stories about Halas' gruff exterior, stern disciplinary techniques and tightwad management abound. But

> **"I knew pro football was a good game, but I had no sense of destiny. We were involved in a matter of survival. Destiny would take care of itself."**
>
> *— George Halas*

former players recall his behind-the-scenes generosity, motivational wizardry and creative concepts. He was the first coach to run daily practices, utilize public address announcers and arrange for games to be carried on radio. Papa Bear literally charted the NFL's course through one crisis after another.

The image remains of Halas roaming the sideline, screaming at officials and players, shaking his rolled-up program and getting swept away by emotion. Football was not a game to him — it was war, an obsessive commitment to winning. His Monsters of the Midway listened well, delivering "modern-era" championships in 1933, '40, '41, '46 and '63. He retired as coach after the 1967 season with 324 wins, a record that has since been topped by Don Shula.

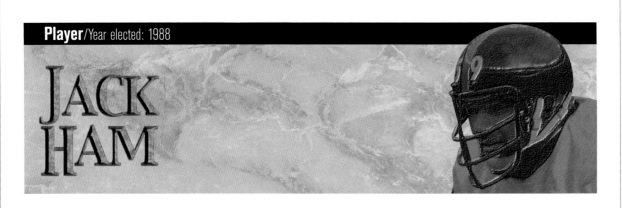

Player/Year elected: 1988

JACK HAM

Born: 12-23-48, Johnstown, Pa. **Ht/Wt:** 6-1/225 **College:** Penn State **Drafted:** 1971, 2nd round, Steelers **Primary position:** LB
Career statistics: Interceptions, 32, 1 TD; 19 fumble recoveries **Teams:** Steelers 1971-82 **Super Bowl champions:** 1974, '75, '78, '79 seasons **Honors:** 75th Anniversary All-Time Team; 1970s All-Decade Team; All-Time NFL Team

He was affectionately called "Dobre Shunka" (Great Ham) by Pittsburgh's Slovak fans. He was respectfully called Master Jack by opponents he faced on Sunday afternoons. By any name, Jack Ham was the brains behind the Steel Curtain brawn, the steadying hand for one of football's great defenses. When trouble loomed, he always was there with the big play.

"I'm a technique guy. I don't go out and beat up on people. That's not me. I try to be consistent and not have a lot of highs and lows. I try to avoid making mistakes. I think being a disciplined player is important so the rest of the players know you'll be in a certain position." —Jack Ham

like an extra defensive back, a role he relished. He loved the challenge of covering fleet running backs and tight ends and his ballhawking ability produced 32 interceptions over a 12-year career that started in 1971. He also recovered 19 opponent fumbles and was a dangerous kick-blocker for the Steelers' special-teams unit.

As the outside linebacker on the left side of a defense fronted by Joe Greene and L.C. Greenwood, the 6-foot-1, 225-pound former Penn State star didn't have to play the power game. He had explosive quickness and the football savvy to diagnose plays, frustrating offensive coordinators who marveled at his anticipation and ability to carve up their game plans. The athletic Ham didn't mind delivering a blow, but he preferred to operate with intelligence and a consistent, unemotional discipline.

Surrounded by Greene, Greenwood, cornerback Mel Blount and fellow linebackers Jack Lambert and Andy Russell, Ham could be used

Ironically, the low-key, quiet Ham, who went out of his way to avoid the spotlight, became one of the most popular players in a city that revered its blue-collar heroes. Ham wasn't as imposing as Lambert and he didn't hit as hard as Greene, but his guile-over-power style still caught the fancy of fans in the Steel City. His athleticism and grace caught the fancy of coaches who redefined the attributes they sought in an outside linebacker.

Ham, an eight-time Pro Bowl selection, played in six AFC title games in eight years and helped the Steelers win four Super Bowl championships in a six-year span. He retired after injury-plagued 1981 and 1982 seasons.

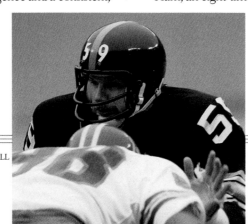

HAM

DAN HAMPTON

Born: 9-19-57, Oklahoma City, Okla. **Ht/Wt:** 6-5/264 **College:** Arkansas **Drafted:** 1979, 1st round, Bears **Primary positions:** DT, DE
Teams: Bears 1979-90 **Super Bowl champion:** 1985 season **Honors:** 1980s All-Decade Team

They ranted, raved, growled, snarled and snorted — 11 intimidating warriors driven to mayhem and destruction. The most passionate of those angry voices belonged to Dan Hampton, the 6-foot-5, 264-pound tackle whose non-stop motor powered Chicago's 1985 defensive machine. The work ethic and motivation of the man they called "Danimal" fueled one of the greatest teams ever assembled and embodied the revival of a proud Bears franchise from 1979-90.

Everybody marveled at Hampton's intense desire to succeed, tunnel-vision pride and ability to play through pain. "He was probably the toughest human being you could ever imagine," former wide receiver Tom Waddle told a *Chicago Daily Herald* reporter, echoing the sentiments of other Bears who watched him sacrifice his body and absorb countless double- and triple-team blocks over a 12-season, surgery-filled career. Near the end, there was little cartilage left in his knees and he seldom practiced, but the game-day motor still hummed.

Hampton relished and earned his "mean and tough" reputation. He was the ultimate team player who accepted punishment to open lanes for his linemates. Defense fueled the 1985 Bears, who allowed a league-low 198 points, shut out two playoff opponents and capped an 18-1 blitz by beating New England in the Super Bowl, but the spotlight focused on Richard Dent, Mike Singletary and William "Refrigerator" Perry — while Hampton labored in the trenches.

The Bears posted 62 regular-season wins and reached the NFC championship game three times in the five-year stretch from 1984-88, thanks in no small part to Hampton.

Mirroring the intensity of coach Mike Ditka, he played with an attitude and demanded that teammates do the same — or answer to him. Hampton cringed at the attention-grabbing antics of quarterback Jim McMahon, but asked only that he deliver on the field, which he usually did.

The former Arkansas All-American, who could run a 5.1-second 40-yard dash before his surgeries, played in four Pro Bowls and posted 82 career sacks, including 11 ½ in both 1980 and 1984.

> "If I was a coach, I'd put my wildest and craziest guys on defense. It takes 10 guys to hold down one insane person."
>
> —*Dan Hampton, 1979, Chicago Sun-Times*

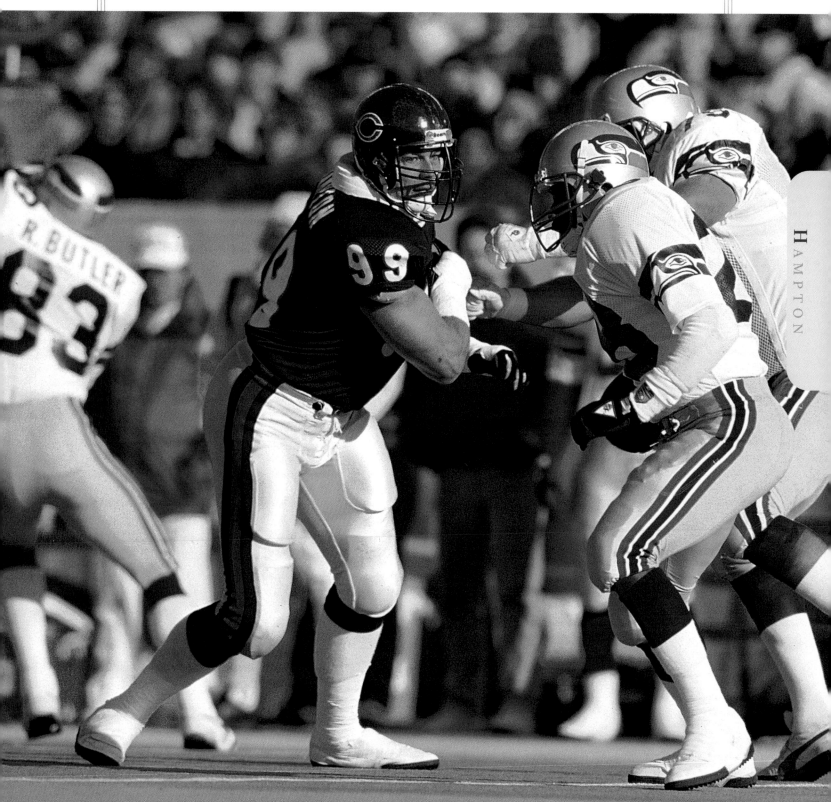

JOHN HANNAH

Born: 4-4-51, Canton, Ga. **Ht/Wt:** 6-2/265 **College:** Alabama **Drafted:** 1973, 1st round, Patriots **Primary position:** OG
Teams: Patriots 1973-85 **Honors:** 75th Anniversary All-Time Team; 1970s All-Decade Team; 1980s All-Decade Team; All-Time NFL Team

Intense. Physical. Intimidating. Relentless. Tough. Adjectives roll off the tongue like defensive linemen rolled off the massive body of New England Patriots offensive guard John Hannah. He was a legend in the football trenches, a grunt-and-groan trailblazer for 13 NFL seasons. When the Patriots needed a tough yard, Hannah made sure they got it.

The 6-foot-2, 265-pound former Alabama All-American was the outstanding run-blocker of his era. Defensive players who did not have their helmet strapped on were in danger of losing it with one of his trademark forearm blows. Hannah intimidated quietly and dominated thoroughly, operating with a ruthless, business-like efficiency that never varied from play to play.

He was at his best when firing out with missile-like force or leading ballcarriers on power sweeps. The sight of a pulling Hannah on one of his full-speed rampages was the worst nightmare of defensive ends and linebackers who were expected to step into his path. Many of the NFL's top defenders dreaded the prospect of facing the nine-time Pro Bowl selection.

Hannah's quickness and physical game were impressive, but no more than the intensity he put into preparation for every game. He was a workaholic who studied the strengths and weaknesses of opponents

> "He's one of the best linemen I've ever played against. ... When you played against John, it was a major challenge. You had to keep your helmet strapped on tight."
>
> —Randy White, 1986, The Boston Globe

and entered every contest with a personal game plan. Hannah's strength was execution and he approached every play as if it would be his last. When the dark-haired giant with the blazing eyes stepped to the line, nobody doubted who was in control.

Not surprisingly, the Patriots thrived with Hannah patroling the middle of their power attack. They posted only three losing records during his 13 seasons and rushed for a single-season-record 3,165 yards in 1978. In 1985, they won an AFC championship before losing to powerful Chicago in Super Bowl XX. Hannah, the son of Herb Hannah and brother of Charley Hannah, both former NFL linemen, retired after his lone Super Bowl appearance.

FRANCO HARRIS

Born: 3-7-50, Fort Dix, N.J. **Ht/Wt:** 6-2/230 **College:** Penn State **Drafted:** 1972, 1st round, Steelers **Primary position:** RB
Career statistics: Rushing, 2,949 att., 12,120 yds., 91 TDs; Receiving, 307 rec., 2,287 yds., 9 TDs **Teams:** Steelers 1972-83; Seahawks 1984 **Super Bowl champions:** 1974 (MVP), '75, '78, '79 seasons **Honors:** 1970s All-Decade Team

He was a small, quick man trapped in a large body, an almost perfect blend of power and finesse. Franco Harris spent 13 seasons trapped between mandates to drive his 230 pounds through tacklers and a personal preference to go around them. Career totals of 12,120 yards and 91 rushing touchdowns suggest he found a happy median, as do the four Super Bowl rings he earned as chief grinder for Pittsburgh's winning machine of the 1970s.

Harris was a quiet, serious, painfully slow-moving personality who shifted into a faster, more-competitive mode when he pulled the Steelers' black helmet over his dark, bearded face. The body suggested power, but Harris had great balance, quick change-of-direction moves and explosive speed. Critics questioned his dancing style and unwillingness to fight for extra yards, but Harris claimed his avoid-unnecessary-contact mentality extended his career.

The former Penn State star, who missed only nine games because of injury, did not punish like Earl Campbell and he wasn't flashy like Tony Dorsett. He

was more like a marathon runner who always reached the finish line. Eight times he topped 1,000 yards in a season, 47 times he topped 100 in a game. His postseason rushing total (1,556) is second all-time; he ranks No. 1 in Super Bowl (354) rushing yards. Harris, who pounded out 158 yards as the MVP of Super Bowl IX, was the man who could get key yards in critical situations.

Harris, versatile enough to catch 307 passes over his 12 Pittsburgh and one Seattle seasons, is remembered for the "Immaculate Reception" he made to defeat Oakland in a first-round 1972 playoff game — the first postseason win in Pittsburgh history. It was a fitting culmination to a storybook 1,055-yard rookie season that inspired formation of "Franco's Italian Army" rooting section.

It's no coincidence the Steelers never had a losing season with Harris on their roster. When the nine-time Pro Bowl selection retired in 1984, he ranked third on football's all-time rushing charts, 192 yards behind Jim Brown and 1,189 behind Walter Payton.

"What Joe Greene meant to (the Steelers') defense—setting the tone—that's what Franco did for our offense. The constant factor became our running game—in bad weather, in good weather, in wind, whatever, you could always count on Harris and our running game."

—*Jack Ham*

MIKE HAYNES

Born: 7-1-53, Denison, Tex. **Ht/Wt:** 6-2/192 **College:** Arizona State **Drafted:** 1976, 1st round, Patriots **Primary position:** DB
Career statistics: Interceptions, 46, 2 TDs; Punt Returns, 112 att., 10.4 avg., 2 TDs **Teams:** Patriots 1976-82; Raiders 1983-89
Super Bowl champion: 1983 season **Honors:** 75th Anniversary All-Time Team; 1980s All-Decade Team

A Sunday afternoon with Mike Haynes was a bonding experience. He didn't limit his introductions to a few well-timed hits or an occasional takedown. When NFL wide receivers got together with the friendliest cornerback in the game, they usually shared a single jersey for 60 excrutiating minutes. Haynes was a smothering presence, the shadow that wouldn't go away.

Few corners in history played tighter than the former Arizona State star, who was an impressive package of speed, quickness and size. The 6-foot-2, 192-pound Haynes was a man-to-man demon who frustrated receivers from his 1976 debut with the New England Patriots to his 1989 final season with the Los Angeles Raiders. He was so dependable that Patriots coach Chuck Fairbanks once remarked, "Mike hasn't seen a ball come his way in over three weeks."

It wasn't that way when Haynes picked off eight passes in a big rookie season that also included two punt returns for touchdowns. It didn't take long for the tall, good-looking Texan to become known as a thinking man's defensive back, a worker who relentlessly studied film and rehearsed his moves based on opponents' tendencies.

> "I think he'd match up with anybody. If I was going to start a football team, he'd be the first corner I'd pick. He had size, speed, great instincts for the game. He had everything you look for in a corner."
>
> —*Steve Grogan, 1997, Akron Beacon Journal*

Haynes was so thorough in his preparation that he often attended meetings for wide receivers and quarterbacks to get an enemy perspective. The result was obvious on Sunday afternoons. He seldom fell for fakes or moves that normally would separate the good receiver from his shadow. Less physical than other defensive backs, Haynes intimidated top pass-catchers in more cerebral ways.

The reputation grew in New England but a 1983 move to Los Angeles really vaulted Haynes into a national spotlight. He teamed with Lester Hayes from 1983-86 as one of the best cornerback tandems in pro football history and he played a big part in the Raiders' Super Bowl XVIII pounding of Washington. The nine-time Pro Bowl selection, who also was known as an electrifying runner after picking off the pass, finished his 14-year career with 46 interceptions.

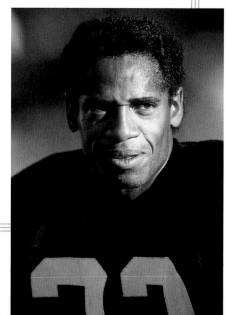

Player/Year elected: 1964

ED HEALEY

Born: 12-28-1894, Indian Orchard, Mass. **Died:** 12-9-78 **Ht/Wt:** 6-3/220 **College:** Dartmouth **Primary positions:** OT, DT, OG
Teams: Rock Island Independents 1920-22; Bears 1922-27 **Honors:** 1920s All-Decade Team

George Halas called him the most versatile tackle of all time. Opponents who had to deal with Ed Healey on a regular basis described him as rough, mean and ruthless, often with more colorful adjectives. No player epitomized the pounding, no-holds-barred ruggedness of 1920s professional football than Big Ed, one of the Chicago Bears' first superstars.

The 6-foot-3, 220-pound Healey was bigger than

most players of his era, a combination of raw power and deceptive speed in a rock-solid body. Fast enough to elude many of his plodding opponents on defense, he usually opted to hammer them into submission with tree-like arms. Strong enough to handle most defensive linemen he faced, Healey was the punishing, go-to blocker in short-yardage situations. He was, simply, a man who enjoyed contact.

Bears player/coach Halas got a first-hand demonstration of Healey's talents from 1920-22, when the former Dartmouth star played for the Rock Island Independents. After one late-season 1922 game in which they had battled one-on-one for 60 excrutiating minutes, Halas, beaten and frustrated, decided to call in a debt from the Rock Island owner. He acquired Healey for $100 — the first player sale in NFL history and one the Papa Bear never regretted.

Over the next five-plus seasons, Healey settled in as one of the league's best players. He seldom missed a start, showed off his vast physical abilities and became a Halas favorite — a football bruiser with an Ivy League mind. One of his signature moments came in 1924 after teammate Oscar Knop, a fullback, intercepted a pass and ran toward the wrong goal line. Healey, amazingly, chased Knop down and tackled him just short of the end zone.

The Bears carved out an impressive 45-12-13 record over Healey's five full Chicago seasons, but never won a championship. In 1926, they were 12-1-3; the following season, they finished 9-3-2. At that point Healey retired to try his hand in the business world.

> "I got a hundred bucks a game from the Bears, which was nice, but the thing I appreciated most about being with them was the clubhouse. At Rock Island, the clubhouse had no showers and seldom a trainer. At Wrigley Field, we had a nice warm place to dress and nice hot showers."
>
> —Ed Healey, from The Chicago Bears, a book by Howard Roberts

Player/Year elected: 1963, charter member

MEL HEIN

Born: 8-22-09, Redding, Calif. **Died:** 1-31-92 **Ht/Wt:** 6-2/225 **College:** Washington State **Primary positions:** C, LB **Career statistics:** Interceptions, 10, 1 TD **Teams:** Giants 1931-45 **Championship teams:** NFL 1934, '38 **Honors:** 75th Anniversary All-Time Team; 1930s All-Decade Team

He was the Lou Gehrig of football, the man who played every minute of every New York Giants game for 15 years. One New York writer called Mel Hein "the greatest two-way player in Giants history," but he probably was shortsighted in his praise. Hein was the prototype center of the professional game's early years, a trend-setting linebacker and a man who developed football techniques that are still in use today.

Hein's first priority was as the "second quarterback" of New York's offense from 1931-45. In the era of single-wing formations, every snap was directed to a tailback positioned away from the line, the equivalent of snapping in today's shotgun formation. Hein, forced to keep his head down longer to ensure accurate delivery, still had the quickness to deliver his block and occasionally

> "I've been around this league a long time and I've never seen a player who made fewer mistakes than Mel. He has a feel for football, an instinctive understanding and grasp of it that allows him to command every bit of action on the field."
>
> —*Steve Owen,*
> *former Giants coach, 1942*

even joined sweeps as one of the first pulling linemen.

Legend has it that Hein never made a bad snap and the techniques he developed have been passed on from center to center for generations. As a mobile 225-pound linebacker, he excelled at pass coverage and used jamming tactics that nobody had seen before. Hein was strong, tough and a 60-minute guarantee for every game, but his greatest asset was the football intelligence he used to develop and master techniques that were well ahead of his time.

Amiable, modest and an "aw shucks" straight-arrow off the field, Hein was the consummate technician on it. He joined the Giants as a $150-per-game hopeful after a good college career at Washington State and served as Giants captain for 10 years, helping the team qualify for seven championship games and win two NFL titles.

The popular Californian, who was honored with "Mel Hein Day" at the end of his career, was selected for four Pro Bowls, a postseason event that was not founded until late in his career. Hein became a charter member of the Pro Football Hall of Fame in 1963.

HEIN

TED HENDRICKS

Born: 11-1-47, Guatemala City, Guatemala **Ht/Wt:** 6-7/220 **College:** Miami (Fla.) **Drafted:** 1969, 2nd round, Colts **Primary position:** LB **Career statistics:** Interceptions, 26, 1 TD **Teams:** Colts 1969-73; Packers 1974; Raiders 1975-83 **Super Bowl champions:** 1970, '76, '80, '83 seasons **Honors:** 75th Anniversary All-Time Team; 1970s All-Decade Team; 1980s All-Decade Team

Some said he was too tall. Others said he was too light. Everybody agreed that the 6-foot-7, 220-pound body Ted Hendricks brought to the field was a little unorthodox for pro football. Everybody, that is, except the Mad Stork himself, who spent 15 seasons making big plays and defying critics as one of the top outside linebackers in the game's history.

The image of a tall, flailing Hendricks rushing the quarterback, leaping high to knock down passes, blocking kicks and wrapping his python-like arms around ballcarriers became a football fixture from 1969-83, first with the Baltimore Colts, then with the Green Bay Packers and Oakland/Los Angeles Raiders. He was at his disruptive best over nine seasons with the Raiders, who gave him the green light to roam the line, blitz on impulse, read the play and react. Nobody could key on him.

And few players could block him. The former University of Miami All-American looked skinny, but he was a well-muscled physical specimen who combined surprising speed with agility. His height was a major obstacle for passing quarterbacks and his long arms pulled down errant passes

> "Ted was one of my favorite players. But the thing was, if you didn't enjoy him, didn't laugh with him, he'd drive you crazy." —*John Madden*

(26 career interceptions) and blocked kicks (25 field goals and extra points). He was master of the unusual play, prompting Raiders defensive coach Charlie Sumner to remark, "At least once a game he'll do something and I won't know how he did it."

The spectacular feats that became Hendricks' on-field trademark were a product of a free-spirit personality that entertained teammates throughout the week and confounded more than one coach. You never knew what to expect from the Guatemala-born star, who was a curious blend of thoughtful intelligence and devil-may-care recklessness.

But what you could count on was the game-day dedication and winning attitude that contributed to four Super Bowl wins (three with the Raiders, one with the Colts) and eight Pro Bowl selections—at least one with each of his teams.

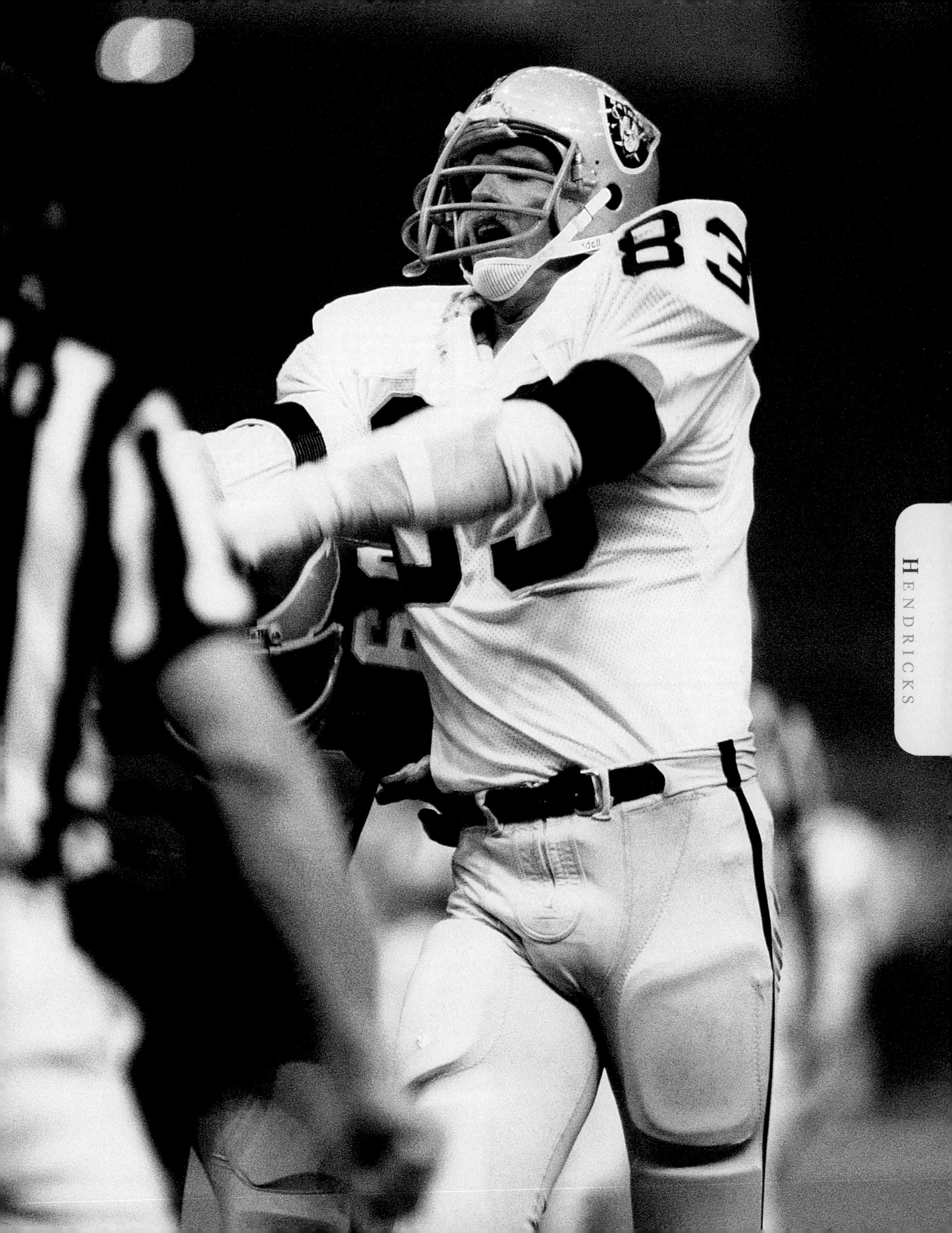
83

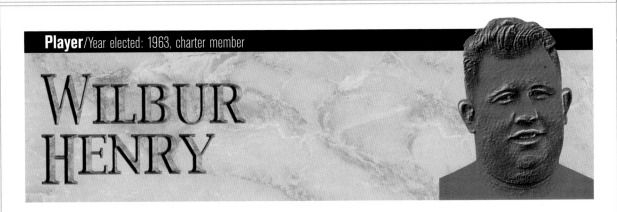

WILBUR HENRY

Born: 10-31-1897, Mansfield, Ohio **Died:** 2-7-52 **Ht/Wt:** 6-0/250 **College:** Washington and Jefferson **Primary positions:** OT, DT
Teams: Canton Bulldogs 1920-26; Giants 1927; Pottsville Maroons 1927-28 **Championship teams:** NFL 1922, '23
Honors: 1920s All-Decade Team

The 250 pounds Wilbur Henry carried on his 6-foot frame were not sculpted by the football gods. He looked flabby and round, worthy of his unflattering nickname "Fats." But that was a cruel illusion. Opponents who bought into the popular misconception, dismissing the bulky two-way tackle as soft, slow and weak, quickly discovered the error of their ways.

Henry, who preferred the nickname "Pete," was one of professional football's first superstars. He also was a key member of the 1922 and '23 Canton Bulldogs, the newly named "NFL's" first two championship teams. Henry is best remembered as a defensive bruiser who cleared out opponents like a bowling ball hitting pins, but he also was a go-to blocker, strong punter and accurate dropkicker — one of the game's first long-range scoring threats.

Henry, who was born in Mansfield, Ohio, was so renowned in his home state that the *Canton Repository* announced his 1920 signing with a huge front-page headline, relegating formation of the American Professional Football Association

> ## "Tackles will come and tackles will go, but never will pro football enthusiasts see the peer of Wilbur Henry."
>
> *— The Canton Repository, 1922*

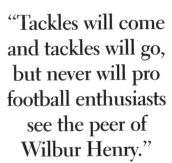

(the future NFL) to an inside page. He had earned All-American honors at Washington and Jefferson College and formed an instant love affair with football-hungry Canton fans.

With 6-foot-2, 233-pound Roy "Link" Lyman joining him on the Bulldogs' line in 1922, Henry powered the Bulldogs to a 10-0-2 record and the city's first championship. But that was just the appetizer. The 1923 team steamrolled opponents en route to an 11-0-1 finish, allowing only 19 points and scoring 246 — 58 by Henry on a tackle-eligible touchdown reception, nine field goals and 25 extra points. In short-yardage situations, coach Guy Chamberlin even used big Pete as a fullback, a la William "Refrigerator" Perry six decades later.

Henry remained in Canton through the 1926 season, when the franchise folded. He played four 1927 games with the eventual champion New York Giants before moving to Pottsville, where he ended his career in '28. The 60-minute star became a charter member of the Pro Football Hall of Fame in 1963.

HENRY

Player/Year elected: 1964

CLARKE HINKLE

Born: 4-10-09, Toronto, Ohio **Died:** 11-9-88 **Ht/Wt:** 5-11/201 **College:** Bucknell **Primary positions:** FB, LB, K, P **Career statistics:** Rushing, 1,171 att., 3,860 yds., 35 TDs; Receiving, 49 rec., 9 TDs; Scoring, 28 FG, 31 PAT, 379 pts.; Punting, 87 att., 40.8 avg. **Scoring champion:** 1938 **Teams:** Packers 1932-41 **Championship teams:** NFL 1936, '39 **Honors:** 1930s All-Decade Team

Proud, fearless and agonizingly stubborn, Clarke Hinkle was a firm believer that the shortest distance between two points is a straight line. Obstacles were welcome, all challenges accepted by Green Bay's little big man, a kamikaze fullback and linebacker who never backed down from a bigger

opponent or a punishing hit. A poster boy for the hard-knock 1930s, Hinkle provided inspiration and versatility for two of the game's most innovative championship teams.

At 5-foot-11 and 201 pounds, Hinkle did not intimidate the bigger defenders and blockers he consistently battled as a 60-minute performer. But opponents marveled at the battering-ram punishment he consistently delivered and the nonstop motor that eventually wore them down. The former Bucknell University star was fast enough to elude contact, too stubborn to back away from it.

His most celebrated battles were against Chicago star Bronko Nagurski, a punishing ballcarrier and linebacker who was 25 pounds heavier and solid as a rock. "I always tried to get him before he got to me," said Hinkle, who would trade haymaker blows with Nagurski for 60 minutes, giving as good as he got.

> "Hinkle was harder to stop than either (Steve) Van Buren or (Tony) Canadeo. ... Steve makes headway only when he is running low, close to the ground. Hinkle had power at all times, whether running low or high."
>
> *— Bulldog Turner, 1951*

The Bronk vs. Hinkle was always an entertaining sub-plot when two of the era's best teams did battle.

But Hinkle's best weapon was his versatility. Operating in Green Bay's single wing backfield with Arnie Herber and later Cecil Isbell, he churned out yardage, blocked, tossed passes to Don Hutson, caught short passes, punted and twice led the league in field goals. He was a defensive scourge, one of the most ferocious tacklers and ballhawks in the league. Polite and mild-mannered off the field, Hinkle transformed into a hard-nosed, determined competitor on it.

With such stars as Hinkle, Herber, Hutson and Isbell operating the NFL's first serious passing offense, the Packers won championships in 1936 and '39, losing to the New York Giants in the 1938 title game. Hinkle, who led NFL scorers with 58 points in 1938, retired in 1941 after 10 outstanding seasons.

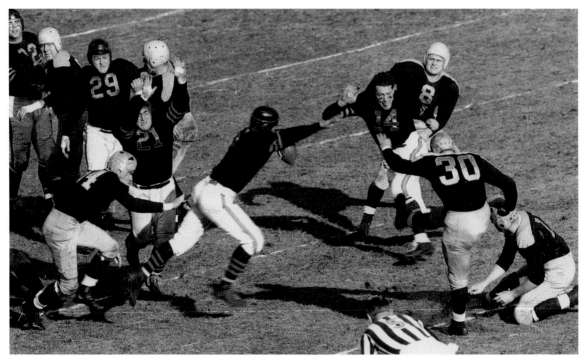

Clarke Hinkle (30) cannot get this field goal attempt past the outstretched arm of a Chicago defender.

ELROY HIRSCH

Born: 6-17-23, Wausau, Wis. **Ht/Wt:** 6-2/190 **College:** Wisconsin, Michigan **Drafted:** 1945, 1st round, Rams **Primary positions:** HB, E, DB **Career statistics:** Rushing AAFC, 370 yds., 2 TDs; Receiving AAFC, 44 rec., 7 TDs; Receiving NFL, 343 rec., 6,299 yds., 18.4 avg., 53 TDs **Receptions leader:** 1951 **Teams:** AAFC Rockets 1946-48; NFL Rams 1949-57 **Championship team:** NFL 1951 **Honors:** 50th Anniversary Team; 1950s All-Decade Team

Start with those Crazy Legs, the long, muscular limbs that appeared to gyrate in six different directions when shifted into warp speed. Elroy Hirsch walked like a duck but ran pass patterns like an awkward young gazelle trying to evade a hungry pursuer. He was quick, elusive and deceptively fast, a deep-threat receiver who terrorized defensive backs for 12 professional seasons. When Crazy Legs turned on the burners, somebody usually got scorched.

"Spectacular" and "colorful" are words usually associated with the former Wisconsin star, who caught 17 touchdown passes in an outstanding 1951 season for the Los Angeles Rams—nine of 44 yards or longer, five of 72-plus yards. Hirsch's speed was complemented by near-perfect timing and long, thin fingers that could pull in over-the-head throws while he was in full stride. Once the ball was secured, nobody caught Hirsch from behind.

The nickname was pinned on a 6-foot-2, 190-pound half-back who displayed elusive running skills as well as susceptibility

to injury during his college career and three years with the Chicago Rockets of the All-America Football Conference. Hirsch changed positions in 1950, his second season with the Rams, and became one of the first ends to move outside as a flanker. For seven years he teamed with Tom Fears as one of first great receiver tandems in football history. Hirsch, a blithe spirit who was infectiously happy, intelligent and always ready with a quick quip or putdown, helped put the word "bomb" in the NFL dictionary. During his big 1951 season, he caught 66 passes for 1,495 yards and a whopping 22.7-yards-per-catch average while helping the Rams win a championship, the second in franchise history.

Hirsch's 18.4-yard career average ranks among the best in NFL history and he once caught touchdown passes in 11 straight 1950 and 1951 games, a record since surpassed. Hirsch, a three-time Pro Bowl selection, retired in 1957 with 343 catches for 6,299 yards and 53 touchdowns in nine NFL seasons.

> "There are plenty of players who can run faster than Hirsch in a straightaway race. But when they carry a football, they lose balance and slow down. Give Hirsch a football and he speeds up. Don't ask me how. He just does."
>
> —*Joe Stydahar, former Rams coach,* 1951

PAUL HORNUNG

Born: 12-23-35, Louisville, Ky. **Ht/Wt:** 6-2/220 **College:** Notre Dame **Drafted:** 1957, Bonus round, Packers **Primary positions:** HB, FB **Career statistics:** Rushing, 893 att., 3,711 yds., 50 TDs; Receiving, 130 rec., 11.4 avg., 12 TDs; Scoring, 66 FG, 190 PAT, 760 pts. **Scoring champion:** 1959, '60, '61 **Teams:** Packers 1957-62, 1964-66 **Championship teams:** NFL 1961, '62, '65, '66 **Super Bowl champion:** 1966 season **Honors:** 1960s All-Decade Team

He could power through the tiniest of holes, catch passes like a wide receiver and throw them like a quarterback while executing Vince Lombardi's famed halfback option. Paul Hornung would stun opponents with his big-play athleticism, then kick the bejabbers out of them with a strong right foot. He was the

"Golden Boy" of Green Bay's golden era, a versatile weapon for powerful Lombardi teams that won five conference titles and four NFL championships from 1959-66.

The wavy blond hair and matinee-idol looks camouflaged Hornung's well-defined football skills—above-average speed, sharp running instincts and a toughness that was always front and center at big moments in big games. Most of all, he was a 6-foot-2, 220-pound scoring machine, a go-to weapon for quarterback Bart Starr.

Hornung led the NFL in scoring three times in nine seasons, setting a still-standing record with 176 points (15 TDs, 15 field goals, 41 conversions) for the 1960 team that lost to Philadelphia in the NFL championship game.

Always explosive, he scored 33 points in one 1961 contest and 19 more in a 37-0 championship game conquest of New York—while on Christmas leave from the Army. He set up Green Bay's only TD in a 16-7

title game win over the same Giants in 1962 with a 21-yard option pass.

The 1956 Notre Dame Heisman Trophy-winning quarterback moved in the social fast lane and paid a price, both in body and reputation. News that Hornung had been suspended for the 1963 season because of gambling activity came as a bombshell, but he quietly served his time, came back strong and helped the Packers win a 1965 championship, scoring five touchdowns in a late-season win over Baltimore. In his 1966 final season, Hornung was a member of the Packers' first Super Bowl winner.

A two-time Pro Bowl participant, the strong-minded Kentuckian retired with 3,711 rushing yards, 1,480 receiving yards and 760 points, almost half coming on 62 career TDs. Interestingly, Hornung teams coached by Lombardi produced a seven-year regular-season record of 69-23-2.

"He may not be the greatest football player in the world, but Paul has the special ability to rise to the occasion and to be the greatest of the great when the games are on the line."

—*Vince Lombardi*

KEN HOUSTON

Born: 11-12-44, Lufkin, Tex. **Ht/Wt:** 6-3/197 **College:** Prairie View A&M **Drafted:** 1967, 9th round, Oilers **Primary position:** DB
Career statistics: Interceptions, 49, 9 TDs; Punt Returns, 51 att., 6.5 avg., 1 TD **Teams:** Oilers 1967-72; Redskins 1973-80
Honors: 75th Anniversary All-Time Team; 1970s All-Time Team

Consistency. Game after game, season after season, that quality separated Ken Houston from the NFL crowd. As a 14-year strong safety for the Houston Oilers and Washington Redskins, pro football's "most underrated superstar" efficiently provided a last line of defense with his special knack for always being in the right place at the right time.

Houston's greatest talent might have been the instinct that helped him make intelligent decisions. But he also was blessed with excellent quickness and speed, the product of strong legs that carried his sinewy 6-foot-3, 197-pound body around the field with long, fluid strides. Houston, a former college linebacker, was a punishing hitter when supporting on the

> ## "Ken Houston is the best player I have ever lined up with."
>
> *— Jake Scott, former Redskins defensive back*

run, a cunning blitzer in passing situations and a first-class ballhawk who was especially dangerous after an interception.

Of his 49 career interceptions, nine were returned for touchdowns—four in 1971 when he also returned a fumble for an Oilers TD. The former Prairie View A&M star also was durable, an ironman who played in 183 straight games before a broken arm ended his 1979 season with Washington. While Houston's performance often escaped the notice of fans, his coaches and teammates marveled at the unwavering work ethic and consistency with which he graded out on film.

The respect Houston commanded was demonstrated by his 12 Pro Bowl selections and the way offensive coordinators avoided him in their weekly game plans. He was a rising star in his first six seasons with the Oilers (1967-72), a proven game-breaker after his trade to Washington. Houston was a captain and defensive signal-caller during part of his eight-year stay with the Redskins.

The only thing missing from Houston's resume was a championship, although he was a member of an Oilers' team that lost to Oakland in the 1967 AFL title game. The quiet, soft-spoken Texan was well known for the charity work he performed in the Houston area, both early in his career and after his 1980 retirement.

Ken Houston bats a pass away from San Francisco's O.J. Simpson (32) in a 1978 game at Washington, D.C.

Big Cal Hubbard (22) helped carry the Green Bay Packers to three straight NFL championships.

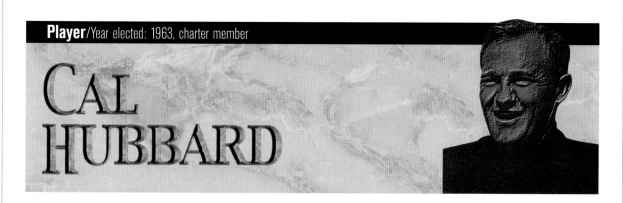

CAL HUBBARD

Born: 10-31-1900, Keytesville, Mo. **Died:** 10-17-77 **Ht/Wt:** 6-3/255 **College:** Centenary, Geneva **Primary positions:** OT, DT, E, LB **Teams:** Giants 1927-28, 1936; Packers 1929-33, 1935; Pirates 1936 **Championship teams:** NFL 1927, '29, '30, '31
Honors: 50th Anniversary Team; 1920s All-Decade Team

He was a big, tough, imposing farmboy with arms of steel and the strength of two Missouri mules. When Cal Hubbard wasn't overwhelming opponents in the trenches, he was finessing them as one of the game's first sideline-to-sideline linebackers. Nobody dominated the early NFL more thoroughly than the 6-foot-3, 255-pound giant who helped carry the New York Giants (1927) and Green Bay Packers (1929, '30, '31) to four championships.

Hubbard, a protege of Centenary College and Geneva College coach Bo McMillin, was bigger than most players of his era. He also was faster, a lethal combination that allowed him to dominate both offensively and defensively—first as a tackle and later as an end and run-stuffing linebacker. Hubbard could break blocking wedges with a sweep of his arms, chase down ballcarriers with his startling quickness and pancake defenders with bulldozing blocks.

"Cal was such a gentle, amiable guy off the field, that you couldn't believe how tough he was," McMillin once said. "Gentle and amiable" didn't

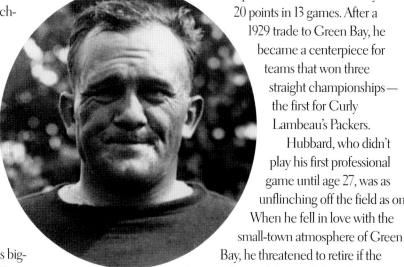

> "Cal Hubbard, going either way, was the greatest I ever saw."
>
> —*Curly Lambeau*

apply to game days. After signing with New York in 1927, Hubbard anchored a Giants championship defense that allowed only 20 points in 13 games. After a 1929 trade to Green Bay, he became a centerpiece for teams that won three straight championships— the first for Curly Lambeau's Packers.

Hubbard, who didn't play his first professional game until age 27, was as unflinching off the field as on. When he fell in love with the small-town atmosphere of Green Bay, he threatened to retire if the Giants didn't trade him there. Every summer from 1928 through his final season in 1936, big Cal honed his skills as a discipline-commanding minor league umpire, anticipating life after football.

Hubbard became an American League umpire in 1936 and retired in 1969 as the A.L.'s supervisor of umpires. The man Bears coach George Halas once described as "the best lineman I ever saw" now holds distinction as the only man to merit Hall of Fame election in both baseball and pro football.

Player/Year elected: 1982

SAM HUFF

Born: 10-4-34, Morgantown, W. Va. **Ht/Wt:** 6-1/230 **College:** West Virginia **Drafted:** 1956, 3rd round, Giants **Primary position:** LB
Career statistics: Interceptions, 30, 2 TDs **Teams:** Giants 1956-63; Redskins 1964-69 **Championship team:** NFL 1956
Honors: 1950s All-Decade Team

"Huff, Huff, Huff. Huff, Huff, Huff." The cheer chugged around Yankee Stadium like a giant steam engine, much the way New York Giants middle linebacker Sam Huff chugged around the field on his typical Sunday search-and-destroy mission. It was a Big Apple love affair, big No. 70 and a city that appreciated its heroes. When Huff delivered another crunching blow, everybody celebrated.

There was a lot to like about the 6-foot-1, 230-pound former West Virginia star, who charmed fans with his warm, engaging personality and dismantled game plans with punishing regularity. Huff was not the fastest or strongest linebacker in the league, but he made up for shortcomings with hard work, dedication, uncanny anticipation and the ability to diagnose plays.

He always seemed to be around the ball, whether blitzing, stuffing a run or making one of his 30 career interceptions on pass coverage, and the blows he delivered were legendary. Longtime Giants fans still recall the bruising battles he waged against two of the game's great running backs—Cleveland's Jim Brown and Green Bay's Jim Taylor. It was rugged hand-to-hand combat, the essence of professional football in the 1950s and '60s.

Huff loved the spotlight and used the New York stage to glamorize the linebacker position. As one of the first defensive players to gain national attention, he was featured on the cover of *Time* magazine at age 24 and in a CBS television documentary called *"The Violent World of Sam Huff"* a few years later. His fame was enhanced by the success of the Giants, who captured one championship and appeared in six title games in his eight New York seasons (1956-63).

The unflinchingly loyal Huff was devastated when his beloved Giants announced a 1964 trade that sent him to Washington, where he played another five successful seasons. Bitter toward the Giants, the five-time Pro Bowler continued to attack ballcarriers with a fury that lasted until 1969, when he retired as a player/coach under Vince Lombardi.

> "You play as hard and as tough as you can, but you play clean. We hit each other hard, sure. But this is a man's game and any guy who doesn't want to hit hard doesn't belong in it."
>
> —Sam Huff

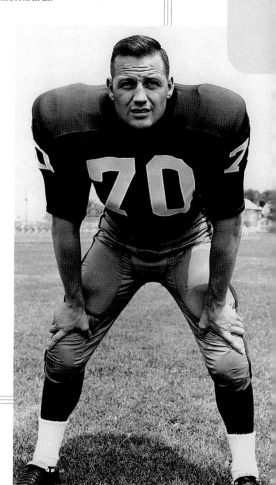

Contributor/Year elected: 1972

LAMAR HUNT

Born: 8-2-32, El Dorado, Ark. **Executive career:** Organizer of American Football League 1960; founder of Dallas Texans franchise 1960; owner of Texans/Chiefs 1960-present

Denied his dream of owning an NFL team, Lamar Hunt built a football empire. The American Football League he pioneered in late 1959 thrived, flourished and merged with the NFL, triggering a new era of professional football prosperity. Team owner, respected NFL power broker, avid sportsman, league builder—the quiet, unpretentious Texas oilman never has been far away from the action.

Hunt will always be remembered as leader of the "Foolish Club," the eight AFL owners who fielded teams for the 1960 season, daring to challenge the established NFL. But he also was a driving force behind the leagues' 1966 merger agreement and the annual AFL-NFL championship game. He built teams that posted an 87-48-5 AFL record, won three championships and represented the league in two of the first four Super Bowls. His Kansas City Chiefs, who began operation as the Dallas Texans (1960-62), won Super Bowl IV, the last game before the merger became official in 1970.

Hunt, the soft-spoken, bespectacled son of Texas oil czar

> **"The American Football League was a challenge. There was a fight, a fight for existence. And there was a challenge to keep it going and overcome the apathy of the fans."** —*Lamar Hunt, 1970*

H.L. Hunt, has remained front and center as Chiefs owner for more than 40 years. Fellow owners know him as a quiet force in the design and development of the modern NFL. As longtime president of the American Football Conference and member of several prominent league committees, Hunt has pushed through legislation, like the 2-point conversion, and helped design the NFL's playoff format.

Hunt also has branched into other sports. He was a founding investor in the NBA's Chicago Bulls and founder of the now-defunct North American Soccer League and World Championship Tennis; his family operates two franchises in Major League Soccer.

Hunt owns 11 championship rings from four professional sports and is a member of three Halls of Fame.

He, fittingly, became the first former AFL figure enshrined at Canton in 1972, and the NFL's annual AFC champion receives the Lamar Hunt Trophy. Not surprisingly, Hunt provided the idea for the name "Super Bowl"—a takeoff from his child's toy Super Ball.

DON HUTSON

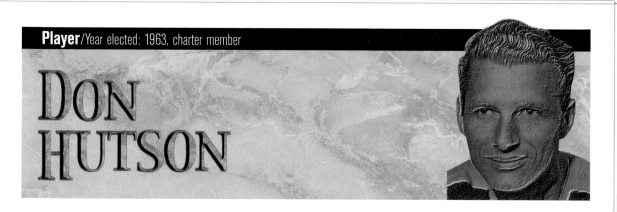

Born: 1-31-13, Pine Bluff, Ark. **Died:** 6-26-97 **Ht/Wt:** 6-1/180 **College:** Alabama **Positions:** E, DB, K **Career statistics:** Receiving, 488 rec., 7,991 yds., 16.4 avg., 99 TDs; Interceptions, 30, 1 TD; Scoring, 7 FG, 172 PAT, 105 TDs, 823 pts. **Receptions leader:** 1936, '37, '39, '41, '42, '43, '44, '45 **Scoring champion:** 1940, '41, '42, '43, '44 **Teams:** Packers 1935-45 **Championship teams:** 1936, '39, '44 **Honors:** 75th Anniversary All-Time Team; 50th Anniversary Team; 1930s All-Decade Team; All-Time NFL Team

He was a gift from the future, a premonition in helmet and cleats. To say Don Hutson was ahead of his time is well beyond understatement. The Green Bay prodigy was professional football's first great receiver, a pass-catching pioneer who helped map the course the game would follow through the second half of the 20th century.

Hutson, the star of Alabama's 1935 Rose Bowl winner, was a nightmare for NFL coaches who were accustomed to defensing the conservative single-wing offenses of the era. He was tall (6-foot-1), elusive and fast, that rare athlete who could find an extra gear and

> ## "There's no easier way of scoring a touchdown than throwing a pass to Hutson."
>
> *—Cecil Isbell,*
> *former Packers quarterback*

explode past helpless defensive backs. Hutson also could outleap most defenders and his big hands and long reach turned poorly-thrown passes into highlight-film touchdowns.

From 1935-45, fans marveled at the sight of the graceful Hutson pulling in long passes and loping into the end zone. He quickly became the centerpiece for

Packers coach Curly Lambeau's innovative quick-strike offense and the driving force behind Green Bay championship teams in 1936, '39 and '44. Not only did Hutson ignite the offense, he also was an accomplished defensive back who made 30 career interceptions and a kicker who scored 193 points.

Over his 11-year career, Hutson led the league in receptions eight times and touchdown catches on nine occasions—still-standing NFL records. His single-season yardage totals consistently topped opposing team totals and most of that yardage was compiled while battling double- and triple-team coverage—unusual strategy at the time. When he recorded the NFL's first 1,000-yard season (1,211) in 1942, 17 of his record 74 catches went for touchdowns.

When Hutson retired, his 488 career catches dwarfed the 298 total of his nearest competitor. His 99 touchdown receptions (and 105 TDs overall) stood as a record for many years, as did his 16.4-yard-per-catch average. The four-time Pro Bowl selection, who once scored 29 points in a single quarter, became a charter member of the Pro Football Hall of Fame in 1963.

JIMMY JOHNSON

Born: 3-31-38, Dallas, Tex. **Ht/Wt:** 6-2/187 **College:** UCLA **Drafted:** 1961, 1st round, 49ers **Primary positions:** DB, WR **Career statistics:** Receiving, 40 rec., 17.3 avg., 4 TDs; Interceptions, 47, 2 TDs **Teams:** 49ers 1961-76 **Honors:** 1970s All-Decade Team

They called him "the lonesome cornerback," a reference to the way Jimmy Johnson was ostracized from the game plans of opposing teams and quarterbacks. It simply made no sense to throw at the best one-on-one cover man in the NFL. Those who did quickly discovered the road to success against San

> ### "I feel Jim is one of the best corners in pro football. I just hope he makes a mistake of some sort so I can get an advantage. He covers all the pass patterns so well."
>
> *— Fred Biletnikoff*

Francisco from 1961-76 curved away from the left side of the 49ers' secondary.

The quiet, soft-spoken Johnson played most of his 16-year career in the shadow of brother Rafer Johnson, the 1960 Olympic decathlon champion and so-called "World's Greatest Athlete." But the 6-foot-2, 187-pound Jimmy also was a gifted athlete with blazing speed and outstanding leaping ability — a standout hurdler and long jumper in addition to football star at UCLA. Drafted by the 49ers as a receiver, he filled an emergency void at safety as a rookie and made five interceptions.

In 1962, Johnson caught 34 passes for 627 yards and four touchdowns. In 1963, he played both offense and defense. He was switched to left corner in 1964 and

spent the next 13 seasons intimidating receivers and quarterbacks, both with his blanket-like coverage and hard-hitting style. Always prepared, Johnson was known for his tunnel-vision concentration and mistake-free instincts.

"Jim doesn't receive much publicity because the opposition avoids him as much as possible," 49ers quarterback John Brodie once said. As a result, Johnson's career interception total (47) was low and he didn't earn All-Pro or Pro Bowl recognition until his ninth season. It didn't help that his 49ers never played in a Super Bowl, losing twice to Dallas in the NFC title game.

But opponents knew he was there, the always cool, never-out-of-position corner with game-breaking abilities. And teammates looked to him as a leader who could bridge the locker room gap between coach and players. Johnson, who teamed on the left side of the 49ers defense for 11 years with Hall of Fame outside linebacker Dave Wilcox, missed only 12 games in 16 years.

JOHN HENRY JOHNSON

Born: 11-24-29, Waterproof, La. **Ht/Wt:** 6-2/225 **College:** St. Mary's (Cal.), Arizona State **Drafted:** 1953, 2nd round, Steelers **Primary positions:** FB, DB **Career statistics:** Rushing, 1,571 att., 6,803 yds., 48 TDs; Receiving, 186 rec., 7.9 avg., 7 TDs **Teams:** 49ers 1954-56; Lions 1957-59; Steelers 1960-65; Oilers 1966 **Championship team:** NFL 1957

The elbows hit flesh like well-aimed hammers and his helmet drove into unprotected ribs like a guided missile. John Henry Johnson didn't simply block opposing defenders, he punished them with all the ferocity he could muster. "John Henry was the meanest man I ever saw," said former Cleveland defensive end Paul Wiggin, who echoed the sentiments of virtually everyone who came in contact with the kamikaze fullback during his 13-year professional career.

Johnson also was an outstanding ballcarrier, a sculpted 6-foot-2, 225-pound blaster with breakaway speed and a crouched, knee-pumping running style. But as one of the best blocking fullbacks in history, he often was asked to sacrifice yards for trench work, a challenge he both endorsed and relished. He loved to inflict pain on bullrushing linebackers and oversized linemen, an overzealous, sometimes-belligerent delight that made him a constant target for revenge.

Johnson, who played one MVP season in the Canadian Football League after leaving Arizona State, played three years (1954-56) with San Francisco, three with Detroit (1957-59) and six with Pittsburgh (1960-65) before finishing his career in 1966 with the AFL's Houston Oilers. He was the enforcer for San Francisco's "Million Dollar Backfield" — a future Hall of Fame quartet that included halfbacks Hugh McElhenny and Joe Perry and quarterback Y.A. Tittle — and a key ingredient for the Lions in their march to the 1957 NFL championship.

But it was the Steelers who gave him his first shot as a feature back and he responded with two 1,000-yard seasons and two more of 787 and 773. He was a dynamic force on short-yardage plays, either as a blocker or runner, and he often played linebacker in goal line situations. Johnson was used by the 49ers at defensive back, a position he could have played with star potential.

The rugged, quiet Californian retired with 6,803 rushing yards, fourth on the all-time list in 1966, and 55 touchdowns. The four-time Pro Bowler also posted a 200-yard rushing game in 1964 against Cleveland.

"There's far more to playing fullback than just running with the football. Everybody wants to run with the ball—that's the quickest way to get the headlines and a lot of newspaper space. But how many times does a back peel off a long run by himself. I'll tell you—absolutely none."

—*John Henry Johnson*

CHARLIE JOINER

Born: 10-14-47, Many, La. **Ht/Wt:** 5-11/185 **College:** Grambling State **Drafted:** 1969, 4th round, Oilers **Primary position:** WR
Career statistics: Receiving, 750 rec., 12,146 yds., 16.2 avg., 65 TDs **Teams:** Oilers 1969-72; Bengals 1972-75; Chargers 1976-86

He was a football scientist, a technician with a plan. When Charlie Joiner stepped on the football field, he wanted everything precise and exact.

That's the way he ran his pass patterns for 18 NFL seasons and that's the way he dissected defenses as one of the premier possession receivers in football history. He was intelligent, disciplined and always precise — Albert Einstein in cleats.

Bill Walsh, who coached Joiner at Cincinnati and San Diego, called him "the most intelligent and perceptive receiver the game has ever seen" — a sentiment shared by numerous defensive backs. The former Grambling star had quick feet, great body control and the ability to slip into the seams of their zones and catch pass after pass. Nobody was

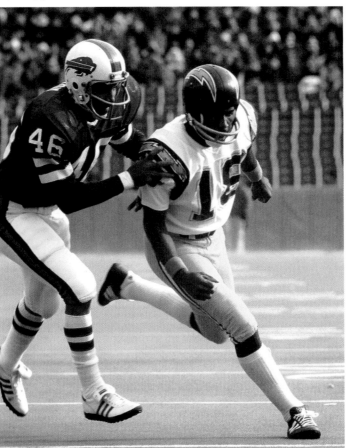

better at reading defenses, a skill he passed on to younger teammates, and nobody hit those seams with more precision or consistency.

At first glance, the 5-foot-11 Joiner appeared too small and too docile to make an NFL impact. But the calm, thoughtful, private demeanor players saw in the locker room turned into fiery, hustling competitiveness on the field. Joiner's career can be measured in two distinct periods: his first seven seasons playing for ball-control offenses in Houston and Cincinnati; his final 11 as part of the "Air Coryell" aerial circus in San Diego.

Before his 1976 trade to the Chargers, Joiner caught 164 passes. With quarterback Dan Fouts throwing to Joiner, John Jefferson, Wes Chandler and Kellen Winslow in San Diego, he caught 586 passes for 9,203 yards and 47 touchdowns while posting four 1,000-yard seasons. The wide-open style was a perfect fit for the always-reliable Joiner, who helped the Chargers win three straight AFC West titles from 1979-81.

When the three-time Pro Bowler retired in 1986 at age 40, he had played more games (239) over more seasons (18) than any receiver in history. He also was the most prolific pass-catcher of all time (750), a record that was shattered by Steve Largent a year later.

> "They call him The Professional, and he's just flat out one of the great wide receivers in the National Football League. Without question, he is the finest technician—running routes and reading coverages."
>
> —*Ernie Zampese, Chargers receivers coach*, 1981

DEACON JONES

Born: 12-9-38, Eatonville, Fla. **Ht/Wt:** 6-5/272 **College:** South Carolina State, Mississippi Valley State **Drafted:** 1961, 14th round, Rams
Primary position: DE **Teams:** Rams 1961-71; Chargers 1972-73; Redskins 1974 **Honors:** 75th Anniversary All-Time Team; 1960s All-Decade Team; All-Time NFL Team

Trying to ignore Deacon Jones was like trying to ignore a parade through your living room. He was colorful, cocky, confident — and athletically gifted, the leader of the Los Angeles Rams' Fearsome Foursome defensive line in the 1960s. Jones was a fast, rugged and mobile sackmaster, a Gino Marchetti-like pass rusher who helped set the standard for modern defensive end play.

Jones was a 6-foot-5, 272-pound unknown when he was selected out of Mississippi Valley State in the 14th round of the 1961 draft. But that changed quickly. Jones played with the same flamboyant personality that he exhibited with reporters and soon became the leader of a devastating line that also included tackles Merlin Olsen and Roosevelt Grier and end Lamar Lundy.

Deacon (a self-ascribed moniker that replaced the "too common" David) became a terror for blockers who were not quick enough to keep him from exploding into the backfield and quarterbacks who had to scramble for their lives. It was Jones who coined the term sack, "you know, like you sack a city — you devastate it," and he popularized the head slap, a maneuver that has since been outlawed by NFL officials.

In an effort to control Jones, teams used double and triple teams, but that strategy simply freed up Olsen, his partner on the best tackle/end combination in NFL history. Jones and Olsen also perfected stunts that confused defenders and usually opened a path for one of them into the opposing backfield. Jones' greatest asset was the sprinter-like speed that allowed him to roam from sideline to sideline, delivering what he called "civilized violence."

Jones, a departure from the stay-at-home defensive linemen of his era, missed only three games over a 14-year career that included brief stops in San Diego and Washington. He earned five consensus All-Pro citations and played in eight Pro Bowls, but never enjoyed the opportunity to play in an NFL championship game or Super Bowl.

> "It used to be that the big defensive linemen just sat in one place and waited for the play to come to them. But mobility is what makes a football player exciting, so I made myself exciting as hell."
>
> —*Deacon Jones*

STAN JONES

Born: 11-24-31, Altoona, Pa. **Ht/Wt:** 6-1/250 **College:** Maryland **Drafted:** 1953, 5th round, Bears **Primary positions:** OG, OT, DT
Teams: Bears 1954-65; Redskins 1966 **Championship team:** NFL 1963

By 1950s standards, Stan Jones was a hulk. He packed 250 pounds of pure, well-defined muscle on a 6-foot-1 frame and dared opponents to take their best shot. Those who tried ran into an immovable object—a Pro Bowl guard for seven of his eight seasons on Chicago's offensive line, a defensive bruiser for four more and the man who proved to skeptical coaches and teammates that weight training and football, unlike oil and water, do mix.

Bears players thought Jones was crazy when they first watched his weight training regimen, a program he had adopted during his high school years in Lemoyne, Pa. But soon they were marveling at his muscular physique and the incredible strength that

> ## "Stan was one strong son of a gun. He could lift the side of a house."
>
> *Fred Williams, former Bears defensive tackle,*
> *1991, Chicago Tribune*

allowed him to block the bigger defensive players of his era. Not only was he the NFL's strongest player, he also was one of its most technically sound and durable linemen—two missed games in his first 11 Chicago seasons.

An All-American for Maryland's 1953 national champions, Jones played his rookie 1954 season at offensive tackle and switched in 1955 to guard, a position he dominated like few others in NFL history. But when the Bears were caught short on defense in 1962, he played both sides of the ball and switched permanently in 1963 to defensive tackle. Manning a position he had not played since college, Jones roughed up blockers, stuffed runners with cat-like quickness and helped the Bears win their first NFL title since 1946.

Reliable, durable and disciplined, Jones was coach George Halas' offensive captain for several years and a later disciple of assistant George Allen's aggressive defensive techniques. He also was popular among teammates, an awesome physical specimen with an upbeat personality and entertaining storytelling abilities.

Jones, who played for the Bears through 1965, asked Halas to trade him to Washington so he could be closer to his Rockville, Md., home. Halas complied and Jones played for the Redskins in 1966 before retiring to take an assistant coaching job with the Denver Broncos.

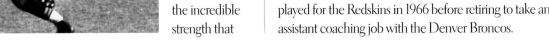

Stan Jones (78) played on a Bears line with Bob Kilcullen (opposite page, left) and John Johnson (right).

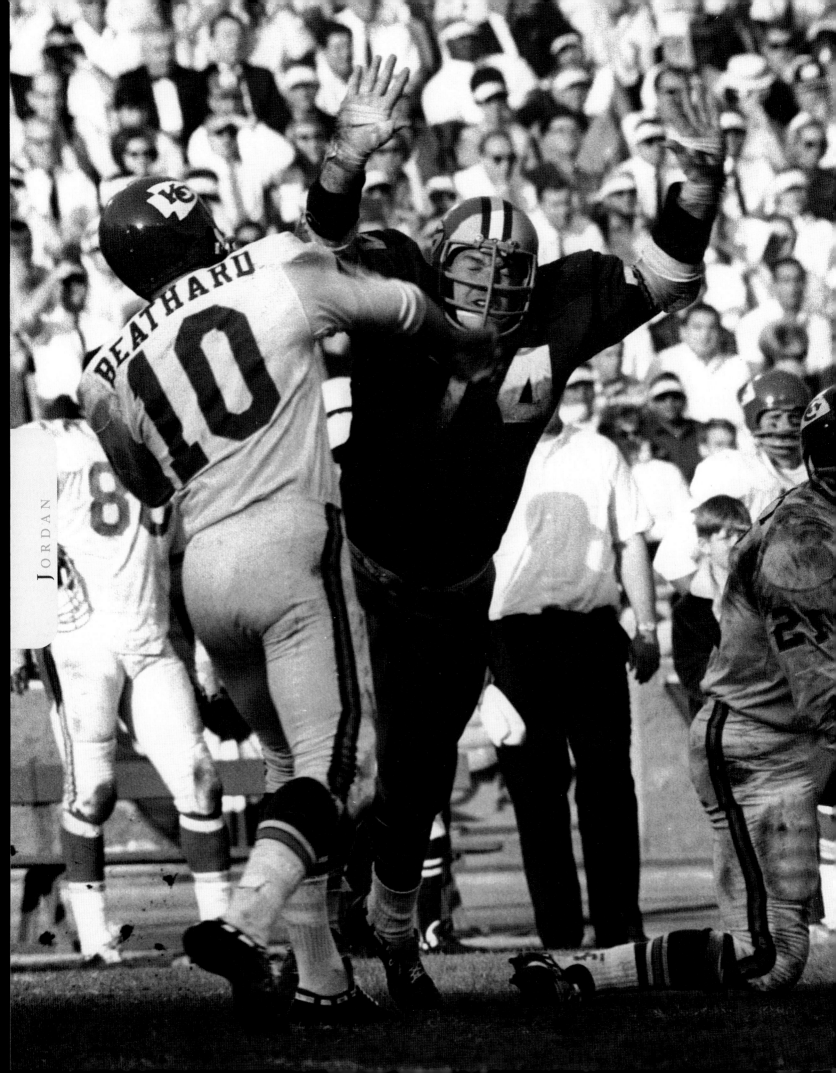
Jordan

HENRY JORDAN

Born: 1-26-35, Emporia, Va. **Died:** 2-21-77 **Ht/Wt:** 6-2/240 **College:** Virginia **Drafted:** 1957, 5th round, Browns **Primary position:** DT **Teams:** Browns 1957-58; Packers 1959-69 **Championship teams:** NFL 1961, '62, '65, '66, '67 **Super Bowl champions:** 1966, '67 seasons

He was an annoying 6-foot-2, 240-pound fly buzzing the bigger and slower offensive guards of his era. No matter how hard or fast they swatted, Henry Jordan would avoid the full force of their blows and resume his hit-and-run pursuit of ballcarriers and quarterbacks. The balding, durable Virginian provided the prototype for a new wave of undersized defensive tackles and an anchor for five Green Bay championship teams from 1959-69.

Jordan was a proponent of the over-under-around pass rush, preferring to let his much larger contemporaries take the through route. If the blocker committed quickly, Jordan was strong enough to jerk him out of the way; if he hesitated, he was quick and agile enough to explode past him. Jordan was smart and unpredictable, a nightmare for guards accustomed to blocking traditional 290-pound NFL tackles.

A defensive front featuring Bill Quinlan and Willie Davis at the ends with Jordan and 255-pound Dave Hanner at the tackles gave coach Vince Lombardi a

> **"After I play Green Bay, my ankles hurt all week. I have to stay up on the balls of my feet against Henry because I never know what he's going to do next. Other tackles I don't have to stay up like that. They don't have Henry's moves."**
>
> —Jim Parker, 1964, *Sport magazine*

ferocious four-man pass rush. But Jordan, unlike his contemporary tackles, had a second gear that allowed him to pursue plays from sideline to sideline. He hit hard, played fast and provided powerful chemistry for one of the best defenses in NFL history.

No one escaped the locker room wit of the former University of Virginia wrestling and football star, who once quipped, "Coach Lombardi is fair. He treats us all the same—like dogs." Jordan took lots of grief about his Y.A. Tittle hair style and was known to trash talk with the enemy. A popular Green Bay figure, Jordan was a renowned after-dinner speaker and goodwill ambassador.

For an undersized tackle, the four-time Pro Bowler was amazingly durable. He missed only two games in his first 12 seasons, including an inauspicious two-year start with Cleveland, and helped the Packers win championships in 1961, '62 and '65 and the first two Super Bowls after the 1966 and '67 campaigns. Green Bay was 103-42-5 during Jordan's 11-year stay.

JORDAN

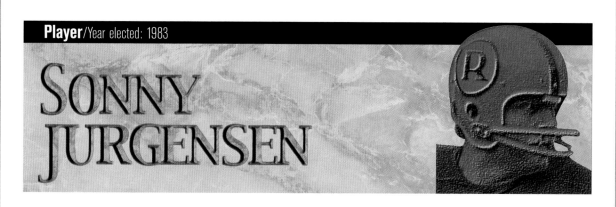

SONNY JURGENSEN

Born: 8-23-34, Wilmington, N.C. **Ht/Wt:** 6-0/200 **College:** Duke **Drafted** 1957, 4th round, Eagles **Primary position:** QB
Career statistics: Passing, 2,433-of-4,262, 32,224 yds., 255 TDs; Rushing, 181 att., 493 yds., 15 TDs **Teams:** Eagles 1957-63;
Redskins 1964-74 **Championship team:** NFL 1960 **Honors:** 1960s All-Decade Team

The dropback form, classic throwing style and sharp, tight spirals were Sonny Jurgensen trademarks. No quarterback looked better while threading the needle with a 30-yard pass and few could match the excitement he generated with a cock of his golden right arm. Jurgensen was a human highlight film for 18 NFL seasons and a passing beacon that brightened the darkness of losing teams in Philadelphia and Washington.

Few would argue that Jurgensen was the NFL's best pure passer over a career that stretched from 1957-74 — seven seasons with the Eagles, 11 as a fan favorite with the Redskins. A classic dropback thrower, the 6-foot, 200-pounder seldom left the pocket and delivered the ball at the last possible instant. Fans with little hope of victory flocked to see Mr. Excitement fire long, short and in-between rockets while dissecting defenses and expertly working the clock.

"All I ask of my blockers is four seconds," said Jurgensen, who complemented his poise under pressure with a free-wheeling lifestyle and fun-loving personality. But the precise timing he displayed on the field was offset by the bad timing that dogged him during his career. Jurgensen played for only eight win-

> "Jurgensen is a great quarterback. He may be the best the league has ever seen. He is the best I've seen. He hangs in there under adverse conditions. He no longer is a young man, but he is all man."
>
> —*Vince Lombardi, 1969*

ning teams — three as a starter. He was Norm Van Brocklin's backup in 1960 when the Eagles won a championship; he was aging and injured in 1972 when George Allen's Redskins advanced to the Super Bowl behind Billy Kilmer.

The proof of Jurgensen's genius is in the numbers. Three NFL passing titles were framed by five 3,000-yard seasons, 25 games of 300-plus yards and five of 400-plus. His 32,224 passing yards and 255 touchdowns rank among the all-time leaders and he once threw TD passes in 23 straight games — five in a single contest twice. Too often, Jurgensen was the only real weapon for weak teams.

When the redhead from North Carolina retired in 1974, he owned an impressive 82.6 passer rating and .571 completion percentage. Jurgensen's well-documented nocturnal escapades only enhanced his Washington status as a real "man of the people."

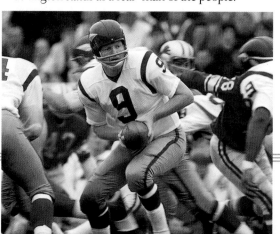

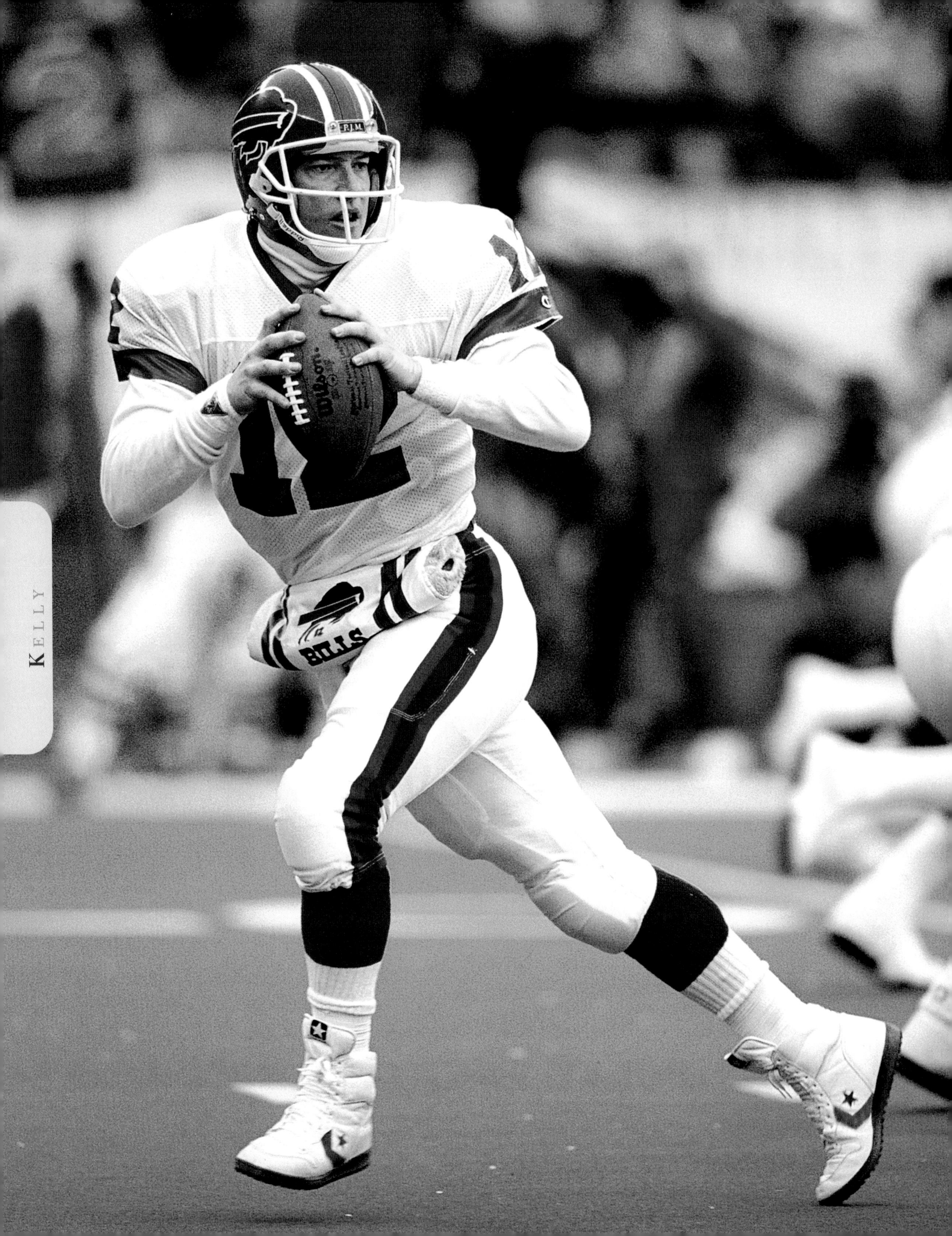
12
Wilson

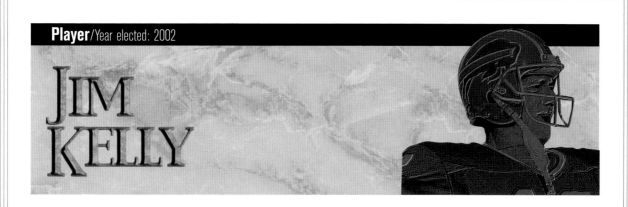

JIM KELLY

Born: 2-14-60, Pittsburgh, Pa. **Ht/Wt:** 6-3/220 **College:** Miami (Fla.) **Drafted:** 1983, 1st round, Bills **Primary position:** QB
Career statistics: Passing, 2,874-of-4,779, 35,467 yds., 237 TDs; Rushing, 304 att., 1,049 yds., 7 TDs **Teams:** USFL Houston
1984-85; NFL Bills 1986-96

Like the city he represented for 11 NFL seasons, Jim Kelly was rugged and tough. He endured howling winds, numbing cold and driving snow; he played with pain and overcame expectations; he challenged and motivated teammates to match his indomitable spirit. Love him or hate him, they followed the game's most intensely competitive quarterback through an unprecedented six-year run that produced a 70-26 record and four straight Super Bowl appearances.

KELLY

Kelly was perfect for Buffalo, a city not far removed in climate and spirit from his blue-collar East Brady, Pa., roots. He was a quarterback with a linebacker's mentality, a cocky, strong-armed, strong-willed competitor with impressive leadership qualities. The 6-foot-3, 220-pounder refused to back down from anybody or anything and the Bills players followed his lead.

Kelly swaggered into Buffalo in 1986, almost three years after he had spurned the Bills for the USFL's Houston Gamblers. The former Miami (Fla.) star and USFL MVP (1984) took quick control of the beleaguered Bills' offense, began posting big passing numbers and won the heart of Buffalo fans with his tenacious mentality and outspoken confidence. By 1989, he was the vocal leader of Marv Levy's high-powered, fast-paced, no-huddle attack.

With Kelly calling the plays and Thurman Thomas operating from Buffalo's innovative one-back sets, the Bills advanced to the AFC championship game in 1988 and made an unprecedented four straight Super Bowl trips from 1990-93, losing each one. The Bills, with their quarterback standing courageously in the pocket and diving into traffic for key first downs, reached the playoffs eight times in 11 seasons and emerged as the AFC's dominant franchise.

Kelly, the only starting quarterback to lose four Super Bowls, overcame that frustration in other ways. He earned four Pro Bowl selections and passed for 35,467 yards and 237 touchdowns while posting an outstanding 84.4 quarterback rating. In 2002, he became the first former USFL player to be inducted into the Pro Football Hall of Fame.

> "He projected such a rugged image and he had the ability to back it up. He was big and tough and not afraid of any challenge. He came to town with huge expectations and he lived up to every one of them."
>
> —*Steve Tasker, former teammate, 2002, Akron Beacon Journal*

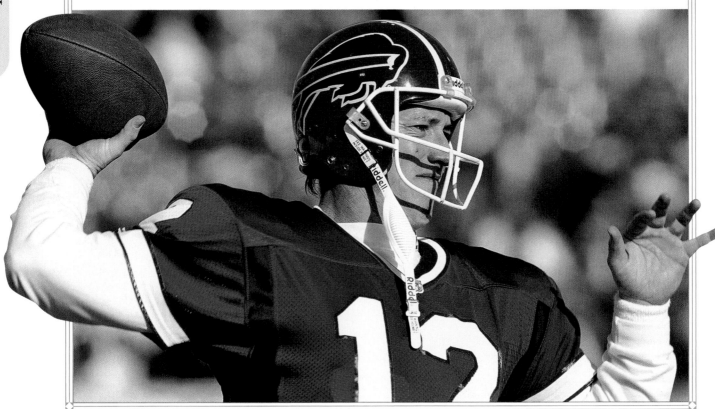

KELLY

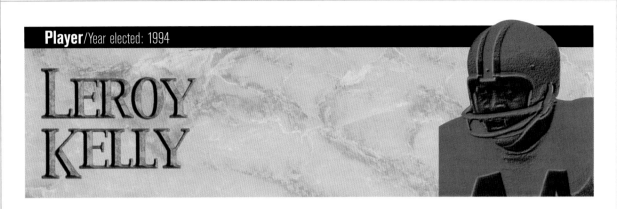

LEROY KELLY

Born: 5-20-42, Philadelphia, Pa. **Ht/Wt:** 6-0/205 **College:** Morgan State **Drafted:** 1964, 8th round, Browns **Position:** RB **Career statistics:** Rushing, 1,727 att., 7,274 yds., 74 TDs; Receiving, 190 rec., 2,281 yds., 13 TDs; Punt Returns, 10.5 avg., 3 TDs; KO Returns, 23.5 avg. **Rushing champion:** 1967, '68 **Teams:** Browns 1964-73 **Championship team:** NFL 1964 **Honors:** 1960s All-Decade Team

The shadow he outran belonged to the great Jim Brown and the eyebrows he raised belonged to surprised Cleveland fans. Fate pushed Leroy Kelly into pro football prominence in 1966, but it was his own legs that carried him to Hall of Fame distinction almost three decades later. He was a quiet, painfully modest, low-key encore to one of the most spectacular first acts in NFL history.

Kelly's story is nothing if not inspiring. Relegated to special teams work and status as one of the NFL's elite return men in 1964 and '65, he was asked to replace an eight-time rushing champion and the game's most renowned player when Brown suddenly retired before the 1966 season. Kelly, who said he never doubted he could handle the job, stepped in and posted three straight 1,000-yard seasons while winning two rushing titles of his own and scoring a three-year total of 42 touchdowns.

While the results were familiar, the styles were not. The 6-foot Kelly weighed 205 pounds, Brown 230; Kelly thrived on quick-hitting trap plays between the tackles, Brown liked to sweep outside; Kelly relied on quickness and cat-like moves, Brown was pure power; Kelly was more versatile, a superior receiver and return

> **"When Leroy became a starter in 1966, it made me that much more effective as a receiver. He was an excellent pass catcher, so the defense couldn't concentrate on me. He froze a lot of linebackers."**
>
> — *Paul Warfield, 1994, Baltimore Sun*

man and even the backup punter.

That versatility played well over a 10-year career that produced 7,274 rushing yards—12,329 on rushing, receiving and returns combined. Considering the eighth-round pick out of tiny Morgan State carried only 43 times over his first two seasons, those numbers are phenomenal. Kelly, one of the best muddy field runners in the game because of his uncanny balance, also scored 90 touchdowns and was selected to six straight Pro Bowls.

The unassuming Philadelphian was a rookie in 1964 when the Browns won an NFL championship and the league's top punt returner in '65 when they advanced to the title game before losing. He twice led Cleveland to the NFL championship game (1968, '69) and averaged 4.2 yards per carry over a career that ended in 1973.

WALT KIESLING

Born: 5-27-03, St. Paul, Min. **Died:** 3-2-62 **Ht/Wt:** 6-2/245 **College:** St. Thomas **Primary positions:** OG, DG **Teams:** Duluth Eskimos 1926-27; Pottsville Maroons 1928; Cardinals 1929-33; Bears 1934; Packers 1935-36; Pirates 1937-38 **Championship team:** NFL 1936 **Honors:** 1920s All-Decade Team

Friends and teammates called him "Big Kies," a reference to a massive 6-foot-2, 245-pound body that sometimes ballooned to 265. But what really set Walt Kiesling apart from other two-way linemen of the 1930s was the surprising speed that allowed him to clear defenders as one of the NFL's first pulling guards. Woe to the tackler who got in the way of the contact-hungry bulldozer on a power sweep!

Kiesling, his prominent belly protruding over his belt, was not the prototypically chiseled muscle man. But few opponents could handle his aggressive charges or counter his strength when stacking up ballcarriers and quarterbacks. Kiesling was most renowned as a blocker over a 13-year playing career for six teams, including an undefeated regular season with the 1934 Chicago Bears and a championship-winning campaign with the 1936 Green Bay Packers.

Kiesling's first taste of success came from 1929-33 with the Chicago Cardinals after three seasons with Duluth and Pottsville. It was Kiesling who led the way during a historic 1929 game against the Bears when Ernie Nevers ran for six touchdowns and scored a still-standing-record 40 points. Big Kies also was an impact blocker for the '34 Bears team that finished the regular season 13-0 before losing to the New York Giants in the NFL championship game.

Kiesling loved pro football and vowed to play "until they wouldn't let me suit up anymore." He was true to his word, remaining active through the 1938 season. When he retired at age 35 after two years at Pittsburgh,

> "He didn't just watch pro football grow from the rocky sandlots, he shoved it along the way. He gave almost half a century to the game."
>
> —*Dick McCann, former director of the Pro Football Hall of Fame*

he became a Pirates assistant, always willing to fill a coaching void at a moment's notice for owner Art Rooney. Three times he stepped in, compiling a 30-55-5 record over nine full and partial seasons.

Kiesling, whose NFL association covered 34 years, is remembered as the coach who delivered Pittsburgh's first winning record (7-4) in 1942 and a co-coach for Steelers teams that combined operations and rosters with the Eagles and Cardinals in consecutive war years.

BRUISER KINARD

Born: 10-23-14, Pelahatchie, Miss. **Died:** 9-7-85 **Ht/Wt:** 6-1/210 **College:** Mississippi **Drafted:** 1938, 2nd round, Dodgers
Primary positions: OT, DT **Teams:** NFL Dodgers 1938-44; AAFC Yankees 1946-47

He was not your average, everyday Bruiser. For 6-foot-1, 210-pound Frank Kinard, actions spoke louder than words or appearance in the trenches of pre-World War II professional football. Undersized and apparently overmatched every time he stepped on the field, the tough guy from Mississippi became the NFL's David-vs.-Goliath poster boy.

What Bruiser lacked in size he made up for with an aggressive, hard-hitting style over a nine-year professional career that started in 1938 with the NFL's Brooklyn Dodgers and ended in 1947 with the All-

> ## "Once Bruiser threw the lead block, there was daylight for the ballcarrier—and Bruiser never missed throwing that block."
>
> *— Joe Stydahar*

America Football Conference's New York Yankees. He never gave an inch, firing his rock-hard body at opponents with savage force, both as a blocker and tackler.

Some players were intimidated by Kinard's violent thrusts; others approached him with understandable caution. Pound for pound, nobody played with more rugged consistency or passion. Kinard also was fast, a 10.4 burner in the 100-yard dash dressed in full gear, and no ballcarrier was safe from his crushing hits or sideline-to-sideline forays.

It was the same speed and raw aggression that had lifted Kinard to two-time All-American status at the University of Mississippi. One of three brothers who played at Ole Miss and in the NFL, Kinard missed one season because of military service and then jumped from the NFL to the new AAFC, becoming the first player to earn All-Pro status in both leagues. Like in Brooklyn, Bruiser was a durable and relentless 60-minute performer for the Yankees.

Kinard never played a postseason game for teams that compiled a 28-43-4 record over his seven Brooklyn seasons. But he was a defensive centerpiece for New York teams that finished 10-3-1 and 11-2-1 while claiming East Division titles before losing to the powerful Cleveland Browns in the AAFC title game. Kinard retired after the 1947 season and returned to Ole Miss, where he served as line coach and later athletic director in a successful post-NFL career.

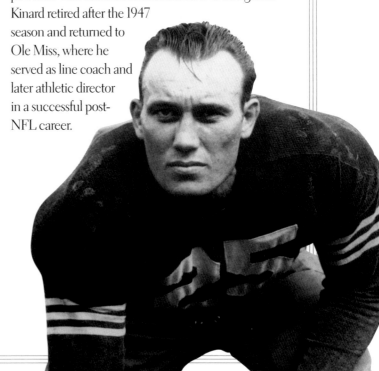

PAUL KRAUSE

Born: 2-19-42, Flint, Mich. **Ht/Wt:** 6-3/200 **College:** Iowa **Drafted:** 1964, 2nd round, NFL Redskins; 12th round, AFL Broncos
Primary position: DB **Career statistics:** Interceptions, 81, 1,185 yds., 3 TDs **Interceptions leader:** 1964 **Teams:** Redskins 1964-67; Vikings 1968-79

He dreamed about becoming the next Willie Mays or Mickey Mantle. But he settled for being Paul Krause, the premier center fielder and ballhawk of professional football. Resilient, resourceful and determined after a baseball-dashing college injury, Krause played 16 years and picked off an NFL-record 81 passes as a trend-setting free safety for the Washington Redskins and Minnesota Vikings. Krause, who appeared destined for baseball stardom before injuring his shoulder during a University of Iowa football game, was at his best as the all-seeing "center fielder" for four Minnesota Super Bowl teams. As the safety valve for Bud Grant's famed "Purple People Eaters" defenses, Krause instinctively read the movement of quarterbacks, the flow of linebackers and direction of blockers to get in position to make a play. Nobody closed faster when the ball was in the air.

"That wasn't gambling," Krause

> "Paul is what free safety means. He sits back there and sees things happen, has great peripheral vision and gets feelings about plays and quarterbacks. He moves to where the action is without endangering his own responsibilities."
>
> —*Bud Grant*, 1975

insisted. "It was being in the right place at the right time." And the 6-foot-3, 200-pound Michigan kid performed that task better than anyone. As a Redskins rookie in 1964, Krause intercepted an NFL-leading 12 passes, returning one for a touchdown. Four seasons with Washington produced 28 interceptions and the first two of eight Pro Bowl selections. Then, apparently because he did not fit the new-wave concept of big-hitting defensive backs, Krause was traded to Minnesota.

Grant marveled at the laid-back, always-in-control demeanor of Krause, who seemed to glide around the secondary and seldom made a mental mistake. He was always around the ball—interceptions in seven straight games, two in one Pro Bowl, one in Super Bowl IV—he was quick to come up on running plays and he was durable, missing only two career games. During his 12 Minnesota seasons, the Vikings reached the playoffs 10 times and played in five NFC title games, winning four.

In his 1979 final season, Krause picked off three passes to break Emlen Tunnell's career interception mark of 79. His 1,185 yards after interceptions rank fourth all time.

K
R
A
U
S
E

CURLY LAMBEAU

Born: 4-9-1898, Green Bay, Wis. **Died:** 6-1-65 **Ht/Wt:** 5-10/187 **Colleges:** Wisconsin, Notre Dame **Primary positions:** TB, E
Teams played: Packers 1921-29 **Teams coached (226-132-22 RS, 3-2 PS):** Packers 1921-49; Cardinals 1950-51; Redskins 1952-53 **Honors:** 1920s All-Decade Team **Executive career:** Founder, general manager of Packers 1921-48

His dark, wavy hair complemented a warm, engaging smile that could light up a room. But Curly Lambeau had no time for social amenities on a football sideline, where he stormed between the 20s, beat himself on the head with animated fury and gestured wildly at no one in particular. Football was no place for pleasantries. ... his Green Bay Packers were doing battle with the enemy.

Nobody took losing more personally or a game more seriously than the man who brought professional football to his hometown, built a company team into a proud dynasty and pioneered the overhead passing game. Intensity, a strong work ethic and stubborn determination colored his three-decade Packers association, both as a player and six-time championship-winning coach.

Lambeau, a former player under Knute Rockne at Notre Dame, organized the Packers for a local packing firm in 1920 and was the team's coach, general manager and halfback in 1921 when it joined the American Professional Football Association, the future NFL. Fascinated by the potential of the forward pass as an offensive weapon, he loaded his

teams with speedy receivers and designed intricate patterns that emphasized quick-strike capabilities.

Lambeau's 1929 Packers won an NFL championship in his final year as a player. His 1930 and '31 teams, with Arnie Herber firing to Johnny (Blood) McNally, also won titles. The 1936, '39 and '44 championship teams, with Herber and Cecil Isbell throwing to Don Hutson, turned Lambeau's farsighted offensive schemes into an artform. A taskmaster who demanded total commitment, the commanding and demonstrative Lambeau remained a Green Bay fixture through 1949 before career-ending two-year stints as coach of the Chicago Cardinals and Washington Redskins.

An avowed enemy of Bears rival George Halas, Lambeau is remembered by Green Bay fans as the team owner who went broke in 1923 and secured a loan from local merchants, thus creating a public nonprofit corporation that still exists. Lambeau, a charter member of the Pro Football Hall of Fame, retired with a 226-132-22 regular-season coaching record.

> "Shake hands with George Halas! That would have been a lie. If I lost, I wanted to punch Halas in the nose. If he lost, Halas wanted to punch me."
>
> —*Curly Lambeau*

LAMBEAU

Player/Year elected: 1990

JACK LAMBERT

Born: 7-8-52, Mantua, Ohio **Ht/Wt:** 6-4/218 **College:** Kent State **Drafted:** 1974, 2nd round, Steelers **Primary position:** LB
Career statistics: Interceptions, 28 **Teams:** Steelers 1974-84 **Super Bowl champions:** 1974, '75, '78, '79 seasons **Honors:** 75th Anniversary All-Time Team; 1970s All-Decade Team; 1980s All-Decade Team

He was the toothless, snarling leader of Pittsburgh's Steel Curtain Defense. When Jack Lambert spoke, everybody listened—or else. Nobody played the role of intimidating middle linebacker better than Jack the Ripper over 11 NFL seasons, six of them as leading man for what many consider the greatest defensive unit ever assembled.

Lambert was taller (6-foot-4) and lighter (218) than most middle linebackers of his era, but his Dick Butkus-like intensity was front and center before every snap. The toothless snarl gave him an almost ghoulish look, as did the eyes that rolled madly inside a dark helmet. An excited voice would bark out defensive signals, arms would pump wildly and legs would quiver uncontrollably in anticipation of the punishment he was about to deliver.

And deliver he did, with vicious consistency. What Lambert lacked in size, he made up for with speed and quickness to the ball. He was a ballcarrier-seeking missile and his height presented problems for quarterbacks trying to throw over the middle. But what set the

> "Jack Lambert demanded total effort from everybody in the organization. He would tell everyone from me on down to the ball boy when he thought something was wrong. He took us to greatness. He was the symbol of our success in the 1970s."
>
> —*Art Rooney*

former Kent State star apart from other middle linebackers was his ability to smother backs and tight ends in passing situations, a talent that produced 28 career interceptions.

Lambert might have played with demonic fervor, but behind that facade was a soft-spoken, sensitive, intelligent leader who served as defensive captain from 1977 until his 1984 retirement. He spent most of his career surrounded by greatness—Joe Greene, L.C. Greenwood, Ernie Holmes up front, Jack Ham and Andy Russell on the outside, Mel Blount in the backfield—and he came to symbolize the work ethic required of a team playing in blue-collar Pittsburgh.

It was no coincidence the Steelers won Super Bowls in four of Lambert's first six seasons. His 13 tackles and fourth-quarter interception keyed the final championship in a Super Bowl XIV win over the Los Angeles Rams. Lambert, who missed only six games because of injury, finished his career with nine straight Pro Bowl appearances.

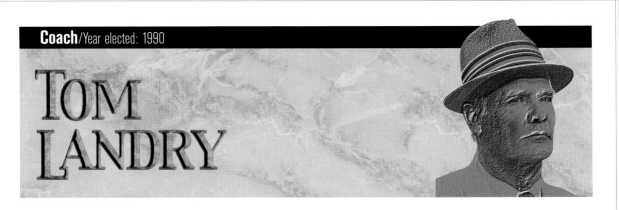

Coach/Year elected: 1990

TOM LANDRY

Born: 9-11-24, Mission, Tex. **Died:** 2-12-2000 **Ht/Wt:** 6-1/195 **College:** Texas **Drafted:** 1947, 18th round, Giants **Primary positions:** DB, P **Career statistics:** Interceptions, 31, 3 TDs; Punting, 338 att., 40.4 avg. **Teams played:** AAFC Yankees 1949; NFL Giants 1950-55 **Teams coached (250-162-6 RS, 20-16 PS):** Cowboys 1960-88 **Super Bowl champions:** 1971, '77 seasons

To millions of fans, he was the stoic, unemotional sideline figure in the felt hat and business suit. But hidden beneath the stone-faced facade of Tom Landry was one of the most active, analytical and innovative coaching minds in NFL history. Master tactician, stern leader and patient builder, nobody better personifies the rise of the Dallas Cowboys from 1960 expansion infant to two-time champion and "America's Team."

From 1960-88, Landry was the only coach Cowboys fans ever knew. The perception of an aloof, colorless, dispassionate Landry was balanced by the imaginative and exciting offenses and defenses he employed while building one of the most successful and popular franchises in history. After struggling through their first six seasons, the Cowboys posted winning records in their next 20 while winning 13

> "You can look at Tom and see agony and joy in his face. If we thought he was throwing tantrums and screaming, we might lose control. He projects confidence, poise and composure to us."
>
> — *Lee Roy Jordan, former Cowboys linebacker*

division titles, five NFC championships and Super Bowls after the 1971 and '77 campaigns.

He did it with a consistent flow of talent supplied by general manager Tex Schramm and a tactical genius that had surfaced years earlier as a New York Giants player and assistant coach. Landry is credited with inventing the umbrella, 4-3 and flex defenses, the multiple and spread offenses and the new-age shotgun operated by quarterback Roger Staubach. He invented

defenses, watched other coaches copy them and then invented offenses to beat them.

Teams playing the Cowboys had to contend with constant offensive motion and movement, complex zone and man-to-man defensive coverages and intricate cat-and-mouse maneuvers from the well-prepared Landry. He always seemed to be one step ahead and the Cowboys became known and admired for their big-play abilities and stirring comebacks.

The tall Texan, a former star for his homestate Longhorns, was a solid defensive back and punter for the AAFC's New York Yankees in 1949 and the Giants from 1950-55. More than three decades later, with the Cowboys under new ownership and coming off a 3-13 season, Landry was fired, sending shockwaves through Dallas. He retired with a 270-178-6 overall record — a win total that ranks behind only Don Shula and George Halas.

LANDRY

NIGHT TRAIN LANE

Born: 4-16-28, Austin, Tex. **Died:** 1-29-2002 **Ht/Wt:** 6-1/194 **College:** Scottsbluff JC **Drafted:** Undrafted **Primary position:** DB
Career statistics: Interceptions, 68, 5 TDs **Interceptions leader:** 1952, '54 **Teams:** Rams 1952-53; Cardinals 1954-59; Lions 1960-65 **Honors:** 75th Anniversary All-Time Team; 50th Anniversary Team; 1950s All-Decade Team; All-Time NFL Team

LANE

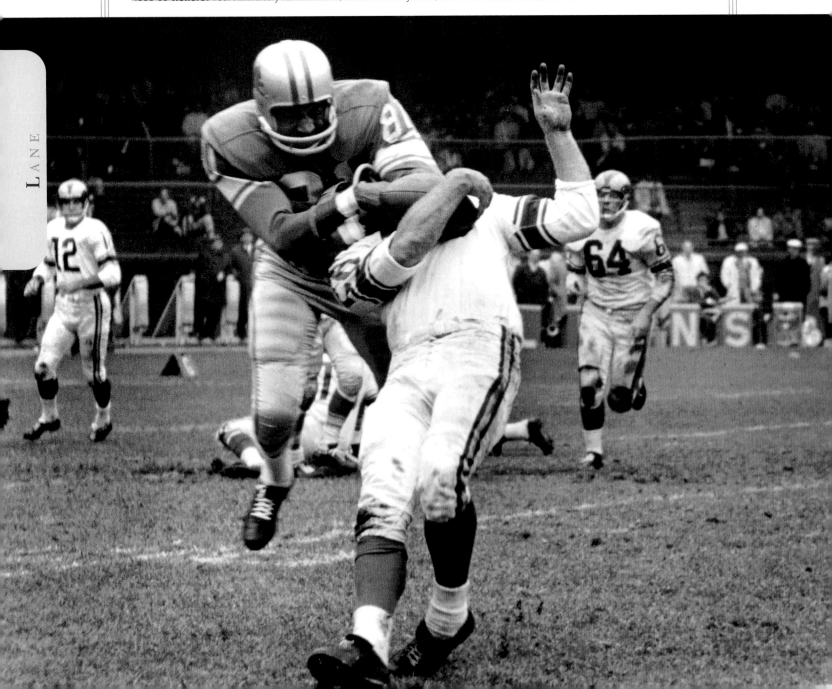

Former Green Bay coach Vince Lombardi called him the greatest cornerback he had ever seen. NFL wide receivers who carried battle scars from his vicious hits called him mean and uncompromising. Love him or hate him, Dick "Night Train" Lane was a defensive force, a fearless ballhawk who disrupted

> ## "Train will always be the Godfather of cornerbacks. He was as large as some linemen of his era. He also was agile and very fast. His tackling was awesome. He did the clothesline and other tackles that just devastated the ballcarrier."
>
> *—Lem Barney, 1999*

passing attacks for 14 outstanding seasons with the Los Angeles Rams, Chicago Cardinals and Detroit Lions.

Incredibly, the 6-foot-1, 194-pound Texan had never played above the junior college level when he showed up at the Rams offices in 1952 and asked for a tryout. Soon he was getting on-the-job training against some of the best NFL receivers in one-on-one situations. His instincts were sharp, his athleticism good enough to make up for the inevitable mistakes and his passion for contact was relentless.

By the end of Lane's rookie season, he had recorded 14 interceptions — a still-standing NFL record — and a pair of return touchdowns. Over the next 13 years, he literally wrote the book on how to play cornerback, experimenting and learning as he went along. Lane developed the reputation as a mean-spirited headhunter who would bring down ballcarriers with clothesline and facemask tackles that prompted legislation to outlaw such tactics. Many receivers, understandably wary, were defeated before the ball was ever snapped.

The flamboyant Night Train, who got his nickname from a popular musical recording of his era, was an impact player who made good things happen with his big-play, gambling style and fierce determination

to win. He was one of the NFL's original ball-strippers and his reputation for dishing out pain was almost legendary.

Happy and fun-loving off the field, he played with an edge that few could match. When he finished his career in 1965 after six years with the Lions, he had 68 interceptions, a figure that still ranks third all time. A member of mostly weak teams, the six-time Pro Bowler played in only one postseason game.

JIM LANGER

Born: 5-16-48, Little Falls, Min. **Ht/Wt:** 6-2/250 **College:** South Dakota State **Drafted:** Undrafted **Primary position:** C
Teams: Dolphins 1970-79; Vikings 1980-81 **Super Bowl champions:** 1972, '73 seasons **Honors:** 1970s All-Decade Team

He thrived as the middle man of Miami's offense for an entire decade, the glue that held together one of the game's consistently outstanding rushing machines. Jim Langer was the perfect center for the near-perfect running attack that fueled the NFL's first perfect team. Nobody better personified the workmanlike consistency of a Dolphins powerhouse that won consecutive Super Bowls, lost a third and posted an historic 17-0 record in 1972.

Langer's success can be attributed to determination and a proud Minnesota work ethic that manifested itself day after day, play after play, over a career that started in 1970 with Miami and ended in 1981 after a two-year stint with the Minnesota Vikings. The 6-foot-2, 250-

> "I believe Jim is the best center we'll face this year. In games I've seen him play, I don't recall him ever making a mistake. Even though he's snapping the ball, he pretty much gets off with the rest of the line. He simply is a fine football player."
>
> *— Bud Grant, Minnesota coach, prior to Super Bowl VIII*

pounder was an undrafted free agent out of South Dakota State who spent two years performing special-teams duty before beating out veteran center Bob DeMarco. From 1972-79, he never missed a game.

Dolphins coach Don Shula watched in amazement as Langer transformed into the league's best center. He was compact and fundamentally sound, quick enough to drive low into bigger defensive linemen and strong enough to move them. Langer studied film relentlessly, communicated with running backs Larry Csonka, Jim Kiick and Mercury Morris and spent extra hours on the practice field with quarterback Bob Griese. He opened holes, protected the passer — and seldom made a mistake.

Miami's high-powered running attack posted league-leading numbers behind Langer, guards Bob Kuechenberg and Larry Little and tackles Wayne Moore and Norm Evans. Langer started for eight seasons and the Dolphins reached the playoffs five times, winning Super Bowls VII and VIII. He was selected for six straight Pro Bowls from 1973-78, at which point a knee injury prompted his request for a trade to his native Minnesota.

Langer, who didn't miss a down in the Dolphins' 1972 season, is a rags-to-riches story—a rise from undrafted obscurity to status as one of the best centers to play the game. According to Shula, he is the best. Ever.

WILLIE LANIER

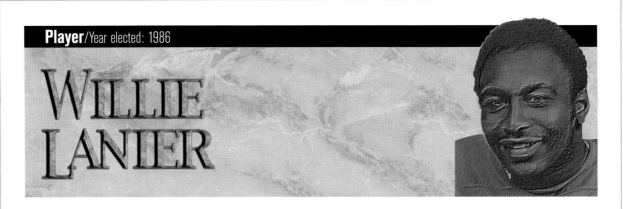

Born: 8-21-45, Clover, Va. **Ht/Wt:** 6-1/245 **College:** Morgan State **Drafted:** 1967, 2nd round, Chiefs **Primary position:** LB
Career statistics: Interceptions, 27, 2 TDs **Teams:** Chiefs 1967-77 **Super Bowl champion:** 1969 season **Honors:** 75th Anniversary All-Time Team

Willie Lanier leans his 6-foot-1, 245-pound body forward, ready to pounce with cat-like quickness. His steely glare locks into the concerned eyes of a quarterback who seems mesmerized by the 34-inch waist, 50-inch chest and 20-inch neck that soon will come crashing toward him like a heat-seeking missile. The fear is overpowering, but nothing compared to the havoc that will unfold once the ball is snapped.

Such was the aura of Lanier, the powerful Virginia-born "Honeybear" who patrolled the middle of Kansas City's defense from 1967-77. He was the first black to find success at the demanding middle linebacker position and he took that success to the highest level of professional football. He was the premier defensive quarterback of the American Football League and he gained Dick Butkus and Ray Nitschke-like star status after the AFL-NFL merger.

The smiling, easy-to-like Lanier literally transformed into a fierce, never-give-an-inch, ballhawking demon when he pulled on his red-and-white No. 63 Chiefs

"It's tough running against a grizzly bear and it's worse if he's a smart one. Lanier against power football is what defense is all about." —*Larry Csonka, 1972*

jersey. He was immovable on runs up the middle and obsessive when tracking down ballcarriers, who usually remembered the intense blows he delivered. And the former small-college All-American from Morgan State was fast enough to make 27 career interceptions while covering tight ends and running backs in passing situations.

Few players dominated a position so thoroughly and coach Hank Stram centered the quick-thinking Lanier in an elite linebacking corps that included Bobby Bell and Jim Lynch. Not surprisingly, the talent-filled Chiefs battled the Oakland Raiders for AFL dominance in the late 1960s and advanced to Super Bowls I and IV, pulling off a shocking upset of a powerful Minnesota team in the 1970 classic. Lanier contributed an interception to that memorable 23-7 victory.

Big Willie's road to the Hall of Fame was paved with All-Pro, All-AFL and All-NFL citations and he was named to eight Pro Bowl games, winning defensive MVP honors in 1972.

STEVE LARGENT

Born: 9-28-54, Tulsa, Okla. **Ht/Wt:** 5-11/187 **College:** Tulsa **Drafted:** 1976, 4th round, Oilers **Primary position:** WR **Career statistics:** Receiving, 819 rec., 13,089 yds., 16.0 avg., 100 TDs **Teams:** Seahawks 1976-89 **Honors:** 1980s All-Decade Team

Call him the master of illusion. When Steve Largent ran pass patterns, he always ended up here and the defender over there. That was the special magic of the record-setting wide receiver, who emptied his bag of tricks over a 14-year career with the Seattle Seahawks. When Largent zigged, everyone else in the stadium usually zagged.

Longtime Raiders cornerback Lester Hayes called him "the master of tomfoolery," a reference to Largent's meticulous, cerebral approach to his craft.

The former Tulsa star did not have great straightaway speed and he was smaller (5-foot-11, 187 pounds) than most receivers, but he made up for those shortcomings with exceptional lateral quickness, great balance, body control and soft hands that seemed to pull balls to him like a magnet.

Covering Largent was a game of cat and mouse. He could run the same pattern on three straight plays and beat the defensive back in three different ways. He would use a move on one play to set up a later one, throw two or three incomprehensible moves into one feint and run unusual routes that played with the defender's mind. Largent was very prepared for every game, the picture of total concentration.

It was all part of a scientific plan, conceived and executed by pro football's ultimate possession receiver. Largent, a 1976 fourth-round Houston draft pick who was cut during training camp by Oilers coach Bum Phillips, joined the expansion Seahawks as an aw-shucks, easy-to-like Oklahoma kid and retired in 1989 as the greatest pass-catcher in NFL history.

When he retired, he owned records for most catches (819), yards (13,089) and touchdowns (100), all marks that have since been broken, and his eight 1,000-yard seasons still rank third behind Jerry Rice and Tim Brown. Largent, who once caught passes in 177 consecutive games, led his team in catches and yards in each of the franchise's first 12 seasons. Never a member of a championship team, Largent did earn seven Pro Bowl selections.

"He was a little guy with a big heart. Steve knew he was going to take a good licking but somehow he must have felt he was going to get up because he never appeared to have the least bit of fear."

—*Mike Haynes, 1995, Seattle Post-Intelligencer*

LARY

YALE LARY

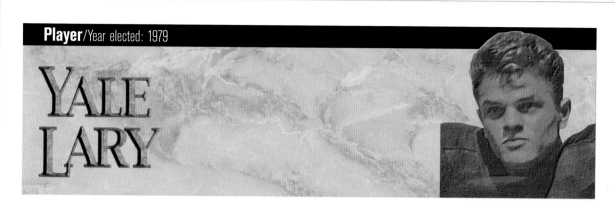

Born: 11-24-30 **Ht/Wt:** 5-11/185 **College:** Texas A&M **Drafted:** 1952, 3rd round, Lions **Primary position:** DB, P
Career statistics: Interceptions, 50, 2 TDs; Punting, 503 att., 44.3 avg. **Teams:** Lions 1952-53, 1956-64
Championship teams: NFL 1952, '53, '57 **Honors:** 1950s All-Decade Team

Some coaches feared his momentum-shifting interceptions; others watched him dictate field position with booming, gravity-defying punts. When Yale Lary really wanted to impact a game, he might throw in a back-breaking return or scamper for a first down on a fake kick. Quietly, efficiently and without fanfare or warning, the multi-talented right safety destroyed opponents for 11 NFL seasons while helping the Detroit Lions win three championships.

It was hard to choose between Lary's exceptional skills as the last vestige of defense for the Lions' secondary or his powerful leg, which produced three punting titles and a spectacular 44.3-yard career average. Few players impacted his team in more ways from 1952-64 and nobody could more consistently dictate the flow of games.

Lary was like a cat, baiting quarterbacks into thinking a receiver was open and then darting over for the interception. He was smart and quick, a defensive strategist who could close rapidly on a receiver or deliver missile-like hits with his 5-foot-11, 185-pound body. Quarterbacks understandably avoided the clever Lary, who still made 50 career interceptions.

> "If I had to pick one defensive back who had everything, it would have to be Yale. He was the smartest and it took him a long way. But the big thing was his quickness, his ability to make a quarterback think he had an open receiver, then recover and intercept. ..."
>
> — *Bobby Layne*

As a punter, the former Texas A&M baseball and football star posted spectacular league-leading averages of 47.1 yards in 1959, 48.4 in 1961 and 48.9 in 1963. His accuracy and hang time discouraged returns, giving the Lions' defense room to maneuver. Lary also was a breakaway punt-return threat, a talent that produced three touchdowns during his first six professional seasons.

Lary, an important member of a powerful defense nicknamed "Chris' Crew" after Hall of Fame safety Jack Christiansen, was a big-play man for coach Buddy Parker's 1952 and '53 Detroit championship teams before spending two years in military service. He returned to help George Wilson's 1957 team win another NFL title.

Lary, a nine-time Pro Bowl selection, was versatile off the field as well as on. He won election to the Texas state legislature in 1958 and served two terms — while he continued playing for the Lions.

DANTE LAVELLI

Born: 2-23-23, Hudson, Ohio **Ht/Wt:** 6-0/199 **College:** Ohio State **Drafted:** 1947, 10th round, Rams **Primary positions:** OE, DE
Career statistics: AAFC Receiving, 142 rec., 2,580 yds., 29 TDs; NFL Receiving, 244 rec., 3,908 yds., 33 TDs **Teams:** AAFC Browns 1946-49; NFL Browns 1950-56 **Championship teams:** AAFC 1946, '47, '48, '49; NFL 1950, '54, '55 **Honors:** 1940s All-Decade Team

His name rolled off the tongue with poetic grace and his Italian flair lit up the football field. Nothing about Dante Lavelli was subtle, from his cocky, center-stage personality to the way he soared above defenders to snag Otto Graham passes. As one-half of the first great receiving tandem in pro football history, Lavelli helped lift the Cleveland Browns from All-America Football Conference infancy to NFL dominance.

The wavy-haired, basso-voiced Lavelli combined

with left end Mac Speedie as the go-get-it receivers for Paul Brown's high-powered Cleveland aerial attacks from 1946-52 — four years in the AAFC, three more in the NFL. With Graham firing away from the T-formation, Speedie lived up to his deep-threat name while Lavelli ran precise patterns and operated in traffic. Always willing to trade blows with defenders,

> "I think Lavelli has the strongest hands I've ever seen. When he goes up for a pass and a defender goes up with him, you can be sure Dante will have the ball when they come down. Nobody can ever take it away from him once he gets his hands on it."
>
> —*Paul Brown, 1949, Sport magazine*

Lavelli had an uncanny knack for going up in a crowd and coming down with the ball.

"He really did have glue fingers," Graham said, referring to the moniker often associated with Lavelli. The 6-foot, 199-pound Ohioan also had a big ego and an unwavering belief that he could catch any pass within his extraordinary leaping range and outfight anybody for the ball. It was not uncommon to hear Lavelli's booming voice calling to Graham as he ran the middle of the field.

The Lavelli-Speedie combination, often called "Cleveland's track stars" by conservative opposing coaches, dominated the AAFC, catching 116 passes for 1,945 yards in 1947. When the Browns moved into the NFL in 1950, they combined for 79 catches and 1,113 yards — big totals for that era. Lavelli, a three-time NFL Pro Bowler before his career ended in 1956, caught a postseason-record 11 passes, including touchdown strikes of 35 and 39 yards, in the Browns' 30-28 championship game victory over Los Angeles in 1950.

Lavelli, who played only three college games for Ohio State because of injury and military service, posted combined AAFC-NFL totals of 386 catches for 6,488 yards and 62 touchdowns.

BOBBY LAYNE

Born: 12-19-26, Santa Ana, Tex. **Died:** 12-1-86 **Ht/Wt:** 6-1/200 **College:** Texas **Drafted:** 1948, 1st round, Bears **Primary position:** QB **Career statistics:** Passing, 1,814-of-3,700, 26,768 yds., 196 TDs; Rushing, 611 att., 2,451 yds., 25 TDs; Scoring, 34 FG, 120 PAT, 372 pts. **Scoring champion:** 1956 **Teams:** Bears 1948; Bulldogs 1949; Lions 1950-58; Steelers 1958-62 **Championship teams:** NFL 1952, '53, '57 **Honors:** 1950s All-Decade Team

He was equal parts George C. Patton and party animal. But whether Bobby Layne was guiding the Detroit Lions to another dramatic victory or his teammates to the nearest bar, there never was any doubt who was in charge. Layne was the ultimate leader, a quarterback who drove the Lions to consecutive NFL championships (1952 and '53) and himself to the edge of physical endurance.

> ## "He was the greatest two-minute quarterback ever. Bobby Layne simply never lost a game. Sometimes, time just ran out on him."
>
> — *Doak Walker*

The husky, round-faced Layne swaggered through a 15-year career that marked him as one of the game's most successful field generals and a relentless carouser. The former University of Texas record-setter ran a huddle like boot camp, castigating teammates for mistakes and prodding them for extra effort. He simply wouldn't tolerate losing and backed up his take-charge demeanor with clever play-calling, a reliable arm that amassed 26,768 passing yards and quick feet that ran for 2,451 yards and 25 touchdowns.

Layne, who played without a facemask, was the first acknowledged master of the two-minute drill, a talent that fit his adventurous, life-on-the-edge personality. He basked in the dramatics of a last-minute victory, then made a beeline for the nearest party, usually with teammates in tow. The fun-loving Layne, complete with colorful quotes delivered in a deep Texas twang, became a bigger-than-life personality during an era when pro football was groping for an identity.

While his playboy image sometimes upstaged his athletic talent, it's hard to deny Layne's football contributions. The 1952 championship broke a 16-year Lions postseason drought. He also led the team through most of a 1957 championship season before sitting out the title game with an ankle injury.

In addition to throwing 196 TD passes, Layne kicked 34 field goals and 120 extra points over a career that included one-year stays with the Chicago Bears (1948) and New York Bulldogs (1949) and a five-plus-year finale (1958-62) in Pittsburgh. One of Layne's more interesting accomplishments came in 1956 when, as a quarterback, he led the NFL in scoring with 99 points.

TUFFY LEEMANS

Born: 11-12-12, Superior, Wis. **Died:** 1-19-79 **Ht/Wt:** 6-0/190 **College:** Oregon, George Washington **Drafted:** 1936, 2nd round, Giants **Primary positions:** HB, DB **Career statistics:** Rushing, 919 att., 3,132 yds., 17 TDs; Passing, 2,318 yds., 25 TDs; Receiving, 28 rec., 3 TDs **Rushing champion:** 1936 **Teams:** Giants 1936-43 **Championship team:** NFL 1938 **Honors:** 1930s All-Decade Team

Inside or out. Over, under, around and through. The path to NFL success never mattered much to Tuffy Leemans, who used all available routes on his journey from the Wisconsin coal mines to the bright lights of New York. He arrived as an unheralded triple threat runner, passer and receiver in 1936 and departed eight years later as a Giants legend—the driving force behind three division title winners and the 1938 NFL champions.

Nothing came easy for Alphonse Emil Leemans, a stocky 6-foot, 190-pound halfback who earned his nickname for the "tough" way he played. Not blessed with breakaway speed, Tuffy attacked defenses with a slashing, hard-nosed running style that was heavy on instinct and short on finesse. He had an uncanny ability to wiggle his hips, make a sudden twist or cut back at the perfect moment to avoid the monster hit. Leemans slithered through the line like a slippery eel,

> "Tuffy Leemans had it all. He could run, pass and catch and he played truly outstanding defense. He was aggressive, dedicated and gave 100 percent at all times to a game he loved. In my opinion, he ranks among the all-time greats."
>
> —Wayne Millner

often turning short-yardage bursts into big gainers.

He also was the primary passer out of the Giants' single wing and a capable receiver. Leemans could play halfback or fullback and return kicks and he was a ballhawking defensive back in coach Steve Owen's two-platoon system. He was the primary ballhandler for teams that posted 8-2-1, 9-1-1 and 8-3-0 records en route to a 1938 championship and title game losses in 1939 and '41.

Leemans, a second-round pick in the first NFL draft, entered the Giants' radar when vacationing Wellington Mara, the son of team owner Tim Mara, saw him play for George Washington University in a game against Alabama. The young Mara talked his father into pursuing Leemans, who justified the confidence by earning MVP honors for the College All-Stars when they played the defending-champion Detroit Lions to a 7-7 tie.

Leemans rushed for an NFL-leading 830 yards as a 1936 rookie and passed for 258 more. But that was his best statistical season in a career that reflected a near-perfect running-passing balance—3,132 rushing yards, 2,318 passing—when he retired in 1943.

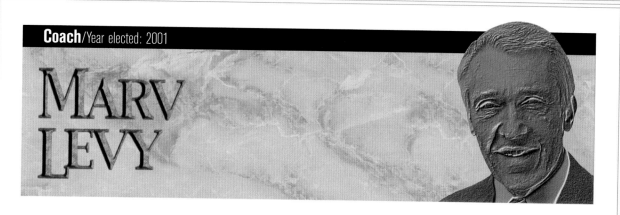

MARV LEVY

Born: 8-3-25, Chicago, Ill. **Teams coached (143-112 RS, 11-8 PS):** Chiefs 1978-82; Bills 1986-97 **Honors:** 1990s All-Decade Team

Fans admired him, opposing coaches envied him and players loved the way he inspired and treated them. Marv Levy's eloquence could be measured by word and action, his ability to motivate and lead by bottom-line results. For 47 years, he was equal parts coach, teacher, father figure, strategist and organizer, the final 12 as the innovative genius behind the swash-buckling Buffalo Bills.

Levy, a cerebral coach with a master's degree in English history from Harvard, is best remembered as the mild-mannered mentor who tamed the "Bickering Bills" and led them to four straight Super Bowls—all losers. He quoted Winston Churchill and Charles Dickens, encouraged innovation and treated his players as professionals, demanding only effort and preparation. Once, when asked if the upcoming Super Bowl was a must-win game for the Bills, Levy responded, "World War II was a must-win." But perspective did not keep him from pursuing perfection. His Buffalo teams, featuring such diverse personalities as Jim Kelly, Bruce Smith, Thurman Thomas and Andre Reed, dominated the AFC, compiling a 112-70 regular-season record and winning six AFC East Division titles and four straight AFC championship games from 1990-93.

The white-haired, always dignified Chicagoan never let convention get in the way of logic. Not blessed with great defensive talent in Kansas City from 1978-82, he ran a 1940s-style Wing-T offense that emphasized ball control. Buffalo's title run was fueled

> ## "Where else would you rather be than right here, right now?"
>
> *—Marv Levy's challenge to his players before every kickoff*

by a fast-paced, no-huddle, passing offense that led the AFC in scoring four straight years. His five seasons as coach of the Canadian Football League's Montreal Alouettes produced two Grey Cup titles.

Wherever he coached, players worked hard for him. He succeeded at the high school level, in the college ranks and as an NFL assistant and one-year USFL coach. When he retired in 1997, two years after fighting off prostrate cancer, he owned a 143-112 NFL coaching mark—and a frustrating but enviable distinction as the only coach to lose four straight Super Bowls.

BOB LILLY

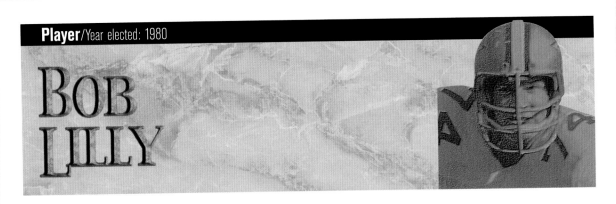

Born: 7-26-39, Olney, Tex. **Ht/Wt:** 6-5/260 **College:** TCU **Drafted:** 1961, 1st round, Cowboys **Primary position:** DT **Career statistics:** 16 fumble recoveries **Teams:** Cowboys 1961-74 **Super Bowl champion:** 1971 season **Honors:** 75th Anniversary All-Time Team; 1960s All-Decade Team; 1970s All-Decade Team; All-Time NFL Team

He is known affectionately as Mr. Cowboy — the first draft pick in Dallas franchise history, the team's first All-Pro, first Pro Bowl selection, first Ring of Honor member and first Hall of Famer. But Bob Lilly also is known in many football circles as the greatest defensive tackle ever to put on a uniform, the centerpiece for the late-1960s Doomsday Defenses that helped an expansion team reach championship heights.

Lilly was a 6-foot-5, 260-pound time bomb that exploded into furious action every time the ball was snapped. Nobody his size could match the

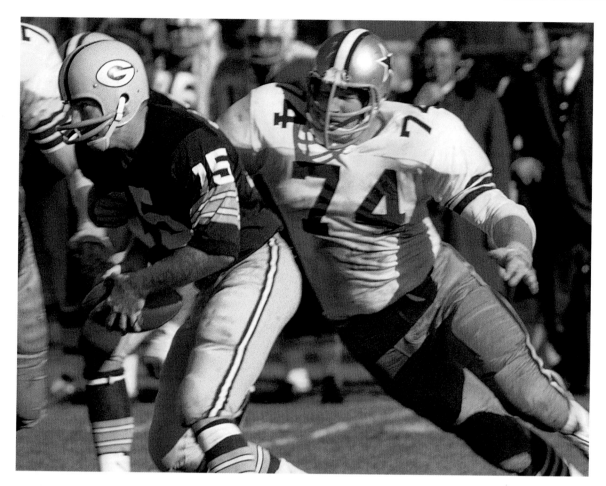

combination of incredible strength and quickness that allowed him to fight through blocks, chase down ball-carriers from sideline to sideline and pressure quarterbacks into errant throws. Double- and triple-team blocking schemes failed to neutralize Lilly's furious rush and competent blockers were brushed aside like giant gnats.

Lilly's ability to pursue so confounded opposing coaches they sometimes elected to run right at him, a ploy that met with only minimal success. Big No. 74 always seemed to be around the ball, no matter what the strategy, and the 16 fumbles he recovered were only a fraction of the miscues he forced with big hits and tackles.

The blond-headed kid from Throckmorton, Tex.,

> ### "He is not enormous but he is strong enough so that there isn't any use arguing with him if he gets hold of your jersey. You just fall wherever Lilly wants."
>
> —*Bob Griese*

an All-American at Texas Christian University, was the foundation upon which an expansion powerhouse was built. He arrived in 1961 with his sleepy, country-boy looks and began a 14-season run in which he never missed a regular-season game while earning 11 Pro Bowl selections.

Lilly was a student of the game, a player who constantly studied film and worked to improve his technique. What he might have lacked in intensity he made up for with hard work and a desire to be the best. As the team's talent level rose quickly in the mid-1960s, so did Lilly's championship hopes — aspirations that were fulfilled with six NFL/NFC title game appearances, two Super Bowls and a championship after the 1971 season.

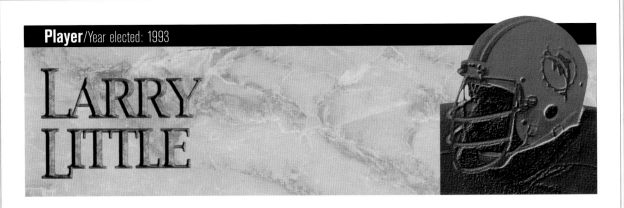

LARRY LITTLE

Born: 11-2-45, Groveland, Ga. **Ht/Wt:** 6-1/265 **College:** Bethune-Cookman **Drafted:** Undrafted **Primary position:** OG
Teams: Chargers 1967-68; Dolphins 1969-80 **Super Bowl champions:** 1972, '73 seasons **Honors:** 1970s All-Decade Team

They called him a sledgehammer, the path-clearing enforcer for Miami's power running attack in the 1970s. Larry Little was the antithesis of his name, a 6-foot-1, 265-pound offensive guard who could out-finesse defensive tackles and overwhelm cornerbacks like a runaway truck. He was the point man for a talented unit that triggered three straight Super Bowl runs and the hatchet man who helped make household names of Larry Csonka, Jim Kiick and Mercury Morris.

Little was fast and quick, a lesson learned by defenders he blocked and unfortunate linebackers and defensive backs who had to deal with him on power sweeps. That's when he was at his intimidating best, pulling to his right and attacking with full-speed ferocity anybody who dared challenge the runner. Little was a rumbling giant who considered every play, every block a matter of respect.

That was a product of the diminutive $750 free-agent bonus Little got from San Diego in 1967 after a college career at tiny Bethune-Cookman. Chargers coach Sid Gillman

> ## "I'm a guard. I do what a guard does. All I'm interested in is knocking people off their feet."
>
> —*Larry Little, 1993, Orlando Sentinel*

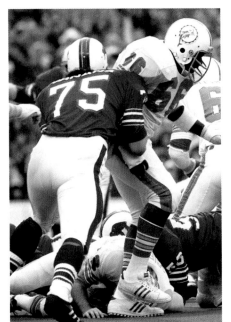

experimented with the 285-pounder at several positions, including fullback, before dealing him to the Dolphins in 1969. It didn't take long for coach Don Shula to get Little down to 265 and make him the durable centerpiece for a line that would clear the way for 2,000-yard rushing seasons every year in the 1970s.

The gregarious, confident Little was a 10-year captain and inspirational role model for younger players. He also was visible in the community, where his charity work became almost as legendary as his power blocks. Little, a five-time Pro Bowl selection, was a force for powerful 1971, '72 and '73 Dolphins teams that lost one Super Bowl and won two others.

The 1972 Dolphins ran for 2,960 yards, posted a 14-0 regular-season record and went on to win the Super Bowl, completing the first undefeated and untied season (including playoffs) in NFL history. The 1973 champions, with Little again playing a major role, finished with 2,521 rushing yards and a 15-2 record.

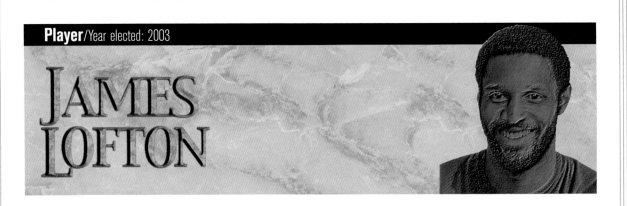

Player/Year elected: 2003

JAMES LOFTON

Born: 7-5-56, Fort Ord, Calif. **Ht/Wt:** 6-3/195 **College:** Stanford **Drafted:** 1978, 1st round, Packers **Primary position:** WR
Career statistics: Receiving, 764 rec., 14,004 yds., 18.3 avg., 75 TDs **Teams:** Packers 1978-86; Raiders 1987-88; Bills 1989-92;
Rams 1993; Eagles 1993 **Honors:** 1980s All-Decade Team

He was the second coming of Don Hutson in Green Bay, a solid contributor to three Super Bowl teams in Buffalo and the game's all-time leader in reception yardage when he retired in 1993. Nobody ever accused James Lofton of keeping a low profile. And nobody ever questioned his big-play impact over a 16-year NFL career that touched five teams and three decades.

It's hard to forget the unusual athleticism, sprinter speed and highlight-reel catches that Lofton delivered over nine Green Bay seasons (1978-86), two with the Los Angeles Raiders (1987-88) and four in Buffalo (1989-92) before career-ending stops with the Los Angeles Rams and Philadelphia. He was, as predicted, a Hutson-like weapon who could create space with lightning-quick moves, work fearlessly over the middle or burn defenders deep. Covering the creative and intelligent former Stanford sprinter and long jumper often had embarrassing consequences.

While playing for weak Packers teams, the 6-foot-3, 195-pound Lofton averaged 59 catches per season, caught 49 touchdown passes and recorded five of his six career 1,000-yard seasons. His 9,656 receiving yards are still a franchise record and he averaged a whopping 18.2 yards per catch, just under his 18.3 career mark. Lofton, who earned seven of his eight Pro Bowl selections with the Packers, led the team in receptions eight times.

But it was as a go-to receiver for Bills quarterback Jim Kelly that Lofton got his first taste of winning. The Bills were 46-18 in his four Buffalo seasons and lost three straight Super Bowls from 1990-92. "He made some electrifying, game-breaking plays for us," former Buffalo coach Marv Levy said when Lofton won election to the Hall of Fame in 2003. He caught 57 passes for 1,072 yards and eight touchdowns in 1991, averaging 18.8 yards per catch.

When Lofton retired, he owned the career receiving yards record of 14,004 and his 764 catches ranked third behind Steve Largent and Art Monk. He currently ranks third in yardage behind active players Jerry Rice and Tim Brown.

"Every time I see (Jerry) Rice play and reflect on Lofton, I think about the similarities. James Lofton was a unique wide receiver."

—*Bart Starr, 2003, Milwaukee Journal Sentinel*

Coach/Year elected: 1971

VINCE LOMBARDI

Born: 6-11-13, Brooklyn, N.Y. **Died:** 9-3-70 **Teams coached (96-34-6 RS, 9-1 PS):** Packers 1959-67; Redskins 1969
Championship teams: NFL 1961, '62, '65, '66, '67 **Super Bowl champions:** 1966, '67 seasons

The very mention of his name stirs emotion, an incongruous mix of love, hate, fear, anger and respect. Vince Lombardi was a volatile, hard-driving pro football genius who attained almost mythical status while creating a pro football dynasty. Few coaches can match the remarkable 10-year legacy of a short, stocky, fire-breathing taskmaster who guided the 1960s-era Green Bay Packers to five championships and wins in the first two Super Bowls.

Lombardi, who first gained notice as a member of Fordham's "Seven Blocks of Granite" line in the mid-1930s, was a dictatorial disciplinarian who demanded total dedication and sacrifice. He preached power football, a "run-to-daylight" philosophy, and pushed, prodded and drove such players as Jim Taylor, Bart Starr, Ray Nitschke, Paul Hornung and Herb Adderley to perfect execution. Lombardi's attention to fundamentals was as relentless as his eye for detail.

Fans remember the Brooklyn-born Lombardi stomping the sideline, his cold, passionate eyes flashing and his toothy grimace locked between a smile and frown. Players remember the trash can-kicking tirades, biting tongue lashings and stiff fines he used to impress intolerance of mediocrity. He dug into his library of football credos ("Winning isn't everything, it's the only thing"; "If you quit during practice, you'll quit during a game") to inspire his troops.

Players blanched at Lombardi's methods, but responded to his tough-love approach. It was all about winning for the former assistant to Army coach Red Blaik and New York Giants coach Jim Lee Howell. Packers teams that had finished 8-27-1 in the three seasons before his 1959 arrival were 89-29-4 in his nine seasons with five championships and one title-game loss.

Lombardi left the sideline for the front office after watching his Packers destroy Oakland in Super Bowl II, but he guided lowly Washington to a 7-5-2 record in a 1969 return. He died a year later of cancer, completing his legacy with a 105-35-6 record, including 9-1 in postseason. Fittingly, the Super Bowl championship trophy was renamed in Lombardi's honor.

"Lombardi treats us all the same—like dogs."

— *Henry Jordan, former Packers defensive tackle*

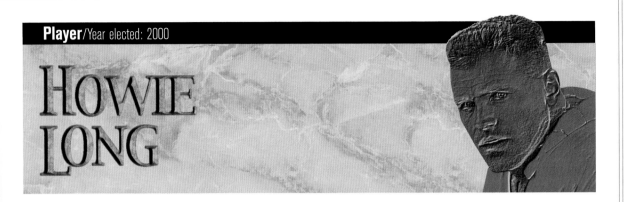

HOWIE LONG

Born: 1-6-60, Somerville, Mass. **Ht/Wt:** 6-5/270 **College:** Villanova **Drafted:** 1981, 2nd round, Raiders **Primary position:** DE, DT
Career statistics: Sacks, 84 **Teams:** Raiders 1981-93 **Super Bowl champion:** 1983 season **Honors:** 1980s All-Decade Team

Don't let that charming, fun-loving personality fool you. Howie Long still has a 6-foot, 5-inch silver-and-black mean streak that stretches from the top of his crew-cut head to the feet on his 270-pound body. The engaging football analyst and television pitch man has come full circle from the one-man wrecking crew that terrorized blockers, ballcarriers and quarterbacks over 13 NFL seasons with the Oakland and Los Angeles Raiders.

> ## "There are guys who are bigger, guys who are stronger, guys who are meaner. But none of them puts it together the way he does."
>
> —Matt Millen, *former Raiders teammate*

Opposing coaches and players who had to deal with the former defensive lineman remember his explosive quickness, surprising speed and bull-like strength. Nobody could match his combination of size and athleticism, and few could fathom his full-throttle intensity. Offensive game plans were constructed with the intimidating Long in mind and he frequently had to fight his way through double- and triple-team blocks.

An unrefined second-round 1981 draft pick out of Villanova, Long quickly grasped the nuances of defensive line play and the swagger that defined the Raiders organization. He was intelligent enough to learn all five line positions and versatile enough to rotate among them from play to play. Blockers never were sure where Long would be positioned, allowing Raiders coach Tom Flores to pick his matchups.

Long made an instant impact for defending Super Bowl-champion Oakland as a 1981 rookie and recorded a career-high 13 sacks in 1983 for the relocated "Los Angeles" Raiders, who pounded Washington 38-9 in Super Bowl XVIII. Big No. 75 became known far and wide as a tenacious, bull-rushing sack man, but he also was a proud and efficient run-stuffer — well-rounded enough to record 84 career sacks and earn eight Pro Bowl invitations.

A former Golden Gloves champion during his youth in the tough Charlestown section of Boston, Long used the superior hand speed he acquired as a boxer to fend off blockers. He also succeeded because of an admirable work ethic and the social skills he turned into a successful broadcasting career.

LONG

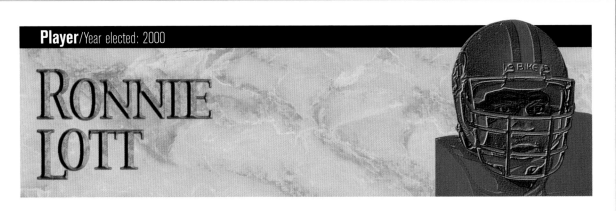

RONNIE LOTT

Born: 5-8-59, Albuquerque, N.M. **Ht/Wt:** 6-0/203 **College:** USC **Drafted:** 1981, 1st round, 49ers **Position:** DB **Career statistics:** Interceptions, 63 **Interceptions leader:** 1986, '91 **Teams:** 49ers 1981-90; Raiders 1991-92; Jets 1993-94 **Super Bowl champions:** 1981, '84, '88, '89 seasons **Honors:** 75th Anniversary All-Time Team; 1980s All-Decade Team; 1990s All-Decade Team; All-Time NFL Team

The footsteps wide receivers often heard in their worst nightmares belonged to Ronnie Lott, who left a black-and-blue imprint on the NFL over an outstanding 14-season career. He was the last line of defense, an enforcer who had to make every hit count. Nobody did that better than Lott and nobody who ventured into his area of concern escaped without paying a stiff price.

Nothing personal, but the talented cornerback-turned-safety took his job seriously. Lott was competitive and resourceful and his never-give-an-inch style inspired the 49ers to four Super Bowl championships in the 1980s. He was a throwback to yesteryear, a ballhawking defender who threw his 6-foot, 203-pound body around like a middle linebacker.

The seemingly reckless abandon with which Lott played was crafted out of his amazing sense and feel for what was happening on every play. Any quarterback who threw a ball into the secondary did so with full

> "I never really had a fear of defensive backs because of my size. Those were the guys you could just run over. But Ronnie, he was a guy who hit like a linebacker, but he'd be coming from 25 yards out with a full head of steam. You wouldn't see him coming, then . . . bam! You're on the 49ers' highlight film."
>
> —Eric Dickerson, 2000,
> *The Press-Enterprise (Riverside, Calif.)*

knowledge that Lott would be ready to pounce. Every receiver who reached for a pass feared the inevitable torpedo-like shot to his ribs.

Many regard Lott as the greatest defensive back ever to play the game. He was a consensus All-Pro early in his career while playing cornerback and again after his 1985 move to free safety. He made the Pro Bowl after a late-career shift to strong safety. During each of those three periods, Lott was generally considered the best player at his position.

The former USC star, who was as gentle and soft-spoken off the field as he was intimidating on it, completed his career in 1994 after 10 seasons with the 49ers and two-year stints with the Los Angeles Raiders and New York Jets. He retired with 63 interceptions in 192 regular-season games (fifth on the all-time list) and added nine more picks in 20 postseason contests. The 49ers' classy and fearless defensive leader also finished with 10 Pro Bowl selections.

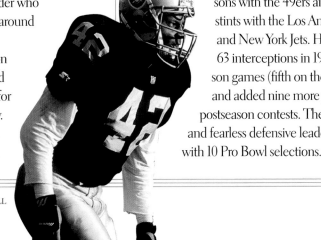

SID LUCKMAN

Born: 11-21-16, Brooklyn, N.Y. **Died:** 7-5-98 **Ht/Wt:** 6-0/197 **College:** Columbia **Drafted:** 1939, 1st round, Bears **Primary positions:** QB, DB, P **Career statistics:** Passing, 904-of-1,744, 14,686 yds., 137 TDs; Interceptions, 17, 2 TDs; Punting, 230 att., 38.4 avg. **Teams:** Bears 1939-50 **Championship teams:** NFL 1940, '41, '43, '46 **Honors:** 1940s All-Decade Team

The first things you noticed about Sid Luckman were his easy smile, square chin, high forehead and dark, rugged good looks. But the smile disappeared when the former Brooklyn street kid pulled a Chicago Bears helmet over his thick, curly black hair and went to work as chief executioner of a George Halas winning machine that produced four NFL championships in the 1940s.

Luckman, a former single-wing star at Columbia University, brought the perfect blend of physical and leadership abilities to his 12-season role as pro football's first successful T-formation quarterback. He was equal parts magician and field general, a gifted ballhandler who could misdirect the defense and set up Chicago runners for big gainers or receivers for his deadly deep-passing attack.

Luckman will forever be linked with contemporary Sammy Baugh as the passing quarterbacks who changed the offensive course of pro football. But Luckman was the first to do it from the formation that would become the rage of the NFL. Luckman, who threw over the top with picture-perfect form, was known for his deep-striking ability while the always-scrambling, off-balance Baugh preferred the controlled possession passing attack.

> "He became a great player simply because he devoted about 400 percent more effort to it than most athletes are willing to do."
>
> — *George Halas*

Luckman, who also was a capable punter and kick returner, was so valuable to the Bears that Halas restricted his running, hoping to avoid injury. So he overpowered opponents in other ways. A typical Luckman performance was delivered in 1943 when he completed 110 of 202 passes for 2,194 yards and 28 touchdowns while leading the Bears to their third championship in four years.

Luckman could be explosive. He ran for one touchdown and passed for another while directing the Bears to an amazing 73-0 victory over Baugh's Washington Redskins in the 1940 NFL title game, dramatically demonstrating the possibilities of the T-formation. He fired a record seven touchdown passes in a 1943 game and five more in a 1943 championship game win over Washington. Luckman, a three-time Pro Bowler, retired in 1950 after passing for 14,686 yards and 137 TDs.

LINK LYMAN

Born: 11-30-1898, Table Rock, Neb. **Died:** 12-16-72 **Ht/Wt:** 6-2/250 **College:** Nebraska **Primary positions:** OT, DT
Teams: Canton Bulldogs 1922-23, 1925; Cleveland Bulldogs 1924; Frankford Yellowjackets 1925; Bears 1926-28, 1930-31, 1933-34 **Championship teams:** NFL 1922, '23, '24, '33

There wasn't an ounce of fat on Roy "Link" Lyman's 6-foot-2, 250-pound body. There was no mistaking the mayhem on his always active mind when he lined up to terrorize the smaller, less-intimidating offensive linemen of the 1920s and '30s. Lyman was a power broker in the early NFL trenches, a rugged and trend-setting performer who anchored four championship teams over an 11-year career.

Everybody shuddered in 1922 when the Nebraska-born Lyman signed with Canton, combining with 250-pound bookend tackle Pete Henry on the Bulldogs' interior line. But whereas Henry overpowered blockers with brute force, Lyman resorted to innovative tactics that would change the way defense is played. Before every snap, after the offensive linemen were set in their stance, the quick-footed Lyman would slide up and down the line, eventually picking a spot to shoot a gap.

Blockers were understandably confused, never knowing where Lyman might strike. Too often, he arrived in the backfield at the moment of the exchange, causing unsettling disruptions and numerous

> "He was the first lineman I ever saw who moved from his assigned defensive position before the ball was snapped. It was difficult to play against him because he would vary his moves and no matter how you reacted, you could be wrong."
>
> — *Steve Owen, former Giants tackle*

fumbles. He forced opponents to adjust to his tactics with new blocking strategies and became more sophisticated with feints that would be followed by looping outside rushes and forward body fakes that would cause edgy blockers to move early.

Offensively, the quick-footed Lyman was restricted to straight-ahead power blocking and occasional tackle-eligible pass plays by coach Guy Chamberlin, another former University of Nebraska star. The 1922 and '23 Bulldogs, with Lyman, Henry and Chamberlin taking center stage, compiled a 21-0-3 record and won consecutive championships; the 1924 Bulldogs, now located in Cleveland and playing without Henry, won a title with a 7-1-1 mark.

Lyman joined the Chicago Bears for a 1926 barnstorming tour and remained with George Halas' team through 1934, minus two seasons he sat out to take care of personal business. With Lyman at tackle, the Bears won the first official NFL championship game in 1933 and lost in the title game a year later.

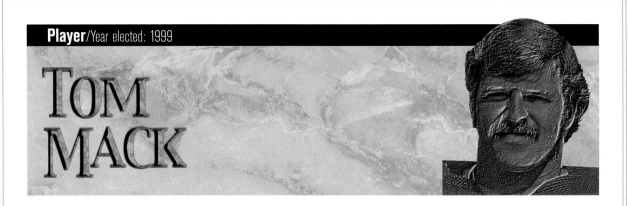

TOM MACK

Born: 11-1-43, Cleveland, Ohio **Ht/Wt:** 6-3/250 **College:** Michigan **Drafted:** 1966, 1st round, Rams **Primary position:** OG
Teams: Rams 1966-78

From 1966-78, the Los Angeles Rams' road to success ran over left guard. That's where runners found the biggest holes, passers got the best protection and mayhem-minded defenders suffered the most frustration, all thanks to Tom Mack. Powerful, strong, proud and durable, the former Michigan star provided a blueprint for how the game's most obscure position should be played.

Work ethic and fierce determination to succeed defined the career of Mack, an undersized 250-pounder who never missed a game (184 straight) during his 13 seasons while earning 11 Pro Bowl selections. He wasn't the greatest athlete and he struggled with blurred vision, but nobody could match his drive and intensity once the game clock started ticking.

He was an especially powerful run blocker and adept pulling guard who could get out front on the sweep — a tribute to his surprising foot speed. Former Rams coach George Allen, who typically shunned

first-year players, called Mack "extremely intelligent" and handed him a starting job in his 1966 rookie season. Nobody was more consistently focused or better prepared during games and few players could claim his level of team success.

It was no coincidence the Rams, who had struggled through seven straight losing seasons before his arrival, posted winning records in 12 of his 13 campaigns (129-48-7), won eight division titles and advanced to four NFC championship games, falling one win short of the Super Bowl each time. They did it with four

coaches, five starting quarterbacks and one left guard—the immovable Mack.

Mack's 1999 Hall of Fame induction was a homecoming of sorts. Born and raised in Cleveland, about an hour away from the Canton-based Hall, Mack was the son of Cleveland Indians second baseman Ray Mack, a

"I've always thought that one of the best things I've had going for me is my speed. I'm not as big and strong as some guards, but one of the things I can do best is block on a sweep." —*Tom Mack*

former double-play partner of Lou Boudreau. The irony is that Mack, an Ohioan, earned All-America honors at Michigan instead of Ohio State because the Buckeyes never offered him a scholarship. He was grabbed by the Rams with the second overall pick of the 1966 draft.

Tom Mack (65) was a big man in the Rams 1960s and '70s football success.

JOHN MACKEY

Born: 9-24-41, New York, N.Y. **Ht/Wt:** 6-2/224 **College:** Syracuse **Drafted:** 1963, 2nd round, NFL Colts; 5th round, AFL Titans
Primary position: TE **Career statistics:** Receiving, 331 rec., 5,236 yds., 15.8 avg., 38 TDs **Teams:** Colts 1963-71; Chargers 1972
Super Bowl champion: 1970 season **Honors:** 50th Anniversary Team; 1960s All-Decade Team; All-Time NFL Team

Nothing could prepare a wide-eyed defensive back for the sight of 224-pound John Mackey, ball tucked safely under a massive arm, rumbling straight at him, full-speed ahead. He was like a runaway truck, a bulldozer on a mission. The big Baltimore Colts tight end was willing to run around, over or through would-be tacklers, and those who successfully brought him down absorbed serious punishment while doing so.

Mackey was a fullback in tight end's clothing. He was a dangerous weapon in the passing arsenal of quarterback Johnny Unitas when most teams used their tight ends primarily as blockers. Mackey had the power to catch short slants, outs and screens and then use his powerul legs to churn out extra yardage. But he also had the speed to go deep, a tight end quality coaches had never had to defend against. He was simply too elusive for the linebackers assigned to cover him and too big for the smaller defensive backs caught in one-on-one situations.

Fullback or tight end? That was the question Baltimore coach Don Shula had to answer in 1963 when Mackey was drafted out of Syracuse University and his decision revolutionized the position. The soft-spoken, mild-mannered New Yorker

was a willing prototype — a devastating blocker against defensive ends and linebackers, a reliable pass catcher and threat to carry on end-around plays.

Mackey's big-play ability was demonstrated in 1966, when six of his nine touchdowns were scored on plays of more than 50 yards. Twice he compiled season averages of more than 20 yards per catch and his 10-year career average of 15.8 was remarkable for a tight end. Baltimore fans remember his 75-yard touchdown catch on a tipped pass from Unitas in the Colts' 16-13 win over Dallas in Super Bowl V.

Big No. 88, a five-time Pro Bowler and member of the Colts' Super Bowl III loser, was voted tight end on the NFL's first half-century team in 1969.

> "He can beat a defense either short or deep. And when he catches the ball, watch out! We came here together as rookies six years ago and he has gotten better every season."
>
> — *Jerry Logan, Colts safety, 1969*

MACKEY

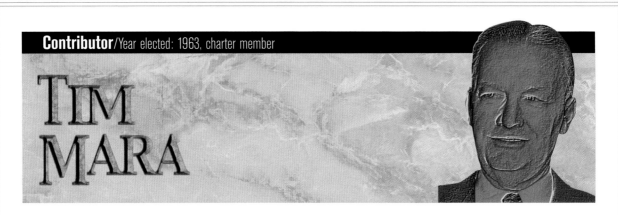

TIM MARA

Born: 7-29-1887, New York, N.Y. **Died:** 2-16-59 **Executive career:** Founder and owner of Giants, 1925-59

Smart, blustery and always willing to roll up his sleeves for a good fight, Tim Mara was a perfect fit for the infant NFL. After more than three decades of scrapping, scraping and finagling for respect, the Giants team he founded was a perfect fit for the New York spotlight he craved. First and foremost, the big Irishman with big ideas was a pioneer who helped mold a struggling little football league into a modern-day corporation.

Mara, a prosperous legal bookmaker, political activist and fight promoter, bought into the vision of NFL president Joe Carr in 1925 when he paid a $2,500 franchise fee to join the 5-year-old circuit. For the rest of his life, he was committed to making the sport grow. A member of the elite ownership fraternity that gave shape to the professional game, Mara was the key figure in the league's all-important New York market.

From a shoestring operation on the verge of collapse in the late 1920s to one of the game's premier franchises at his death in 1959, Mara never backed down from

> "I didn't know much about football. I never went to college and had not seen a football game. However, I felt that if it were any good at all, a New York franchise was a bargain at the price."
>
> — *Tim Mara*

his challenge. He staged creative promotions to stay afloat, signed attractive stars to generate headlines and established strong rivalries with teams in Chicago, Washington and Green Bay. Mara was resourceful — he once bought the Detroit Wolverines franchise to get triple-threat halfback Benny Friedman — while surviving costly bidding wars against two rival leagues (the AFL in 1926 and AAFC from 1946-49), the Great Depression and World War II.

For a man who knew more about racetracks and boxing than football, Mara was amazingly successful. His Giants won championships in 1927, '34, '38 and '56 — and lost in the NFL title game eight times. He passed his football obsession to sons Jack and Wellington, a Hall of Famer who is still active as the Giants president and co-chief executive officer.

Tim Mara, one of the league's early brokers with Carr, George Halas, Curly Lambeau and George Preston Marshall, became a charter member of the Pro Football Hall of Fame in 1963.

Contributor/Year elected: 1997

WELLINGTON MARA

Born: 8-14-16, New York, N.Y. **Executive career:** Co-owner of Giants 1930-65; owner of Giants 1965-present; NFC president 1984-present **Front-office titles:** Secretary 1938-40; vice president and secretary 1945-58; vice president 1959-65; president 1966-90; president and co-chief executive officer 1991-present

His name is synonymous with New York Giants football; his NFL memories predate most of the circuit's 32 teams. Wellington Mara has spent a lifetime observing, scouting, organizing, building and leading his team and professional football through a remarkable period of growth and prosperity. Like the father he emulated, Wellington is a New York giant—both in thought and deed.

> ## "Over the years, one thing has never changed. I loved the game then, and I love it just as fiercely now."
>
> — *Wellington Mara, 1997, The Atlanta Journal and Constitution*

At age 9, he was on the bench for the first home game played by the Giants—the team his father, Tim Mara, had organized to compete in the NFL's important New York market. At age 14, Wellington was listed as the team's co-owner along with older brother Jack. At age 22, the Fordham-educated Wellington was full-time secretary and the brains behind personnel procurement and all football matters.

Mara was responsible for discovering and signing star halfback Tuffy Leemans in 1936 and he is credited for engineering trades and draft picks that brought such stars as Y.A. Tittle, Andy Robustelli, Del Shofner, Dick Modzelewski, Frank Gifford and

Roosevelt Brown to a New York team that played in five NFL championship games from 1958-63. When his father died in 1959, his role expanded into the business side; when brother Jack died in 1965, "Duke" (as in Duke of Wellington) became a front-office force and the team's chief decision-maker.

The quiet, painfully self-effacing Mara has never wavered from his belief that the good of the NFL takes precedent over the needs of its teams. As an important ally of commissioner Pete Rozelle, he served as chairman of the NFL Management Council, president of the NFC and worked as a member of the powerful Competition Committee. The proud octogenarian, who has watched his Giants win six NFL championships (two Super Bowls) and lose 12 times in the title game, remains an influential figure as the Giants' president and co-chief executive officer.

A devoutly religious father of 11, Wellington joined Tim as the first father-son combination in the Pro Football Hall of Fame in 1997.

GINO MARCHETTI

Born: 1-2-27, Smithers, W.Va. **Ht/Wt:** 6-4/244 **College:** San Francisco **Drafted:** 1952, 2nd round, Yanks/Texans **Primary position:** DE
Teams: Texans 1952; Colts 1953-64, 1966 **Championship teams:** NFL 1958, '59 **Honors:** 75th Anniversary All-Time Team;
50th Anniversary Team; 1950s All-Decade Team

Call him the dominator, the intimidator, the terminator. Gino Marchetti was all that and more. He was to the defensive end position what Sammy Baugh was to quarterback, Don Hutson to receiver and Lawrence Taylor to outside line-backer. He was the prototype, the standard by which future generations of defensive ends would be judged.

Marchetti combined size (6-foot-4, 244), agility and amazing big-man quickness in his 13-year role as the Baltimore Colts' chief run-stuffer and pass rusher. He became the first defensive end specialist in the early 1950s, when coaches were phasing out two-way players. And he introduced the concept of a defensive end pressuring the quarterback—a function he performed with demonic fervor.

Marchetti, playing with obsessive emotion, was big and fast enough to overpower anybody who blocked his path to the quarterback. His relentless charges were executed with a wild passion that spread fear throughout the league and his explosiveness off the snap confounded double- and triple-team blocking tactics.

> "My goodness gracious, Gino would just knock your butt off every time. He was the toughest, cleanest ballplayer I can remember from my many years in the league. There's never been another one like him."
>
> — *Bobby Layne*

Trying to block Marchetti was like trying to stop a steamroller moving at warp speed. He simply overwhelmed some of the best offensive tackles in the game.

Marchetti's menacing aura was enhanced by the dark-bearded jaws and piercing eyes that flashed at offensive linemen from inside his Colts helmet. And the legend grew with stories of how he had played half of one game with a separated shoulder and another game two weeks after undergoing surgery for an appendicitis.

The big Californian, who fought during World War II in the Battle of the Bulge at age 18 before attending the University of San Francisco, helped the Colts capture consecutive NFL championships in 1958 and '59. Late in the classic 1958 title game victory over the New York Giants, Marchetti suffered a broken leg and was forced to watch pro football's first sudden-death overtime from the sideline. The big man who played in 10 Pro Bowls and earned All-Pro honors every year from 1957-62 retired after the 1966 season.

GEORGE PRESTON MARSHALL

Born: 10-11-1896, Grafton, W. Va. **Died:** 8-9-69 **Executive career:** Owner of Redskins 1932-69

He stormed through pro football like a category-5 hurricane—loud, blustery, quick-tempered and painfully contentious. But any controversy generated by George Preston Marshall was more than tempered by his imaginative, outrageous and daring showmanship. For a sport and league in dire need of color and promotional flair, the longtime Redskins owner was like a hard-to-swallow breath of fresh air.

From the moment in 1932 when the laundry entrepreneur bought a piece of the Boston Braves franchise to his death in 1969 as longtime owner of the Washington Redskins, Marshall was a pro football force. He was creative and passionate, a visionary who pushed and prodded his fellow owners to make the NFL more fan friendly and the games more fun.

Marshall, who moved his Redskins to the nation's capital after the 1936 season, championed such innovations as the two-division format with winners meeting in an annual championship game, the rule that legalized passing from anywhere behind the line of scrim-

> ## "He's irascible, violent, opinionated, a dictator and completely uninhibited. He has an almost psychopathic passion for football. But he's colorful and good copy. I like him, but I wouldn't want to work for him."
>
> —*Bob Addie, former Washington Post columnist*

mage and the moving of the goal post to the goal line, which produced more field goals. When the television era arrived, Marshall fought for local blackouts.

But Marshall was at his best while promoting his Redskins. He loved to stage gala halftime shows and created the Redskins marching band, a 110-piece unit outfitted in colorful tribal regalia. When Texas Christian University quarterback Sammy Baugh was drafted in 1937, he paraded him around town in cowboy boots and a 10-gallon Stetson—a publicity blitz that helped draw 20,000 fans to the team's inaugural game at Griffith Stadium. Other owners watched and learned.

Players and coaches, who often ran plays and made substitutions at the owner's whim, didn't like him. But they won NFL titles in 1937 and '42 behind Baugh and lost in four other championship games before the team fell on hard times in the 1950s and '60s. Still the fans came, a tribute to the ingenuity and determination of the game's first promotional genius.

OLLIE MATSON

Born: 5-1-30, Trinity, Tex. **Ht/Wt:** 6-2/220 **College:** San Francisco **Drafted:** 1952, 1st round, Cardinals **Primary positions:** RB, DB
Career statistics: Rushing, 1,170 att., 5,173 yds., 40 TDs; Receiving, 222 rec., 14.8 avg., 23 TDs; KO Returns, 143 att., 26.2 avg., 6 TDs; Punt Returns, 65 att., 3 TDs **Teams:** Cardinals 1952, 1954-58; Rams 1959-62; Lions 1963; Eagles 1964-66 **Honors:** 1950s All-Decade Team

Optimistic Chicago Cardinals fans labeled him "The Messiah," envious Bears coach George Halas called him a "wonder player" and the Los Angeles Rams wanted him so badly they traded nine players to get him. That Ollie Matson labored in the obscurity of losing teams over a 14-year NFL career did not diminish the lightning-bolt speed that made coaches drool and gave him distinction as one of pro football's most feared breakaway threats in the 1950s and '60s.

Matson was the near-perfect blend of power and speed—a 6-foot-2, 220-pound former silver and bronze medal-winning sprinter for the 1952 U.S. Olympic team. He could slash through the middle or power his way for short yardage, but he was at his best when running outside. One block, one missed tackle and he might be gone. He was explosive and intelligent, a talented receiver who also utilized his speed as a 1952 defensive back.

The former University of San Francisco All-American might have been most dan-

> ## "I don't think there's another man in football who's that big and that fast. ..."
>
> —*Clark Shaughnessy, 1959*

gerous as a punt and kickoff returner—talents that produced nine touchdowns. His career total of 12,799 combined yards (5,173 rushing, 3,285 receiving, 4,341 returns) could have been higher, but he was always the focal point of defensive game plans while playing for teams that compiled a 59-127-6 record. Matson, who never played in a postseason game, enjoyed his greatest success for the Cardinals in 1955 when he led the NFL in punt returns and 1956 when he ran for a career-best 924 yards.

But the proud, soft-spoken "Messiah" never was able to lead the lowly Cardinals to the Promised Land and the Rams, after giving up eight players and a draft choice to get him in 1959, sank to an 11-39-2 mark over the next four seasons as his playing time dwindled. Matson made career-ending stops in Detroit and Philadelphia.

The Texas-born Californian with the thin mustache and prominent jaw retired in 1966 with 73 career touchdowns and five Pro Bowl selections.

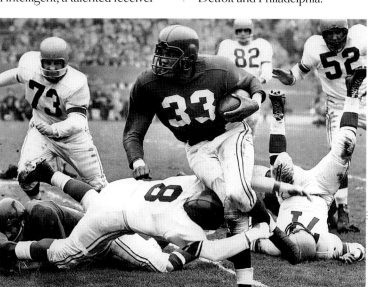

DON MAYNARD

Born: 1-25-35, Crosbyton, Tex. **Ht/Wt:** 6-1/180 **College:** Texas Western **Drafted:** 1957, 9th round, Giants **Primary position:** WR

Career statistics: Receiving, 633 rec., 11,834 yds., 18.7 avg., 88 TDs **Teams:** Giants 1958; Titans/Jets 1960-72; Cardinals 1973

Championship teams: NFL 1958; AFL 1968 **Super Bowl champion:** 1968 season **Honors:** All-Time AFL Team

There never was any doubt about Don Maynard's sprinter speed or ability to catch a football. The trick was getting him to do it the company way. Coaches tried for 15 frustrating seasons to tame the rebellious and independent Texan, who free-lanced and improvised his way to lasting fame as the go-to receiver for New York Jets quarterback Joe Namath.

The former Texas Western track and football star raised eyebrows when he arrived for his rookie training camp with the 1958 New York Giants wearing a plaid shirt, jeans, cowboy boots, silver belt buckle and long sideburns. That first New York stay lasted only one season, but he returned to New York in 1960 with the Titans of the new American Football League — an association that would last through 1972.

What coach Weeb Ewbank inherited when he took over the renamed Jets in 1963 was a receiver with stunning change-of-pace moves — a pattern free-lancer who routinely forced quarterbacks to adjust. But speedy No. 13 also had a great knack for getting open, which suited the talented Namath when he arrived in 1965. They quickly established a big-play rapport and clicked for 244 completions, 4,789 yards and 39 touchdowns over their first four seasons.

Off the field, the 6-foot-1, 180-pounder was the atypical New York sports hero—non-

> **"If I had to prepare to cover a guy like Maynard, my first thought would be to devise several ways to get double coverage on him. He'd kill you one-on-one. The biggest thing is his speed and change of pace."**
>
> — *Walt Michaels, Jets defensive backs coach, 1967*

smoking, non-drinking, frugal and seldom seen, the opposite of Namath. On the field, they formed a swashbuckling duo. Maynard capped a 1,297-yard 1968 season by catching six passes for 118 yards and two TDs in the AFL title-game win over Oakland. In the Jets' Super Bowl III upset of Baltimore, a hobbled Maynard willingly served as decoy while George Sauer caught eight passes for 133 yards.

Maynard, who made 633 career receptions for 11,834 yards and 88 touchdowns before retiring as the game's all-time leading receiver in 1973 after one St. Louis season, played in two of the biggest games in pro football history — the Giants-Colts 1958 championship game and the Jets' 1969 Super Bowl win. He retired with five 1,000-yard seasons and 50 100-yard receiving games.

Maynard (13) pulls in a TD pass against Oakland in the 1968 AFL title game.

GEORGE MCAFEE

Born: 3-13-18, Corbin, Ky. **Ht/Wt:** 6-0/177 **College:** Duke **Drafted:** 1940, 1st round, Eagles **Primary positions:** HB, DB, P **Career statistics:** Rushing, 341 att., 1,685 yds., 22 TDs; Receiving, 85 rec., 16.0 avg., 11 TDs; Punt Returns, 112 att., 12.8 avg., 2 TDs; Punting, 39 att., 36.7 avg. **Teams:** Bears 1940-41, 1945-50 **Championship teams:** NFL 1940, '41, '46 **Honors:** 1940s All-Decade Team

Now you see him, now you don't. George McAfee twisted, turned, darted, cut and juked his way through the 1940s NFL, a ball-carrying wizard for the magically inclined Chicago Bears teams of that era. George Halas gushed about his highlight-film dashes, Red Grange called him the greatest broken-field run-

George McAfee (5), who doubled as a defensive back, was part of a swarming Bears defense that posted a 73-0 win over Washington in the 1940 NFL championship game. Fellow Hall of Famer Sid Luckman is tackling Jimmy Johnston.

ner of all time and fans lamented the war-dictated brevity of his electrifying career.

The 6-foot, 177-pound McAfee was a barrage of hip twists, head fakes and change-of-direction cuts as he maneuvered with choppy strides past open-field tacklers. He was equally elusive in traffic, a quick-stepping artist who could give tacklers a leg or hip and pull away with a sudden burst to daylight. McAfee's slight build only added to his deception and his finely chiseled features gave him a cover-boy veneer.

When the No. 1 draft pick arrived in 1940 after an All-America season at Duke, the star-studded Bears were beginning a four-year run that would net three championships and one title game loss. But Halas couldn't ignore the all-around talents of the quiet Kentuckian, who could run, catch, throw and punt. The lefthanded and leftfooted McAfee also was a ballhawking defender who posted 25 career interceptions.

In his first NFL game, McAfee stunned Green Bay with a 93-yard kickoff return, a touchdown run and a TD pass. His first two years were filled with big plays—stirring punt and kickoff returns, interception runbacks, dramatic runs. McAfee scored touchdowns in each of the Bears' championship game wins—and then he was gone, literally, to fight more serious battles in World War II.

He didn't return until 1945 and was limited to six games in his first two seasons back because of injury and sickness. A healthy McAfee still was exciting and dangerous from 1947-50, but his skills had diminished after losing five peak seasons. One lasting memory from his six full campaigns is a 12.8-yard punt return average, a still-standing NFL record.

> ## "The highest compliment you can pay a ballcarrier is just to compare him to McAfee."
>
> —*George Halas*

MIKE MCCORMACK

Born: 6-21-30, Chicago, Ill. **Ht/Wt:** 6-4/250 **College:** Kansas **Drafted:** 1951, 3rd round, Yanks **Primary positions:** OT, DT, LB
Teams: New York Yanks 1951; Browns 1954-62 **Championship teams:** NFL 1954, '55

He protected Otto Graham, opened holes for Jim Brown and performed various leadership roles over nine outstanding seasons under legendary coach Paul Brown. Nobody ruled the Cleveland trenches more skillfully than big-hearted Mike McCormack, a 6-foot-4, 250-pound Irishman who was equal parts diplomat and enforcer. When a big play was needed or a game was on the line, the road to Browns success often ran directly over right tackle.

Brown often referred to his reliable captain as "the finest offensive lineman I ever coached"—a powerful sentiment backed up by many of McCormack's contemporaries. He was surprisingly fast for a big man, allowing him to pull on power sweeps, and he was equally adept at run or pass blocking. Disciplined, smart and dedicated to Brown's team-first philosophy, McCormack provided an extension of his coach on the field and even-keeled leadership in the clubhouse.

Brown thought so much of McCormack that he engineered a stunning 15-player trade in

> **"We could have played Mike at middle linebacker or on the defensive line, but his No. 1 niche was offensive right tackle. He was an excellent pass protector but he could also blow people out of there."**
>
> —*Paul Brown*

1953 to get him—10 Browns for five Baltimore Colts, the team that had evolved over a two-year period from the New York Yanks. McCormack, who had earned the first of six career Pro Bowl selections as a two-way 1951 rookie for the Yanks, was serving a two-year military hitch when he received the news.

The former University of Kansas star was quickly tabbed to replace retired Bill Willis at middle guard, a linebacker in Cleveland's defensive scheme. McCormack was big and fast enough to handle that role for the Browns' 1954 championship team and he even stole the ball from Detroit quarterback Bobby Layne to set up a touchdown in a Cleveland title-game rout. He earned another championship ring as an offensive tackle in 1955 and stayed at that position through his 1962 retirement.

The good-natured Chicagoan, a favorite on the Cleveland after-dinner speakers circuit, later served as a head coach at Philadelphia, Baltimore and Seattle and front-office executive at Seattle and Carolina.

TOMMY MCDONALD

Born: 7-26-34, Roy, N.M. **Ht/Wt:** 5-9/175 **College:** Oklahoma **Drafted:** 1957, 3rd round, Eagles **Primary position:** WR **Career statistics:** Receiving, 495 rec., 8,410 yds., 17.0 avg., 84 TDs; KO Returns, 51 att., 20.7 avg. **Teams:** Eagles 1957-63; Cowboys 1964; Rams 1965-66; Falcons 1967; Browns 1968 **Championship team:** NFL 1960

Like a scared jackrabbit negotiating a thorny briar patch, Tommy McDonald scurried, darted and dashed through 12 breathless and exciting NFL seasons. He was a 5-foot-9, 175-pound quick-strike receiver who could ignite an offense with his enthusiasm and light up a locker room with his boundless energy. Nobody played the game with more zeal than the diminutive kid from New Mexico, who was living proof that football success can come in small packages.

For most of his seven years with the Philadelphia Eagles, McDonald was the go-to target for quarterbacks Norm Van Brocklin and Sonny Jurgensen. Fans marveled at his ability to streak across the middle, make a fingertip catch without losing stride and weave past frustrated tacklers. He was fearless and proud, a tough competitor who took crunching hits, bounced up defiantly and scurried back to the huddle.

One of the last players without a facemask, the colorful McDonald was an incessant talker who needled opponents and constantly lobbied his quarterback for passes. He also

> ## "He's one of the greatest competitors I've ever seen. I've never known anyone with more intense desire."
>
> — *Nick Skorich, Eagles coach, 1961*

flashed his elusiveness on punt and kickoff returns. When the popular McDonald cut off the sleeves of his jersey to "extend my reach," kids throughout Philadelphia could be spotted wearing sleeveless jerseys and practicing his trademark "bounce-up" after hits.

From 1958-60, McDonald caught 115 Van Brocklin passes for 2,250 yards and 32 touchdowns. When Van Brocklin retired after the Eagles' 1960 championship season, McDonald and Jurgensen combined for an even more prolific three-year stretch: 163 catches, 3,021 yards, 31 TDs. His 1,144 yards and 13 touchdown catches led the NFL in 1961; his 237 yards in a 1961 game against the Giants set a still-standing Eagles record.

Amazingly, McDonald missed only three games during a career that included stops at Dallas, Los Angeles, Atlanta and Cleveland before he retired in 1968 with 85 touchdowns, six Pro Bowl selections and a superlative 17-yards-per-catch average. And his professional success followed a dream college career at Oklahoma. With McDonald at halfback, the Sooners never lost a game and won two national championships.

HUGH MCELHENNY

Born: 12-31-28, Los Angeles, Calif. **Ht/Wt:** 6-1/195 **College:** Washington **Drafted:** 1952, 1st round, 49ers **Primary position:** HB
Career statistics: Rushing, 1,124 att., 5,281 yds., 38 TDs; Receiving, 264 rec., 12.3 avg., 20 TDs; Punt Returns, 126 att., 7.3 avg., 2 TDs; KO Returns, 83 att., 23.1 avg. **Teams:** 49ers 1952-60; Vikings 1961-62; Giants 1963; Lions 1964 **Honors:** 1950s All-Decade Team

His broad shoulders tapered gradually to a narrow waist and powerful legs that could stop, start, cut, juke and change direction at the blink of a defender's eyes. When Hugh McElhenny zigged, everybody else often zagged over a magical 13-year NFL career. He was a touchdown waiting to happen, the purest combination of running back speed, power, quickness and instinct ever conceived when he introduced himself to San Francisco fans in 1952.

McElhenny, an every-play breakaway threat, was labeled "the best runner in the history of the National Football League" by then commissioner Bert Bell. To 49ers coach Buck Shaw, his No. 1 draft pick was a perfect complement for fullback Joe Perry in one of the fastest backfields ever assembled. Perry was the explosive ballcarrier, McElhenny the dangerous runner-receiver-return man over a nine-year association that brought fans through the turnstiles and produced combined totals of 10,210 rushing and 3,698 receiving yards.

The 6-foot-1, 195-pounder was at his best in the open field. The 49ers loved to give him the ball on draw plays, screens and swing passes that allowed "The King" to use his quick bursts and wide assortment of feints. Few defenders could deliver a solid open-field blow and McElhenny's terrific peripheral vision allowed him to avoid blind-side threats.

The trick with McElhenny was containment—a difficult prospect over 60 minutes. The Chicago Bears found that out in a 1952 game when McElhenny,

"Hugh McElhenny is the greatest of them all. I played fullback with the (AFL's) Chicago Bulls against Red Grange in five different games. Grange was an elusive but soft runner. McElhenny has a better change of pace, is two seconds faster and more than 20 pounds heavier than Grange, which gives Mac a lot more power."

—Red Strader, 49ers coach, 1955

quiet for most of the day, burned them on a 94-yard punt return. He could go all the way any time and when he wasn't handling the ball, he was a valuable decoy for quarterback Y.A. Tittle.

The former University of Washington star scored 51 of his 60 career touchdowns with the 49ers before making career-ending stops at Minnesota, New York and Detroit. Never a champion, he did reach the 1963 title game with the Giants while serving as a backup. When he retired in 1964, he left with 11,369 combined yards — 5,281 rushing, 3,247 receiving and 2,841 on returns.

JOHNNY MCNALLY (BLOOD)

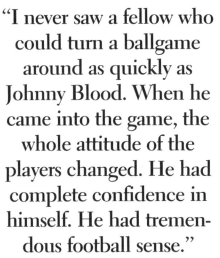

McNALLY

Born: 11-27-03, New Richmond, Wis. **Died:** 11-28-85 **Ht/Wt:** 6-0/185 **College:** St. John's (Min.) **Primary position:** HB, DB **Career statistics:** Scoring, 49 TDs, 296 pts. **Scoring champion:** 1931 **Teams:** Milwaukee Badgers 1925; Duluth Eskimos 1926-27; Pottsville Maroons 1928; Packers 1929-36; Pirates 1937-38 **Championship teams:** NFL 1929, '30, '31, '36 **Honors:** 1930s All-Decade Team

Strong, fast and athletically superior to most of the NFL players he competed against in the 1920s and '30s, Johnny Blood attacked football with the same free-wheeling passion he lived his life. Opponents feared the quick-strike potential of a dangerous playmaker; coaches and teammates endured the clowning and antics of an off-centered personality. Lovable, vexing and unpredictable, the wild man from Wisconsin cut a legendary swath through pro football's formative era.

Born John Victor McNally, he opted for the "Blood" alias to preserve his college eligibility. The name, picked off a marquee advertising a Rudolph Valentino movie, soon became synonymous with big-play heroics and colorful behavior as Blood made early career stops at Milwaukee, Duluth and Pottsville before hooking up with Green Bay. From 1929-36, Blood helped Curly Lambeau's Packers win four championships.

The 6-foot, 185-pound halfback could break open

> "I never saw a fellow who could turn a ballgame around as quickly as Johnny Blood. When he came into the game, the whole attitude of the players changed. He had complete confidence in himself. He had tremendous football sense."
>
> —*Don Hutson, 1963, Sports Illustrated*

games with his speed, slithering runs, acrobatic catches and ballhawking defensive play. He was the exceptional receiver of his era and his special instinct and versatility allowed him to strike as a runner, pass catcher, return man or defender. Blood scored his 49 career touchdowns in every conceivable manner and had an uncanny knack for delivering spectacular plays in game-deciding situations.

Off the field, he was a hard-drinking, Shakespeare-quoting daredevil who disregarded training rules and curfews. He once jumped a 6-foot air shaft, eight stories above an open courtyard, so he could burst dramatically through Lambeau's hotel window. The Packers coach quietly seethed over newspaper accounts of other Blood stunts as well as his occasional on-field clowning and lackadaisical effort. But Blood offset his transgressions by leading the Packers to titles in 1929, '30, '31 and '36.

Blood, who ended his career in 1939 as coach of the Pittsburgh Pirates, completed his college degree at St. John's (Min.)—a quarter century after his graduating class—and later taught economics and history there. He became a charter member of the Pro Football Hall of Fame in 1963.

Player/Year elected: 1964

MIKE MICHALSKE

Born: 4-24-03, Cleveland, Ohio **Died:** 10-26-83 **Ht/Wt:** 6-0/210 **College:** Penn State **Positions:** OG, DG, LB **Teams:** AFL Yankees 1926; NFL Yankees 1927-28; Packers 1929-35, 1937 **Championship teams:** NFL 1929, '30, '31 **Honors:** 1920s All-Decade Team

It was the body, that compact 6-foot, 210-pound mass of muscle that could plow through a brick wall — or a 250-pound opponent. August "Mike" Michalske attacked football from a low center of gravity, whether mixing it up in the trenches or dazzling blockers with his unconventional tactics. The former Penn State All-American was a strong and resourceful two-way guard, a creative contributor to Green Bay teams that won three straight NFL championships from 1929-31.

The former fullback, small for a lineman of any era, attacked defenders low and hard — a broad-based blocker with superior strength, perfect balance and relentless determination. It was difficult to avoid his bull-like charge, almost impossible to move him from side to side. But Michalske was more celebrated for his defensive contributions during pro football's early years.

As a centerpiece for Curly Lambeau's championship Packers teams, Michalske became famous for his blitzing ability as a combination lineman-linebacker. No quarterback or ballcarrier was safe from his lightning charge and Michalske made life even more difficult by working out creative stunts with teammate Cal Hubbard, another future Hall of Famer. The players criss-crossed, set picks, changed positions before the snap — anything to create confusion.

> **"I just didn't get hurt. Don't ask me why. It got so the guys on the team began kidding me about getting paid by the minute."**
>
> *— Mike Michalske*

Michalske's professional career began as a blocker for Red Grange with the New York Yankees of the short-lived American Football League. He played two more seasons with the Yankees (now in the NFL) before signing a free-agent contract with the Packers after the New York team folded. Lambeau considered Michalske so important to Green Bay's success that he paid him more than quarterback Arnie Herber.

Nicknamed "Iron Mike" because of his 60-minute durability over an 11-year pro career, Michalske urged Lambeau to find fullbacks he could convert into guards, taking advantage of their speed and compact explosiveness. Lambeau successfully heeded his advice many times. Michalske, who was born in Cleveland, became the first guard to enter the Ohio-based Hall of Fame in 1964.

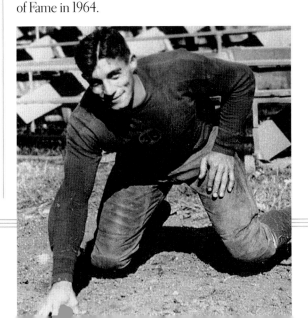

WAYNE MILLNER

Born: 1-31-13, Roxbury, Mass. **Died:** 11-19-76 **Ht/Wt:** 6-0/190 **College:** Notre Dame **Drafted:** 1936, 8th round, Redskins
Primary positions: OE, DE **Career statistics:** Receiving, 124 rec., 12.7 avg., 12 TDs **Teams:** Redskins 1936-41, 1945
Championship team: NFL 1937 **Honors:** 1930s All-Decade Team

Sammy Baugh appreciated his sure hands and quick-strike pass catching abilities. Cliff Battles was thankful for his traffic-clearing blocks. Redskins coach Ray Flaherty liked everything about Wayne Millner, who crafted a rewarding seven-year NFL career around quickness, power, determination and near-perfect instincts as one of the game's last two-way ends.

Flaherty, in fact, was so excited to learn that the Notre Dame All-American had been picked up in the inaugural 1936 draft that he dashed off a telegram to Boston owner George Preston Marshall offering his resignation if the Redskins failed to win the championship. With Millner in the lineup, Battles rushed for 614 yards, the defense allowed 9.2 points per game and the Redskins advanced to the NFL title game, where they lost to Green Bay, 21-6.

Flaherty did return in 1937, the team's first season in Washington, and his Redskins delivered his championship, thanks primarily to the extraordinary passing of rookie quarterback Baugh. His primary target was the 6-foot, 190-pound Millner, who caught nine passes for 160 yards and two electrifying touchdowns (55- and

78-yard strikes) in Washington's 28-21 title game victory over Chicago.

As a receiver, Millner had a knack for finding the open seams in a secondary and enough speed to turn a short pass into a long gainer. He was particularly tough in the clutch, a go-to target when everything was on the line. Millner was fundamentally sound as a blocker and defender who could maneuver bigger opponents out of position with quickness and clever footwork. Opposing quarterbacks and ballcarriers paid the price when their blockers underestimated Millner's explosive charge.

From 1936-41, Millner and Baugh formed a dangerous passing combination from the Redskins' single-wing formation. After three years of military duty in World War II, Millner returned in 1945 for one final season before beginning a long football association as a coach and scout. His career totals of 124 receptions for 1,578 yards were Redskins records when he retired.

> "I always knew if I could get out in the open, Wayne would be there to throw a block for me. It was Wayne's blocks that determined whether or not I would get away for a long run."
>
> —*Cliff Battles, from Richard Whittingham's book,* The Washington Redskins

Millner (right) with teammate Sammy Baugh.

BOBBY MITCHELL

Born: 6-6-35, Hot Springs, Ark. **Ht/Wt:** 6-0/195 **College:** Illinois **Drafted:** 1958, 7th round, Browns **Primary positions:** HB, WR
Career statistics: Rushing, 513 att., 2,735 yds., 18 TDs; Receiving, 521 rec., 7,954 yds., 15.3 avg., 65 TDs; Punt Returns, 69 att., 10.1 avg., 3 TDs; KO Returns, 102 att., 26.4 avg., 5 TDs **Receptions leader:** 1962 **Teams:** Browns 1958-61; Redskins 1962-68

He was pro football's ultimate weapon, a dangerous running back, pass-catching wizard and dazzling return man over 11 electrifying seasons. Nobody personified "big play potential" more than Bobby Mitchell, a two-position star who earned lasting fame for his heart-stopping exploits and historical recognition for his trailblazing efforts as the first black player in Washington history.

Mitchell's versatility was legendary and the numbers he posted spectacular. The speedy 6-footer began his career in 1958 as the four-year backfield mate of Cleveland great Jim Brown; he spent his final seven seasons in Washington as a go-to receiver for Norm Snead and Sonny Jurgensen. Listed among his career exploits are a 232-yard rushing game, 218-yard receiving effort, 98- and 92-yard kickoff returns, 90-yard touchdown run, 99-yard pass play and 78-yard kickoff return.

If not for Brown, the 195-pound Mitchell would have been the centerpiece of a Cleveland offense that had dominated the NFL through much of the 1950s. But Brown handled the primary running load while Mitchell was used in change-of-pace situations and as a receiver out of the backfield. After the 1961 season, coach Paul Brown traded Mitchell to Washington for the draft rights to Syracuse star Ernie Davis—and Mitchell began life anew as a Redskins flanker.

His eye-popping moves and deep-strike speed made him a perfect fit for that role. His quiet, unassuming personality allowed him to endure the slings of discrimination while breaking Washington's color barrier. No longer playing in the shadow of Brown, Mitchell emerged as an exciting playmaker for a franchise badly in need of a talent transfusion.

The former seventh-round draft pick out of Illinois never lacked for excitement. He piled up 14,078 combined yards and scored 91 touchdowns—18 rushing, 65 receiving, 3 on punt returns and 5 on kickoffs. His 72 catches for 1,384 yards led the NFL in 1962; his 1,436 receiving yards led in '63. The four-time Pro Bowl selection served in Washington's front office after his 1968 retirement, retiring as assistant general manager in 2003.

> "He had tremendous speed, the ability to shift his weight without faltering and he could stop and start at full speed. ... (Drafting Mitchell) was really one of the best moves we ever made."
>
> —*Paul Brown*

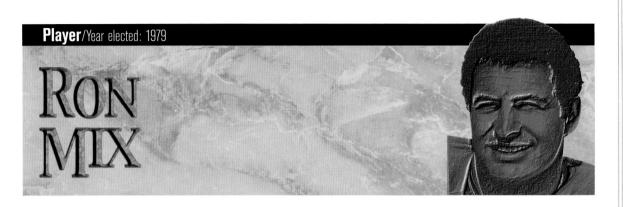

RON MIX

Born: 3-10-38, Los Angeles, Calif. **Ht/Wt:** 6-4/255 **College:** USC **Drafted:** 1960, 1st round, AFL Patriots; 1st round, NFL Colts
Primary position: OT **Teams:** Chargers 1960-69; Raiders 1971 **Championship team:** AFL 1963 **Honors:** All-Time AFL Team

Like any "Intellectual Assassin," Ron Mix put a lot of thought into his craft. Then he suited up and took care of physical responsibilities in a decade-long quest to make the pro football world safe for Chargers running backs. Mix was a charmer and destroyer, a contradictory and finely tuned giant who earned respect as the premier offensive tackle in American Football League history.

From 1960-69, the 6-foot-4, 255-pound Californian provided an anchor for Sid Gillman's high-powered Los Angeles and San Diego Chargers offenses. Mix was big and fast, a quick-strike artist who could blow defensive ends away from the hole or pull on power sweeps. Defenders marveled at his every-play intensity and the multi-hit determination that kept rushers away from his quarterback.

San Diego fans remember Paul Lowe's

dramatic 58-yard touchdown run in the Chargers' 51-10 AFL championship game win over Boston in 1963. What they might not have noticed is a pulling Mix escorting his back downfield, mowing down three different Patriots without ever leaving his feet. Early in Mix's career, he was a no-frills pounder; he evolved into one of the game's most fundamentally sound technicians.

Mix, who was assessed only two holding penalties in his entire career, debunked the stereotype of football linemen as grunting, monosyllabic giants. He was articulate, personable and intelligent, a handsome, broad-shouldered physical specimen who would later become an attorney. Mix, who played collegiately at USC in his native Los Angeles, had planned to play only long enough to get a stake, but his love for the game grew as his skills improved.

"When you're running behind Mix, it's like you're a little kid and your big brother is protecting you from the wolves."

—*Paul Lowe, former Chargers running back*

Mix, who played in five of the first six AFL championship games, retired after the 1969 season but made a one-season comeback with the Oakland Raiders in 1971. When he left the game for good, Mix claimed distinction as an eight-time AFL All-Star and nine-time All-AFL tackle. He later was named to the All-Time AFL team.

JOE MONTANA

Born: 6-11-56, New Eagle, Pa. **Ht/Wt:** 6-2/200 **College:** Notre Dame **Drafted:** 1979, 3rd round, 49ers **Position:** QB **Career statistics:** Passing, 3,409-of-5,391, 40,551 yds., 273 TDs; Rushing, 1,676 yds., 20 TDs **Teams:** 49ers 1979-90, 1992; Chiefs 1993-94 **Super Bowl champions:** 1981 (MVP), '84 (MVP), '88, '89 (MVP) seasons **Honors:** 75th Anniversary All-Time Team; 1980s All-Decade Team

His gunslinger name fit the cool, calculating manner in which he shot down opposing defenses. It was part of the Joe Montana charisma, a mystique that permeated the NFL for 15 successful seasons. He was the blond, blue-eyed kid from Notre Dame who revived a franchise, carved out a Super Bowl legacy and built a reputation as the greatest pressure quarterback of all time.

Montana was a football surgeon, an artist who could carve up a defense with patience and relentless precision. His arm strength and speed were only slightly above average, but his quick feet and quicker mind were perfect matches for San Francisco and coach Bill Walsh's

> "I just hope now they'll stop saying, 'He's right up there with the best.' He's the greatest big-game player I've seen, period."
>
> —*Randy Cross, former 49ers center, after Super Bowl XXIII*

complicated short-passing offense. He had a sixth sense that allowed him to evade rushers and he could throw on the run with uncanny, mistake-free accuracy.

Montana, who piled up big yardage, high completion percentages and victories while throwing to Jerry Rice and a host of other talented receivers in the 1980s, might have combined all aspects of quarterback play better than anyone in history. He was a great passer (40,551 yards in his career, 5,772 more in postseason play), a dangerous scrambler (1,676 yards, 20 touchdowns), a masterful play-caller and an unquestioned leader.

Montana took the postseason-starved 49ers to four Super Bowls, won them all and claimed a record three Super Bowl game MVPs. He threw 122 Super Bowl passes without an interception and posted a record six 300-yard postseason passing games. The image of Montana executing a near-perfect drive in the final moments of a big game will forever be etched in the fabric of NFL history.

Super Joe led 31 fourth-quarter comeback victories, including playoffs, and his late-game heroics lifted teammates to higher performance levels. With a game on the line, Montana had no peer. When the eight-time Pro Bowl selection left San Francisco after an almost two-year layoff with elbow problems, he came back and led Kansas City to the AFC championship game before retiring in 1994.

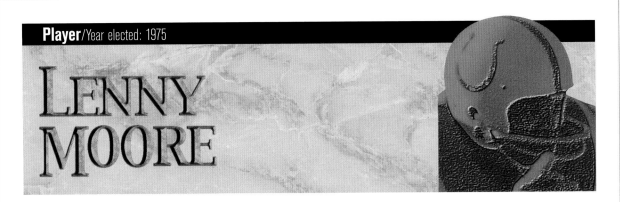

LENNY MOORE

Born: 11-25-33, Reading, Pa. **Ht/Wt:** 6-1/191 **College:** Penn State **Drafted:** 1956, 1st round, Colts **Primary positions:** HB, WR
Career statistics: Rushing, 1,068 att., 5,174 yds., 63 TDs; Receiving, 363 rec., 6,039 yds., 16.6 avg., 48 TDs; KO Returns, 18 att., 25.2 avg. **Scoring champion:** NFL 1964 **Teams:** Colts 1956-67 **Championship teams:** NFL 1958, '59 **Honors:** 1950s All-Decade Team

Now you see him, now you don't. That was the magic of Lenny Moore, who bobbed, dipped, weaved and twisted his way through NFL defenses for 12 successful seasons. The speedy Rocket from Reading, Pa., was a master of deception, whether taking a handoff or catching a pass from Baltimore quarterback Johnny Unitas—a combination that cut a swath through the team's record books from 1956-67.

At first glance, Moore was an unlikely candidate to cut swaths through anything. He stood 6-foot-1 and carried 191 pounds on spindly legs that looked like they might snap at first contact. But the body proved to be as durable as the yardage totals he would pile up— first as a combination flanker/halfback and later as a runner who could catch passes out of the backfield. He finished his career with 12,393 combined yards (running, receiving and returns) and 113 touchdowns, which ranked second only to Jim Brown's 126 for a number of years.

The secret to Moore's durability was a shifty, jitterbug running style that kept tacklers from making solid contact. He would catch Unitas slants over the middle, make two or three lightning-quick moves and end

> ## "A tackler just never gets a good shot. His feet go up and down so fast you can hardly see them hit the ground." —*Gino Marchetti*

up with another big gainer. Or he could go deep with his sprinter speed, a threat that complemented Raymond Berry's talents as a possession receiver. As a halfback, he would dart into the line, legs always pumping, and suddenly break free, like a spider going in 10 different directions.

The former Penn State star, who was called "Slats" because of the way he taped the top of his high-top shoes, enjoyed his best season in 1958, when he totaled 1,536 rushing-receiving yards and 14 touchdowns for the NFL-champion Colts. He added 1,268 yards and eight touchdowns a year later before catching a 59-yard TD strike from Unitas in a championship game win over New York.

The seven-time Pro Bowl selection, who once scored touchdowns in a league-record 18 straight games, put together his last big season in 1964 when he scored a league-leading 20 TDs.

MOORE

MARION MOTLEY

Born: 6-5-20, Leesburg, Ga. **Died:** 6-27-99 **Ht/Wt:** 6-1/232 **College:** South Carolina State, Nevada-Reno **Drafted:** Undrafted **Primary positions:** FB, LB **Career statistics:** Rushing AAFC, 489 att., 3,024 yds., 6.2 avg., 26 TDs; Rushing NFL 339 att., 1,696 yds., 5.0 avg., 5 TDs **Rushing champion:** NFL 1950 **Teams:** AAFC Browns 1946-49; NFL Browns 1950-53; Steelers 1955 **Championship teams:** AAFC 1946, '47, '48, '49; NFL 1950 **Honors:** 75th Anniversary All-Time Team; 1940s All-Decade Team

His football destiny was charted at Canton, Ohio, in the 1930s and fulfilled many years later in the same city. Somewhere between his childhood and Hall of Fame election, Marion Motley discovered that superior athletic abilities could carry him to lasting fame as a social pioneer and a great fullback. But his ticket to greatness would not come without a price.

Motley, a hulking 6-foot-1, 232-pound bulldozer, made his professional debut with the Cleveland Browns of the newly formed All-America Football Conference in 1946, joining teammate Bill Willis as the first blacks in the pro game since the early 1930s. Although they endured untold hardships and bigotry in the months preceding the 1947 baseball debut of Jackie Robinson, they never received equal credit for their social breakthroughs.

So Motley made a different kind of impact on the field. A rookie at age 26, he became a

one-man wrecking crew for the talented Paul Brown-constructed team that would dominate the AAFC and NFL over his eight Cleveland seasons. Motley was a human freight train when he carried the ball on sweeps or up the middle on his patented draws and trap plays. He was a relentless blocker on runs, a one-man wall for quarterback Otto Graham on passes and a capable receiver. He also was an outstanding linebacker and kickoff-return man in the AAFC.

When the Browns were accepted into the NFL in 1950, opponents got their first look at the new-era fullback—a blocker and elusive runner instead of a traditional line plunger. They designed defenses to stop him, but he still led the league in rushing. In one amazing game, Motley rushed for 188 yards on 11 carries, a whopping 17.09-yards-per-carry average.

When Motley retired after the 1953 season (he made a brief 1955 comeback for Pittsburgh), he had compiled a 5.7-yard rushing average in the AAFC/NFL and his teams had won five league championships and lost in the title game three times.

> **"I tackled Motley head-on (on the first day of the Browns' 1946 training camp). I felt like I was being hit by a truck. He had huge thighs. From that point on, I tried to tackle him from the side, drag him down. He was a load."**
>
> *—Lou Groza*

MIKE MUNCHAK

Born: 3-5-60, Scranton, Pa. **Ht/Wt:** 6-3/281 **College:** Penn State **Drafted:** 1982, 1st round, Oilers **Primary position:** OG
Teams: Oilers 1982-93 **Honors:** 1980s All-Decade Team

Watching Mike Munchak carry out a blocking assignment was like viewing a well choreographed how-to video. Every movement was exact, every detail of the play scientifically analyzed by the NFL's premier offensive line technician. Failure to execute was never an option for the 6-foot-3, 281-

> "I looked over at practice every day to see what Munch was doing. There was a built-in standard of excellence for me. I consider myself a high achiever, and I didn't have to look far to see what I wanted to achieve."
>
> —*Bruce Matthews, 2001, The Associated Press*

pound blocking machine over an amazingly consistent 12-year career with the Houston Oilers.

Nobody spent more hours in the weight and film rooms than Munchak, who approached his offensive guard duties like a head coach dissecting his next opponent. He didn't just concentrate on the player he might be blocking; he learned the strengths and weaknesses of every defender—the better to recognize blitzes, tell-tale rushing patterns and other helpful nuances. He was as fanatical in execution as he was in preparation.

Oilers strength and conditioning coach Steve Watterson described Munchak's blocking fundamentals as almost robotic. For a huge, well muscled man, he had a low center of gravity with powerful legs and quickness that allowed him to maneuver defenders away from the hole. But Munchak was at his best as a textbook pass blocker who could stand up a rusher and take him out of the play.

The former Penn State star, a first-round draft pick in 1982, became an instant starter for the Oilers—a prelude to the 1983 arrival of bookend guard Bruce Matthews. When quarterback Warren Moon arrived in 1984, the foundation was in place for a high-powered passing offense that would lead the team to seven straight playoff appearances from 1987-93 under coaches Jerry Glanville and Jack Pardee.

Bright, articulate and always ready to share knowledge with teammates, Munchak was the epitome of focus and intensity when he stepped on the field. He seldom said anything during his 159 career games, preferring to speak with actions that earned him nine Pro Bowl selections. The kid from Scranton, Pa., who retired in 1993 after nine knee surgeries and chronic shoulder problems, is the current offensive line coach for the Tennessee Titans.

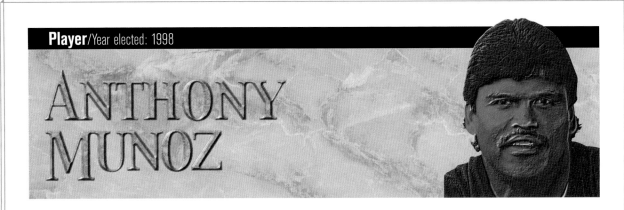

ANTHONY MUNOZ

Born: 8-19-58, Ontario, Calif. **Ht/Wt:** 6-6/278 **College:** USC **Drafted:** 1980, 1st round, Bengals **Primary position:** OT
Teams: Bengals 1980-92 **Honors:** 75th Anniversary All-Time Team; 1980s All-Decade Team; All-Time NFL Team

He was a human avalanche, 278 pounds of beef caving in on a helpless defender. When Anthony Munoz attacked, the physical onslaught continued until somebody was on the ground. The Cincinnati Bengals' Raging Bull snorted and pawed his way through the NFL for 13 outstanding seasons, drawing near-universal praise as the best offensive tackle in the game's history.

The 6-foot-6 former USC star was an intimidating physical presence. But the neanderthal body also moved around the field with surprising quickness and agility. "His head alone weighs 200 pounds," marveled one scout on draft day in 1980, but the secret to Munoz's success was the huge, powerful legs that gave him the leverage to move any defensive end he might face. He played offense with the attack mentality of a defender.

Not surprisingly, the Bengals directed their power running attack over tackle through most of the 1980s, piling up league-best rushing totals in 1988 and '89.

Munoz also cleared a path to Super Bowl appearances after the 1981 and 1988 seasons — both of which

> ## "Anthony Munoz was the epitome of what an NFL offensive lineman should be. I've never seen one better."
>
> —*Mike McCormack*

ended in close losses to the San Francisco 49ers. James Brooks and Ickey Woods became 1,000-yard rushers while following the blocks of the big Californian.

Finesse was not part of Munoz's game. He drove some defenders 10 yards off the line, waffled others into submission and guarded quarterbacks Ken Anderson and Boomer Esiason like a protective big brother. Munoz's quickness, toughness and consistency impressed coaches, teammates and opponents, earning him 11 straight Pro Bowl invitations and gushing testimonials.

The ferocious dedication he exhibited on the field was contrasted by the quiet, polite, unassuming personality that won him friends and praise throughout the Cincinnati community. When he won the NFL's prestigious Man of the Year award in 1991, a smile lit up the normally scowling face. When he retired after the 1992 season, a different kind of smile could be seen on the faces of most NFL defensive coordinators, who had never seen the charitable side of big No. 78.

GEORGE MUSSO

Born: 4-8-10, Collinsville, Ill. **Died:** 9-5-2000 **Ht/Wt:** 6-2/270 **College:** Millikin **Primary positions:** OG, OT, DG **Teams:** Bears 1933-44 **Championship teams:** NFL 1933, '40, '41, '43

He was THE Monster of the Midway, the biggest, baddest and most intimidating of the Chicago Bears who dominated the NFL from 1933-44. Competing against George Musso was like trying to wrestle a starving 270-pound gorilla. He was king of the trenches and anchor of a 12-year dynasty, the man most likely to succeed in any one-on-one or two-on-one battle.

"George was the outstanding lineman of his time," said former Washington coach Ray Flaherty, who marveled at Musso's unusual combination of size and speed. On offense, he excelled as a run-blocking tackle or guard who could pull on sweeps while clearing holes for the likes of Bronko Nagurski, Red Grange, George McAfee and Sid Luckman. On defense, he was the impenetrable wall in the middle of the line, the literal stopping point for most opposing runners.

But there was much more to Musso than intimidation and toughness. He was affectionately known by teammates as "Big Bear" and coach George Halas looked to him for clubhouse chemistry. "He was a great team leader," said Halas, who relied on Musso as his longtime captain and even asked him to deliver big-game pep talks. His fired-up teammates usually responded.

Musso, a star for tiny Millikin College in 1932,

> "George was one of the finest guards ever in professional football. He was tough, mobile, agile and intimidating, with an indomitable competitive spirit."
>
> *—George Halas*

almost was cut by Halas during a 1933 tryout. But Big Bear persevered, Papa Bear relented and the Chicago Bears prospered. Playing on a line that matched him with such future Hall of Famers as end Bill Hewitt, tackle Joe Stydahar and guard/tackle Bulldog Turner, Musso helped the Bears power their way to NFL championships in 1933, 1940, 1941 and 1943 and title-game losses in 1934, 1937 and 1942.

Over Musso's career, the Bears compiled an amazing 104-26-6 record, winning seven Western Division titles. The impressive 60-minute star also holds distinction as the only person to play football against two future presidents— Ronald Reagan, a guard for Eureka College in 1929, and Gerald Ford, when the Bears played the College All-Stars in 1935.

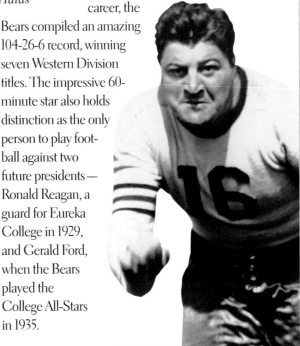

BRONKO NAGURSKI

Born: 11-3-08, Rainy River, Ontario **Died:** 1-7-90 **Ht/Wt:** 6-2/226 **College:** Minnesota **Primary positions:** FB, DT, LB **Career statistics:** Rushing, 633 att., 2,778 yds., 4.4 avg., 25 TDs; Passing, 32-of-77, 474 yds., 7 TDs **Teams:** Bears 1930-37, 1943
Championship teams: NFL 1932, '33, '43 **Honors:** 75th Anniversary All-Time Team; 1930s All-Decade Team

Bronko Nagurski was the stuff of which legends are made — a Bunyanesque fullback who journeyed from a farm near Rainy River, Canada, to national acclaim as a two-position All-American at the University of Minnesota and folk-hero status with the Chicago Bears. The rock-solid 6-foot-2, 226-pounder was bigger than most linemen of his era, a human steamroller with massive arms and hands, a size-19 neck and powerful shoulders that punished tacklers.

Nagurski bulled his way through the NFL with head down, legs churning and bodies flying. It often took four defenders to make a tackle: two to grab hold and slow him down, one to knock him off balance and another to finish him off. He also was a devastating defensive tackle/linebacker and one of the great 60-minute

> "When you blocked for Bronko, you either threw a good block or you got out of the way. If you didn't, Bronko would run right up your back."
>
> *— George Musso*

players of all time.

Born Bronislaw Nagurski in 1908, he adopted the more colorful "Bronko" and rode it to stardom. His career rushing total of 2,778 yards could have been considerably higher if Bears coach George Halas had not valued him as a powerful blocker for the other thoroughbred backs he had stockpiled on his roster. Halas also loved the havoc Nagurski created on defense.

Lost in the shadow of Nagurski's reputation as the ultimate power runner was his ability as a pioneer passer. It was Nagurski who made the championship-securing touchdown pass to Red Grange in a 1932 indoor playoff battle against Portsmouth, and he came back in the NFL's first official championship game a year later to throw for two TDs in a Chicago victory over New York. Nobody could dominate a game so thoroughly.

The man who came to symbolize the raw power and brute force of professional football played from 1930-37, when he left the Bears in a salary dispute with Halas. He returned six years later to help the war-strapped Bears and contributed a touchdown run in their 1943 championship game win over Washington. Nagurski became a Hall of Fame charter member in 1963.

JOE NAMATH

Born: 5-31-43, Beaver Falls, Pa. **Ht/Wt:** 6-2/200 **College:** Alabama **Drafted:** 1965, 1st round, AFL Jets; 1st round, NFL Cardinals
Primary position: QB **Career statistics:** Passing, 1,886-of-3,762, 27,663 yds., 173 TDs; Rushing, 140 yds., 7 TDs **Teams:** Jets 1965-76; Rams 1977 **Championship team:** AFL 1968 **Super Bowl champion:** 1968 (MVP) season **Honors:** All-Time AFL Team

There were imperfections: A stoop-shouldered slouch, spindly legs and knees held together by rubber bands. But the rest of Joe Willie Namath was a masterpiece, from his long black hair, million-dollar smile and white shoes to the roguish charm he dispensed in large doses. And there was that arm, the weapon he used to win over fans and slay opponents for 13 seasons, all but one at center stage with the New York Jets.

Brash, bold, cocky, flamboyant, stylish — all the adjectives applied to Broadway Joe, who never met a party he didn't like or a defensive back he couldn't beat. The skinny 6-foot-2 kid from Alabama captured the heart of New Yorkers when he rejected NFL overtures in 1965 and signed a stunning contract with the

AFL's Jets, and he shocked the football world four years later when he took the Jets to Super Bowl III, brashly predicted a victory over heavily-favored Baltimore — and delivered.

That victory captured the essence of Namath, the fun-loving playboy who brought instant respect to the AFL and credibility to the still-young Super Bowl series. He was that rare athlete who affected the game in ways that far exceeded his accomplishments. Everybody remembers the leadership, clever play-calling and excitement he brought to the field, but it was the superstar aura, the near-perfect form, the needle-threading passes and the confident swagger that set him apart.

Namath's Super Bowl moment was complement-

> "People ask me all the time (about Namath). I tell them whatever you hear about his football ability, multiply it; whatever you hear about his night life, divide it. ... He's as dedicated a football player as I've ever met. He doesn't believe he can be beaten, even if the score is 28-0."
>
> *—Don Maynard, 1972*

ed by a steady stream of 300- and 400-yard passing games. When he sandwiched the first 4,000-yard passing season in NFL history (1967) between two 3,000-yard campaigns, fans gasped in amazement. Nothing, it seemed, was beyond the reach of his powerful right arm.

But the bad knees and other injuries took their toll, as did weak Jets teams that failed to post a winning record after 1969. After an injury-plagued 1977 season with the Los Angeles Rams, the five-time Pro Bowl selection retired with 27,663 passing yards and 173 TD passes.

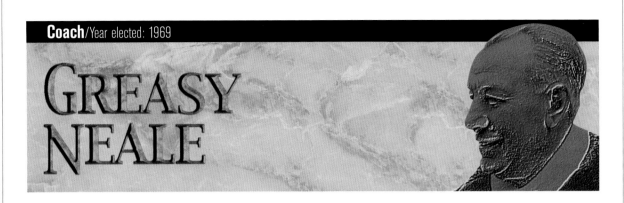

Coach/Year elected: 1969

GREASY NEALE

Born: 11-5-1891, Parkersburg, W. Va. **Died:** 11-2-73 **Teams coached (63-43-5 RS, 3-1 PS):** Eagles 1941-50
Championship teams: 1948, '49

It was a rite of winter: White-haired, coatless Greasy Neale, pacing to and fro on the Philadelphia sideline, gesturing angrily toward players, yelling indignantly at officials and bemoaning, for everybody to hear, the injustice of life — and football — in general. The tone of his booming voice and the half scowl on his long, thin face suggested, usually inaccurately, that his team was losing.

The Eagles didn't do that all too often from 1944-49, when the irascible Neale was guiding them to a 48-16-3 record, three Eastern Division titles and consecutive NFL championships. Behind the argumentative exterior of the always colorful West Virginian was an innovative mind belonging to one of the most clever offensive strategists in NFL history.

Neale, one of the first coaches to recognize the possibilities of George Halas' T-formation, built his offense around quarterback Tommy Thompson, ends Jack Ferrante and Pete Pihos and bruising running

> **"I think I was a success as a coach because I wasn't afraid to borrow something that worked for someone else. People in the stands never asked you where you got it. They only want to know if you got it."** — *Greasy Neale*

back Steve Van Buren. He added wrinkles — the triple reverse, fake reverses — and implemented the famed Eagle Defense (a predecessor to the 4-3) that would dominate the NFL for three seasons. The 1948 and '49 Eagles became the first NFL team to post consecutive title-game shutouts.

Neale's NFL coaching legacy evolved from an unusual career that included eight seasons as a major league outfielder for Cincinnati (1916-22, '24) and successful coaching stops at six colleges. His greatest baseball highlight was the .357 average he posted in the Reds' scandal-marred 1919 World Series win over the Chicago White Sox; his greatest college feat was coaching Washington & Jefferson College to a 0-0 tie with powerful California in the 1922 Rose Bowl. Neale also played and coached in the pre-1920s semipro and professional football leagues under an assumed name.

Neale's star finally faded in 1950 when his aging defending champions struggled to a 6-6 record and lost twice to NFL newcomer Cleveland — the team that had won all four titles in the disbanded All-America Football Conference. Neale was fired with a 10-year record of 63-43-5.

Neale (right) with players Steve Van Buren (left) and Al Wistert.

ERNIE NEVERS

Born: 6-11-03, Willow River, Min. **Died:** 5-3-76 **Ht/Wt:** 6-0/205 **College:** Stanford **Primary positions:** FB, LB, K **Career statistics:** Rushing, 38 TDs; Passing, 25 TDs; Scoring, 7 FG, 52 PAT, 301 pts. **Scoring champion:** 1929 **Teams:** Duluth Eskimos 1926-27; Cardinals 1929-31 **Honors:** 1920s All-Decade Team

The golden-blond hair, ruggedly handsome face and sculpted 205-pound hardbody were perfect accessories for football's classic 60-minute warrior. But the Ernie Nevers legend was better defined by his deep-rooted intensity and insatiable competitive hunger. Nobody could dominate a game more thoroughly than the do-everything fullback who gained stature as a 1920s marquee rival for Jim Thorpe and Red Grange.

Nevers might have been the best runner-passer-kicker-blocker-tackler combination the game has ever produced. He was a dangerous single-wing offensive threat and hard-hitting linebacker who controlled opponents with sideline-to-sideline speed. There seemingly was nothing the 6-foot Minnesotan could not do and no ends to which he wouldn't go to succeed.

In the 1925 Rose Bowl while playing for Stanford, Nevers rushed for more than 100 yards on two broken ankles in a 27-10 loss to Notre Dame. In his 1926 NFL rookie season for Duluth, the Eskimos played a brutal 29-game exhibition and regular-season schedule to showcase Nevers and he played all but 29 of a possible 1,740 minutes. On Thanksgiving Day in 1929 for the Chicago Cardinals, he scored a still-standing NFL-record 40 points in a 40-6 win over the Chicago Bears.

> ## "He was better than Jim Thorpe. He had more desire and determination and could do a lot of things Thorpe couldn't."
>
> — *Pop Warner*

The thick shoulders and classic athleticism belied the open, almost docile friendliness with which Nevers approached life. Soft-spoken and modest off the field, he was hard-edged and ferocious when showcasing his multi-sport talents — five NFL seasons, three as a major league pitcher for the St. Louis Browns, one as an early era professional basketball player in Chicago. Nevers surrendered two home runs to Babe Ruth during the New York Yankee star's 60-homer explosion in 1927.

Nevers' 1926 ironman routine was followed by a second Duluth season, a year off because of a back injury and three years with the Cardinals, two as player-coach. Despite his short NFL career, the Blond Bull was honored as a charter member of the Pro Football Hall of Fame in 1963.

OZZIE NEWSOME

Born: 3-16-56, Muscle Shoals, Ala. **Ht/Wt:** 6-2/230 **College:** Alabama **Drafted:** 1978, 1st round, Browns **Primary position:** TE
Career statistics: Receiving, 662 rec., 7,980 yds., 47 TDs **Teams:** Browns 1978-90 **Honors:** 1980s All-Decade Team

Ozzie Newsome's road to the Hall of Fame was not paved with yellow bricks and it passed through the giant-infested NFL, not a place filled with Munchkins. But that didn't diminish the accomplishments of this real, live "Wizard of Oz," whose fantasy-like career helped define the football personality of a city and redefine the position he played.

Newsome was a wide receiver trapped in a tight end's body. So Cleveland coach Sam Rutigliano drafted the 6-foot-2, 230-pound Alabama wideout in 1978 and introduced him to a new position. In his first professional game, the first time Newsome touched the ball, he sprinted 33 yards for a touchdown on a reverse. Soon he was a favorite target of quarterback Brian

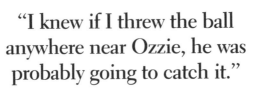

> ## "I knew if I threw the ball anywhere near Ozzie, he was probably going to catch it."
>
> — *Bernie Kosar, 1999, The Associated Press*

Sipe in the Browns' "Kardiac Kids" passing attack.

Only contemporary San Diego tight end Kellen Winslow could match Newsome's combination of size and speed. A position that traditionally had required blocking skills became a focal point in Cleveland's sophisticated offense and Newsome often overmatched the linebackers assigned to cover him. He had big, soft hands, uncanny leaping ability and instincts to work the middle of the field. If Sipe or Bernie Kosar threw the ball anywhere near Newsome, he would go and get it.

The likable, always-professional Oz bridged two exciting eras of Cleveland football. When the Kardiac Kids fell short on Sipe's infamous "Red Right 88" end zone interception in a 1980 playoff loss to Oakland, Newsome was the intended receiver. When the Kosar-led Browns fell one win short of Super Bowls in 1986, '87 and '89, he was front and center. As frustrated Browns fans suffered, Newsome's popularity never waned.

Over 13 Cleveland seasons, he caught a then tight end-record 662 passes for 7,980 yards and 47 touchdowns. He led the Browns in receiving five straight years, posted two 1,000-yard seasons and caught at least one pass in 150 straight games. Sometimes lost in the shuffle was his durability. Newsome, a three-time Pro Bowl selection, played in 198 of a possible 201 games before retiring in 1990.

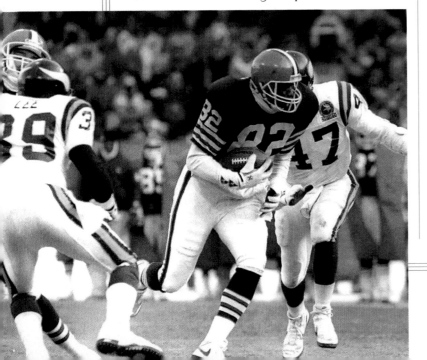

Player/Year elected: 1978

RAY NITSCHKE

Born: 12-29-36, Elmwood Park, Ill. **Died:** 3-8-98 **Ht/Wt:** 6-3/235 **College:** Illinois **Drafted:** 1958, 3rd round, Packers **Position:** LB
Career statistics: Interceptions, 25, 2 TDs **Teams:** Packers 1958-72 **Championship teams:** NFL 1961, '62, '65, '66, '67 **Super Bowl champions:** 1966, '67 seasons **Honors:** 75th Anniversary All-Time Team; 50th Anniversary Team; 1960s All-Decade Team

Forget the rumors: Ray Nitschke never ate barbed wire or spit nails. Nor could he take responsibility for many other outrageous stories that circulated throughout his 15-year NFL career. Nitschke's legacy, however, is based on legendary feats and it's tightly intertwined with Vince Lombardi's Green Bay Packers—a team he led to five championships (including victories in the first two Super Bowls) over a seven-year period of the 1960s.

Off the field, Nitschke was a tall, balding, intelligent, thoughtful and conservative businessman, complete with horn-rimmed glasses and traditional suit. On the field, he was a ferocious, no-nonsense, body-slamming middle linebacker, eyes blazing from inside a battered helmet and venom spewing from his toothless snarl. The 6-foot-3, 235-pound Nitschke who entertained rabid Green Bay fans on Sunday afternoons had the strength, quickness, lateral speed and toughness to back up the animalistic aura that intimidated opponents.

To say the former University of Illinois star was

> **"Ray's the core of the Packers. He's such an inspiration. He's a real hustler and talker. He gives 100 percent all the time."**
>
> —*Bill Pellington, former Colts linebacker*

the heart of the Packers' defense during the team's glory years is an understatement. Nitschke inspired greatness among teammates with his all-out hustle, never-wavering enthusiasm and leader-by-example mentality. He played mean and his reputation as one of the greatest run-stuffing linebackers of all time was well deserved. He also was a cat-like pass defender who rattled receivers and ran back 25 interceptions for 385 yards.

The image of a scowling Nitschke, blood spattered on his No. 66 uniform and white tape wrapped tightly around various parts of his body to hide and protect numerous injuries, will live long in Green Bay football lore. So will the role he played as the leader of a defense that led the NFL in fewest points allowed during three of the Packers' five championship seasons.

Curiously, he was selected for only one Pro Bowl over his outstanding career. But he did earn MVP honors in the 1962 title game and claimed a spot on the NFL's 75th Anniversary All-Time Team selected in 1969.

"If (the 49ers) had played (the Steelers) with the rules in effect that governed the game in the '70s, no way we'd beat them. No way anybody would. They were too good defensively."

—*Bill Walsh, 1993, Cleveland Plain Dealer*

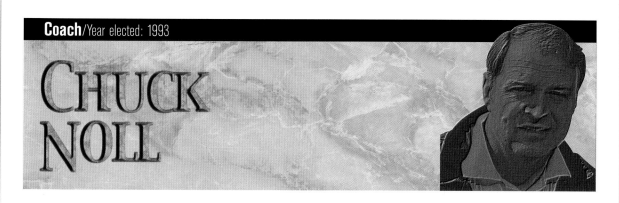

Coach/Year elected: 1993

CHUCK NOLL

Born: 1-5-32, Cleveland, Ohio **Ht/Wt:** 6-1/220 **College:** Dayton **Drafted:** 1953, 20th round, Browns **Primary positions:** LB, OG
Teams played: Browns 1953-59 **Championship teams:** NFL 1954, '55 **Teams coached (193-148-1 RS, 16-8 PS):** Steelers
1969-91 **Super Bowl champions:** 1974, '75, '78, '79 seasons **Honors:** 1980s All-Decade Team

Dull, bland and passionately reticent, Chuck Noll worked hard to avoid the spotlight he so justly deserved. He was the quietly efficient coaching genius of the 1970s, the tactical wizard behind the Steel Curtain who redefined the football aspirations of a forlorn franchise. The Pittsburgh Steelers transformed from lamentable losers to four-time Super Bowl champions under Noll, who could run but never hide from his 23-year winning legacy.

Noll considered himself a teacher and builder and his successful career was forged through shrewd drafts, expert talent evaluation and his ability to tap into player strengths. He was a technician and organization man, not comfortable patting players on the back but unflinchingly fair. Motivation, he believed, was a player responsibility and he filled his rosters with "self-starters."

Noll-planned drafts in 1969 and the early 1970s produced such players as Joe Greene, L.C. Greenwood, Mel Blount, Jack Ham, Dwight White, Mike Wagner and Jack Lambert for his impenetrable Steel Curtain defenses; Terry Bradshaw, Franco Harris, Lynn Swann, John Stallworth and Mike Webster for his efficient ball-control offenses. From 1972-79, the Steelers were 88-27-1 and won seven AFC Central titles; in the six-year span from 1974-79, they dominated the NFL and won four Super Bowls.

Noll played for two Paul Brown championship teams in his hometown Cleveland (1954, '55) and served as an assistant under Chargers coach Sid Gillman and Baltimore's Don Shula. His first Steelers team in 1969 finished 1-13. But soon the Steelers were improving, thanks to the influx of strong, fast, hard-hitting young players molded into a confident and disciplined unit by the grim but ever-upbeat Noll.

Off the field, he was a gourmet cook, gardener and pilot who enjoyed fine wine, classical music, literature and scuba diving. On the field, his passion was in the preparation and execution of game plans, not the spoils of winning. The enigmatic Noll remained true to that passion through the 1991 season, when he retired with a 193-148-1 record and 16-8 mark in 12 playoff appearances.

LEO NOMELLINI

Born: 6-19-24, Lucca, Italy **Died:** 10-17-2000 **Ht/Wt:** 6-3/264 **College:** Minnesota **Drafted:** 1950, 1st round, 49ers **Primary positions:** OT, DT **Teams:** 49ers 1950-63 **Honors:** 50th Anniversary Team; 1950s All-Decade Team

His oak tree-like forearms were extensions of thick, powerful shoulders that could squeeze any obstacle into quick submission. Life never seemed complicated for big, hulking Leo Nomellini, who bulldozed and head-slapped his way through 14 ironman seasons as a premier mover and shaker in the football trenches. Leo the Lion is most fondly remembered as one of the game's last 60-minute performers and one of the San Francisco 49ers' first superstars.

Nobody could match the combination of physical strength and intimidation the 6-foot-3, 264-pounder brought to the NFL from 1950-63. He was a superbly conditioned two-way tackle with speed, agility and animal-like reflexes that allowed him to overpower or outfinesse frustrated opponents. He could attack a defensive end with a bull-like charge one play, zip around him on the next. Offensively, Nomellini was a pile-driving blocker and dedicated pass protector.

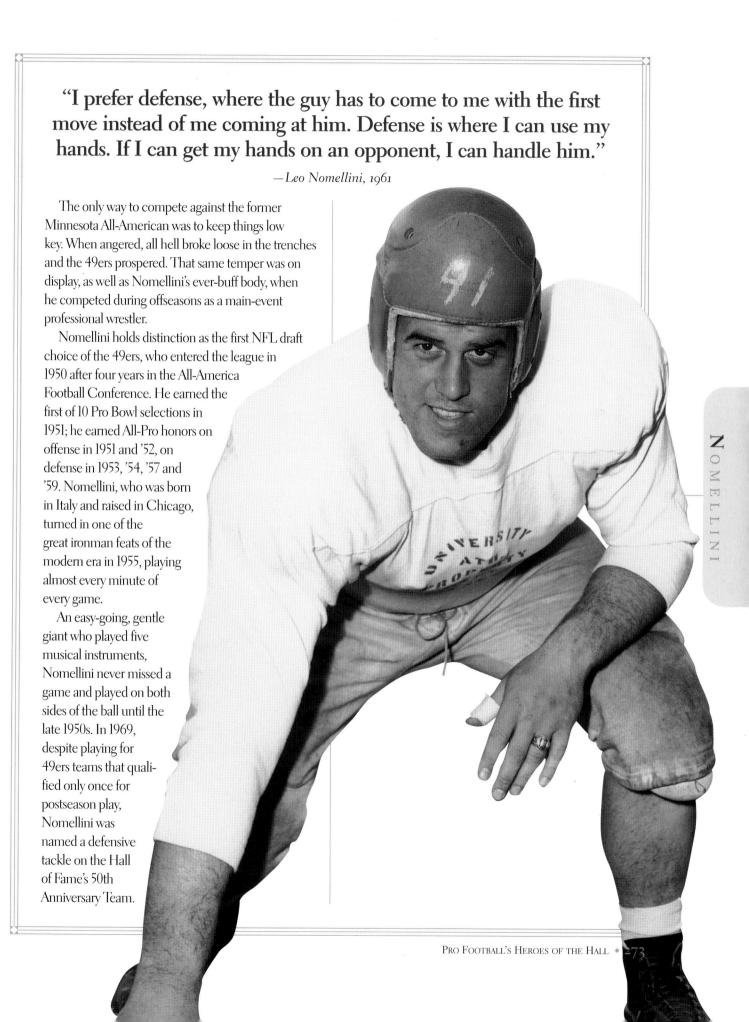

> "I prefer defense, where the guy has to come to me with the first move instead of me coming at him. Defense is where I can use my hands. If I can get my hands on an opponent, I can handle him."
>
> *—Leo Nomellini, 1961*

The only way to compete against the former Minnesota All-American was to keep things low key. When angered, all hell broke loose in the trenches and the 49ers prospered. That same temper was on display, as well as Nomellini's ever-buff body, when he competed during offseasons as a main-event professional wrestler.

Nomellini holds distinction as the first NFL draft choice of the 49ers, who entered the league in 1950 after four years in the All-America Football Conference. He earned the first of 10 Pro Bowl selections in 1951; he earned All-Pro honors on offense in 1951 and '52, on defense in 1953, '54, '57 and '59. Nomellini, who was born in Italy and raised in Chicago, turned in one of the great ironman feats of the modern era in 1955, playing almost every minute of every game.

An easy-going, gentle giant who played five musical instruments, Nomellini never missed a game and played on both sides of the ball until the late 1950s. In 1969, despite playing for 49ers teams that quali-fied only once for postseason play, Nomellini was named a defensive tackle on the Hall of Fame's 50th Anniversary Team.

MERLIN OLSEN

Born: 9-15-40, Logan, Utah **Ht/Wt:** 6-5/270 **College:** Utah State **Drafted:** 1962, 1st round, Rams **Primary position:** DT
Teams: Rams 1962-76 **Honors:** 75th Anniversary All-Time Team; 1960s All-Decade Team; 1970s All-Decade Team

Watching Merlin Olsen play football was like watching a surgeon in an operating room. No wasted motion, precise and near-perfect technique, absolute confidence and self-control. The former Utah State All-American performed his operations on Sunday afternoons for 15 NFL seasons, carving

> ## "We never got a bad game from Merlin Olsen. You always got a good game from Oly and, more often than not, you got a great game."
>
> —*George Allen*

up linemen, quarterbacks and game plans that struggled to deal with one of the greatest defensive lines ever assembled.

As the stabilizing force and charter member of the Los Angeles Rams' Fearsome Foursome defensive front wall in the 1960s, the 6-foot-5, 270-pound Olsen was a prototypical tackle with incredible upper body strength, explosive speed and the agility to out-maneuver blockers. But the real secret to his success came from within—the Phi Beta Kappa classroom skills he used to dissect the game and the players he competed against.

Off the field, Olsen was a gentle giant who spoke with soft, measured words about topics ranging from finance to politics. On the field, he played with control

and discipline, unwilling to get caught up in the emotion and animalistic violence that sometimes dominated his occupation. He worked for 10 years as the left-side partner of Hall of Fame end Deacon Jones, form-

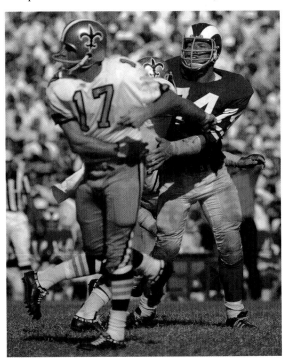

ing one of the great pass-rushing, run-stuffing combinations in NFL history.

Jones was the colorful, speed-rushing playmaker. Olsen was the quiet, steady practitioner who stayed at home and covered up for his partner. The Rams' linemen worked innovative stunting and looping maneuvers that had never been tried, many conceived by the analytical Olsen. The big, blond-headed Mormon from Logan, Utah, became a starter in the third game of his 1962 rookie season and played in 208 regular-season contests, the final 198 in succession.

Extraordinarily consistent, Olsen earned a record 14 straight Pro Bowl invitations, five unanimous All-NFL selections and six straight citations as team MVP. He never played in a championship game or Super Bowl before retiring in 1976, but he did gain post-football acclaim as an actor and broadcaster.

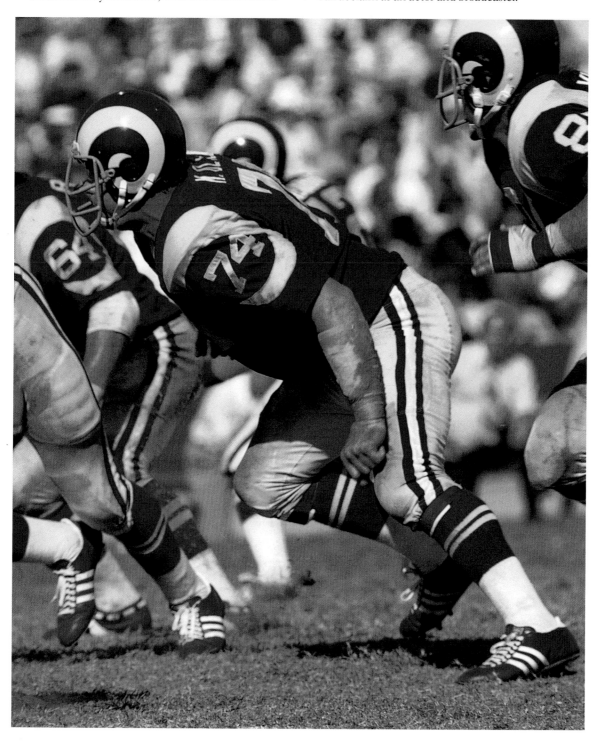

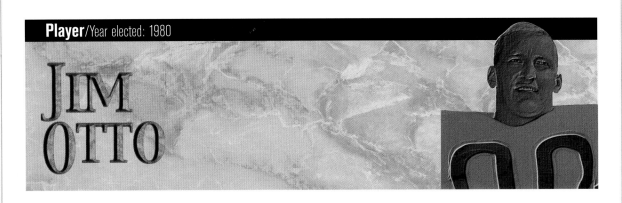

JIM OTTO

Born: 1-5-38, Wausau, Wis. **Ht/Wt:** 6-2/250 **College:** Miami (Fla.) **Drafted:** 1960, 1st round, Raiders **Primary position:** C
Teams: Raiders 1960-74 **Championship team:** AFL 1967 **Honors:** All-Time AFL Team

He was a charter member of the American Football League, an Oakland Raider original and the only All-AFL center in the league's 10-year existence. Nobody exhibited more domination of a position over a 15-year stretch than Jim Otto. Despite 10 broken noses and numerous knee operations, the Raiders' Ol' Double Zero always answered the bell, starting in all 210 of his team's regular-season games, all 13 postseason contests and 12 Pro Bowls.

Life could have been a lot different for the big, blue-eyed kid from Wausau, Wis. Undrafted after his college career at Miami (Fla.), he showed up in 1960 at the Raiders' first tryout camp weighing an unimpressive 205

> **"He loved to win. He led by example and he set the tempo. He gave the Raiders an image of hard discipline, hard work and hard-nosed football."**
>
> —*George Blanda*

pounds and quickly showed the heart and determination that would propel him to all-star status. By 1961, he had beefed up his 6-foot-2 frame to 250 and attracted NFL attention with overpowering performances against bigger nose tackles and faster linebackers.

Otto, whose star recognition was enhanced by the two big zeroes he wore on his uniform jersey, was an outgoing, easy-to-like charmer whose oversized head (size 8½ helmet) was covered by platinum blond hair. But on the field, he was an old-school competitor who used superior speed and techniques to range well beyond the usual blocking assignments for centers. Described by one opponent as "meaner than a bear and tougher than an old boot," Otto was the signal-caller for an outstanding Raiders line that was fortified in the late 1960s by fellow Hall of Famers Art Shell (tackle) and Gene Upshaw (guard).

Otto's pride and leadership were instrumental in the Raiders' transformation from AFL doormat to one of pro football's most successful franchises. With him in the middle, they won seven division titles in an eight-year span from 1967-74, appeared in six AFL or AFC title games and secured a 1967 AFL championship, losing to Green Bay in Super Bowl II. From 1963 through Otto's retirement in 1974, the Raiders posted an impressive 115-42-11 regular-season record.

OTTO

STEVE OWEN

Born: 4-21-1898, Cleo Springs, Okla. **Died:** 5-17-64 **Ht/Wt:** 5-10/235 **Primary positions:** OT, DT **Teams played:** Kansas City Cowboys 1924-25; Cleveland Bulldogs 1925; Giants 1926-31, 1933 **Championship team:** NFL 1927 **Teams coached (151-100-17 RS, 2-8 PS):** Giants 1931-53 **Championship teams:** NFL 1934, '38 **Honors:** 1920s All-Decade Team

He was the John McGraw of New York football, the fundamentals-preaching player/coach who bridged the professional game's formative and modern eras. Drawling, tobacco-chewing Steve Owen, all 235-plus pounds of him, was a gridiron Giant, both in stature and philosophy. Over three remarkable decades, Stout Steve earned respect in the NFL trenches as well as the rooms where innovative game plans and strategies are formulated.

Nobody embodied the hard-knock, chin-busting mentality of football more than Owen, a powerful two-way tackle from 1924-33 with the Kansas City Cowboys, Cleveland Bulldogs and Giants. He butted heads with the likes of George Halas, Jim Thorpe and Link Lyman at an All-Pro level, helping the Giants win a 1927 championship. By 1931, he was a player-coach who emphasized fundamentals, hard work and defense.

Anybody who considered Owen a hopeless conservative was not paying attention. His mind was quick and creative and he fathered such concepts as the A-formation, the umbrella defense and the two-

> ## "Football is a game played down in the dirt and it always will be that way. So there's no use getting fancy about it."
>
> *—Steve Owen*

platoon system that triggered the era of specialization. While his offenses focused on such basics as ball control and power running, his stifling defenses were marks of creative genius.

The umbrella, a predecessor to today's 4-3, was revolutionary. It was the first defense that could successfully slow down Cleveland coach Paul Brown's high-powered passing offenses and other coaches quickly adopted it. Never wavering from his simple approach to the game, Owen choreographed the rise of professional football in the game's biggest market while bringing fans eight Eastern Division championships and two NFL titles.

The first came in the Giants' 1934 "Sneakers Game" win over Chicago; the second came in 1938. The simple, unassuming Oklahoman, who coached such Hall of Fame greats as Mel Hein, Tuffy Leemans, Emlen Tunnell and Tom Landry, retired after the 1953 season with a 151-100-17 record. In his 30-year association with the Giants, 23 as coach, Owen never signed a contract, working instead on a yearly handshake agreement.

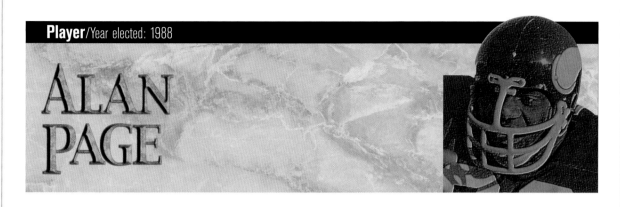

ALAN PAGE

Born: 8-7-45, Canton, Ohio **Ht/Wt:** 6-4/245 **College:** Notre Dame **Drafted:** 1967, 1st round, Vikings **Primary position:** DT
Teams: Vikings 1967-78; Bears 1978-81 **Honors:** 1970s All-Decade Team

Call him the thinking man's defensive tackle, a destroyer who only employed contact as a means to an end. Alan Page never wore arm pads during his 15-year NFL career because he planned to go around blockers, not hit them. He relied on intelligence, speed and explosive quickness to win the battle of the trenches, a style that helped him redefine the position over a career that started with the Minnesota Vikings in 1967 and ended 218 games later in Chicago.

The 6-foot-4, 245-pound Page was thinner than most tackles, but he also was quicker and faster. The Notre Dame All-American played like a linebacker in a three-point stance, an aggressive attack man who didn't need brute force to blow past a blocker. Page's strengths were quickness off the snap and pursuit—a sideline-to-sideline determination to chase down the ball.

His uncanny ability to get into the backfield gave him distinction as the game's first outstanding pass-rushing tackle and a dangerous kick-blocker. Page, a free-lancer within the Vikings' defensive system, became the centerpiece for the famed "Purple People Eaters" defense that carried Minnesota to Super Bowls after the 1969, 1973, 1974 and 1976 seasons—all losses. Page and end Jim Marshall formed a dynamic right side through most of the 1970s, with Carl Eller operating on the left.

With the unemotional Page often controlling the flow of games from 1968-77, the Vikings were 104-35-1. The quick-striking tackle was a perennial All-NFC or All-Pro pick, the Associated Press'

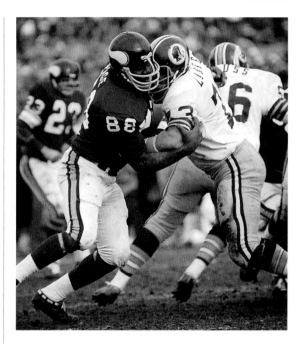

"A defensive player should think of himself more as an aggressor, not as a defender. I've got a job to do and my job is not to sit back and wait and then react to what the offense does. My job is to go after them. If you are going to make a mistake, make it aggressively."

—*Alan Page*

1971 MVP and a four-time NFC Defensive Player of the Year. Through all his success, the nine-time Pro Bowler professed a take-it-or-leave-it feeling about football and earned a law degree before finishing his career.

The low-key Canton, Ohio, native also became fascinated with running and competed in marathons, a pastime that contributed to his late-career drop to 220 and his 1978 breakup with the Vikings. He played his final 58 games for the Bears.

ACE PARKER

Born: 5-17-12, Portsmouth, Va. **Ht/Wt:** 5-11/175 **College:** Duke **Drafted:** 1937, 2nd round, Dodgers **Primary positions:** QB, DB, P
Career statistics: Passing NFL, 273-of-603, 3,935 yds., 22 TDs; Rushing NFL, 423 att., 1,108 yds., 10 TDs; Punting, 123 att., 39.5 avg.; Interceptions, 7, 2 TDs **Interceptions leader:** 1940 **Teams:** NFL Dodgers 1937-41; NFL Braves 1945; AAFC Yankees 1946

It was easy to spot him in the crowd. Clarence "Ace" Parker was the little guy with the ready smile, steady arm and quick, active feet that always seemed to be a step or two ahead of frustrated pursuers. Few players performed with more fun-loving abandon than the multi-talented Virginian, a two-sport star whose football legacy was the life he injected into a struggling Brooklyn franchise.

As a triple-threat halfback, punter, kicker, return man and ballhawking defender, Parker arrived in 1937 and helped turn the 7-year-old Dodgers into an NFL contender. He had a zest for the game, an exciting flair that sent an unprecedented buzz through a borough devoted to baseball. He called all signals and handled the ball in the Dodgers' single wing offense. He was smart, instinctive and creative, the "quarterback" who could impact games from anywhere on the field.

The 5-foot-11, 175-pound Parker was neither fast nor athletically superior to most of the players he competed against. But he

> ## "You can kick Ace Parker in the head and you can break both his ankles. But you can never break his heart."
>
> — *Tim Mara*

had the knack for making a perfect cut or throw, the playmaking instinct many star-quality players lacked. His masterpiece season was 1940 when he passed for 817 yards and 10 touchdowns while scoring five more. The Dodgers finished 8-3, a game behind first-place Washington, and Parker earned MVP honors.

Ironically, football was his destiny, not his choice. He wanted to play baseball for Connie Mack's Philadelphia Athletics and even hit a home run in his first major league at-bat off Boston's Wes Ferrell in 1937, but a two-year average of .179 redirected his attention to football. He played five years of his war-interrupted career with the Dodgers and single seasons with the NFL's Boston Yanks (1945) and New York of the All-America Football Conference (1946).

Parker's final season was memorable. The former Duke star passed for eight touchdowns, scored four more and led the Yankees to a division title. They lost in the AAFC championship game, 14-9, to the powerful Cleveland Browns.

JIM PARKER

Born: 4-3-34, Macon, Ga. **Ht/Wt:** 6-3/273 **College:** Ohio State **Drafted:** 1957, 1st round, Colts **Positions:** OG, OT **Teams:** Colts 1957-67 **Championship teams:** NFL 1958, '59 **Honors:** 75th Anniversary All-Time Team; 1950s All-Decade Team; All-Time NFL Team

The straightest path to Johnny Unitas made a half-circle detour around left tackle. Big Jim Parker wouldn't have it any other way. He was the quarter-back's blind-side protector, the man entrusted with the continued good health and welfare of Baltimore's most valuable property. And he diligently made sure nobody violated that trust over 11 outstanding NFL seasons.

Parker is considered by many the greatest offensive tackle in pro football history—and the greatest offensive guard. He spent his first 5½ seasons working over the league's big and fast defensive ends and the next 5½ at guard, where his blocking responsibilities changed considerably. It didn't seem to matter. The big man from Macon, Ga., was a Pro Bowl regular from 1959-66 and a Hall of Famer in the making no matter where the Colts positioned him.

The 6-foot-3, 273-pound Parker, Baltimore's first-round pick out of Ohio State in 1957, was not only the biggest man of his day, he was the fastest big man. He was a human avalanche when he exploded off the line on a straight running play and a relentless bulldozer when he cleared traffic on power sweeps, which came all too often for opposing linebackers and defensive backs.

But Parker was at his best as an immovable pass-blocker. His massive body, great balance, quick feet and superior blocking technique held back all rushers, the more the merrier. Unitas could perform his high-

powered passing magic without fear of blind-side hits and, not surprisingly, the Parker-Unitas pairing coincided with the Colts' rise to prominence in the 1950s.

They won consecutive NFL championships in 1958 and '59 and regrouped after a four-year falloff to reach the league title game in 1964. Consciencious, hard-working and durable (he didn't miss a game over his first 10 seasons), Parker became the model that young offensive linemen studied to learn their craft. In 1973, he was elected to the Hall of Fame as the first lineman to play exclusively on offense.

> "I loved playing next to Jim. He was the best, man. He played every position along the line and was great at all of them. He was one of those guys who just punished you. He smothered you."
>
> —*John Mackey, 1999*

WALTER PAYTON

Born: 7-25-54, Columbia, Miss. **Died:** 11-1-99 **Ht/Wt:** 5-10/200 **College:** Jackson State **Drafted:** 1975, 1st round, Bears
Primary position: RB **Career statistics:** Rushing, 3,838 att., 16,726 yds., 110 TDs; Receiving, 492 rec., 4,538 yds., 15 TDs;
Passing, 8 TDs; KO Returns, 17 att., 31.7 avg. **Rushing champion:** 1977 **Teams:** Bears 1975-87 **Super Bowl champion:** 1985
season **Honors:** 75th Anniversary All-Time Team; 1970s All-Decade Team; 1980s All-Decade Team; All-Time NFL Team

"Sweetness" was an illusion nurtured by Chicago Bears fans who watched Walter Payton perform for 13 NFL seasons. Blurred by the 16,726 yards he piled up as the second most prolific runner in football history were the thousands of bruises, headaches and battered egos he left on his trail of tears. There was nothing sweet about Payton's running style. His nickname stood for hard work, hustle, enthusiasm and total effort.

> "It's his legs. He's got the strongest legs I've ever seen. They are like springs. ... If he had played on good teams, oh my gosh, I can't imagine what he would have done."
>
> — *Bobby Beathard, former Redskins G.M., 1984*

Every Payton run started with the trademark first-step burst that carried him into the hole, where he could accelerate to daylight or explode into a tackler with aggressive, punishing force. Every Payton run ended with the 5-foot-10, 200-pounder grinding, scrapping, fighting, battling for one more yard. No one in history ran harder, play after play, and nobody did more with modest speed than the blue-collar star former Bears coach Mike Ditka called "the most complete football player I ever saw."

The superbly-conditioned former Jackson State star also was an outstanding receiver and a threat to break open a game with the halfback pass, which he threw eight times for touchdowns. Need a block? Payton could deliver with the enthusiastic drive of a fullback, a role he relished even more than his ball-carrying exploits. His powerful legs and sledgehammer arms were feared weapons, as was the delight he took in clearing a hole.

A playful, figety clubhouse prankster off the field, Payton became a yardage machine when he pulled on his No. 34 jersey. Among his 77 100-yard performances was a then single-game-record 275-yard effort in 1977 against the Vikings and his 21,803 combined rushing/pass-catching yards accounted for 125 touchdowns, 110 on the ground. When he retired in 1987, he owned the NFL rushing record, a mark he held until Emmitt Smith passed him in 2002.

Payton, a nine-time Pro Bowler, missed only one game in 13 seasons. He earned his only championship ring as a member of the powerful 1985 Bears, who defeated New England in Super Bowl XX.

PAYTON

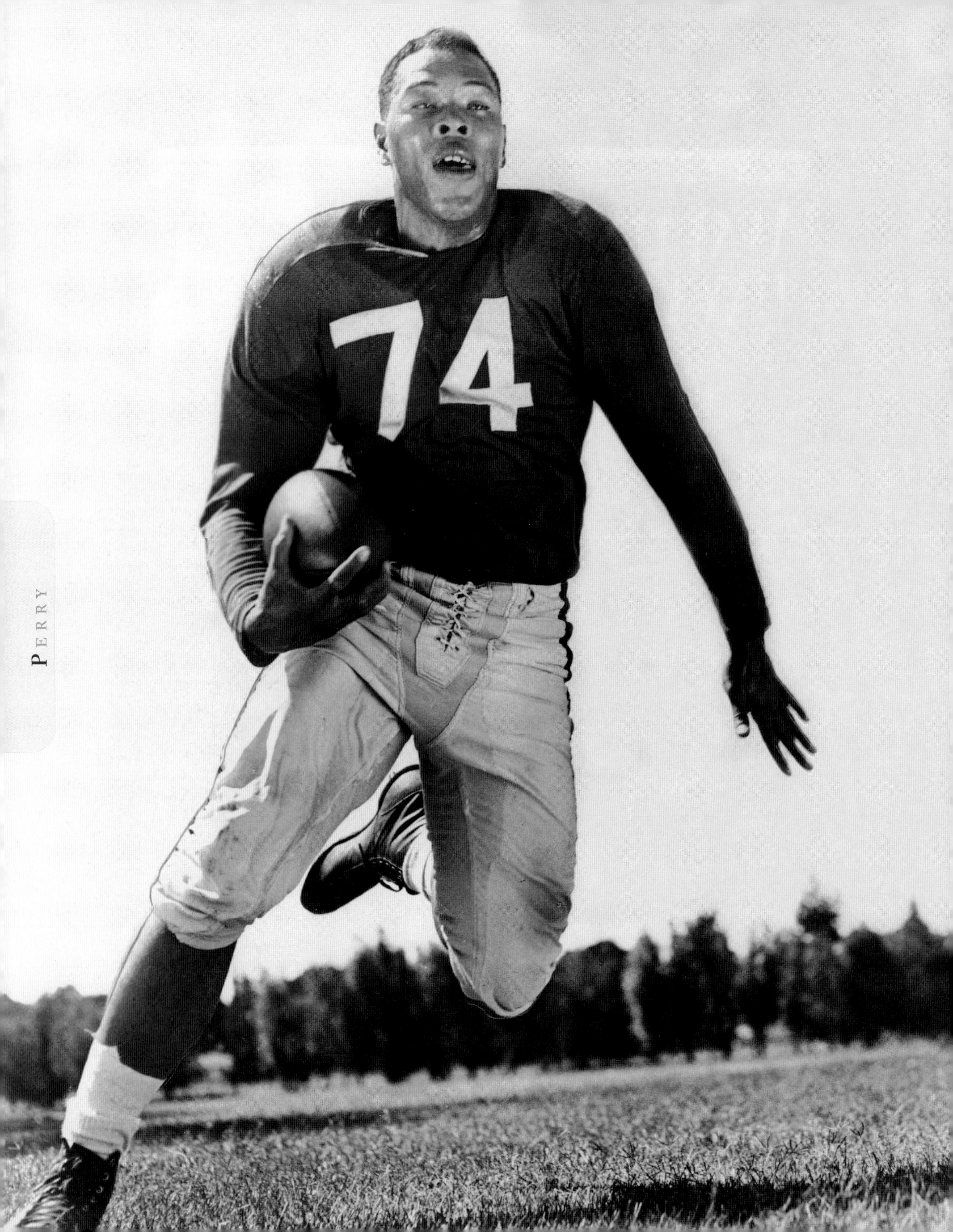
74

JOE PERRY

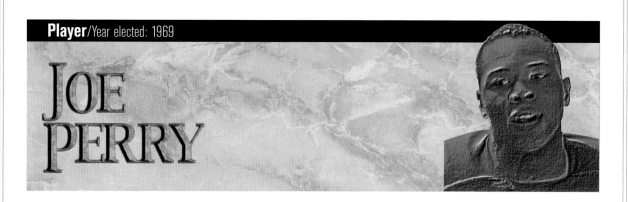

Born: 1-27-27, Stevens, Ark. **Ht/Wt:** 6-0/200 **College:** None **Drafted:** Undrafted **Positions:** FB, DB **Career statistics:** Rushing AAFC, 192 att., 1,345 yds., 18 TDs; Rushing NFL, 1,737 att., 8,378 yds., 53 TDs; Receiving NFL, 241 rec., 1,796 yds., 8 TDs **Rushing champion:** NFL 1953, '54 **Teams:** AAFC 49ers 1948-49; NFL 49ers 1950-60, 1963; Colts 1961-62 **Honors:** 1950s All-Decade Team

They called him "The Jet" and his explosive bursts threatened to shatter the NFL sound barrier. The vapor trails that followed Joe Perry for 16 seasons remain embedded in the memory of opponents who chased them from 1948-63. So does his role as one of the first black superstars in professional football and a worthy predecessor to Jim Brown as the game's all-time rushing champion.

The 6-foot, 200-pound youngster with long sprinter legs and a quiet self-confidence played 14 of his professional seasons with generally weak San Francisco teams—two in the All-America Football Conference and the balance in the NFL. Spotted on a Navy service team during World War II, he joined the 49ers as a raw rookie in 1948, one of the few players who did not play college football, and had to learn the tricks of his position on the job—feints, hesitation moves, twists and turns.

He learned them well. Perry was good enough to lead the AAFC in 1949 with 783 rushing yards and he topped NFL rushers

> "Joe can do everything. He can run, he has power and, best of all, he can think. If something goes wrong with a play and Joe is carrying the ball, he'll figure out something else in a split second. We wouldn't be where we are today if we didn't have Joe Perry."
>
> —*Buck Shaw, 49ers coach, 1952*

in 1953 and '54, posting the first consecutive 1,000-yard seasons in NFL history. He was lightning in a bottle, a breakaway threat on every play, and he teamed in the same explosive 49ers backfield with Hugh McElhenny for nine seasons.

Off the field, Perry was a modest, soft-spoken gentleman who could have had his choice of 14 colleges to study engineering; on the field, he was strong enough to endure verbal and physical abuse from fans and players who fought the breakdown of racial barriers. He seldom gave in to distractions and played through injuries as one of the most durable backs of his era.

Perry was traded to Baltimore in 1961 and returned to San Francisco for a final season in 1963. Late in his career, he held the all-time NFL rushing record before being overtaken by Brown; when he retired, his 9,723 rushing yards (8,378 NFL, 1,345 AAFC) were the most ever posted by a professional back. He also caught 260 passes and scored 513 career points.

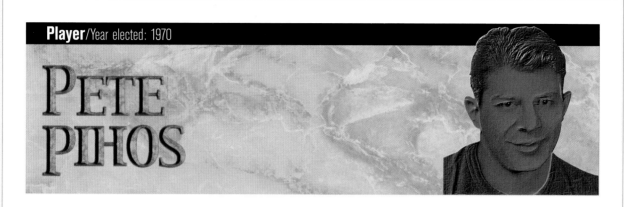

PETE PIHOS

Born: 10-22-23, Orlando, Fla. **Ht/Wt:** 6-0/210 **College:** Indiana **Drafted:** 1945, 3rd round, Eagles **Primary positions:** E, DE
Career statistics: Receiving, 373 rec., 5,619 yds., 15.1 avg., 61 TDs **Receptions leader:** 1953, '54, '55 **Teams:** Eagles 1947-55
Championship teams: NFL 1948, '49 **Honors:** 1940s All-Decade Team

A man of the trenches, Pete Pihos was uncomfortable with the skill-position quickness and talent he packed into a 6-foot, 210-pound body. Contact was his addiction and he always preferred to run through obstacles, not around them. The "Golden Greek" never lost that rugged edge from 1947-55, either as a defensive end or a "skilled" pass catcher who helped fuel a three-year Philadelphia Eagles championship run.

Pihos looked at the world from dark eyes and a ruggedly handsome face that was topped by jet black hair. His squinting glare personified a sometimes gruff personality and the attacking football style that served him well as a hard-charging defensive end and devastating run-blocker. Pihos' motor was always revved and bigger opponents learned never to underestimate the power of his missile-like blows.

But it was as a receiver that Pihos claimed special distinction. He did not have superior speed, but his clever moves, excellent timing and

> **"Without Thomason and Burk, great passers both, I would be just Pihos, another defensive end in pro football. They are the guys who fire the shots. I just try to catch 'em."**
>
> — *Pete Pihos, 1953*

sure hands made him a favorite target of Eagles quarterbacks Tommy Thompson, Bobby Thomason and Adrian Burk. Pihos often looked awkward in execution, but he seldom dropped a pass and ran like a body-crunching fullback.

The former Indiana University star was a two-way end for Eagles teams that won three straight Eastern Division championships from 1947-49 and consecutive NFL titles. His 31-yard touchdown pass from Thompson in the 1949 title game opened the scoring in a 14-0 win over Los Angeles. When the two-platoon system reached Philadelphia in 1952, he devoted one season to defense and his final three to becoming the NFL's top pass-catcher.

Pihos, who missed only one game in nine seasons, led the league with 63 catches for 1,049 yards and 10 touchdowns in 1953. He also led in receptions the next two years (60, 62) while scoring 17 TDs. When he retired at age 32 with 373 catches, opposing coaches were surprised—and relieved. Pihos played his final career game, fittingly, in the 1956 Pro Bowl—his sixth straight selection to the postseason classic.

SHORTY RAY

Born: 9-21-1884, Highland Park, Ill. **Died:** 9-16-56 **Executive career:** NFL's Technical Advisor on Rules and Supervisor of Officials 1938-52

To NFL players whose careers were affected by his astute judgments, he was known affectionately as "Shorty." To league officials and coaches who understood and appreciated his far-reaching vision, he was a 5-foot-6, 136-pound clipboard-carrying giant. Nobody had a more lasting impact on the game of football than diminutive Hugh Ray, who spent a quarter century stabilizing, refining and making it fit for

all levels. When Ray was approached by the NFL in 1938, he quickly accepted the duo role of Technical Advisor on Rules and Supervisor of Officials.

The marriage lasted 15 years and Shorty became an NFL institution. A master of detail, he traveled to games and practices, always armed with stopwatch, clipboard, binoculars and charts, to observe and find ways to improve the product. He streamlined rules,

"At one time, officials couldn't score over 95 percent on a written test even with a rulebook at their elbow. Now they can score better than 95 percent without using a rulebook."

—Shorty Ray (center, left photo)

public consumption.

Too small to play the game he had learned at the University of Illinois, Ray dedicated his life to standardizing its rules and conduct of play. Officiating became his first passion and he spent two decades preaching the need for a universal code. Ray acted on his instincts in 1925 when he founded the American Officials Organization and began conducting rules-interpretation clinics for all sports.

Four years later, Ray was asked by the National Federation of High School Athletic Associations to write a football rules book. Soon his intuitive code was being used as the standard for football conduct at

suggested ways to make the game more pleasing to fans, conducted preseason educational clinics for players and coaches and made safety recommendations.

Ray carefully screened officials, requiring them to score 95 or better on written rules tests, and tutored them on field procedures—always demanding high performance. His stopwatch readings were legendary, allegedly prompting more than 300,000 notations aimed at improving game-conduct techniques that would give the NFL a faster-paced appeal.

The cerebral and energetic Ray retired because of poor health in 1952 and died four years later at age 71.

DAN REEVES

Born: 6-30-12, New York, N.Y. **Died:** 4-15-71 **Executive career:** Owner Cleveland Rams 1941-45; Los Angeles Rams 1946-71

He was a New York-born Irishman with big ideas and determination to match. When Cleveland Rams owner Dan Reeves forced the NFL to accept his 1946 franchise relocation to the West Coast, he broke a barrier to growth and prosperity while redrawing the boundaries of everyone's imagination. Nobody more creatively altered the course of professional sports in America than the handsome little rich man with the Hollywood flair.

Reeves, heir to the founder of a lucrative grocery store chain in New York, shocked the football world when he announced, shortly after his Rams had defeated Washington in the 1945 NFL championship game, that he would move his team to Los Angeles. Reeves was upset over lack of support and saw the West Coast as a new frontier. Owners refused to approve what they saw as a bold and risky venture until he threatened to withdraw from the league.

Reeves opened the floodgate to West Coast expansion. Soon he was butting heads with the Los Angeles Dons and San Francisco 49ers of the new All-America Football Conference. Baseball's Dodgers and Giants headed west. So did basketball's Lakers and Warriors. Financial success followed, thanks in large part to Reeves' ground-breaking innovations.

He organized the NFL's first full-time scouting staff and his intricate evaluation system revolutionized the sport. He broke the NFL's color barrier in 1946 by signing former UCLA star Kenny Washington, pioneered television broadcasting and filled his front office with talented idea men who lifted public relations to a new level. Reeves also gave fans a Hollywood touch — bright uniforms, exciting passing attacks and colorful players like Norm Van Brocklin and Elroy "Crazy Legs" Hirsch.

Over three decades (1941-70), his teams won seven division or conference titles and two championships while drawing numerous 80,000-plus crowds to the massive L.A. Coliseum. But his legacy is tied more closely to the barriers he shattered and the growth he triggered as one of the game's visionary figures.

> **"Dan broke the barrier. I very well remember sitting in at the league meetings with my father and brother when Dan had to overcome the severest of opposition from all sides, particularly the Giants, in order to get permission to make the move. But the fact is, it was Dan who took the 'first small step' that became the 'giant leap' for organized sports."**
>
> —Wellington Mara,
> *Giants owner, from the book Los Angeles Rams by Steve Bisheff*

MEL RENFRO

Born: 12-30-41, Houston, Tex. **Ht/Wt:** 6-0/190 **College:** Oregon **Drafted:** 1964, 2nd round, NFL Cowboys; 10th round, AFL Raiders
Primary position: DB **Career statistics:** Interceptions, 52, 3 TDs; Punt Returns, 109 att., 7.7 avg., 1 TD; KO Returns, 85 att., 26.4 avg., 2 TDs **Interceptions leader:** 1969 **Teams:** Cowboys 1964-77 **Super Bowl champions:** 1971, '77 seasons

He was a Deion Sanders prototype, without the hype. Mel Renfro was a multi-threat athlete who could influence games with uncanny ballhawking instincts, smothering man-to-man coverage and electrifying returns. Former Dallas coach Tom Landry remembered the quiet Texan as one of the game's most talented and versatile skill position players, a valuable weapon for Cowboys teams that won two of the four Super Bowls they reached from 1964-77.

According to Landry, the 6-foot, 190-pound Renfro could have been an All-Pro at any skill position. He had been an All-American running back and two-way star at the University of Oregon when the Cowboys drafted him in 1964. Loaded with offensive talent, Landry plugged the speedy Renfro in at free safety and watched the rookie intercept seven passes, lead the NFL in punt and kickoff returns and earn the first of 10 straight Pro Bowl invitations.

There was none of Deion's flash in the always controlled and confident youngster who inspired teammates with his quiet professionalism. A gifted ballcarrier, he satisfied those needs as an early career return man and with eye-popping dashes after interceptions. Landry even moved him briefly to running back in 1966, but decided his value was greater on defense.

Renfro remained at free safety through 1969 and spent his last eight seasons shutting down the NFL's top receivers as a phys-

> ## "There couldn't possibly be a better cornerback in football week in and week out than Mel Renfro. You see what he does on passes, though not very much because teams don't throw at him too often. But watch him force a running play. He's so quick. I've never seen anything like him on film or anywhere else."
>
> *—Gene Stallings, 1973*

ical, man-to-man cornerback. Teammate Charlie Waters called him the best ever at the position and quarterbacks refused to throw his way. Renfro had the coveted ability to neutralize any receiver and he always seemed to know what the opponent was going to do.

The Cowboys' career interceptions leader (52) was a member of teams that won nine division titles, appeared in four Super Bowls and fell one game short of four others — including a loss to Green Bay in the 1967 Ice Bowl. His 1970 NFC championship game interception helped preserve a victory over San Francisco that lifted the Cowboys into their first Super Bowl.

Player/Year elected: 1992

JOHN RIGGINS

Born: 8-4-49, Seneca, Kan. **Ht/Wt:** 6-2/240 **College:** Kansas **Drafted:** 1971, 1st round, Jets **Primary position:** RB **Career statistics:** Rushing, 2,916 att., 11,352 yds., 104 TDs; Receiving, 250 rec., 2,090 yds., 12 TDs **Teams:** Jets 1971-75; Redskins 1976-79, 1981-85 **Super Bowl champion:** 1982 (MVP) season **Honors:** 1980s All-Decade Team

You could always spot John Riggins, who shocked NFL conservatives with his creative hair styles, outlandish statements and indomitable free spirit. It also was hard to miss the tree-trunk legs that supported 240 pounds of farm-bred muscle and churned out yardage for one of football's great workhorse fullbacks. Life was never dull for the big kid from Kansas who found happiness as a five-time 1,000-yard rusher and Super Bowl MVP.

Riggins showed up at his first New York Jets training camp in 1971 sporting a mohawk haircut and gold pearl earring, prompting coach Weeb Ewbank's "it won't look too bad when he puts his helmet on" comment. Over the next 14 years, Riggins' over-the-top behavior was more than offset by a superb work ethic, fiery determination and a hard-nosed running style that helped make the Jets competitive and the Washington Redskins reach championship heights.

The 6-foot-2 Riggins was a prototype fullback. He could pound out tough yards, punish tacklers, catch passes, block and go outside with his 4.5 speed. He also was an intelligent goal line bulldozer who seldom fumbled. His 11,352 career rushing yards and 104 rushing touchdowns testify to his durability. So do the 1,347 yards and then-record 24

TDs he posted in 1983.

Fans remember Riggins as the maverick who sat out the 1980 season in a contract dispute with the Redskins and returned under new coach Joe Gibbs to lead the team to consecutive Super Bowls. He topped 100 rushing yards and scored two touchdowns in each of the two NFC championship games and earned MVP honors in Super Bowl XVII by rushing for 166 yards and a game-turning 43-yard TD against Miami.

Off the field, Riggins made news with unpredictable behavior and several celebrated drinking incidents. On it, he was a model of consistency if not conformity. The former Kansas University star retired in 1985 with a 3.9-yard-per-carry average and 250 catches for 2,090 yards. Only four running backs and six players have scored more touchdowns than Riggins' 116.

"You see John's personality, his sense of humor, and then you look at how he produced on the field and you see why he's a leader. He has a great outlook on life, and he can do it all on the field."

—*Joe Gibbs, 1992, Chicago Tribune*

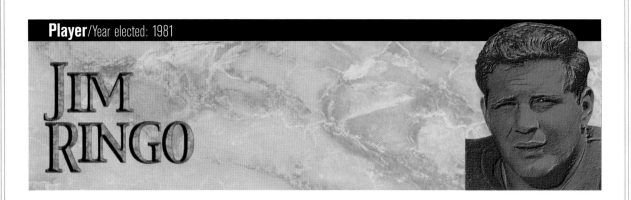

JIM RINGO

Born: 11-21-31, Orange, N.J. **Ht/Wt:** 6-2/235 **College:** Syracuse **Drafted:** 1953, 7th round, Packers **Primary position:** C
Teams: Packers 1953-63; Eagles 1964-67 **Championship teams:** NFL 1961, '62 **Honors:** 1960s All-Decade Team

Too small to survive in the NFL trenches, Jim Ringo simply gritted his teeth and defied logic for 15 body-crunching seasons. Not only did he survive as an undersized center in the land of giants, he earned respect as the model to which all others were compared. From 1953-67, Ringo provided a foundation for Vince Lombardi's Green Bay dynasty and started 182 consecutive games for the Packers and Philadelphia Eagles.

The 6-foot-2 Ringo reported to his first Packers training camp in 1953 as a 211-pound rookie out of Syracuse and he never weighed more than 235 while blocking much larger defensive linemen. But what Ringo lacked in size he made up for with quickness, near-perfect mechanics and a tenacity that frustrated less-inclined opponents. When Lombardi took over the struggling Packers in 1959, he built around his savvy center.

As the team's talent level increased, so did Ringo's role. He was the recognized leader of the offense, an enforcer who demanded total team effort and chastised anybody who gave less. He determined blocking

"He's one of the all-time greats. He blocks low—at the ankles. He can make blocks most centers can't make. And he's a great leader."

—*Sam Huff, 1967, Newsweek magazine*

assignments on every play, pulled on sweeps, defiantly protected quarterback Bart Starr and smartly picked up blitzes and other defensive trickery. Short-yardage plays typically went through the center of the line.

And Ringo was always there. In 1957 while suffering from mononucleosis, he spent Monday through Friday in the hospital for five straight weeks while playing on Sundays. He played through bronchial pneumonia, a staph infection, bad knees, a dislocated shoulder and other injuries to continue his streak. After his rookie season, Ringo never missed a game—and he seldom played at less than All-Pro form.

The quiet, wavy-haired Ringo was a member of three straight Western Conference championship teams from 1960-62 and helped Lombardi win his first two NFL titles. After Lombardi traded Ringo to the Eagles in 1964, he played four more seasons and earned the last three of 10 Pro Bowl invitations. Fittingly, his final professional game was in that classic, after the 1967 campaign.

ANDY ROBUSTELLI

Born: 12-6-25, Stamford, Conn. **Ht/Wt:** 6-1/230 **College:** Arnold College **Drafted:** 1951, 19th round, Rams **Primary position:** DE
Career statistics: 22 fumble recoveries **Teams:** Rams 1951-55; Giants 1956-64 **Championship teams:** NFL 1951, '56

Fans recall the fiery passion and dogged determination that defined Andy Robustelli's 14-year professional career. But teammates point to the leadership intangibles and chemistry he brought to Los Angeles and New York teams that played in eight NFL championship games. Physical, smart and inspirational, few players could match the total football essence of the hard-charging defensive end from tiny Arnold College.

Robustelli is best remembered as the humble leader of a late-1950s Giants "Fearsome Foursome" line that included Jim Katcavage, Dick Modzelewski and Rosey Grier. That defensive front helped the Giants win a 1956 championship and finish as runners-up five

> ### "Andy hits you so hard your bones rattle. But he's not malicious and he always plays fair."
>
> — *Bobby Layne, 1962*

more times before Robustelli retired in 1964. But before New York, the 6-foot-1, 230-pounder was an unsung sparkplug for Rams teams that won a 1951 championship and reached the title game four years later.

Wherever the dark-haired, stoop-shouldered Robustelli played, he drew raves with his cat-like quickness, uncanny instincts and bone-rattling hits. In five seasons with the Rams, he was the unsung 19th-round draft pick who rose to All-Pro heights because of his contagious energy and football savvy. In nine campaigns with the Giants, he was the passion-inspiring defensive captain who helped younger teammates find the road to success.

Robustelli was a serious football student who spent long hours honing his skills and preparing his body for the rigors of NFL line play. Opponents feared his pass-rushing ability and teammates marveled at his instinctive knack for finding the ball. He recovered 22 fumbles and scored five defensive touchdowns while missing only one of a possible 176 games.

The man who was considered a longshot when drafted out of Arnold College, a now-defunct teachers preparatory school in his home state of Connecticut, played in seven Pro Bowls and was honored in 1962 by the Maxwell Club as the NFL's best player. The Giants thought so much of Robustelli they used him as a player-coach in his final three seasons.

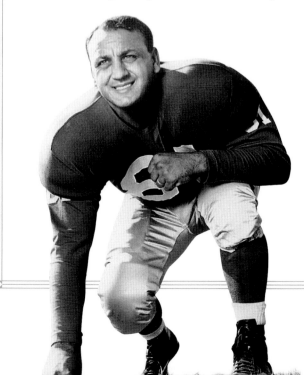

ART ROONEY

Born: 1-27-01, Coulterville, Pa. **Died:** 8-25-88 **Executive career:** Founder and owner of Steelers 1933-40, 1946-88; co-owner of Steelers 1941-46

Pittsburgh fans complained to him, booed him, suffered with him and embraced him as the lovable patriarch of a long-awaited football dynasty. Art Rooney was nothing if not patient over his 56-year association with the Steelers, a club he founded with an NFL entry fee of $2,500 in 1933. His team took 10 years to post its first winning record and 40 to win its first divisional title, but it needed only a six-season span to win four Super Bowls.

Success was a long time coming for the cigar-chomping Rooney, a humble man of the people who never balked in his belief that professional football would someday gain stature and popularity among the nation's sports enthusiasts. As a pioneer in the NFL's infancy and a member of the league's inner circle, he promoted that success by spending top dollar for talent and helping mold policies and rules that would make the game more attractive.

It was a hard road. Rooney, the son of a North Side Pittsburgh saloon keeper and hotel owner, dabbled in minor league baseball, boxing and semipro football in the 1920s. He also bet seriously on horse racing, a fascination rivaled only by his love for professional football when he founded the Pittsburgh Pirates (renamed Steelers in 1940) and doggedly pulled his team through the Depression and war years.

Fans might have questioned the Steelers' ineptitude,

> ## "I'll tell you something from the bottom of my heart. I'd pay to lose money just to keep in this game. I love it that much."
>
> —*Art Rooney*

but they never doubted Rooney's desire to win. He gave them Whizzer White, the NFL's 1938 rushing leader and future Supreme Court justice, and such Hall of Famers as Johnny Blood, Bill Dudley and Bobby Layne. Nothing worked. As the Steelers stumbled, Rooney was perceived as the patient, benevolent owner—revered and loved by his players and fellow owners.

The stumbling ended in 1974 when the Steelers, rebuilt by sons Dan and Arthur Jr., won their first Super Bowl. They won three more in the decade under coach Chuck Noll, a winning legacy "lovable loser" Rooney took to his deathbed in 1988.

DAN ROONEY

Born: 7-20-32, Pittsburgh, Pa. **Executive career:** Various front-office jobs with Steelers 1955-74; President of Steelers 1975-present

In Pittsburgh football, he's "the other Rooney," the unsung architect of a team that won four Super Bowls in a six-year span of the 1970s. Dan Rooney, the quintessential organizational genius, is the natural extension of a father who operated his beloved franchise with passion, if not always sound business acumen. It's hard to ignore the accomplishments of a lifelong football brat who changed the fortunes of the Steelers while helping to modernize the expanding NFL.

Dan, who first visited a Steelers' locker room at age 5, watched and learned as the team his father founded in 1933 struggled to even post a winning record. Art Rooney was the colorful and benevolent patriarch of Steelers football, a friend to all and larger-than-life figure in Pittsburgh and the inner circle of the NFL. But his teams never won and respect was tempered by years of frustration.

Dan, with the help of younger brother Arthur Jr., changed that. He joined the front office after his graduation from Duquesne in 1955 and became team president 20 years later. In between, he and

> "Dan helped build and manage one of the premier franchises in sports and he has been a tremendous contributor to the overall success in the league."
>
> —*Commissioner Paul Tagliabue, 2000, The Associated Press*

Art Jr. reorganized the franchise, introducing sound business principles, delegating authority and building an impressive scouting operation. The breakthrough came with the 1969 hiring of coach Chuck Noll. The draft would yield nine future Hall of Fame players in six years and provide the cornerstone for the 1970s Super Bowl run.

Under Dan's leadership, the Steelers have won 16 AFC Central Division titles, four of five Super Bowls and fallen a game short of the January classic six times. While lacking his father's raffish personality, he has quietly affected league policy as a behind-the-scenes power broker and member of numerous committees.

Rooney was chairman of the NFL's negotiating committee in 1976 and '82 and a key figure in the league's breakthrough collective bargaining agreement. He also headed the expansion committee that added teams in Seattle and Tampa in 1976, helped craft league policy for increasing TV and marketing revenues and has served on the NFL's powerful Management Council.

ROONEY

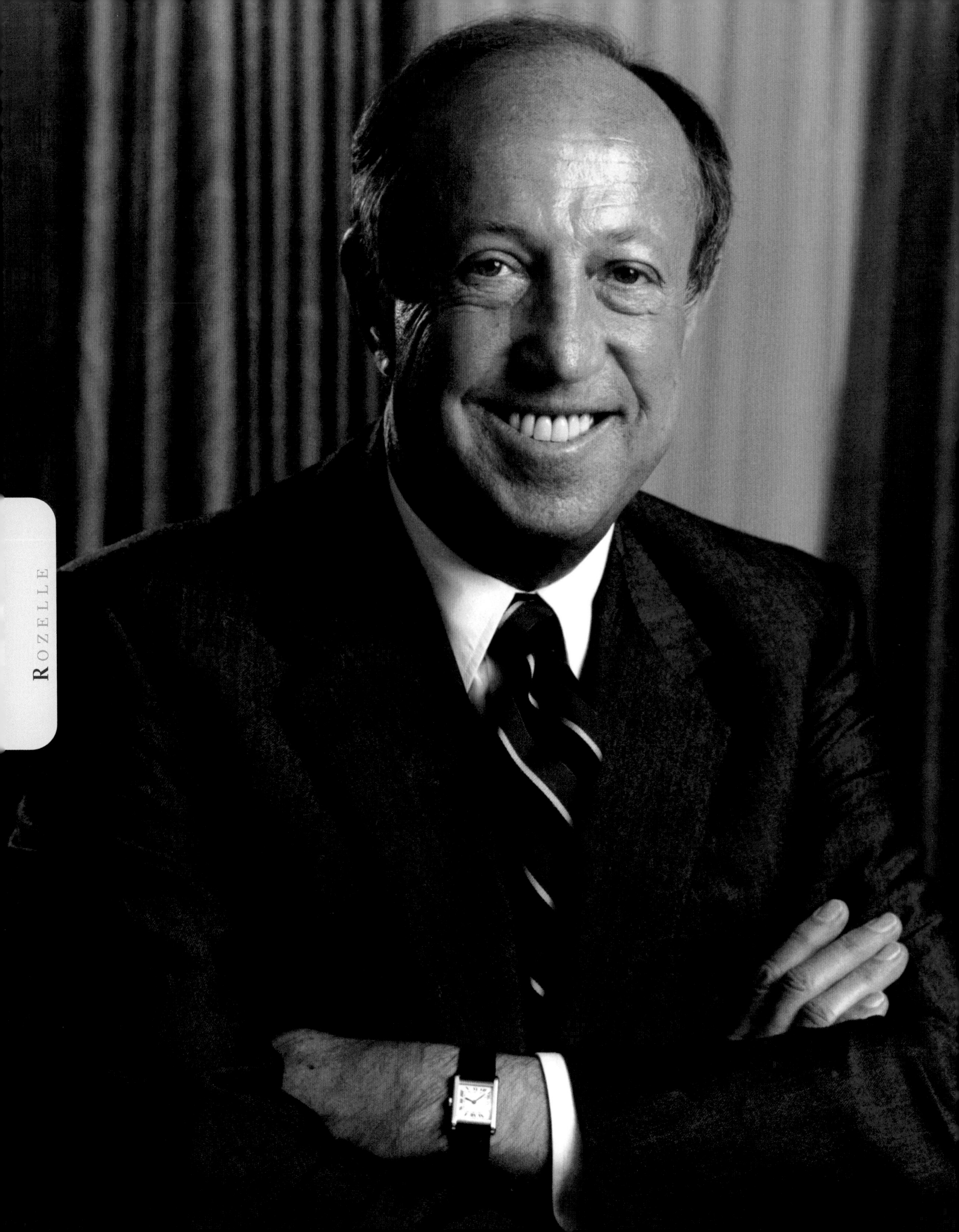

PETE ROZELLE

Born: 3-1-26, South Gate, Calif. **Died:** 12-6-96 **Executive career:** Commissioner of NFL 1960-89

He was a football visionary, the "compromise commissioner" who presided over the NFL's rise from regional obscurity to national obsession. Pete Rozelle's impact on the growth and popularity of professional football can be measured in television dollars, revenue-sharing stability and surging fan interest. He was the game's guiding light, a public relations genius who repackaged a tired sport into a glitzy, multi-million-dollar entertainment industry.

Rozelle's name was barely on the radar screen in 1960 when NFL owners, trying to replace deceased commissioner Bert Bell, struggled through 23 futile ballots over a nine-day span before finally tabbing the 33-year-old Los Angeles general manager as a stunning choice. Over the next three decades, the former Rams public relations director delivered equally stunning results while staking legitimate claim as the premier commissioner in sports history.

Using his "iron fist in a velvet glove" approach, the smooth, unflappable Rozelle set about forging an ownership union that would work toward the common good of the league. He recognized the significance of television and talked big-market owners into a revenue-sharing plan for TV contracts that became a foundation for growth and prosperity. The conciliatory and resourceful Rozelle quickly earned the trust and respect of a football community while preaching image and integrity.

As television became the backbone for NFL growth, Rozelle worked to satisfy Congress on anti-trust laws, oversaw an unprecedented sports-leagues merger with the AFL, mollified players, helped negoti-

> ### "On the tough decisions, the owners always voted right and it was due to Pete's leadership. He convinced us to vote in the best interest of the NFL. We'll be paying tributes the rest of our lives to the leadership of Pete Rozelle."
>
> *—Hugh Culverhouse, former Tampa Bay owner, 1989*

ate an historic collective bargaining agreement and presided over expansion. The 13-team NFL he inherited in 1960 had grown to 28 by his retirement in 1989 while player rosters and salaries mushroomed, game attendance soared and football became America's most-watched sport.

Rozelle helped the NFL deal with strikes, maverick owners, a gambling crisis, another rival league (the USFL) and drugs, never losing his television-friendly smile. Nothing pleased the amiable Californian more than the league's expanding community involvement and the growth of the Super Bowl into an annual sports classic.

ROZELLE

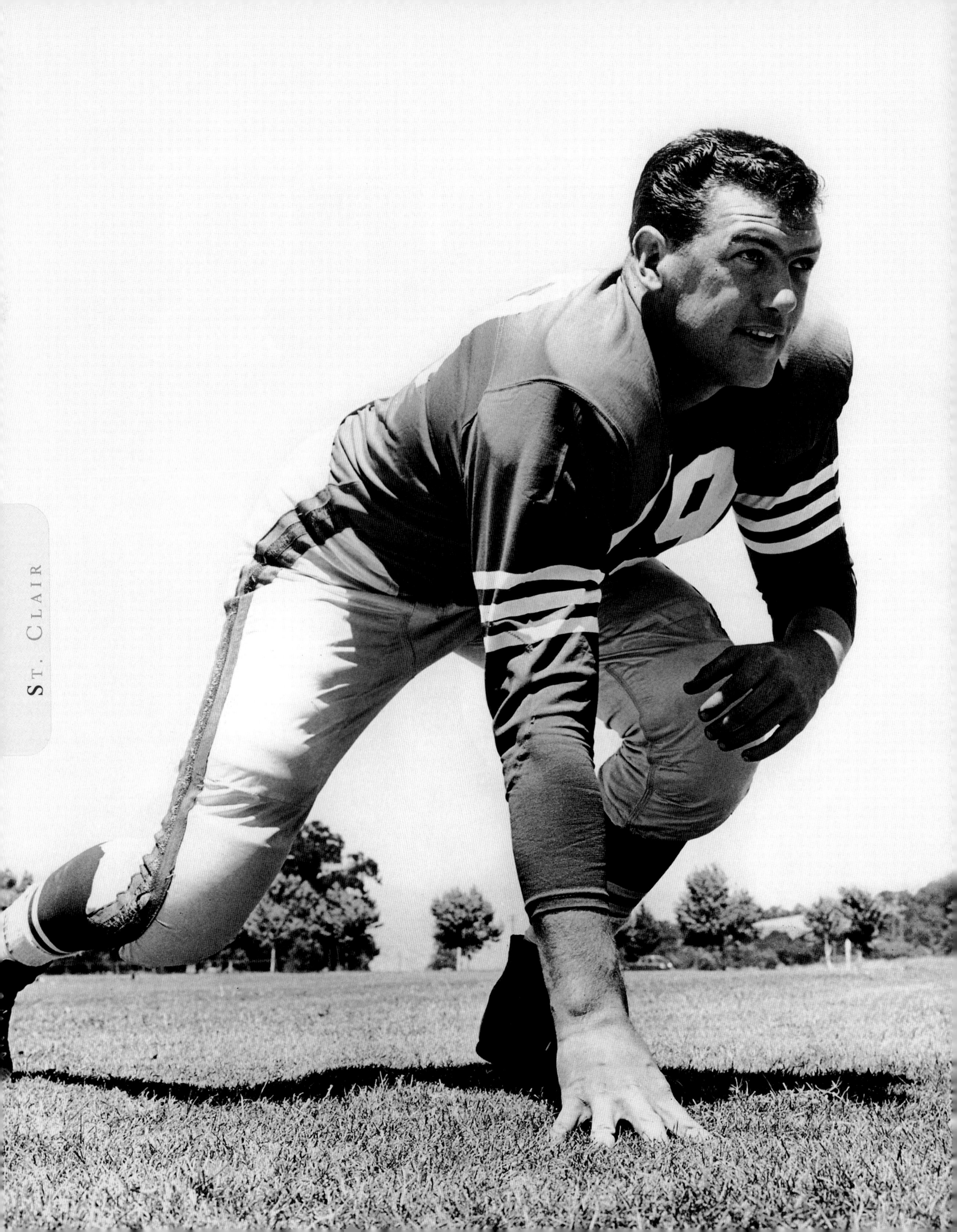

BOB ST. CLAIR

Born: 2-18-31, San Francisco, Calif. **Ht/Wt:** 6-9/265 **College:** San Francisco, Tulsa **Drafted:** 1953, 3rd round, 49ers **Primary position:** OT **Teams:** 49ers 1953-63 **Honors:** 1950s All-Decade Team

The 6-foot-9, 265-pound body was enough to scare the bejabbers out of overmatched defensive linemen. Bob St. Clair's almost fanatical love for hitting and violent contact only added to their displeasure. So did the eccentric reputation of a San Francisco monster who liked his meat raw and his football basic over 11 colorful seasons from 1953-63.

The brute power of the NFL's tallest offensive tackle was well documented by defenders who were on the receiving end of St. Clair's bulldozing blocks. Stories of him chomping on pieces of raw steak, chicken or liver, blood dripping down his chin, were legendary—and not exaggerated. He was a flamboyant, charming and quick-to-smile free spirit who enjoyed a popularity denied most linemen.

The 49ers' third-round 1953 draft choice out of Tulsa was a muscular physical specimen with a chest and biceps that measured larger than future heavyweight boxing champion Sonny Liston. St. Clair was fast, able to pull as a lead blocker on sweeps, and he was a ferocious hitter and kamikaze special-teams performer. Former Giants linebacker Sam Huff described him as a "big python I couldn't get around."

"The Geek" is best remembered as the front man for San Francisco's "Million Dollar Backfield" of Y.A. Tittle, Joe Perry, Hugh McElhenny and John Henry Johnson. It's no coincidence that Tittle, Perry and McElhenny posted the bulk of their Hall of Fame numbers over a nine-season stretch (1952-60) while operating behind St. Clair. Despite his eccentricities, St. Clair was a natural leader who served as a 49ers captain while doubling as mayor of Daly City, Calif.

The former San Francisco street kid was renowned for his battles against Baltimore Colts defensive end Gino Marchetti, a former college teammate at the University of San Francisco, and his ability to play through injuries. But relentless double- and triple-teaming eventually took a toll on the five-time Pro Bowler, who retired in 1963 after spending his entire career with a team that played only one postseason game.

> "The game is built around roughness. There is a personal thrill out of knocking a man down, really hitting him. It is the only satisfaction a lineman has. It gets you up, hitting a man. It gives you a jolt of the old adrenalin." —*Bob St. Clair*

Player/Year elected: 1977

GALE SAYERS

Born: 5-30-43, Wichita, Kan. **Ht/Wt:** 6-0/198 **College:** Kansas **Drafted:** 1965, 1st round, NFL Bears; 1st round, AFL Chiefs **Primary position:** RB **Career statistics:** Rushing, 991 att., 4,956 yds., 5.0 avg., 39 TDs; Receiving, 112 rec., 9 TDs; Punt Returns, 27 att., 14.5 avg., 2 TDs; KO Returns, 91 att., 30.6 avg., 6 TDs **Rushing champion:** 1966, '69 **Scoring champion:** 1965 **Teams:** Bears 1965-71 **Honors:** 75th Anniversary All-Time Team; 50th Anniversary Team; 1960s All-Decade Team; All-Time NFL Team

Catching up with Gale Sayers was a 60-minute task. If he didn't burn you with one of his gliding, stutter-stepping bursts up the middle, he probably would get you with a reception, a halfback pass or an electrifying return. He was lightning just waiting to strike, an offensive weapon just waiting to be unleashed. If Sayers wasn't the most prolific all-around performer in NFL history, he probably ran a close second.

It all started with his powerful legs. The 6-foot, 198-pound former Kansas star could hit the hole with his long, low stride, sidestep traffic and accelerate to daylight. Sayers was a master at reversing directions or wiggling and squirming his way through a swarm of tacklers. He seemed to have a variety of gears. Just when a tackler thought Sayers was going full speed, he

> **"Sayers is the greatest player I've ever seen. That's right—THE greatest. I've never been more impressed with one player."**
>
> — *Dick Butkus, 1965*

turned it up a notch and exploded into the open.

Sayers became the most celebrated newcomer in NFL history when he scored a rookie-record 22 touch-downs in 1965—14 on the ground, six via the pass, one on a kickoff return and one on a punt return. Included in that total were the record-tying six he scored in a memorable game against San Francisco—four on runs, one on an 80-yard pass and one on an 85-yard punt return. He followed that with a 1,231-yard sophomore season and the first of two rushing titles.

But the magic would end after a much-too-short 68-game career, thanks to a series of knee injuries. When the quiet, self-confident Sayers was forced to retire after two 1971 games at age 28, the city of Chicago mourned. He finished with incredible averages of 5.0 yards per run, 11.7 per catch, 30.6 per kickoff return and 14.5 per punt return. His 9,435 combined yards (running, receiving, returns) and 56 touchdowns (six on kickoff returns) were produced in only five full seasons.

Sayers, who was named the outstanding back in three of four Pro Bowl appearances, never played in a postseason game.

JOE SCHMIDT

Born: 1-19-32, Pittsburgh, Pa. **Ht/Wt:** 6-1/220 **College:** Pittsburgh **Drafted:** 1953, 7th round, Lions **Primary position:** LB **Career statistics:** Interceptions, 24, 2 TDs **Teams:** Lions 1953-65 **Championship teams:** NFL 1953, '57 **Honors:** 1950s All-Decade Team

It was hard not to notice Joe Schmidt, whose 18-inch neck, 48-inch barrel chest and concrete-block shoulders dominated a stocky 220-pound frame. He was the guy in the middle of the defense firing obscenities at teammates, trying to throw them into a rage before every snap; the guy standing in the trench-

> ## "If I were to start a team from scratch and had my pick of one player, I'd select Joe Schmidt to form the core of my team."
>
> —*Norm Van Brocklin*

es, whipping his team of horses. Schmidt was to the Detroit Lions defense what Bobby Layne was to the offense — the quarterback and unquestioned field general.

Big No. 56 was a perfect fit for his role as one of the game's first middle linebackers. He had surprising speed with sideline-to-sideline mobility, the strength to fight off bigger offensive linemen and the ability to read plays and react with lightning-quick accuracy. When Schmidt drove low and hard into a ballcarrier, everybody recognized the distinctive "pop."

Schmidt might have appeared to play at the boiling point, but his fury was controlled and his instinct for the ball remarkable. He was a serious captain who studied opponents and tendencies with religious fervor. The intangibles came as a surprise to the Lions, who grabbed the blond-haired Pittsburgh star with a

seventh-round pick in the 1953 draft.

It didn't take long for the aggressive youngster to draw notice as a punishing tackler while playing outside linebacker, and his ballhawking abilities surfaced when he moved to the middle in 1955. Schmidt's ability to drop back in pass coverage took pressure off a quality Lions' secondary that included future Hall of Famers Jack Christiansen and Yale Lary. Conversely, their coverage abilities allowed Schmidt to take intelligent gambles.

With Schmidt forming the heart of a big-play defense, Detroit rolled to NFL championships in 1953 and 1957 and fell one game short in 1954. He continued calling defensive signals until he ended his 13-year career after the 1965 season. When he retired, Schmidt had 24 interceptions, nine Pro Bowl selections and undying acclaim as one of the most beloved sports heroes in Detroit history.

TEX SCHRAMM

Born: 6-2-20, San Gabriel, Calif. **Executive career:** General manager of Los Angeles Rams 1951-56; President and general manager of Dallas Cowboys 1960-89; President of World League of American Football 1989-90

His first Dallas team finished 0-11-1, his last 3-13. In the 27 seasons between expansion and the late-1980s demise of the star-blessed Cowboys, Texas E. Schramm created one of the most remarkable winning legacies in NFL history. Not only was he the architect and doting father of America's Team, the innovative "Tex" also was a leader in professional football's transformation into a glitzy, multi-million dollar enterprise.

> ## "You've got to remember, Tex is the guy who started the organization from scratch. He's the guy who did the hiring."
>
> — *Tom Landry*

Schramm was the president and general manager Clint Murchison hired to build his expansion Cowboys in 1960. Over the next 28 years, the forceful Californian made his Dallas franchise the envy of professional sports and the prototypical marketing tool for the new television-friendly NFL. "Smooth" and "classy" became catch phrases for an organization that gave us computized scouting, Dallas Cowboys Cheerleaders and the widely read Dallas Cowboys Weekly.

Schramm also gave us Tom Landry, the Cowboys' only coach from 1960 through 1988. Together, Schramm and Landry gave Dallas fans 20 straight winning records, 13 division titles, 12 NFC championship game appearances and two winners in five Super Bowls. Scouting, drafts, player evaluation, front-office hiring — everything was a science under the visionary Schramm.

The former Los Angeles Rams publicity director and general manager, the man who hired future commissioner Pete Rozelle in 1952, also had a major impact on the NFL. It was Schramm who entered secret negotiations with Kansas City owner Lamar Hunt that led to the 1970 merger of the NFL and American Football League. And it was Schramm, as chairman of the NFL's Competition Committee, who championed the six-division format with playoff wildcards. Other Schramm innovations include the referee microphone for communicating on-field decisions, the 30-second play clock, wider sideline borders and wind-direction strips on goalposts.

Between jobs with the Rams and Cowboys, Schramm was the CBS-TV executive who arranged the first network coverage of Olympics competition in 1960. His Cowboys association ended in 1989 in a new-ownership purge and he served until 1990 as president of the World League of American Football.

LEE ROY SELMON

Born: 10-20-54, Eufaula, Okla. **Ht/Wt:** 6-3/256 **College:** Oklahoma **Drafted:** 1976, 1st round, Buccaneers **Primary position:** DE
Teams: Buccaneers 1976-84 **Honors:** 1980s All-Decade Team

From an Oklahoma farm to the pantheon of professional football, Lee Roy Selmon never deviated from historic destiny. He was the cornerstone of a franchise, the first pick in the first draft by the expansion Tampa Bay Buccaneers. For nine NFL seasons, the big-hearted defensive end chased his dream with relentless passion while earning the love of a city and helping his team rise from an 0-26 doormat to the brink of Super Bowl glory.

The 6-foot-3, 256-pound Selmon was a marked man from the moment he stepped into the trenches for the lowly Bucs in 1976. As their only big-play defender, he was the focus of game plans and the target of double- and triple-team blocks. Opponents worked hard to negate the perfect blend of speed,

quickness, strength and agility that, no matter what the strategy, showed up on highlight films with eye-popping consistency.

Fans loved to watch Selmon fight through blocks to crush a ballcarrier or record one of his 78 career sacks. No matter the score, the passion was always there. Teammates—and even opponents—were equally astonished by the soft-spoken, always upbeat personality of a man who drew universal acclaim as a "genuinely nice guy" who never complained or lost his temper.

One of nine children who grew up in Eufaula, Okla., the easy-going Selmon played for two national championship teams at Oklahoma and won both the Outland and Lombardi trophies his senior year. But soon Lee Roy

and older brother Dewey were starters for the expansion Bucs, who went from the ignominy of an 0-26 beginning to the ecstasy of a 10-6 record, NFC Central Division title and a playoff run that fell one win short of the Super Bowl in 1979.

Selmon, a six-time Pro Bowl performer who retired in 1984 because of a back injury, played for one more division winner and was named Associated Press defensive player of the year in 1979. He earned Hall of Fame honors despite playing for a team that was 44-88-1 during his career.

> "He was almost unblockable. I can't imagine anyone being better. He was the heart of our team. At a time when we were pretty fair, he was what made us pretty fair."
>
> —John McKay, 1995, *The Associated Press*

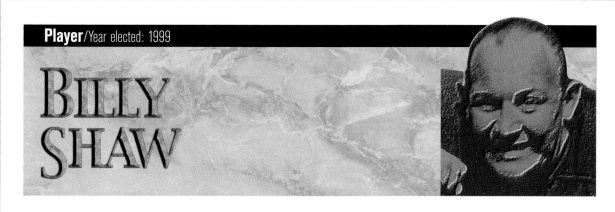

Player/Year elected: 1999

BILLY SHAW

Born: 12-15-38, Natchez, Miss. **Ht/Wt:** 6-2/258 **College:** Georgia Tech **Drafted:** 1961, 2nd round, AFL Bills; 14th round, NFL Cowboys
Primary position: OG **Teams:** Bills 1961-69 **Championship teams:** AFL 1964, '65 **Honors:** All-Time AFL Team

The 258 pounds Billy Shaw carried on his 6-foot-2 frame provided the foundation for consecutive Buffalo championship teams. The loyalty and determination he displayed during a rock-like nine-season career symbolized a more significant foundation that supported the 10-year American Football League. He was an AFL original, a standout pulling guard who earned Hall of Fame glory in a league known for its high-powered passing attacks.

While longtime San Diego star Ron Mix is generally regarded as the best offensive lineman in AFL history, Shaw might have been its premier run-blocker. He was compact, tough, strong and fast enough to stay ahead of Buffalo runners while pulling on sweeps. Shaw also was a relentless pass blocker, always resourceful and smart enough never to get beaten twice by the same tactic.

> "Of all the offensive linemen I played for in my 10 years, other than tackle Ron Mix, my old roommate with the Chargers, Billy Shaw is the greatest lineman in the history of the American Football League. He ranked right there, parallel with Mix."
>
> — *Jack Kemp, 1999, The Buffalo News*

The Mississippi-born Shaw, who played collegiately at Georgia Tech, stepped into Buffalo's lineup as a 1961 rookie and remained the team's go-to blocker for nine years. He was especially prominent from 1964-66 when the well-grounded Bills posted a 31-9-2 record, won three straight Eastern Division titles and two AFL championships.

Not readily apparent to outsiders was the impact Shaw had on teammates. At age 22, in his second professional season, he was elected offensive captain of the Bills, an honor he never relinquished. He was a popular and classy leader, both on the field and off, and a blue-collar plugger who enthusiastically displayed his athleticism on the kicking and return teams. Like the Buffalo offenses Shaw played for, he was a workmanlike performer—powerful but never flashy.

Shaw, an eight-time All-Star, was the first Hall of Famer who played exclusively in the AFL. He had an opportunity after his 1969 retirement to sign a three-year contract with the NFL-merged Houston Oilers for more money than he had made in his entire Buffalo career, but he declined saying, "I could not envision myself putting on somebody else's uniform. I was a Buffalo Bill."

ART SHELL

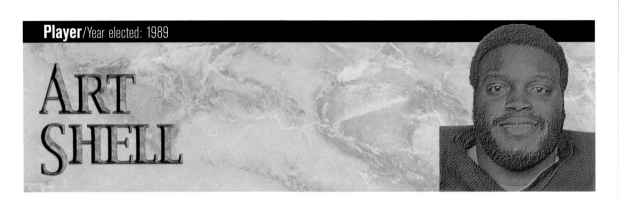

Born: 11-26-46, Charleston, S.C. **Ht/Wt:** 6-5/265 **College:** Maryland-Eastern Shore **Drafted:** 1968, 3rd round, Raiders **Primary position:** OT **Teams:** Raiders 1968-82 **Super Bowl champions:** 1976, 1980 seasons **Honors:** 1970s All-Decade Team

It was a fundamental rule, understood and followed by every defensive player in the NFL: Do not make Art Shell mad. The Oakland Raiders' hulking offensive tackle was intimidating enough in his "kill-you-softly, gentlemanly" mode. Arouse the bear and pay the price — a price that was exacted over 15 seasons with methodical and relentless consistency.

The quiet, introspective Shell was listed at a brutish 6-foot-5 and 265 pounds, but the weight fluctuated as high as 310 — a figure he wouldn't confirm. He never played the role of tough guy, preferring to let his strength and quickness speak for itself. He would greet opponents with flashing brown eyes, his wide, trademark smile and the words, "Let's have a great game." Then he would run them into the ground for 60 sometimes-painful minutes.

There was never anything personal with the former Maryland-Eastern Shore star. He was simply doing his job, one he took very seriously. He was extremely physical, he never got rattled and he knew the offensive assignments of every teammate, a result of the game film he studied for hours every night. Shell and guard Gene Upshaw dominated the left side of the Raiders line for 14 seasons, operating as a well-oiled machine whether run blocking or protecting the passer.

The Shell/Upshaw dominance was on display in Super Bowl XI when the Raiders rushed for 266 yards, most of them over the left side, right at perennial All-Pro Minnesota defenders Alan Page and Jim Marshall. Shell spent most of the game blocking Marshall, who finished his long afternoon without a tackle — or an assist.

Fans became accustomed to such efforts from the shy kid from South Carolina, who led the Raiders to 11 playoff appearances, nine championship game appearances and two Super Bowl wins from 1968-82. Shell also played in eight Pro Bowls. In 1989, almost seven years after his retirement, Shell became coach of the Raiders — the first black field boss in the post-World War II era.

> "He was one of those quiet leaders who commanded respect just by being a great player. He never, ever acted like a tough guy."
>
> —*John Madden*

Coach/Year elected: 1997

DON SHULA

Born: 1-4-30, Grand River, Ohio **Ht/Wt:** 5-11/190 **College:** John Carroll **Drafted:** 1951, 9th round, Browns **Position:** DB **Career statistics:** Interceptions, 21 **Teams played:** Browns 1951-52; Colts 1953-56; Redskins 1957 **Teams coached (328-156-6 RS, 19-17 PS):** Colts 1963-69; Dolphins 1970-95 **Championship team:** NFL 1968 **Super Bowl champions:** 1972, '73 seasons

The chiseled jaw, heart-stopping glare and mistake-triggering tirades were Don Shula trademarks. So were the record 347 victories delivered by the game's most celebrated coach over an incredible 33 NFL seasons with the Baltimore Colts and Miami Dolphins. The gruff exterior, the unwavering discipline, the complete dedication—all were tools of the trade for pro football's ultimate field general.

"I'm no miracle worker and don't make me out to be one. I don't have a magic formula that I'm going to give to the world as soon as I can write a book. I'm not a person with a great deal of finesse. I'm about as subtle as a punch in the mouth."

—*Don Shula*

sons, his Dolphins finished under .500 twice; he coached 19 playoff teams, 20 that recorded 10 or more wins, and won 11 AFC East titles; he coached in a record six Super Bowls, winning two.

Shula's masterpiece was 1972, when his Dolphins finished 17-0—the only perfect season in NFL history—and defeated Washington in Super Bowl VII. His 1973 Miami team (15-2) also won a Super Bowl and his Dolphins posted a 112-44-1 record in the decade. Perhaps Shula's greatest accomplishment was his ability to adapt to the ever-changing style of play, from the grind-it-out offenses of his Baltimore and early Miami teams to the wide-open passing attacks he later employed with quarterback Dan Marino.

Playing for Shula was a life-changing experience. He was methodically prepared, down to the smallest detail, and intolerant of mistakes. His intensity was manifested by roaring tirades and long, strenuous practices. Shula demanded the same uncompromising work ethic from his players that he had exhibited from 1951-57 as a defensive back in Cleveland, Baltimore and Washington.

The numbers Shula posted from 1963, when he took the Colts coaching reins at age 33, through 1995, his 26th season with the Dolphins, are staggering. His 328 regular-season wins are the most in history; his Colts posted winning records in each of his seven sea-

The Ohio-born Shula also was a forerunner in the use of zone defenses, zone blitzing, situation substitution and a roving pass-rush specialist. He was the first coach to have three-a-day practices, including the now-common "walk-through." One memory Shula would like to erase is the New York Jets' stunning victory over his powerful Colts in Super Bowl III.

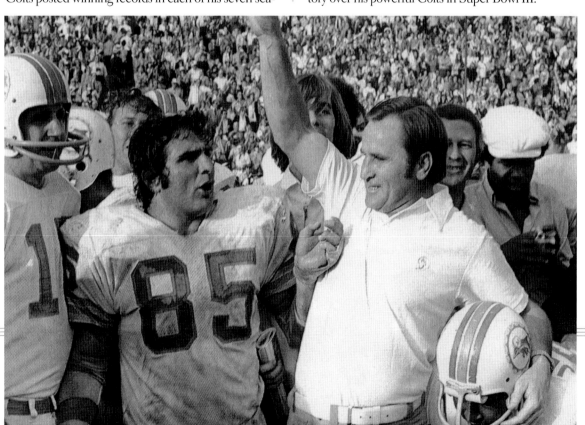

O. J. SIMPSON

Born: 7-9-47, San Francisco **Ht/Wt:** 6-1/212 **College:** USC **Drafted:** 1969, 1st round, Bills **Position:** RB **Career statistics:** Rushing, 2,404 att., 11,236 yds., 61 TDs; Receiving, 203 rec., 14 TDs; KO Returns, 33 att., 30.0 avg., 1 TD **Rushing champion:** 1972, '73, '75, '76 **Scoring champion:** 1975 **Teams:** Bills 1969-77; 49ers 1978-79 **Honors:** 75th Anniversary All-Time Team; 1970s All-Decade Team

Like any good thoroughbred, O.J. Simpson was a creature of timing. He knew precisely when to cut, dart, slash and accelerate to the finish line — and he knew how to do it with style. The aura, the memory of a humpback, forward-leaning Simpson high-stepping his way through an opponent's secondary remain indelibly locked in the minds of everyone who saw him over a sometimes-agonizing, often-amazing 11-year career.

Simpson was a charmer who could light up a stadium with a 90-yard run or a room with his 100-watt personality. On the field, he was the Juice, Buffalo's swashbuckling 6-foot-1, 212-pound lightning rod who might punish a tackler one play, zip past him the next. Off the field, he was outgoing and accommodating, blessed with a million-dollar smile and Hollywood good looks that would translate into lucrative commercial endorsements and a post-football acting career.

O.J., the high-profile 1968 Heisman Trophy winner from USC, was restricted during nine Buffalo seasons by weak teams that qualified only once for the playoffs. But that didn't

> **"(O.J.) slithers, he hurdles, he accelerates and changes directions. Use all the adjectives you can think of and then at the end of them add on a bleep-bleep."**
>
> —*Dwight White, Steelers defensive end,* 1975

keep him from storming the NFL while running behind an "Electric Company" offensive line specially constructed by coach Lou Saban to showcase his talents. O.J. won the first of four rushing titles in 1972 while beginning a five-season rampage that would net an incredible 7,699 yards and 54 touchdowns.

Simpson's signature season was 1973, when he posted three 200-yard games and gained immortality by becoming the first 2,000-yard rusher in NFL history. But some consider his 1975 season, which produced 2,243 yards (1,817 rushing, 426 receiving) and 23 touchdowns, even better. A 1,503-yard 1976 campaign ended a memorable five-year run filled with All-Pro, MVP, Player of the Year and Pro Bowl citations that lifted the graceful O.J. to legendary status.

Simpson never approached such numbers again. The six-time Pro Bowl selection retired in 1979, after two injury-plagued seasons in San Francisco, with 11,236 rushing yards, 2,142 receiving and 990 on 33 kickoff returns.

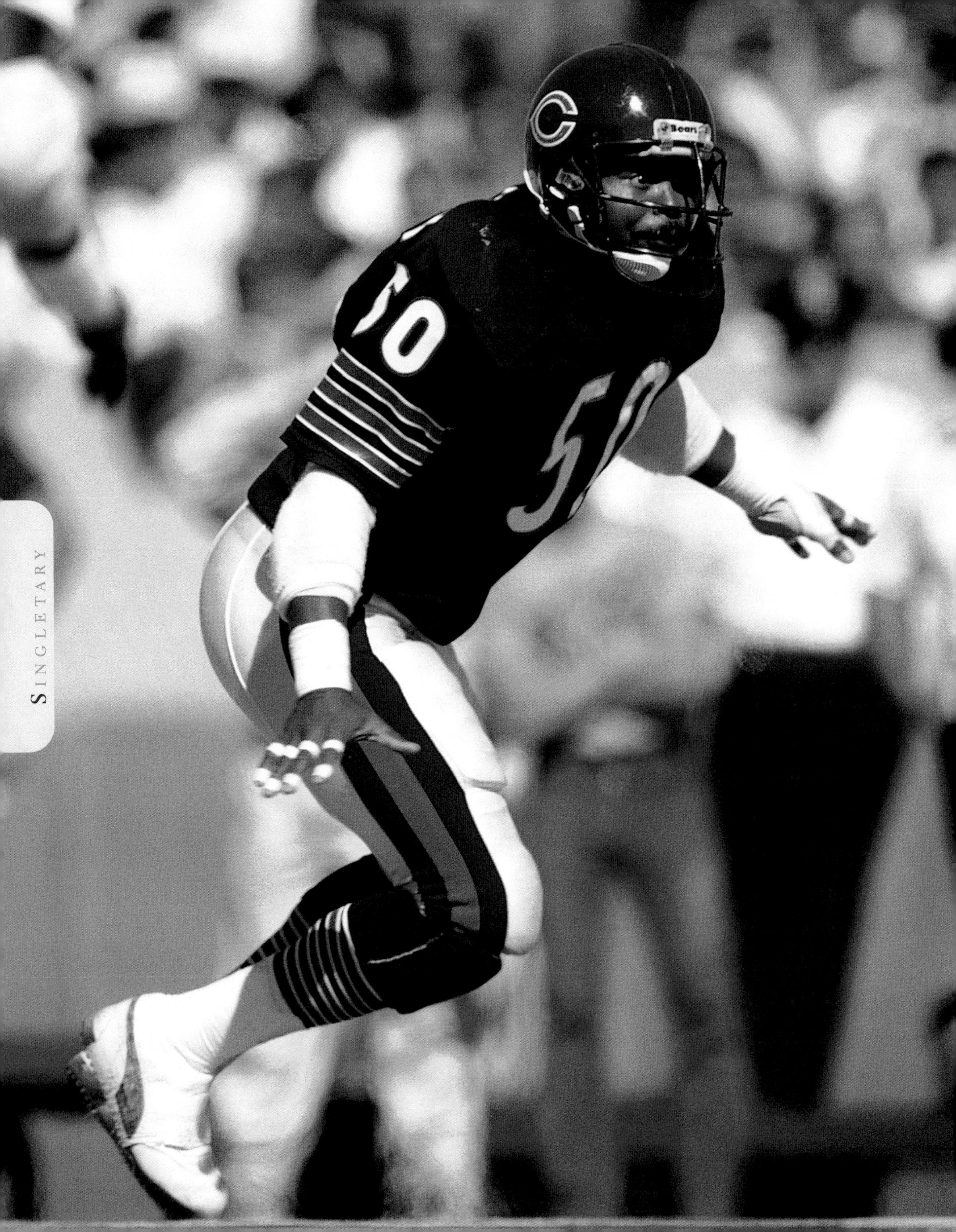
Bears
50
50

MIKE SINGLETARY

Born: 10-9-58, Houston, Tex. **Ht/Wt:** 6-0/230 **College:** Baylor **Drafted:** 1981, 2nd round, Bears **Primary position:** LB
Teams: Bears 1981-92 **Super Bowl champion:** 1985 season **Honors:** 1980s All-Decade Team

Former teammates remember the inspirational speeches, the fiery and demonstrative pregame diatribes that usually resulted in at least minor damage to furniture. Intensity never was a problem for Mike Singletary, who listened to Bach and Beethoven to get "pumped-down" for opponents. If success can be measured by sheer will and determination, the Chicago Bears' No. 50 could match up with anybody who ever played the middle linebacker position.

Singletary needed that kind of edge to overcome deficiencies in size (6-foot, 230) and speed. What he couldn't do when he came out of Baylor University in 1981 he learned through obsessive dedication. He hated coming out of games in third-down situations so he spent countless hours after practice working on coverage techniques that eventually allowed him to become a complete player. He approached the game like a coach, studying film to learn tendencies and memorizing the nuances of every position.

Singletary, who was built like a fireplug with thick neck and a powerful upper body, was a walking contradiction. Off the field, he looked at life through thick-rimmed glasses and spoke in the soft, thoughtful tones of a high school math teacher. On the field, he was constant motion, totally focused and dedicated to getting the man with the ball. He was at his best as a run-stuffer who could throw his body into the fray with total disregard for life or limb.

Nobody could match the relentless desire and enthusiasm that kept Singletary in the lineup for all but two games over a 12-year career. The man who was "too small and too slow" earned 10 Pro Bowl selections and acclaim as a middle linebacker in the throwback mold of Dick Butkus.

Singletary's happiest moment came in 1985 when he quarterbacked a defense that allowed an NFL-low 12.3 points per game and helped the Bears complete an 18-1 season with a victory over New England in Super Bowl XX. Singletary recovered two fumbles in the 46-10 championship-securing rout.

> **"Nobody studied any harder, nobody worked any harder to make the Bears a good defense than Mike Singletary. It became a passion to him."**
>
> —*Mike Ditka, 1998, The Associated Press*

SINGLETARY

Player/Year elected: 2001

JACKIE SLATER

Born: 5-27-54, Jackson, Miss. **Ht/Wt:** 6-4/277 **College:** Jackson State **Drafted:** 1976, 3rd round, Rams **Primary position:** OT
Teams: Rams 1976-95

Snarling, snorting and growling were never part of Jackie Slater's game-day routine. He was a quiet assassin, a silent-but-deadly hit man who methodically inflicted pain for 20 NFL seasons. Slater also was the consummate professional and the go-to offensive tackle who opened holes for seven different 1,000-yard rushers in his long career with the Los Angeles and St. Louis Rams.

Teammates were inspired by Slater's relentless drive to be the game's best blocker and the every-play passion he displayed through practices as well as games. The 6-foot-4, 277-pound giant, whose work ethic

matched his powerful frame, loved to play and never missed an opportunity to improve. When the agile and surprisingly quick Slater fired out from his three-point stance, defenses parted for appreciative running backs.

Former Rams defensive end Jack Youngblood, a long-time teammate and practice opponent, marveled at Slater's nonstop search for perfection. "Jackie didn't want to just beat you, he wanted to dominate you," Youngblood said. And that was true from his 1976 rookie season through 1995, his one-game, career-ending campaign in St. Louis.

The soft-spoken Slater was a backup for teams that appeared in two NFC championship games in his first three years. But he was a starter by 1979, when the Rams advanced to the franchise's first Super Bowl and lost to Pittsburgh, despite Slater's outstanding effort against Steeler defender L.C. Greenwood. In 1983, when Slater earned the first of seven Pro Bowl invitations, the Rams allowed only 23 sacks and Eric Dickerson rushed for a rookie-record 1,808 yards. Dickerson, thanks in no small part to Slater, exploded for 2,105 yards a year later.

Mississippi-born Slater, the oldest of five brothers, attended Jackson State in his hometown, primarily because of the recruiting efforts of Walter Payton. He spent three seasons blocking for the future NFL rushing champion before playing 259 games with the Rams—the first NFL player to spend 20 seasons with one team.

"He was so much of a leader in the way he went about his craft that people began to use him as a role model. I certainly did. Within our own team, he was the guy everybody admired."

—*John Robinson, former Rams coach,* 2001, *The Associated Press*

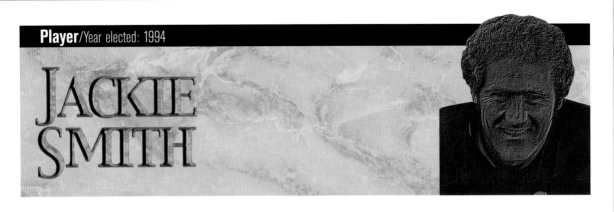

JACKIE SMITH

Born: 2-23-40, Columbia, Miss. **Ht/Wt:** 6-4/235 **College:** Northwestern State (La.) **Drafted:** 1963, 10th round, Cardinals **Primary positions:** TE, P **Career statistics:** Receiving, 480 rec., 7,918 yds., 16.5 avg., 40 TDs; Rushing, 38 att., 327 yds., 3 TDs; Punting, 127 att., 39.1 avg. **Teams:** Cardinals 1963-77; Cowboys 1978

The snarling post-tackle disgust and intimidating glare were Jackie Smith trademarks. So were the bulldozing blocks and locomotive-like runs that personified the double-edged talents of the NFL's new-era tight end from 1963-78. He was a 6-foot-4, 235-pound physical contradiction, a shockingly efficient pass catcher who helped redefine a position.

Before Smith and Baltimore's John Mackey, tight ends were primarily blockers. After witnessing their surprising blend of size, speed and power, coaches looked for more athletic big men who could provide an extra pass-receiving option and stretch defenses. Smith, a 10th-round after-thought 1963 draft pick by the St. Louis Cardinals, could neutralize ends, outrun linebackers and intimidate safeties.

It's unlikely big No. 81 ever expected to fill such a role when he was drafted out of Northwestern State (La.)—a long-striding hurdler who filled out scholarship requirements by playing football. But he caught nine passes for 212 yards and two touchdowns in his third professional game and remained a Cardinals' starter through 1977. He became feared throughout the league, a ferocious runner who preferred to punish tacklers rather than run around them.

Off the field, Smith was an ever-pleasant and courteous Southern gentleman; during games, he was combative and belligerent, a dependable receiver who took every tackle as a personal affront. Smith, who also doubled for three years as a punter, was the dependable third-down option for four St. Louis coaches, including creative Don Coryell. Although he played only two postseason games for St. Louis, he earned five straight Pro Bowl invitations and topped 40 receptions seven times, making 56 catches for 1,205 yards in a 1967 masterpiece.

Ironically, the signature play of Smith's 210-game career came after St. Louis—when he dropped a sure Super Bowl XIII TD pass from Dallas quarterback Roger Staubach in a 35-31 loss to Pittsburgh. The memory of Smith writhing in anguish overshadows his career total of 480 catches for 7,918 yards and 40 touchdowns—tight end records when he retired after the 1978 season.

"I just don't like to get tackled. When that defensive man tackles me, it means he's beaten me. I'm just not going to give up. I'm not going to give him that satisfaction. ... I hate to get beat."

—*Jackie Smith, 1968*

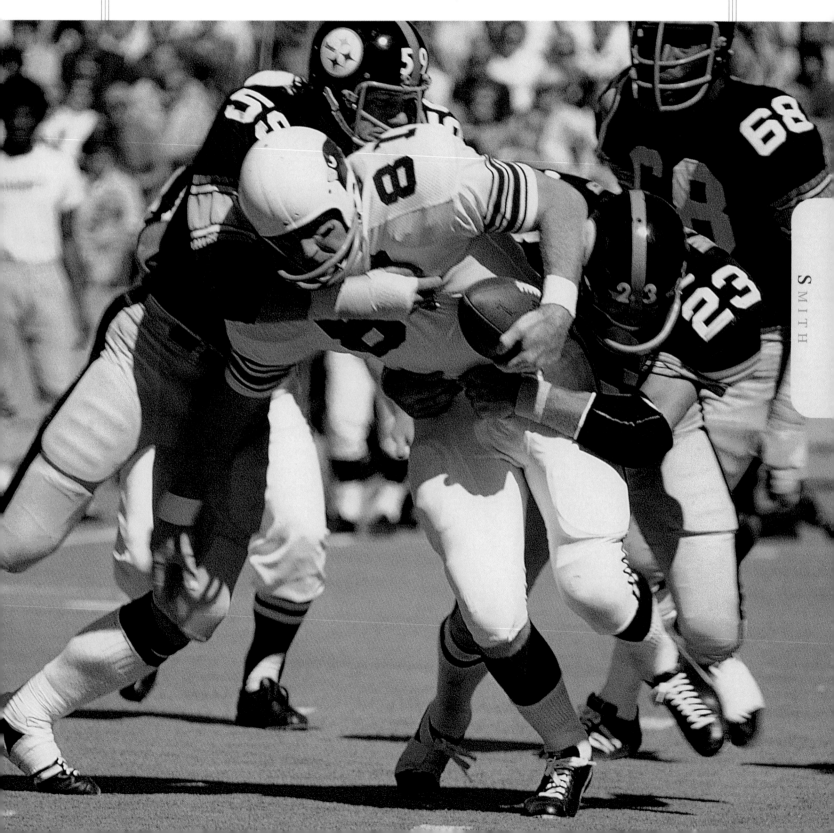

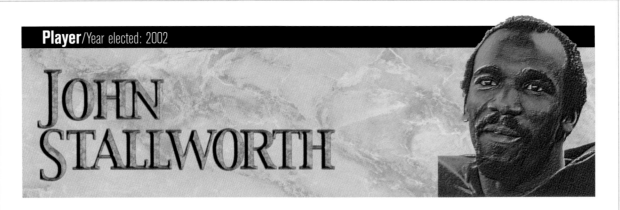

Player/Year elected: 2002

JOHN STALLWORTH

Born: 7-15-52, Tuscaloosa, Ala. **Ht/Wt:** 6-2/202 **College:** Alabama A&M **Drafted:** 1974, 4th round, Steelers **Primary position:** WR
Career statistics: Receiving, 537 rec., 8,723 yds., 16.2 avg., 63 TDs **Teams:** Steelers 1974-87 **Super Bowl champions:** 1974, '75, '78, '79 seasons

To Pittsburgh fans, he was the subtle big-game warrior and pass-catching hero of two Super Bowls. To the rest of the pro football world, Terry Bradshaw's "other receiver" was an unsung alternative to the always-flashy and charismatic Lynn Swann. The real John Stallworth was an exceptional talent who overcame his fate-imposed anonymity with 14 years of workmanlike efficiency and go-to dependability.

Swann was picked in the first round, Stallworth in the fourth of a 1974 Steelers draft that yielded four future Hall of Famers. Over the next nine seasons, they formed one of the most productive receiver tandems in NFL history while helping the Steelers win four Super Bowls. Swann, the Southern Cal product, was sleek, fast and flamboyant, prone to making spectacular, acrobatic catches; Stallworth, from little Alabama A&M, was strong, fast and seldom dropped a pass.

The 6-foot-2, 202-pound Stallworth was a practice workhorse who ran precise routes and used his powerful legs to break tackles and set up big-gainers. Intelligent and a meticulous planner, his soft-spoken and quiet personality belied the pride and passion that produced three 1,000-yard seasons, an impressive 16.2-yard reception average and 63 receiving touchdowns. Even though he was forced to share catches with Swann, he still holds numerous Pittsburgh receiving marks.

But Stallworth's greatest asset was an ability to elevate his game. In the Steelers' Super Bowl XIII win over Dallas, he caught three passes for 115 yards and two touchdowns, one a 75-yarder; in a Super Bowl XIV win over Los Angeles, he

"Do you realize that if Stallworth was in the West Coast offense, if he was catching underneath and people were picking for him and such, with his strength and size, there's no telling what he would have done? He had big, strong thighs. He had deceiving speed. He was strong enough to catch those slants and he never had alligator arms."

—*Lionel Taylor, former Steelers receiving coach, 2002, Pittsburgh Post-Gazette*

caught three for 121, including a 73-yard TD bomb. He holds the Super Bowl record with a 24.4-yard reception average and he's the only player in history to catch TD passes in eight straight postseason games.

In 1987, five years after Swann had retired, Stallworth also called it a career. He left the game with 537 career receptions, four Pro Bowl appearances and respect as one of the NFL's great big-game performers.

BART STARR

Born: 1-9-34, Montgomery, Ala. **Ht/Wt:** 6-1/200 **College:** Alabama **Drafted:** 1956, 17th round, Packers **Primary position:** QB
Career statistics: Passing, 1,808-of-3,149, 24,718 yds., 152 TDs; Rushing, 247 att., 15 TDs **Teams:** Packers 1956-71 **Championship teams:** NFL 1961, '62, '65, '66, '67 **Super Bowl champions:** 1966 (MVP), '67 (MVP) seasons **Honors:** 1960s All-Decade Team

Contrary to popular belief, perfection did not come easily for Bart Starr. He was an unlikely success story, a legend spawned on the sideline at the University of Alabama, in the 17th round of the NFL draft and from deep on the depth chart of a struggling franchise. Starr ran a quarterback sneak on professional football, rising to Hall of Fame prominence as the perfect field general for the near-perfect team of the 1960s.

On the surface, Starr's long and prosperous association with Vince Lombardi's colorful, blue-collar Green Bay Packers seemed strange. He was a Southern-bred boy, an always-polite "yes sir, no sir" kind of guy with no vices and deep religious

convictions. But when Lombardi took the Packers reins in 1959, the qualities he saw in Starr were a perfect match for his ball-control vision—quiet, calculating and always under control, both physically and emotionally.

Handed control of the meticulous, grinding Green Bay offense in 1960, Starr led the Packers on an eight-year winning odyssey that produced an 82-24-4

> ## "Nothing seems to rattle him. You can never get him mad, and that's what we like to do, get the quarterback all excited. You can hit Starr as hard as you want and he never seems to lose his cool."
>
> *— Joe Schmidt*

record, six title-game appearances and five championships, including wins in the first two Super Bowls. Starr took Lombardi's well-conceived game plans and executed them with cool efficiency, deviating from script only with perfect audibles. Norm Van Brocklin, after watching Starr carve up his Minnesota Vikings in one game, called him "the smartest quarterback in pro football."

Unlike swashbuckling, gambling contemporary Johnny Unitas, Starr was conservative and always threw the high-percentage pass. He could lull an opponent to sleep with his ball-control game plan, then deliver a third-and-one touchdown dagger. His accuracy was uncanny (a 57.4 percent career completion rate) and he once threw 294 passes without an interception.

Starr, who finished his 16-year career in 1971 with 24,718 passing yards, will always be remembered for his championship-securing touchdown dive in the waning seconds of the Packers' 1967 Ice Bowl victory over Dallas. He also was MVP of the first two Super Bowls.

ROGER STAUBACH

Born: 2-5-42, Cincinnati, Ohio **Ht/Wt:** 6-3/200 **College:** Navy **Drafted:** 1964, 10th round, NFL Cowboys; 16th round, AFL Chiefs
Primary position: QB **Career statistics:** 1,685-of-2,958, 22,700 yds., 153 TDs; Rushing, 410 att., 2,264 yds., 5.5 avg., 20 TDs
Teams: Cowboys 1969-79 **Super Bowl champions:** 1971 (MVP), '77 seasons **Honors:** 1970s All-Decade Team

Don't be fooled by the clean-cut, All-American boy-next-door image. Roger Staubach, the always-polite U.S. Naval Academy graduate and Vietnam veteran, was a football warrior who could break your heart without remorse. He could do it on the ground, through the air or in the huddle, a winning combination he supplied for 11 successful seasons as quarterback of the Dallas Cowboys.

Former coach Tom Landry called him "the greatest competitor I have ever seen," a quality that showed up over and over in Staubach's ability to engineer comeback victories. He did it 23 times in his career, 14 times in the final two minutes of games. Staubach once wiped out a 12-point deficit with two touchdown passes in the final 78 seconds of a 1972 playoff win over San Francisco. In a 1975 playoff battle against Minnesota, his desperation 50-yard bomb to Drew Pearson — the now-famous "Hail Mary pass" — gave the Cowboys a shocking 17-14 win.

That was the essence of Staubach, who ranks as one of the greatest passer/runner/leader quarterbacks of all time. Game plans were carefully designed to contain Roger the Dodger, who was especially dangerous on third-down plays. He could scramble away from defenders and throw accurately on the run. His daring forays, the opposite of his soft-spoken, disciplined off-field personality, gave the Dallas offense an extra dimension.

Staubach's success is amazing, considering he fulfilled a four-year Navy commitment and did not turn professional until age 27. He played 11 years, threw for 22,700 yards and 153 touchdowns and ran for 2,264 yards and 20 TDs. In his nine years as a starter, the Cowboys won 73 percent of their games, reached the playoffs eight times, won four NFC championship games and captured two of four Super Bowls.

The four-time Pro Bowl selection and 1963 Heisman Trophy winner earned MVP honors in Super Bowl VI. Fittingly, Staubach's last regular-season pass in 1979 was a seven-yard, game-winning TD throw to Tony Hill with 39 seconds remaining.

> "Every Cowboy, offense and defense, looked to him. They all felt that as long as he was in the game they had a chance to win. To tell you the truth, his opponents felt the same way."
>
> — *Jim Hanifan, Cardinals coach, 1980*

ERNIE STAUTNER

Born: 4-20-25, Prinzing-by-Cham, Germany **Ht/Wt:** 6-2/235 **College:** Boston College **Drafted:** 1950, 2nd round, Steelers **Primary positions:** DT, DE, OG **Career statistics:** 21 fumble recoveries; 3 safeties **Teams:** Steelers 1950-63 **Honors:** 1950s All-Decade Team

A fist to the mouth, forearm to the ear, knee to the stomach—all were Ernie Stautner calling cards, a signal that his special brand of trench warfare had begun. And things only got worse over the next 60 minutes. Nobody could make life more difficult for offensive linemen than the body-crunching Pittsburgh strongman, who never stopped handing out punishment over a legendary if not prosperous 14-year NFL career.

Stautner, an undersized 6-foot-2, 235-pound defensive tackle who was rejected as "too small" by New York Giants coach Steve Owen, became something of a folk hero to long-suffering Steelers fans. With oaken arms, powerful shoulders and a low center of gravity, he pounded on bigger blockers and anchored a respectable defense. Opponents discovered quickly that a matchup against Stautner meant a bruising battle for survival.

His motor never stopped and the intimidation factor rose with every blow he delivered. Stautner was intense and aggressive, a man who competed with a championship-level drive. His teams posted only

> "That man ain't human. He's too strong to be human. He keeps coming, coming, coming. Every time he comes back, he's coming harder."
>
> —*Jim Parker*

four winning records and never qualified for postseason play from 1950-63, but that didn't stop Big Ernie from dominating his position with mobility, cunning and that fear-inducing strength.

Rejected by Notre Dame after fighting for the Marine Corps in World War II, Stautner became an offensive and defensive star at Boston College before going to Pittsburgh in the 1950 draft. The Bavarian-born tackle went on to earn nine Pro Bowl invitations while starting 168 of a possible 174 games, often battling through painful injuries while eagerly filling voids at defensive end and offensive guard when the situation dictated.

The three career safeties and 21 fumbles he recovered are tributes to his aggressiveness and determination. His 23-year post-playing career association with the Dallas Cowboys gives substance to his football acumen. As Dallas defensive coordinator and line coach, Stautner was credited with developing the famed "Doomsday Defense" that helped the Cowboys reach five Super Bowls in the 1970s.

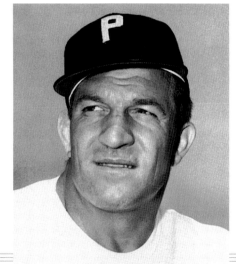

S T A U T N E R

JAN STENERUD

Born: 11-26-42, Lillestrom, Norway **Ht/Wt:** 6-2/190 **College:** Montana State **Drafted:** 1966, 3rd round, Chiefs **Primary position:** PK
Career statistics: 1,699 pts., 373-of-558 FGs, 580-of-601 PAT **Teams:** Chiefs 1967-79; Packers 1980-83; Vikings 1984-85
Championship team: AFL 1969 **Super Bowl champion:** 1969 season **Honors:** 75th Anniversary All-Time Team; All-Time NFL Team

The mild-mannered enthusiasm, good-natured charm and wide-eyed wonder were Jan Stenerud trademarks for 19 NFL seasons. So was the powerful right leg that produced 1,699 points, even though the former Norwegian ski jumper never fully understood the game he sometimes dominated. Nobody traveled a more unusual road to greatness than the first full-time kicker to earn distinction in the Pro Football Hall of Fame.

Stenerud will be remembered primarily for the 13 outstanding seasons he gave the Kansas City Chiefs from 1967-79. Not only was the Danny Kaye lookalike deadly from 30-40 yards, he was surprisingly accurate from 50-55. Stenerud was a weapon Chiefs coach Hank Stram could deploy from anywhere in enemy territory, a bomb he could drop on demoralized defenders.

Such hard-edged notions never connected with Stenerud, who lived his first 19 years in Norway, playing soccer and dreaming of becoming a champion ski jumper. It was that latter talent that brought him on scholarship

> **"When we first saw Jan Stenerud, we were in awe. ... He started kicking and I heard guys coming into the locker room. They were saying, 'Get out here. You've got to see this guy. He's one-stepping and popping them 60 yards, kicking them out of the end zone.' "**
>
> —*Len Dawson, 1983, The Kansas City Times*

to Montana State University; but it was that soccer leg that gained him American renown when he connected on 18-of-33 field goal attempts, including a then college-record 59-yarder, for the football team.

Stenerud, who did not witness his first professional game until age 21, was a slender, 6-foot-2 soccer-style kicker with the ability to learn quickly. While Stenerud did not fully grasp the intricacies of football, that didn't stop him from becoming a straight-arrow scoring machine. Ten times he kicked 20 or more field goals in his 13 Chiefs seasons and he never missed a game because of injury or illness. His three field goals, one a 48-yarder, helped the Chiefs upset Minnesota in Super Bowl IV.

Seven times Stenerud topped 100 points in a career that also included stints in Green Bay and Minnesota. He kicked 17 field goals of 50-plus yards, including a career-best 55-yarder against Denver in 1970. The six-time Pro Bowler retired in 1985 with 373 field goals, an NFL record at the time.

STEPHENSON

DWIGHT STEPHENSON

Born: 11-20-57, Murfreesboro, N.C. **Ht/Wt:** 6-2/255 **College:** Alabama **Drafted:** 1980, 2nd round, Dolphins **Primary position:** C
Teams: Dolphins 1980-87 **Honors:** 1980s All-Decade Team

Alabama's Bear Bryant once called him "the greatest center I've ever coached." So did Miami's Don Shula. Teammates and opponents marveled at the unrelenting ferocity he unleashed after every snap of his massive wrists. Dwight Stephenson was a human destroyer, a protector of quarterback Dan Marino and the perfect middle man for one of the better offensive lines of the 1980s.

The finely-chiseled Stephenson was like an angry panther when he snapped the ball and exploded his 6-foot-2, 255-pound body into a startled defender. He was strong, fast and devoted to the challenge of becoming the best center in NFL history. Stephenson seemed to operate at a new level of intensity and the Dolphins constructed their blocking schemes around his ability to handle nose tackles and linebackers one-on-one. Trying to get past big No. 57 was like trying to wrestle a bear.

Run-blocking or pass-blocking, the North Carolina native was equally proficient. He was a tire-

> "Man, I've never seen anyone like him. I just don't know how he does it, how he can snap the ball with one hand and be off exploding into his block all in one motion."
>
> —*Mike Charles, former Dolphins teammate, 1985*

less worker who approached every practice as if it was the Super Bowl and worked out during offseasons as if his life depended on it. Coaches marveled at his play every time they broke down game film and he once went two seasons without allowing a sack.

Tenacious as Stephenson was on the field, he was gentle and friendly off it. A deeply religious man with a charming smile, he winced every time teammates talked up his sometimes amazing feats.

Like the time he took out two rushers at the same time, one with each forearm. Or the time he blocked a defender out of the end zone.

Stephenson, a five-time Pro Bowl selection by age 30, saw his eight-year career come to a premature end in 1987 when a hit to the knee tore his anterior cruciate ligament. He retired without a championship, although he helped the Dolphins win four AFC East titles and played in two Super Bowls—losses to Washington and San Francisco.

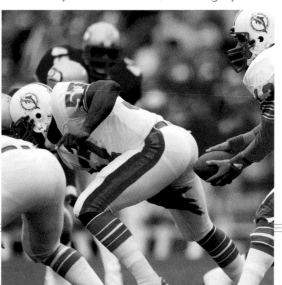

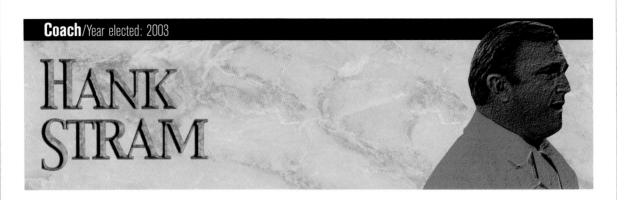

Coach/Year elected: 2003

HANK STRAM

Born: 1-3-24, Chicago, Ill. **Teams coached (131-97-10 RS, 5-3 PS):** Texans/Chiefs 1960-74; Saints 1976-77 **Championship teams:** AFL 1962, '66, '69 **Super Bowl winner:** 1969 season

The energy that emanated from Hank Stram's compact 5-foot-8 body lit up Kansas City for more than a decade. The ideas and innovations that flowed from his football-savvy mind changed pro football strategy and the way the game is played. The winningest coach in American Football League history also was an articulate salesman who helped bring credibility to a new league on the eve of its merger with the NFL.

The image of Stram, wandering the sideline in his three-piece suit, waving his rolled-up game plan and excitedly calling signals into a wireless microphone, is a Super Bowl IV classic. His willingness to wear the mike was a breakthrough for NFL Films, a step forward in Super Bowl popularity and an example of Stram's public relations savvy. The Chiefs' shocking upset of powerful Minnesota provided an inspirational

> "He knew how to win. A lot of people thought we always had the best talent, but that wasn't always the case. He knew how to take advantage of our strengths and the opponents' weaknesses."
>
> — *Len Dawson, 2003, The Kansas City Star*

ending to the AFL's 10-year existence.

Stram, the straight-shooting former college assistant who built Lamar Hunt's Dallas Texans/Kansas City Chiefs into an AFL power, was an outstanding organizer, motivator and talent evaluator. But he is best remembered as a strategist who gave football such concepts as the tight I-formation, the moving pocket, the stack defense and zone coverages to combat the wide-open offenses of the AFL. Stram was a master of the play-action pass and confusing pre-snap offensive formation shifts.

He also was a disciplinarian who encouraged diversity during an era in which racial barriers still existed. Outstanding black players like Abner Haynes, Buck Buchanan, Bobby Bell, Willie Lanier and Otis Taylor provided a firm foundation for teams that won 124 games—87 in the AFL—and three championships.

Stram coached his Chiefs in the first Super Bowl, a 35-10 loss to Green Bay that made his Super Bowl IV upset all the sweeter. He remained in Kansas City through 1974 before coaching a weak New Orleans team for two seasons. Stram retired to the CBS Radio broadcast booth in 1977 with a 131-97-10 regular-season record.

STRAM

KEN STRONG

Born: 8-6-06, West Haven, Conn. **Died:** 10-5-79 **Ht/Wt:** 5-11/210 **College:** NYU **Positions:** HB, DB, K **Career statistics:** Rushing, 24 TDs; Receiving, 7 TDs; Passing, 6 TDs; Punt Returns, 2 TDs; Scoring, 38 FG, 166 PAT, 484 Pts. **Scoring champion:** 1933 **Teams:** Staten Island 1929-32; Giants 1933-35, 1939, 1944-47 **Championship team:** NFL 1934 **Honors:** 1930s All-Decade Team

To New York Giants fans, he's the legendary hero of one of the most memorable games in team history. To his 1930s-era contemporaries, Ken Strong was a versatile, point-producing tailback whose potentially spectacular career was diminished by acrimonious contract battles. Not diminished was the Red Grange and Ernie Nevers-like aura Strong brought to the field and to one of the game's first glamour franchises.

There was little Strong couldn't do athletically. The compact 5-foot-11, 210-pounder had sprinter speed, Grange-like elusiveness and Nevers-like toughness. He was an outstanding passer, punter, placekicker and defensive back who could beat you in a variety of ways. He also was an outstanding baseball prospect who played in the New York Yankees' system until a wrist injury ended his two-sport aspirations.

The former New York University star could have stepped into the Giants' football spotlight in 1929, but he stubbornly elected to sign with Staten Island when the New Yorkers failed to meet his salary demands. He ended up with the Giants when the Stapletons folded four years later and played three seasons before jumping to the outlaw American Football League, again because of a salary dispute. That cost him three NFL seasons—two under contract to the short-lived AFL, one more to suspension.

But when he did play, he kept fans on the edge of their seats. Strong topped NFL scorers with 64 points in 1933 and led the Giants to Eastern Division titles in 1933, '34 and '35. The 1934 Giants defeated powerful Chicago, 30-13, when Strong scored 17 points—a 38-yard field goal, two extra-point kicks and second-half touchdown runs of 42 and 11 yards—in the famed "Sneakers" championship game on an icy Polo Grounds field.

Reinstated from suspension in 1939, Strong played for the division-winning Giants before retiring after suffering a serious back injury. He returned in 1944 as a war-time kicking specialist and helped the Giants win two more division titles before retiring in 1947 with 484 career points.

> "Strong was the greatest all-round player of all time. I've never seen a football player in his class."
>
> — *Walter Steffen, former coach at Carnegie Tech*

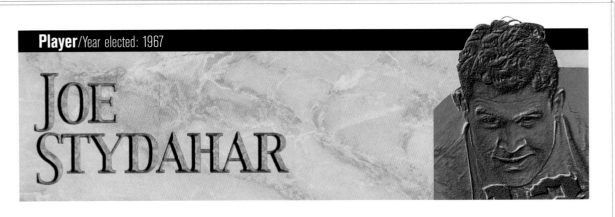

JOE STYDAHAR

Born: 3-17-12, Kaylor, Pa. **Died:** 3-23-77 **Ht/Wt:** 6-4/230 **College:** Pittsburgh, West Virginia **Drafted:** 1936, 1st round, Bears **Primary positions:** OT, DT **Teams:** Bears 1936-42, 1945-46 **Championship teams:** NFL 1940, '41, '46 **Honors:** 1930s All-Decade Team

He was Jumbo Joe to friends and teammates, a Monster of the Midway to fans and enemies of powerful Chicago teams. Everything about Joe Stydahar was huge, from the 6-foot-4, 230-pound body he used to batter opponents to the quality of his work as one of the game's great two-way tackles. Nobody provided a more powerful anchor for the Bears' colorful 1940s championship dominance than the hard-nosed son of a West Virginia coal miner.

Stydahar was so tough he refused to wear a helmet until forced to do so by NFL rules. He measured his success by missing teeth and never backed away from the elbow-flinging battles in the trenches. He was big and remarkably fast, a bulldozing blocker and impenetrable defensive wall for runners who marveled at his 60-minute intensity.

From 1936, when Stydahar became George Halas' first pick in the inaugural draft, through 1942, he formed a formidable front line with future Hall of Famers George Musso and guard Danny

> "Once we decided to stop Joe. We worked up a play just for him, called it the Stydahar Special. It was a trap play and on paper it sure looked like we had him. Dick Todd was the ballcarrier. Well, I called the play, Joe ran over two Redskin linemen and hit Todd so hard we thought he'd killed him. That was the last time we used the Stydahar Special."
>
> — *Sammy Baugh*

Fortmann. Bulldog Turner joined the mix in 1940 and the Bears won consecutive championships and three in four years. Musso and Fortmann were gone in 1946 when Stydahar, who missed the team's 1943 title run because of military duty, helped the Bears to their final championship of the decade.

Gentle and easy-going off the field, the curly-haired Stydahar turned nasty when play began. He was a relentless hit man and demanding performer who was known to reprimand underachieving teammates, a quality that served him well in his post-player life as a championship-winning coach of the Los Angeles Rams. The ever-intense Stydahar refused to play football during his two-year Navy hitch because "I just don't have the heart to play against these kids. They're just too damned small."

It was no coincidence the Bears compiled a 72-25-2 record during Stydahar's nine NFL seasons, winning five Western Division titles and three championships. Jumbo Joe also earned four Pro Bowl invitations.

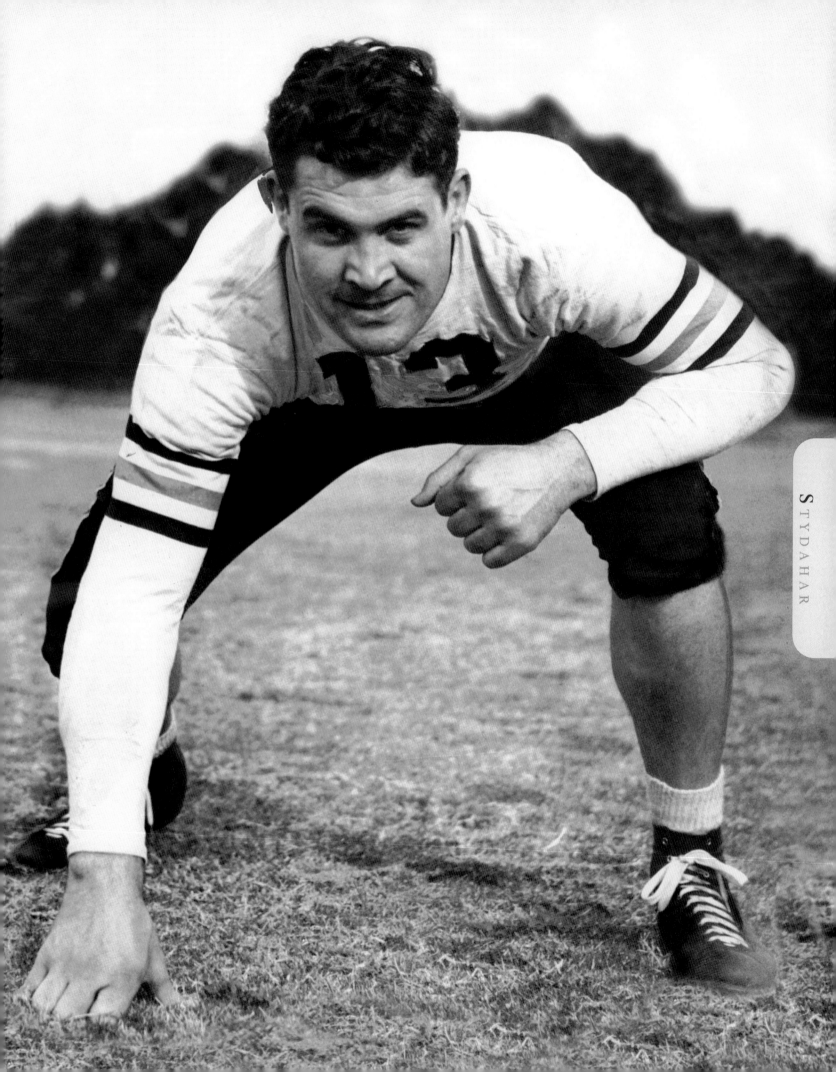

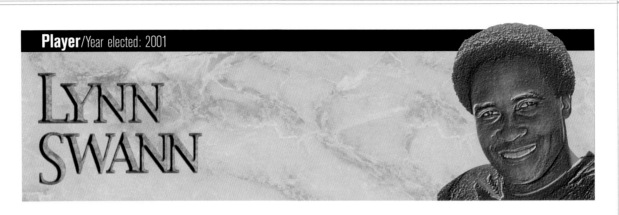

LYNN SWANN

Born: 3-7-52, Alcoa, Tenn. **Ht/Wt:** 5-11/180 **College:** USC **Drafted:** 1974, 1st round, Steelers **Primary position:** WR **Career statistics:** Receiving, 336 rec., 5,462 yds., 16.3 avg., 51 TDs; Punt Returns, 61 att., 12.1 avg., 1 TD **Teams:** Steelers 1974-82 **Super Bowl champions:** 1974, '75 (MVP), '78, '79 **Honors:** 1970s All-Decade Team

He was grace under fire, a soaring, sensitive paragon of athletic expression amid the violence and chaos of the NFL. Nobody personified the dramatic and elegant virtues of professional football more than Lynn Swann, who helped turn pass-catching into an artform and the Pittsburgh Steelers into four-time Super Bowl champions. And nobody was more closely associated with big-game magic than the Steel City's "Astaire in cleats."

The smooth Swann, who benefited from a dance and gymnastics background, did not build his career around regular-season statistics and the traditional blue-collar Pittsburgh work ethic. He was the acrobatic go-to receiver who could dive, leap and soar for the

spectacular catch, the fearless clutch target for Terry Bradshaw passes when everything was on the line. The bigger the game, the better he performed.

Statistics show Swann never ranked high in catches or yardage over a nine-year career that stretched from 1974, when he was selected as a first-round pick out of Southern Cal, through 1982, when he retired with a modest 336

receptions. His Steelers featured a balanced offense and Swann shared catches with future Hall of Famer John Stallworth. His career was a classic example of quality over quantity.

In a Super Bowl X victory over

> **"The mark of a good player is being able to play in big games, and nobody played better in big games than Lynn Swann."**
>
> —*Chuck Noll, 2001,*
> *The Associated Press*

Dallas, MVP Swann caught four passes for 161 yards and a touchdown. On one highlight-film play, he leaped for a Bradshaw bomb, tipped the ball to himself and pulled it in while falling over the defender. In Super Bowl XIII against the same Cowboys, he caught seven passes for 124 yards and a TD. In Super Bowl XIV versus the Los Angeles Rams, he caught five for 79 yards and a score.

The 5-foot-11, 180-pound Swann, a stylish, friendly athlete with a camera-ready smile, balanced the glitzy catches with sure-handed, over-the-middle toughness. Injuries that forced a premature retirement didn't diminish the photogenic work of the three-time Pro Bowler who inspired a whole new generation of receivers.

Player/Year elected: 1986

FRAN TARKENTON

Born: 2-3-40, Richmond, Va. **Ht/Wt:** 6-0/190 **College:** Georgia **Drafted:** 1961, 3rd round, NFL Vikings; 5th round, AFL Patriots
Primary position: QB **Career statistics:** Passing, 3,686-of-6,467, 47,003 yds., 342 TDs; Rushing, 675 att., 3,674 yds., 5.4 avg., 32 TDs **Teams:** Vikings 1961-66, 1972-78; Giants 1967-71

Off the field, Fran Tarkenton was a Boy Scout athlete, the articulate, straight-arrow son of a Methodist minister. On the field, he was a daring, improvising, scrambling 190-pound quarterback who played Russian roulette with 270-pound defensive linemen. He was a novelty in the 1960s, a record-set-

> **"He runs as if he is in a basketball game. He takes all the skill away from the defensive back. He makes you cover a man for five or six seconds and that's too long. Once the pattern is over, you are fighting for your life."**
>
> *—Erich Barnes, former Browns cornerback*

ting field general in the 1970s. During an 18-year NFL career that propelled him to the top of every major passing chart, Tarkenton revolutionized the way his position was played.

Tark's 1961 debut season with the expansion Minnesota Vikings served notice to defenders throughout the league. He darted, turned, juked and ran for his life from giants who were bent on destruction but gasping for the fortitude to continue their chase. Every game against Tarkenton was exhausting, a defensive marathon. He flitted around the field like a butterfly, a startling departure from the era's dropback passers who stood bravely in the pocket.

The catch-me-if-you-can style was a product of Tarkenton's uncanny sixth sense, quick feet and ability to throw accurately on the run. His arm was not strong, but he had great

touch. His scrambles were not planned, but they often created big plays. There was no way to defend against the offensive fireworks Tarkenton was capable of setting off.

For his first 11 seasons with weak Minnesota and New York Giants teams, Tarkenton was simply a quarterback. For his last seven with the beefed-up Vikings, he was a consummate field general capable of generating lots of points. From 1973-78, the former University of Georgia star led the Vikings to six straight NFC Central titles and three Super Bowls, all losses.

When the nine-time Pro Bowl selection retired at age 38, he was the NFL's all-time leading passer with 47,003 yards and 342 touchdowns, a figure that still ranks No. 2. But he also had run for 3,674 yards, an impressive 5.4 average, and 32 touchdowns. Incredibly, the durable Tarkenton did not miss a game because of injury until 1976, his 16th season.

CHARLEY TAYLOR

Born: 9-28-41, Grand Prairie, Tex. **Ht/Wt:** 6-3/210 **College:** Arizona State **Drafted:** 1964, 1st round, Redskins **Primary positions:** WR, RB **Career statistics:** Receiving, 649 rec., 9,110 yds., 14.0 avg., 79 TDs; Rushing, 442 att., 1,488 yds., 11 TDs **Receptions leader:** 1966, '67 **Teams:** Redskins 1964-77 **Honors:** 1960s All-Decade Team

New York Giants scout Emlen Tunnell called Washington rookie Charley Taylor "the best back to come into the NFL since Ollie Matson and Hugh McElhenny." Taylor envisioned himself as the next Jim Brown. But Redskins coach Otto Graham looked past the obvious athleticism, the natural instincts and the explosive breakaway speed to spot a wide receiver in running back's clothing, a big-play machine that would dissect opposing secondaries for 13 relentless seasons.

Graham's wise 1966 switch was fought bitterly by Taylor, who had run for 755 yards and caught 53 passes for 814 more in an outstanding 1964 rookie season. But it didn't take long to see that the 6-foot-3, 210-pound Taylor, isolated against smaller defensive backs and catching passes from Sonny Jurgensen, was a big play waiting to happen. The speed and quickness that got him to the holes ahead of his blockers as a

> "I'd throw him that short sideline pass and he'd come by me twice before he turned upfield. He'd go by me to the right and I'd get out of the way. Then he'd bring a whole crowd back from the other direction."
>
> —*Sonny Jurgensen, 1978, Washington Post*

TAYLOR

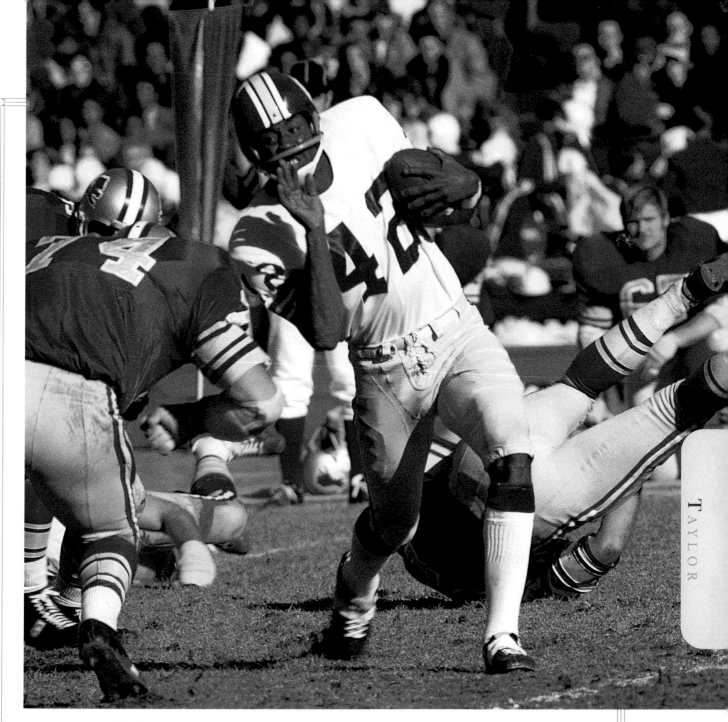

runner became a lethal weapon on pass routes and runs after receptions.

The former Arizona State star blossomed quickly, catching a league-leading 72 passes for 1,119 yards and 12 touchdowns in a breakout 1966 season. He led the league again in 1967 with 70 catches — the third of seven times he would top the 50 plateau. No one, including Taylor himself, would again question his move to wide receiver.

It wasn't long before the hard-working Taylor was known as an outstanding technician who could go short or long with sure hands and the ability to impro-

vise on broken plays. But the always-smiling Texan took most pride in his all-round game, which he punctuated with fierce downfield blocking. With Jurgensen passing to Taylor and Bobby Mitchell, the Washington offense gained stature, especially in a 1972 season that ended with a loss to Miami in Super Bowl VII.

Taylor's always positive attitude and popularity earned him a captain's stripe under coach George Allen before he retired in 1977 as the most prolific receiver in history with 649 catches, good for 9,110 yards. The eight-time Pro Bowl selection also scored 90 touchdowns, 79 through the air.

Player/Year elected: 1976

JIM TAYLOR

Born: 9-20-35, Baton Rouge, La. **Ht/Wt:** 6-0/215 **College:** LSU **Drafted:** 1958, 2nd round, Packers **Position:** FB **Career statistics:** Rushing, 1,941 att., 8,597 yds., 83 TDs; Receiving, 225 rec., 1,756 yds., 10 TDs **Rushing champion:** 1962 **Teams:** Packers 1958-66; Saints 1967 **Championship teams:** NFL 1961, '62, '65, '66 **Super Bowl champion:** 1966 season **Honors:** 1960s All-Decade Team

Vince Lombardi called it "running to daylight." Defenders targeted by the smash-mouth, body-punishing assaults of Jim Taylor called it all-out warfare. To Green Bay's ever-relentless and intense No. 31, it was basic, old-style, pain-inflicting, in-your-face football, the hard-edged kind that separates championship teams from contenders.

There was nothing fancy about the 6-foot, 215-pound Taylor once he wrapped his powerful arms around a Bart Starr handoff. He hit the hole fast, searched out a tackler and charged at him like a raging bull. Contact only inspired the former LSU star, who squirmed, crawled and curled for extra yardage, then mauled, kicked and threw elbows as he got to his feet. He further antagonized opponents with taunts challenging their manhood and tackling ability.

Not blessed with great speed, Taylor's quick, punishing bursts and tree-stump legs made him perfect for short-yardage runs, quick swing passes and power sweeps. Teams that didn't gang tackle paid a stiff price and those that did became susceptible to Green Bay's

speedier backs and Starr's surgical aerial attack. Taylor, a workhorse who consistently topped 200 carries, posted five straight 1,000-yard seasons (1960-64) and led the NFL in 1962 with 1,474 yards and 19 touchdowns. Only Cleveland contemporary Jim Brown stood between him and more rushing titles.

Taylor spoke with a charming Southern drawl, but his scowling, square-jawed countenance reflected his burning intensity. He never played at less than full-throttle from 1958-66 with the Packers and a final 1967 season with New Orleans. The prototypical fullback was a centerpiece for ball-control teams that won four championships and he scored touchdowns in Green Bay's 1962 title-game win over New York and Super Bowl I victory over Kansas City.

Taylor's career numbers and tough, no-pretense style mirrored the championship aura of the teams he anchored. He rushed for 8,597 yards and caught 225 passes for 1,756. He also scored 93 touchdowns and earned five Pro Bowl invitations.

"If you give a guy a little blast, maybe the next time he won't be so eager. Football is a game of contact. You've got to make them respect you. You've got to punish them before they punish you."

—Jim Taylor

LAWRENCE TAYLOR

Born: 2-4-59, Williamsburg, Va. **Ht/Wt:** 6-3/237 **College:** North Carolina **Drafted:** 1981, 1st round, Giants **Primary position:** LB
Career statistics: Interceptions, 9, 2 TDs; Sacks, 132.5 **Teams:** Giants 1981-93 **Super Bowl champions:** 1986, '90 seasons
Honors: 75th Anniversary All-Time Team; 1980s All-Decade Team; All-Time NFL Team

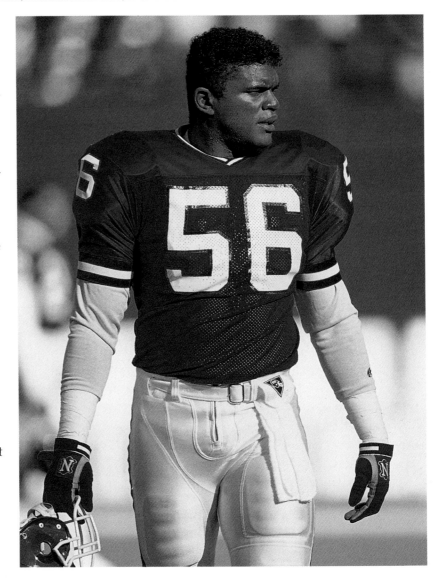

Hall of Famers shook their heads in disbelief, opponents eyed him with nervous anticipation and fans marveled at the way he threw big, tough players around like rag dolls. When Lawrence Taylor stepped onto the field, everybody noticed. The riveting eyes, imposing glare and intimidating, perfectly-sculpted body were merely appetizers for the savage rage he would unleash on every play.

The 6-foot-3, 237-pound New York Giants outside linebacker could disrupt a game plan without moving one of his well-defined muscles. Players would look for him from the corner of their eye, listen for him and sense his presence. Linemen forgot counts, quarterbacks dropped snaps and blockers jumped offsides. When LT did go into action, he could dominate capable linemen, chase down ballcarriers on both sides of the field and fight through triple-team blocks to record one of his patented quarterback take-downs.

The former North Carolina star jumped quickly into the spotlight, earning defensive player of the year

> ## "If there ever was a Superman in the NFL, I think he wore No. 56 for the Giants."
>
> — *Joe Theismann, 1999, The Associated Press*

honors as a 1981 rookie. By his second season, he already had become the standard by which future line-backers would be judged. He made pass rushing a function of the position and literally changed the way defense was played, prompting former Raiders coach

John Madden to call him "the most dominant defensive player I've ever seen." His search-and-destroy abilities were fueled by an anger that might someday be matched, but never surpassed.

With big No. 56 providing a defensive anchor, the Giants transformed from also-ran into serious contender. Playoff runs in 1986 and 1990 culminated with Super Bowl victories, another measure of his impact on the game. With his every-play intensity, position-altering athleticism and the inspiration he provided teammates, LT altered the way an entire franchise was perceived.

Taylor, as imposing off the field as on, fought through a series of personal problems that included a drug suspension and rehabilitation during his 13-year career. He retired in 1993 with 10 Pro Bowl selections and 132.5 career sacks.

Player/Year elected: 1963, charter member

JIM THORPE

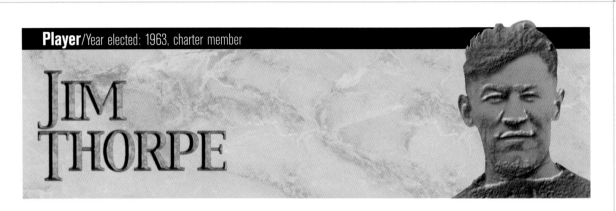

Born: 5-28-1888, Prague, Okla. **Died:** 3-28-53 **Ht/Wt:** 6-1/190 **College:** Carlisle **Primary positions:** FB, DE, K, P **Teams:** Canton Bulldogs 1920, 1926; Cleveland Indians 1921; Oorang Indians 1922-23; Rock Island Independents 1924-25; Giants 1925; Cardinals 1928 **Honors:** 50th Anniversary Team; 1920s All-Decade Team

He guards the main entrance to the Pro Football Hall of Fame museum, threatening to deliver one of his dreaded stiff-arms or to trample anyone in his path. The lifesize statue of Jim Thorpe prepares visitors for their nostalgic trip into pro football past, much as the real Thorpe prepared fans for pro football future eight decades ago. The name and legend still are powerful, his exploits are recounted with flair and exaggeration. But what cannot be exaggerated is Thorpe's role as the game's first great running back, its

first gate attraction and its spiritual guru.

Thorpe had gained worldwide acclaim as a collegiate football hero for the Carlisle Indian School and a double-gold medal winner in the 1912 Olympics before he played his first professional football game in 1915 for the Canton Bulldogs. The thick-armed kid with the moon face, thick black hair, 42-inch chest

> **"Jim Thorpe could have made any team in any league. What's more, he would have been the best player on that team. He would have been the best player in the league. There wasn't anything he couldn't do better than anyone else."**
>
> —*Jimmy Conzelman, 1963*

and penetrating black eyes was first and foremost a great athlete, maybe the most versatile of the first half century. He complemented his football career by playing 289 games of major league baseball, primarily with the New York Giants.

Those who competed against Thorpe remember a high-stepping, stiff-arming muscle man who could run the sweep with outstanding speed, slam down defenders or shed tacklers with an unusual hip twist. A Native American of Sac and Fox Indian heritage, the 6-foot-1, 190-pound Thorpe also was a gifted passer, a devastating blocker and a kicker who could dominate games with long punts, placements or drop kicks.

The greatness of Thorpe cannot be measured by numbers or team accomplishments. After the NFL (called the American Professional Football Association for two years) was organized in 1920, he wandered from team to team until 1928, finally retiring at age 41. But his most lasting contributions were as the first president of the APFA/NFL and as the unparalleled gate attraction who kept the new league afloat during its formative years.

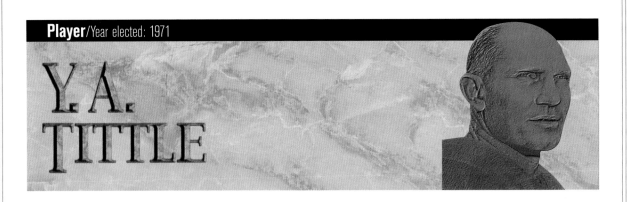

Y.A. TITTLE

Born: 10-24-26, Marshall, Tex. **Ht/Wt:** 6-0/200 **College:** LSU **Drafted:** 1948, 1st round, Lions **Primary position:** QB **Career statistics:** Passing AAFC, 309-of-578, 4,731 yds., 30 TDs; Passing NFL, 2,118-of-3,817, 28,339 yds., 212 TDs; Rushing AAFC, 81 att., 246 yds., 6 TDs; Rushing NFL, 291 att., 999 yds., 33 TDs **Teams:** AAFC Colts 1948-49; NFL Colts 1950; 49ers 1951-60; Giants 1961-64

The bald head, double-initial first name and indestructible right arm were trademark features of an NFL icon. So was the memory of Y.A. Tittle standing boldly in the pocket, calm amid chaos, as he waited, waited, waited for that inevitable open receiver. Nobody waited more fearlessly or played with more passion than the affectionately named "Bald Eagle," whose 17-year career provided a blueprint for both admiration and frustration.

Yelverton Abraham Tittle was the smart, durable and creative quarterback who lit up the All-America Football Conference as a 1948 rookie with the Baltimore Colts and finished his career in 1964, after three near-miss championship seasons with the New York Giants. In between, the former LSU star spent 10 years trying to ignite the struggling San Francisco 49ers.

The ever-modest Tittle, sometimes overshadowed in an era that produced such quarterback heavyweights as Johnny Unitas, Otto Graham, Bart Starr and Norm Van Brocklin, threw for a whopping 33,070 career yards and 242 touchdowns. It was all in the wrist for No. 14, a 6-footer who defied fundamentals with a long throwing stride but frustrated defenders with sidearm, overhand or underhand passes, whatever the situation might dictate.

It wasn't unusual to see Tittle, after missing an open receiver, fling his helmet to the ground, revealing his bald head. Neither was it unusual to see him ranked among the league's top passers while throwing for double-digit touchdowns. Playing in a talented backfield that included Joe Perry and Hugh McElhenny, Tittle led the 49ers to seven winning records from 1951-60 but only one playoff appearance.

Tittle is best remembered as the aging quarterback who passed for 8,641 yards and 86 TDs while leading the Giants to a 33-8-1 record and three straight Eastern Conference crowns from 1961-63. But each time they came up short in the NFL title game. Tittle's New York legacy included a record-tying seven touchdown passes in a 1962 game, a then record 36 TD throws in 1963, two league MVPs (1961, '63) and two of his six Pro Bowl appearances.

> ### "Y.A. just loves to play this game. He really gets fired up. And this is great for our young people because they get fired up, too."
>
> *—Frank Gifford, 1963*

GEORGE TRAFTON

Born: 12-6-1896, Chicago, Ill. **Died:** 9-5-71 **Ht/Wt:** 6-2/235 **College:** Notre Dame **Primary positions:** C, DL **Teams:** Staleys 1920-21; Bears 1923-32 **Championship teams:** NFL 1921, '32 **Honors:** 1920s All-Decade Team

Red Grange called him "the toughest, meanest, most ornery critter alive." Such high praise from the game's premier halfback only encouraged Chicago teammate George Trafton, a 6-foot-2, 235-pound man-child who lifted roughhousing and center play to new heights in the early NFL. Big George reveled in his brawling, no-holds-barred, roughneck reputation while building his 12-season Hall of Fame credentials around a technically superior and innovative style of play.

Late hits, dirty tricks, cheap shots — nothing was sacred for the player known in NFL circles as "The

Brute." Trafton loved a good fight and the loosely enforced rules of the early game did not discourage his colorful antics. His penchant for contact and violence led him to moon-

> ## "Trafton was the only guy who claimed he was the world's greatest at his position—and actually was."
>
> — *Jimmy Conzelman*

lighting careers in professional wrestling and boxing, where he once lost on a 54-second knockout to Primo Carnera.

Trafton's physical play and nightlife escapades often overshadowed his football talents. He was surprisingly fast and agile and his strength was legendary. He also was shrewd, a formula blocker and tackler who could outwit opponents and recognize defensive tendencies. Bears coach George Halas thought so highly of his center that he made him a team captain and Green Bay coach Curly Lambeau, an avowed enemy during Trafton's playing career, hired him as an assistant after his 1932 retirement.

But Trafton's biggest impact was made on the field. He was the first center to snap the ball with one hand and the first defender to roam the line of scrimmage before a snap, a technique that disrupted opponents' blocking assignments. Trafton was a 60-minute performer who missed surprisingly few games, even though he might have been the NFL's most-hated player.

Trafton often boasted he was the game's best center, which he probably was from 1920 when he joined Halas' Decatur Staleys until his 1932 retirement as a two-time champion with the hometown Chicago Bears. The always defiant Trafton, one of the first to wear No. 13, was an all-league selection eight times.

CHARLEY TRIPPI

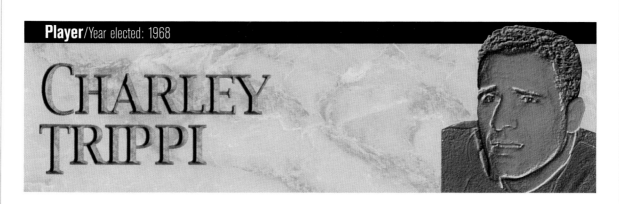

Born: 12-14-22, Pittston, Pa. **Ht/Wt:** 6-0/185 **College:** Georgia **Drafted:** 1945, 1st round, Cardinals; 1947, special selection, AAFC Yanks
Positions: HB, QB, DB, P **Career statistics:** Rushing, 3,506 yds., 23 TDs; Receiving, 130 rec., 11 TDs; Passing, 2,547 yds., 16 TDs; Punt Returns, 63 att., 13.7 avg., 2 TDs **Teams:** Cardinals 1947-55 **Championship team:** NFL 1947 **Honors:** 1940s All-Decade Team

Call him a one-man wrecking crew. Opponents who watched Charley Trippi pass, run, kick, catch, return and defend certainly did, with understandable admiration. Nobody better personified "multi-talented" than the former triple-threat Georgia star, who "wrecked" the All-America Football Conference's hopes for parity with the NFL when he signed a breakthrough $100,000 contract with the Chicago Cardinals in 1947.

Trippi's big-dollar signing, orchestrated by Cardinals owner Charles W. Bidwill at the expense of the AAFC's New York Yanks, was an important victory for the NFL in its bitter war for player talent against the upstart new league. It also marked a dramatic reversal of fortune for one of the game's most forlorn franchises, which immediately won a Western Division title and NFL championship.

Jimmy Conzelman, coach of the 1947 Cardinals,

> "Trippi carried the ball only three times, but that was enough to convince everybody he will get along all right in professional football."
>
> —*Chicago Tribune, 1947, reporting on Trippi's Chicago debut*

called Trippi "the greatest player I coached in 17 years." And it did not take long for opponents to discover the wisdom of that praise. The well-muscled 6-foot, 185-pounder could play quarterback, running back and defensive back, position switches he made willingly throughout his nine-year career while returning kicks and serving as Cardinals punter. He wasn't the fastest runner, most-accurate thrower or longest kicker, but nobody could match his combination of skills and game-breaking instincts.

Trippi, the most sought-after athlete of his day, completed a "Dream Backfield" that included quarterback Paul Christman, fullback Pat Harder and halfbacks Marshall Goldberg and Elmer Angsman. The 9-3 Cardinals advanced to the 1947 championship game and defeated Philadelphia, 28-21, thanks to a 44-yard touchdown run and 75-yard punt return by Trippi and two 70-yard TD runs by Angsman. The 11-1 Cardinals lost the 1948 title to the Eagles, 7-0, in a driving snowstorm.

The quiet, sleepy-eyed son of a Pennsylvania coal miner played until 1955, when he suffered a career-ending head injury while trying to tackle Pittsburgh's John Henry Johnson. He retired with 7,148 combined yards and 37 touchdowns. Trippi, who also threw 16 TD passes, still holds the Cardinals' record of 5.1 yards per carry.

EMLEN TUNNELL

Born: 3-29-25, Bryn Mawr, Pa. **Died:** 7-23-75 **Ht/Wt:** 6-1/187 **College:** Toledo, Iowa **Drafted:** Undrafted **Position:** DB **Career statistics:** Interceptions, 79, 1,282 yds., 4 TDs; Punt Returns, 258 att., 8.6 avg., 5 TDs; KO Returns, 46 att., 26.4 avg., 1 TD **Teams:** Giants 1948-58; Packers 1959-61 **Championship teams:** NFL 1956, '61 **Honors:** 50th Anniversary Team; 1950s All-Decade Team

Forget the smile and ever-cheerful demeanor Emlen Tunnell brought to his job. There really was a scheming con man, master thief and destructive weapon rolled into that innocent-looking 187-pound body. The zest and abandon that made him the most popular player in the locker room for 14 NFL seasons also fueled his rise to Hall of Fame recognition as one of the great defensive backs and kick return men of all time.

Tunnell, an undrafted University of Iowa ballhawk who paid his way to New York in 1948 and asked the Giants for a tryout, became one of the first defense-only stars of the game. The first black player in the Giants' post-World War II era also went on to distinction as the NFL's first black assistant coach and pro football's first black Hall of Famer. Innovative and always willing to gamble, he is credited with developing many of the pass-coverage techniques for the safety position.

Emlen the Gremlin was an interception waiting to happen. He would lull quarterbacks and receivers into a sense of security and then zip into the path of the ball. Some of his 79 career interceptions (No. 2 all-time) could be attributed to cat-like reactions, but many were the result of his

> "He had brains. He knew what was going on out there. He could cover, tackle, do it all. He was so knowledgeable about the position and the defensive schemes he played in."
>
> —*Raymond Berry, 1999*

free-lancing instincts and ability to read plays. Tunnell, who once played in 126 consecutive games, became the centerpiece for the Giants' famed "Umbrella Defense" that revolutionized defensive play by dropping linebackers into pass coverage.

But Tunnell was at his dangerous best when he dropped back to receive punts, a job he fearlessly performed 258 times as one of the NFL's first great punt returners. He was accurately labeled "offense on defense," a moniker he justified with 4,706 career yards on interception runbacks, punt returns and kickoff returns combined. Tunnell, who played for the 1956 championship team in New York and another in his career-ending 1961 season at Green Bay, was selected to nine Pro Bowls.

BULLDOG TURNER

Born: 3-10-19, Plains, Tex. **Died:** 10-30-98 **Ht/Wt:** 6-2/235 **College:** Hardin-Simmons **Drafted:** 1940, 1st round, Bears
Primary positions: C, LB **Career statistics:** Interceptions, 17, 2 TDs **Interceptions leader:** 1942 **Teams:** Bears 1940-52
Championship teams: NFL 1940, '41, '43, '46 **Honors:** 1940s All-Decade Team

To fully grasp the football prowess of Clyde "Bulldog" Turner, you had to watch him run. His 6-foot-2, 235-pound hardbody and Bunyanesque strength were impressive; so were his unerring instincts, quickness and agility. But it was that halfback speed, the ability to churn his thick, powerful legs in the NFL fast lane, that set the burly Texan apart from other top-line centers.

From the moment he made his first Chicago appearance in 1940, a No. 1 draft pick out of little Hardin-Simmons College wearing cowboy boots and a ten-gallon hat, he was "Bulldog," the drawling, steer-wrestling center from Sweetwater, Tex. From the moment Bears coach George Halas witnessed his exceptional speed, Turner was a sideline-to-sideline linebacker.

Few players have matched that two-way

> "He just controlled the middle of the line of scrimmage. Easily the best center to come along for years and years."
>
> *— Jim Parmer, former NFL player and scout, 1998, Chicago Tribune*

combination. And nobody has done it with the sustained success of Turner, a savvy, free-wheeling leader of four Bears championship teams over 13 NFL seasons. Defenders dreaded the bulldozing blocks he delivered as the centerpiece of a Monsters of the Midway line that at one point included future Hall of Famers George Musso, Joe Stydahar and Danny Fortmann. Opposing coaches marveled at his 17 career interceptions.

One, against Washington's Sammy Baugh in 1947, was returned 96 yards for a touchdown. A league-leading eight came in 1942. Most were the result of quarterbacks underestimating Turner's speed. When Halas was short of halfbacks because of war-time shortages in 1944, he used Turner in one game and watched him break a 48-yard touchdown run.

Turner was a shrewd student of the game who enhanced his value by learning different positions. It was not uncommon to see Halas use him at guard or tackle, although it was as a center that he made his greatest impact. Turner, a serious, no-nonsense performer, succeeded New York's Mel Hein as the top NFL center and earned four Pro Bowl invitations. After he retired in 1952, he served as a Bears assistant and later coached the AFL's New York Titans.

JOHNNY UNITAS

Born: 5-7-33, Pittsburgh, Pa. **Died:** 9-11-2002 **Ht/Wt:** 6-1/195 **College:** Louisville **Drafted:** 1955, 9th round, Steelers
Primary position: QB **Career statistics:** Passing, 2,830-of-5,186, 40,239 yds., 290 TDs; Rushing, 450 att., 1,777 yds., 13 TDs
Teams: Colts 1956-72; Chargers 1973 **Championship teams:** NFL 1958, '59 **Super Bowl champion:** 1970 season
Honors: 75th Anniversary All-Time Team; 50th Anniversary Team; 1960s All-Decade Team; All-Time NFL Team

The distinctive stoop shoulders were sandwiched by crew-cut hair and black, high-top shoes. It was easy to pick Johnny Unitas out of a football crowd. It also was easy to watch the talented Baltimore quarterback pick apart defenses with commanding, unwavering confidence over 18 NFL seasons (1956-73) while gaining status as one of the most fabled stars in pro football history.

The 6-foot-1 Unitas was a master craftsman, an unlikely looking athlete who overcame physical limitations with impressive intangibles. He wasn't fast, but he knew when and how to run. His arm was not as strong as some, but he threw with incredible touch and timing. What Unitas did have was courage, coolness under fire and the ability to lead, a quality Baltimore teammate John Mackey acknowledged when he said, "It's like being in the huddle with God."

The no-nonsense former Louisville quarterback was a pocket passer who showed daring and courage when standing in against a rush. He also was a play-calling genius who could mentally dissect a defense, make the perfect audible and get the ball to the right player. He showed unwavering control when a game was on the line and was masterful when racing the clock, an ability that vaulted him into prominence when he led the Colts to their classic 1958 championship game overtime victory over the New York Giants.

Unitas, a Pittsburgh native, was as tough as the city of his birth. When No. 19 was barking signals, everybody knew who was in control. Unitas was the most decorated passer in football history when he retired in 1973 after one season in San Diego. He left with then-record totals of 2,830 completions, 40,239 yards and 290 touchdowns, but he'll always be remembered for the 47 straight games in which he threw at least one TD pass—a still-standing record.

Johnny U., a 10-time Pro Bowler, played on three championship teams, including Baltimore's winner in Super Bowl V.

> **"The thing that makes Unitas is his physical courage. He is the bravest man I've known in football."**
>
> —*Merlin Olsen*

GENE UPSHAW

Born: 8-15-45, Robstown, Tex. **Ht/Wt:** 6-5/255 **College:** Texas A&I **Drafted:** 1967, 1st round, Raiders **Primary position:** OG
Teams: Raiders 1967-81 **Championship team:** AFL 1967 **Super Bowl champions:** 1976, '80 seasons **Honors:** 75th Anniversary All-Time Team; 1970s All-Decade Team

It was a religious experience, a broom-waving moment for Oakland fans. Big No. 63 would step back at the snap, move laterally to his left and sprint ahead of a Raiders' ball-toting convoy. First a defensive back would show up on Gene Upshaw's radar screen, then a linebacker—targets for annihilation. Then a bulldozing block would send bodies flying and clear the way for another successful power sweep.

Upshaw was Oakland's Big Sweeper and masterful left offensive guard for 15 seasons, a line fixture from the 1967 day he was drafted out of tiny Texas A&I by Al Davis. Upshaw was targeted for guard duty, even though his 6-foot-5, 255-pound body was much bigger than the fire-plug-like players who traditionally manned the position. Davis was looking for somebody who could block monster Kansas City tackle Buck Buchanan (6-7, 270) and their one-on-one battles became football classics.

The intelligent, intense and always-dedicated Upshaw was equally proficient as a straight-ahead blocker or pass protector, a

> "I figured if (Buck) Buchanan was going to play for the Chiefs for the next 10 years, we better get some big guy who could handle him. So we got Upshaw. Those two guys put on some stirring battles over the years." —*Al Davis*

14-year linemate of Hall of Fame tackle Art Shell. He also was a team leader, coach John Madden's choice as offensive captain in 1969—his third NFL season. Upshaw provided a liaison between an admiring Davis and the team's players, who looked to him for advice.

His intelligence carried over to the way he consistently approached his work.

The mild-mannered Upshaw could knock over writers with his thunderous laugh or defenders with his savage blocks. It's no coincidence the Raiders won an AFL championship in his rookie 1967 season and went on to post a 157-56-7 regular-season record over his 15-year career. Upshaw also played in 10 AFL/AFC title games and helped the Raiders win two Super Bowls before retiring in 1981.

The seven-time Pro Bowl selection, who started 207 straight games before being sidelined once in his final season, went on to post-playing distinction as the highly respected executive director of the NFL Players' Association.

Player/Year elected: 1971

NORM VAN BROCKLIN

Born: 3-15-26, Eagle Butte, S.D. **Died:** 5-2-83 **Ht/Wt:** 6-1/190 **College:** Oregon **Drafted:** 1949, 4th round, NFL Rams; 11th round, AAFC Hornets **Primary position:** QB **Career statistics:** Passing, 1,553-of-2,895, 23,611 yds., 173 TDs; Rushing, 11 TDs **Teams:** Rams 1949-57; Eagles 1958-60 **Championship teams:** NFL 1951, '60 **Honors:** 1950s All-Decade Team

The long-range missiles he fired at NFL defenses were no less spectacular than the fireworks he set off with his legendary tantrums. Norm Van Brocklin was a prototypical "mad" bomber who carved up opponents with a powerful right arm and teammates with a biting tongue. Nobody left a more indelible mark than the colorful Dutchman, who powered two different teams to NFL championships from 1949-60.

Van Brocklin was a notoriously bad loser who snarled his way through nine seasons with the Los Angeles Rams. He spent his early career fretting about

> "He was the reincarnation of General Patton. He went at every game as if he were leading his men across the Rhine, and God help anybody who let him down. Patton slapped his troops; Dutch kicked his in the rear end."
>
> —*Dick Lynch, former Giants defensive back*

his role while sharing quarterback duties with multi-talented Bob Waterfield and feuded throughout his later Rams career with coach Sid Gillman. But that didn't stop him from leading the team to four NFL championship games.

Van Brocklin was the master of the long strike, a big play waiting to happen. He couldn't run and his ball-handling skills were suspect. But he was an intelligent strategist, a gifted punter and, oh, could he throw. The 6-foot-1 Dutchman exploded for 554 yards — a still-standing NFL record — and five touchdowns in a 1951 game against the New York Yanks and his clutch 73-yard TD pass to Tom Fears decided the Rams' 24-17 title-game win over Cleveland in 1951.

The former Oregon star was endearingly outspoken and quick to laugh in the locker room, but his on-field sarcasm was legendary when teammates dropped a pass or blew an assignment. His problems with Gillman stemmed from a burning desire to call his own plays. When Van Brocklin retired in frustration after the 1957 season, the Rams traded him to Philadelphia and coach Buck Shaw gave him full rein.

Van Brocklin rewarded him by leading the Eagles to the 1960 championship and earning league MVP honors. He retired after the season with 23,611 passing yards, 173 touchdowns and nine Pro Bowl selections before spending 13 of the next 14 seasons as the volatile coach of the expansion Minnesota Vikings and Atlanta Falcons. His final coaching mark was 66-100-7.

STEVE VAN BUREN

Born: 12-28-20, La Ceiba, Honduras **Ht/Wt:** 6-0/200 **College:** LSU **Drafted:** 1944, 1st round, Eagles **Position:** RB **Career statistics:** Rushing, 1,320 att., 5,860 yds., 69 TDs; Receiving, 45 rec., 3 TDs **Rushing champion:** 1945, '47, '48, '49 **Teams:** Eagles 1944-51 **Championship teams:** NFL 1948, '49 **Honors:** 75th Anniversary All-Time Team; 1940s All-Decade Team

He was easy to spot. Broad shoulders, strong upper body, a slim, tapered waist and powerful legs supported a 6-foot, 200-pound frame, making Steve Van Buren stand out in any crowd. He was especially noticeable when he tucked a football under his big right arm, the signal to defensive players throughout the NFL that the "Movin' Van" was getting ready to rumble.

Van Buren, simply stated, was the best running back of the 1940s, a worthy successor to the Jim Thorpe/Bronko Nagurski power-running style and the predecessor to coming stars Marion Motley, Jim Brown and Jim Taylor. The Philadelphia Eagles star was a no-nonsense, up-the-middle runner with enough speed to make a cut on unsuspecting defenders and enough power to run over them.

Van Buren, who was born in Honduras and raised in New Orleans, approached his craft with a shy, country kid modesty, even after a spectacular senior season at LSU in which he led the country in rushing. Philadelphia coach Greasy Neale, recognizing the steamroller power, agility and speed combination Van Buren brought to the field, designed an offense around him and watched his Eagles win three straight division titles and consecutive championships in 1948 and '49.

Neale also watched Van Buren win four rushing and scoring titles in a record-setting career. He led the league in 1947 with 1,008 yards and exploded for a season-record 1,146 two years later. Van Buren was front and center in the Eagles' consecutive title-game wins, scoring the game's only touchdown on a five-yard run in 1948 and sloshing through the mud for 196 yards in 1949.

When Van Buren retired after the 1951 season with a record 5,860 yards, he also held records for rushing attempts, rushing touchdowns, most touchdowns in a season, most years leading the league in rushing and most yards gained in a title game. The versatile Van Buren also was an accomplished receiver and scored five touchdowns on kickoff and punt returns.

> "Thorpe was a bigger man than Van Buren, outweighed him by 10 pounds and was two inches taller. Yet Steve does the same things as Thorpe. There is one difference. When Thorpe hit, he did so with his knees. Steve uses the shoulder—and with terrific power."
>
> —*John Kellison, Eagles line coach, 1948*

VAN BUREN

DOAK WALKER

Born: 1-1-27, Dallas, Tex. **Died:** 9-27-98 **Ht/Wt:** 5-11/173 **College:** SMU **Drafted:** 1949, 1st round, NFL Boston Yanks; 9th round, AAFC Browns **Positions:** HB, DB, K **Career statistics:** Rushing, 1,520 yds., 12 TDs; Receiving, 152 rec., 21 TDs; KO Returns, 38 att., 25.5 avg.; Scoring, 49 FG, 183 PAT, 534 pts. **Scoring champion:** 1950, '55 **Teams:** Lions 1950-55 **Championship teams:** NFL 1952, '53

To college football-crazed Texans, he was a genuine American folk hero. To more practical-minded Detroit fans, he was a too small, too slow overachiever who led the Lions to consecutive championships. From college legend to professional superstar, 5-foot-11, 173-pound Doak Walker shot down skeptics and defied the law of averages with his fairy tale exploits.

Few players can match the collegiate aura of Walker, a three-time All-American and 1948 Heisman Trophy-winning halfback for SMU in his hometown of Dallas. He was the soft-spoken, ever-modest and polite boy next door who could run, pass, kick, handle returns and play defensive back. The fans loved his gritty determination and uncanny ability to make big plays.

Professional scouts were not so sure Walker's size and seemingly modest skills—a jack of all trades, a master of none—would translate in the NFL. But he scored an NFL-best 128 points and earned the first of five Pro Bowl invitations during an incredible 1950 rookie season and never stopped producing. Over his six-year career, Walker notched entries in every possible statistical category—rushing, passing, receiving, punt and kickoff returns, punting, placekicking, interceptions—and the Lions won three conference titles and 1952 and '53 championships.

Ironically, the low-key Walker was a high school teammate and close friend of Lions quarterback Bobby Layne, the acknowledged leader of a swashbuckling team that played as hard off the field as on. What Walker lacked in color he made up for as the team's point-producer and playmaker. His big-play heroics included a 67-yard TD run in a 1952 title-game win over Cleveland, an 11-point effort in Detroit's 17-16 title-game win over the Browns in 1953 and an 18-point explosion (TD receptions of 66 and 53 yards) in a 1954 showdown win over San Francisco.

Walker, whose immense popularity opened the door for the pro game in Dallas, furthered his aura by retiring after the 1956 Pro Bowl, at age 29, to pursue business interests. His 534 points (34 touchdowns) ranked third all-time when he left.

> "Doak is a lot faster than he looks out there. He's quick and he's always moving. Nobody gets much of a shot at him. Tacklers learn Doak is running in high gear after he's past them."
>
> —*Hunchy Hoernschemeyer,*
> *former Detroit teammate*

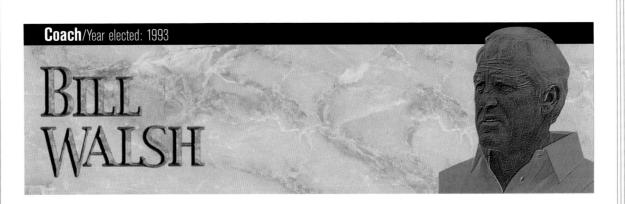

Coach/Year elected: 1993

BILL WALSH

Born: 11-30-31, Los Angeles, Calif. **Teams coached (92-59-1 RS, 10-4 PS):** 49ers 1979-88 **Super Bowl champions:** 1981, '84, '88 seasons **Honors:** 1980s All-Decade Team

He is the official savior of San Francisco football, the man who lifted a franchise from 35 years of desolation to Super Bowl ecstasy. By the time Bill Walsh completed his 10-year run as the NFL's "offen- sive genius," his 49ers were well established as the "Team of the '80s." Passing guru, team builder, master tactician — the smooth, white-haired Californian also will be remembered as the man who turned pro foot-

> ## "Adversity can be a great motivator. But football, as anything else, is always a series of problems and your success will depend on how you are prepared and how you handle those problems."
>
> *— Bill Walsh*

ball into a hip and trendy artform.

But don't call Walsh an innovator. He was a self-described "learner," a coach who assimilated the ideas of football past into his more sophisticated game plans. He worked as an assistant for eight years under Paul Brown at Cincinnati. The "West Coast" passing game he introduced came from field-stretching concepts he learned under Sid Gillman at San Diego. He field tested his ideas at Stanford before becoming 49ers coach and general manager in 1979.

Walsh built a team that had made only four playoff appearances into a contender through astute draft picks and trades. The man who developed quarterbacks Ken Anderson (Cincinnati) and Dan Fouts (San Diego) turned 1979 third-round pick Joe Montana into the league's best field general, a perfect trigger man for his short-to-moderate, ball-control passing game. In 1981, his third season, the 49ers posted the first of six NFC West titles and went on to beat Cincinnati in Super Bowl XVI.

Walsh's teams reflected the calm, self-confidence of a cosmopolitan coach. He was the master of preparation, a clipboard-carrying fanatic who scripted the first 25 plays of his intricate game plans. Walsh's system was complex but his managing style relied on intelli-

gent players who took responsibility for their actions.

The 49ers lost in the 1983 NFC championship game and won Super Bowl titles after the 1984 and '88 seasons, at which point Walsh retired with a 92-59-1 regular-season record. The players he left behind won another Super Bowl for rookie coach George Seifert, a former Walsh assistant.

PAUL WARFIELD

Born: 11-28-42, Warren, Ohio **Ht/Wt:** 6-0/188 **College:** Ohio State **Drafted:** 1964, 1st round, NFL Browns; 4th round, AFL Bills
Primary position: WR **Career statistics:** Receiving, 427 rec., 8,565 yds., 20.1 avg., 85 TDs **Teams:** Browns 1964-69, 1976-77;
Dolphins 1970-74 **Championship team:** NFL 1964 **Super Bowl champions:** 1972, '73 seasons **Honors:** 1970s All-Decade Team

Paul Warfield's pass routes weren't diagrammed; they were choreographed. His graceful, prancing style seemed more appropriate for a ballet than a football field. He jigged. He jagged. A quick cut left, a fake right, then whoosh! He was gone. For 13 NFL seasons with Cleveland and Miami, Warfield danced his way through enemy secondaries and into the hearts of appreciative fans.

The misfortune of Paul Warfield is that he never got a chance to play in a passing offense. His sprinter's speed, magic moves, soft hands and elusive running ability could have garnered big numbers in a vertical attack. But the Browns (1964-69, 1976-77) and Dolphins (1970-74) were winning division titles and championships with run-oriented systems that benefit-ed greatly from Warfield's presence as a constant home run threat.

The numbers tell the story. Warfield's 427 career receptions netted 8,565 yards and a whopping average of 20.1. His one-touchdown-per-five-catches ratio ranks second all-time only to Don Hutson. The former Ohio State star was dangerous at all times and demanded constant double-team attention, which kept opponents from stacking the line. But he was used more often as a blocker, a job the 188-pounder handled with surprising efficiency.

The shy, introverted Warfield endured without complaint. Despite his limited role, he was a big fan favorite with the Browns, who posted a 59-23-2 record over his first six seasons while winning one NFL championship. It was more of the same after a stunning 1970 trade to Miami. The Dolphins posted a 57-12-1 record en route to consecutive Super Bowl wins and three AFC championships during his five seasons. But they ran almost 70 percent of the time during their perfect 1972 campaign and Warfield caught only 29 passes.

His efforts did not go unnoticed. Warfield, who spent the 1975 season playing in the ill-fated World Football League, was selected for eight Pro Bowls and earned five All-NFL citations in a career that ended in 1977 after a two-year return stint with Cleveland.

> "I've thrown to a lot of receivers in my time. Warfield definitely ranks right at the top. He has fluid moves and any time he gets one-on-one, he's gone. He is the complete player. He is a great blocker. He never makes a mistake."
>
> —*Earl Morrall,*
> *Dolphins quarterback, 1972*

WARFIELD

BOB WATERFIELD

Born: 7-26-20, Elmira, N.Y. **Died:** 3-25-83 **Ht/Wt:** 6-2/200 **College:** UCLA **Drafted:** 1944, 3rd round future, Rams **Positions:** QB, DB, K, P **Career statistics:** Passing, 814-of-1,617, 11,849 yds., 97 TDs; Rushing, 13 TDs; Interceptions, 20; Punting, 315 att., 42.4 avg.; Scoring, 60 FG, 315 PAT, 573 pts. **Teams:** Rams 1945-52 **Championship teams:** NFL 1945, '51 **Honors:** 1940s All-Decade Team

The giant "S" Bob Waterfield wore on his chest was hidden beneath his No. 7 Rams jersey. But there was no hiding the incredible athletic skills that separated the 6-foot-2, 200-pound superman from other post-World War II NFL stars. The quarterback-placekicker-punter-safety was a dangerous big-play scoring threat who gave new meaning to the professional football concept of versatility.

Waterfield will always be remembered as the rookie quarterback who earned league MVP honors while leading the Cleveland Rams to a 1945 championship and a contributor to the Los Angeles Rams' 1951 title. He was a clever ballhandler who could throw short or deep, fool everybody with a well-timed bootleg and inspire teammates with his poise under pressure. Waterfield was well-known for performing late-game miracles in a variety of ways.

The former UCLA star was an outstanding punter who posted a career 42.4-yard average, a kicker who connected on 60 field goals and a touchdown-maker who fired 97 scoring passes and ran for 13 more. The sometimes-aloof, soft-spoken Waterfield scored 573 career points and even

> "He was the greatest footballer I ever saw. Not only was he mechanically the best, but when he walked into the huddle and called a play, he gave you the sureness that this was it. This would work."
>
> —*Elroy "Crazy Legs" Hirsch*

doubled as a safety over his first four seasons, making 20 interceptions.

The irony is that Waterfield, with his amazing arsenal of talents, was forced to share quarterbacking duties from 1950-52 with another future Hall of Famer—Norm Van Brocklin. Waterfield, the quiet loner, and Van Brocklin, the fiery Dutchman, each played half of every game and combined for 3,601 passing yards in 1950, 3,291 in 1951. Waterfield, who had thrown 37- and 53-yard touchdown passes in the Rams' 1945 title-game victory, fired an 82-yard bomb in a 1950 championship game loss to Cleveland and contributed a field goal and three extra points in a 24-17 win over the Browns in 1951.

Waterfield, who also is remembered for his highly publicized 25-year marriage to movie star Jane Russell, retired in 1952, after his eighth pro season—perhaps discouraged by the quarterback split. He later returned as Rams head coach, but managed only a 9-24-1 record over three seasons.

ARNIE WEINMEISTER

Born: 3-23-23, Rhein, Saskatchewan **Died:** 6-29-2000 **Ht/Wt:** 6-4/235 **College:** Washington **Drafted:** 1945, 17th round, Dodgers
Primary positions: DT, OT **Teams:** AAFC Yankees 1948-49; NFL Giants 1950-53

Punch him, hold him, double- or triple-team him—nothing could keep Arnie Weinmeister from his appointed rounds. And no matter how hard and fast opponents ran away, they couldn't elude the hard-charging Giants defensive tackle. Few players dominated a position more impressively than the Canadian-born enforcer, who entranced New Yorkers during an all-too-brief NFL cameo from 1950-53.

"He couldn't be blocked," said Cleveland quarterback Otto Graham, who heard Weinmeister's footsteps for two years in the All-America Football Conference and four more in the NFL. "He was very agile and could cover almost everything all over the field." The combination quickness, strength, agility and aggressiveness of this 6-foot-4 monster was special. But the shocking footspeed he used to chase down opponents is what set him apart.

Weinmeister, carrying 235 pounds, could outrun most NFL halfbacks and he might have been the first defensive tackle who could operate from sideline to sideline. Giants assistant Jim Lee Howell enjoyed pitting his rookie

> "Arnie was bigger than most who played at that time and he had great speed. He could go from sideline to sideline because he was probably the fastest lineman in the league. He could outrun most of our big backs." —*Tom Landry*

receivers in a training camp 100-yard dash against Weinmeister, who never lost. Few blockers could stop his explosive defensive charge and quarterbacks made a lot of hurried throws while running for their life.

Weinmeister, a former University of Washington fullback whose college career was interrupted by two-plus years of military service, turned pro in 1948 as a two-way tackle for the AAFC's New York Yankees. When the AAFC folded, he signed with the Giants and became the anchor for coach Steve Owen's innovative Umbrella Defense. Weinmeister's relentless rush allowed Owen to drop his ends into coverage and his instinctive ability to diagnose plays disrupted opponent game plans.

The Giants posted 10-2 and 9-2-1 records with Weinmeister and he earned All-NFL and Pro Bowl recognition in all four NFL seasons. The bubble burst for New York fans after the 1953 campaign when Weinmeister signed with British Columbia of the Canadian Football League for an extra $3,000, ending his outstanding NFL career after 46 games.

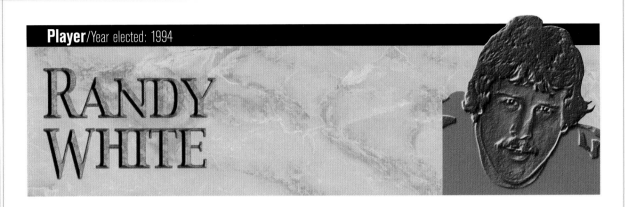

Player/Year elected: 1994

RANDY WHITE

Born: 1-15-53, Wilmington, Del. **Ht/Wt:** 6-4/257 **College:** Maryland **Drafted:** 1975, 1st round, Cowboys **Primary position:** DT, LB
Teams: Cowboys 1975-88 **Super Bowl champion:** 1977 (co-MVP) season **Honors:** 1980s All-Decade Team

They called him "manster" — as in half man, half monster. Randy White didn't just beat up on offensive opponents, he destroyed them. He was a 6-foot-4, 257-pound Jekyll-Hyde personality in a defensive tackle's body, the demon who could single-handedly dismantle game plans. To the Dallas fans he entertained every Sunday for 14 seasons, he was the second coming of Bob Lilly in the middle of the Doomsday Defense.

No right-thinking offensive coordinator could plan for Dallas without first neutralizing White, the former Outland Trophy winner from Maryland. That usually took two or three blockers, good news for other Cowboys defenders. When opponents chose instead to run away from White, which they often did, he could chase them down with surprising lateral quickness.

It was that quickness that prompt-ed coach Tom Landry to position his prize rookie at middle linebacker in 1975, an experiment he discarded after two seasons. White, an obses-sive weightlifter, also was the strongest man on the Dallas roster, a quality he used efficiently in his more-familiar tackle slot. The strength allowed him to shed blockers like rag dolls and the quickness allowed him to rush with a stop-me-if-you-can scorn. When big No. 54 broke through the line, quarterbacks had a serious decision to make — quickly.

Off the field, White was quiet, shy and soft-spoken, an easy-to-like giant. On the field he was "just plain

> ## "Randy was the toughest, most intense player I ever coached. His own teammates didn't want to practice against him because he didn't know what practice speed was."
>
> —Ernie Stautner, 1994, *Philadelphia Daily News*

mean," a reflection of the intensity that pushed him to 100 percent effort on every play. With White operating at peak efficiency from right tackle, the Cowboys rolled to five championship game appearances and two Super Bowls from 1977-82. The pass-rushing combination of White and Harvey Martin was so dominant in a Super Bowl XII victory over Denver that it shared MVP honors — an unusual award for defensive players.

White, who missed only one game in 14 seasons, earned nine Pro Bowl appear-ances and eight All-Pro citations before retiring after the 1988 season.

DAVE WILCOX

Born: 9-29-42, Ontario, Ore. **Ht/Wt:** 6-3/240 **College:** Boise State, Oregon **Drafted:** 1964, 3rd round, NFL 49ers; 6th round, AFL Oilers **Primary position:** LB **Career statistics:** Interceptions, 14, 1 TD **Teams:** 49ers 1964-74

Opponents called him "The Intimidator" and swore that even his routine hits could have been recorded on a Richter Scale. When Dave Wilcox lined up as the NFL's premier outside linebacker, physical punishment was as inevitable as a California earthquake. Before the Joe Montana-Jerry Rice-Ronnie Lott gold-rush era in San Francisco, some of the biggest blows for 49ers success were struck by big No. 64.

It was easy to appreciate the 6-foot-3, 240-pound Wilcox, who attacked ballcarriers from 1964-74 with a near-perfect combination of physical abandon and situation-savvy restraint. One of the bigger outside men of his era, he was strong enough to keep tight ends from getting off the line, fast enough to cover the NFL's speedier backs. Most of Wilcox's

> ## "As a coach, you have the great players that stick out. He was certainly the best I ever coached. Speaking as an old Marine, he's a guy you want next to you."
>
> — *Mike Giddings, former 49ers linebackers coach, 2000, The Associated Press*

strength was in his broad shoulders and long, far-reaching arms, which he used to swat away pesky blockers.

The former University of Oregon star was as smart as he was physical. Always prepared for an opponent, he let unerring instincts guide his play and seldom gave in to emotion. He was an outstanding open-field tackler known for his big hits, but he also knew when not to leave his feet, using his powerful arms to bulldog ballcarriers. He could be devastating, as in 1973 when he made 104 tackles (13 for loss) and two interceptions while forcing four fumbles and recovering another.

The 49ers could never get over the hump during Wilcox's 11 pro seasons, recording five winning records and losing twice to Dallas in the NFC championship game. But that didn't stop the soft-spoken, easy-to-smile Wilcox from garnering recognition — seven Pro Bowl invitations and All-Pro selections. Wilcox, former tight end Mike Ditka said, helped convince him to hang up his cleats.

Few offenses dared venture to the left side of San Francisco's defense, where Wilcox roamed in tandem with future Hall of Fame cornerback Jimmy Johnson. Wilcox also was a hard-nosed ironman who played 153 of a possible 154 games.

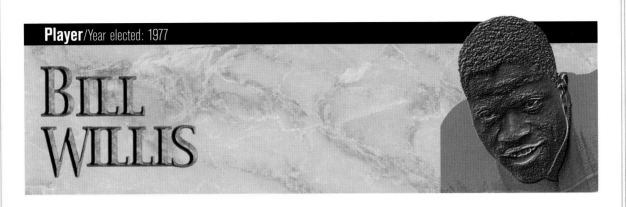

BILL WILLIS

Born: 10-5-21, Columbus, Ohio **Ht/Wt:** 6-2/215 **College:** Ohio State **Drafted:** Undrafted **Primary positions:** DG, OG **Teams:** AAFC Browns 1946-49; NFL Browns 1950-53 **Championship teams:** AAFC 1946, '47, '48, '49; NFL 1950 **Honors:** 1940s All-Decade Team

He was cat-quick, befitting the panther-like crouch from which he sprung at unfortunate centers assigned to block him. Bill Willis also was tough and proud, befitting his pioneer effort in crossing professional football's longtime color barrier. Cleveland's undersized middle guard was a perfect fit for Paul Brown's 1946 vision of a perfect team, skin color and racial conventions be damned.

Willis, a member of Brown's 1942 Ohio State championship team, was football coach and athletic director at Kentucky State College when he asked for a tryout with Brown's new All-America Football Conference team. Brown agreed and watched Willis bolt over, around and through center Mo Scarry on four straight plays in a stunning training camp drill. No Browns player protested when Willis was signed as pro football's first black since the early 1930s.

The Cat, who later was joined on that 1946 team by black fullback Marion Motley, was central to the Browns' four-year domination of the AAFC and early success in the reorganized NFL. At 6-foot-2 and 215, Willis was the lightest member of a talented defensive line. But centers had problems

> **"About the first guy that ever convinced me that I couldn't handle anybody I ever met was Bill Willis. They called him The Cat. He would jump right over you."** —*Bulldog Turner*

reacting to his legendary quickness, head-wrenching forearms and creative moves. Brown sometimes dropped Willis behind the line so he could react to the play and utilize his speed—football's pioneer middle linebacker.

With Willis leading the charge, it's no coincidence the Browns dominated the AAFC in scoring defense and topped the NFL in four of their first six seasons. He also was a popular teammate who kept his ear-to-ear smile while enduring both on- and off-field abuse. It was hard to ignore Willis, who earned all-league honors in seven of his eight seasons (1946-53) and played in three Pro Bowls.

Willis is best remembered for a game-saving tackle in the 1950 conference playoff game against New York, setting the stage for the Browns' first NFL championship. He also played for four AAFC champions and three teams that lost in the NFL title game.

WILLIS

LARRY WILSON

Born: 3-24-38, Rigby, Idaho **Ht/Wt:** 6-0/190 **College:** Utah **Drafted:** 1960, 7th round, Cardinals **Primary position:** DB **Career statistics:** Interceptions, 52, 5 TDs **Interceptions leader:** 1966 **Teams:** Cardinals 1960-72 **Honors:** 75th Anniversary All-Time Team; 1960s All-Decade Team; 1970s All-Decade Team; All-Time NFL Team

He was the bane of every quarterback's existence, the player most likely to deliver physical and mental pain. His 6-foot, 190-pound body was a cleverly-disguised wrecking machine. Whether dashing madly into an opposing backfield as pioneer of the safety blitz or aggressively defending against the pass, Larry Wilson spent 13 seasons spreading his special kind of fear around the NFL.

It was a fear born of respect for the oft-described "toughest player in the game." Wilson was a football bulldog, a free safety who played through incredible pain and never conceded a down.

Former New York Giants coach Allie Sherman called the blond-haired St. Louis Cardinals star "the goingest player I ever saw." Others called him the NFL player who coaxed more out of his abilities than any other.

It was Wilson's reckless style that inspired St. Louis defensive coordinator Chuck Drulis' innovative idea for the safety blitz — code name "Wildcat." From 1960-72, the former University of Utah halfback shot the gaps of NFL offensive lines, making life miserable for quarterbacks and setting himself up for nasty blows from much-bigger blocking backs. The gambling maneuver demanded superb timing and courage, qualities Wilson included on his football resume.

When Wilson stayed back in coverage, he was a different kind of Wildcat — a great open-field tackler and an instinctive pass defender with an uncanny knack for getting to the ball. Runners dreaded the sight of Wilson approaching on a kamikaze charge. Receivers

> "He's the key to the Cardinal secondary. He is aggressive and unbelievable, the most fearless blitzer ever. No offense is going to get a line on him. He is everywhere. He is a great player."
>
> —*Tom Landry*

braced for Wilson's tear-inducing shots to the ribs.

Over his Hall of Fame career, the eight-time Pro Bowl selection intercepted 52 passes, including a league-leading 10 in 1966. But it was one he made in 1965 that brought him everlasting fame. Wilson, playing against the advice of doctors with casts on both of his broken hands, leaped high to block a pass by Pittsburgh quarterback Bill Nelsen, cradled the deflection in his arms and ran the ball back 35 yards. The play was vintage Larry Wilson.

KELLEN WINSLOW

Born: 11-5-57, St. Louis, Mo. **Ht/Wt:** 6-5/250 **College:** Missouri **Drafted:** 1979, 1st round, Chargers **Primary position:** TE
Career statistics: Receiving, 541 rec., 6,741 yds., 12.5 avg., 45 TDs **Receptions leader:** 1980, '81 **Teams:** Chargers 1979-87
Honors: 75th Anniversary All-Time Team; 1980s All-Decade Team

Miami coach Don Shula once called him "Superman." Former San Diego quarterback Dan Fouts described him as the finest tight end ever to play football. Kellen Winslow inspired such exultations from those who watched him perform from 1979-87 in a Hall of Fame career that was cut short by a knee injury.

Critics argued that Winslow was really a wide receiver disguised as a tight end, a beneficiary of the wide-open passing offense constructed by Chargers coach Don Coryell. He would sometimes split wide as a third receiver or go in motion. Other times he would drop into a slot. Always he was one of three primary receivers for the Hall of Fame-bound Fouts, a member of the prolific pass-catching trio that also included John Jefferson and Charlie Joiner.

Winslow did not revolutionize the tight end position, but he did take it to a different level. At 6-foot-5 and 250 pounds, he provided an inviting target and his strong, springy legs allowed him to catch passes over smaller defenders. He was a mouth-watering combination of size, speed and athleticism, a fine-tuned version of the John Mackey/Mike Ditka tight end.

But what separated Winslow from his predecessors was his big, soft hands and deceptive speed — a

> **"You hear it all the time from coaches and general managers. They'll be looking for a tight end in the draft and they'll say, 'We'd like to have another Kellen Winslow.'"**
>
> *—Dan Fouts, 1995,*
> *The Kansas City Star*

byproduct of his "elephant stride." His pass-catching proficiency opened eyes in 1980 when he led NFL receivers with 89 catches (a then tight end record) for 1,290 yards and he followed that with a league-leading 88 for 1,075 yards in 1981.

The former Missouri All-American was dedicated and explosive. He caught a record-tying five touchdown passes in a 1981 win over Oakland; his exhausting 13-catch, 166-yard effort in a classic January 1982 overtime playoff win over Miami vaulted him to national prominence and inspired Shula's appraisal.

The articulate, outspoken Winslow pulled in every ball he should and many that seemed beyond his unlimited reach.

The five-time Pro Bowler, who had just turned 30, finished his career in 1987 with 541 catches for 6,741 yards and 45 touchdowns.

Player/Year elected: 1968

ALEX WOJCIECHOWICZ

Born: 8-12-15, South River, N.J. **Died:** 7-13-92 **Ht/Wt:** 6-0/235 **College:** Fordham **Drafted:** 1938, 1st round, Lions **Primary positions:** C, LB **Career statistics:** Interceptions, 19, 1 TD **Teams:** Lions 1938-46; Eagles 1946-50 **Championship teams:** NFL 1948, '49 **Honors:** 1940s All-Decade Team

He was hard as a rock, which made him a fitting relic of the Fordham "Seven Blocks of Granite" offensive line that included Vince Lombardi. When big Alex Wojciechowicz reached out and touched someone, it left a lasting impression. He was a rugged 6-foot, 235-pound enforcer who experienced the extreme joy of victory and agony of defeat over a 13-year career in Detroit and Philadelphia.

There was nothing fancy about the hard-hitting "Wojie," who doubled as a center and linebacker for the struggling Lions from 1938-46. He was powerful and compact, a broad-based snapper with a low center of gravity and the quickness to bulldoze defenders. But he also had surprising defensive speed, which allowed him to rush the quarterback, chase down ball-carriers and even handle pass coverage. His linebacker skills would later help the Eagles reach championship heights.

Wojciechowicz had his moments in Detroit—a team-record seven interceptions in 1944—but his teams barely challenged respectability. When the Lions unexpectedly released him early in the 1946 season, Eagles coach Greasy Neale signed the fun-loving ironman and turned him into a defensive specialist. Wojciechowicz, positioned on the outside of Neale's creative "7-4" alignment, was given the job of "chucking" the end to keep him from becoming part of the play.

He was so good at his new job that he routinely covered the opponent's best receiver. Whether

> ## "(Wojciechowicz's style of play) involved hands and feet and arms and maybe even fingernails, plus some conversation."
>
> —*Allie Sherman, former Eagles assistant coach*

destroying their timing or covering them after release, Wojciechowicz shut down some of the NFL's best pass-catchers. Not coincidentally, the Eagles' defense thrived and Philadelphia enjoyed a three-year stretch (1947-49) in which it won consecutive Eastern Division titles and two championships.

Wojie was equal parts locker room comedian and on-field crazy. One opponent described him as "a thousand elbows put together without a plan." Wojciechowicz retired with 19 interceptions after the 1950 season, never an All-Pro or Pro Bowl selection because of his unfortunate career and position parallel with New York's Mel Hein and Chicago's Bulldog Turner.

Player/Year elected: 1989

WILLIE WOOD

Born: 12-23-36, Washington, D.C. **Ht/Wt:** 5-10/190 **College:** USC **Drafted:** Undrafted **Primary position:** DB **Career statistics:** Interceptions, 48, 2 TDs; Punt Returns, 187 att., 7.4 avg., 2 TDs **Interceptions leader:** 1962 **Teams:** Packers 1960-71 **Championship teams:** NFL 1961, '62, '65, '66, '67 **Super Bowl champions:** 1966, '67 seasons **Honors:** 1960s All-Decade Team

WOOD

He was a 190-pound gnat who annoyed and buzzed some of the great quarterbacks in football history. Pound for pound, Green Bay safety Willie Wood created more offensive turmoil than most of his contemporaries in the colorful and rugged 1960s. He was the go-to ballhawk, the buck-stops-here last line of defense for a Packers team that won five championships, including the first two Super Bowls, during a fairy-tale 12-year career.

Nobody was more consistent for Vince Lombardi's Packers than the 5-foot-10 Wood, an undrafted USC quarterback who had to earn a roster spot during a 1960 training camp tryout. He won over the Packers with his hard-nosed desire and superior athleticism while learning a position he had never played. Lombardi was especially impressed with his instincts and leaping ability, which Wood displayed by easily dunking the ball over the goal-post crossbar.

Wood primarily returned punts for the 1960 Packers, although he was burned for two touchdown passes by Baltimore great Johnny Unitas in a late-season start. By 1961, however, he was the starting right safety who went on to play 154 straight games through his 1971 retirement. Wood provided a preview of his big-play future with five 1961 interceptions and two punt-return TDs and he earned the first of eight Pro Bowl invitations while posting a league-leading nine interceptions a year later.

Wood did not have sprinter speed, but his uncanny instincts were always front and center. His 48 career interceptions were visible reminders of his ballhawking ability. The bruises he delivered with hard hits were more subtle. No Packers defender produced more crucial big plays than Wood, who was admired for his work ethic and upbeat honesty.

Wood's signature moment came in Super Bowl I when he intercepted Kansas City quarterback Len Dawson and returned the ball 50 yards, setting up a touchdown that turned a 14-10 Packers lead into a 35-10 rout. After he retired, he coached briefly in the World Football League and Canadian Football League.

> "Wood sets the style for the Packer type of defense. Willie gives them the ability to call one defense and get many interpretations of it. He smells a play and takes off, strictly on his own, to break up a play he should never even have been near."
>
> —Raymond Berry

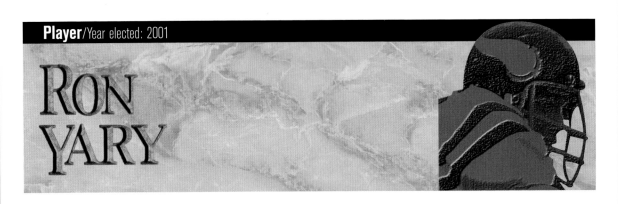

RON YARY

Born: 8-16-46, Chicago, Ill. **Ht/Wt:** 6-5/255 **College:** USC **Drafted:** 1968, 1st round, Vikings **Primary position:** OT
Teams: Vikings 1968-81; Rams 1982 **Honors:** 1970s All-Decade Team

As the blue-collar blocker for one of pro football's premier blue-collar teams, Ron Yary was an enticing blend of size, speed, quickness, strength and toughness. But defenders who had to deal with Minnesota's 6-foot-5, 255-pound right tackle from 1968-81 were more intimidated by his simmering intensity. Every game, every play was a career-defining battle for the fire-breathing warrior who helped clear a path to four Super Bowls.

Few opponents could match Yary's every-play intensity, which came with a trademark grunt, fundamental precision and unyielding determination. He was an outstanding run-blocker who would get upset when plays were called to the other side of the line, a rugged pass protector who engaged in fierce battles with the best defensive ends of his era. Minnesota practices were never dull with Yary doing mortal combat with equally intense teammate Carl Eller.

No one ever questioned the heart of the rangy youngster who arrived in Minnesota as the 1968 first overall draft pick out of USC, winner of the Outland Trophy. Yary was quiet and modest, an obviously intelligent kid with a relentless work ethic. When coach Bud Grant, known for his reluctance to play rookies, kept him on the bench in 1968, Yary brooded. But by 1969, he was an offensive

> ## "If you saw him line up, if you just looked at him, he didn't seem like a great physical specimen. He was big enough, tall enough, strong enough. But it's when he played that you said, 'Holy smokes, he just knocked that man backwards.' Or in his pass protection, that his feet were too good. That's when you saw the real Ron Yary."
>
> —*Bud Grant, 2001, The Associated Press*

centerpiece for the 12-2, Super Bowl-bound Vikings. Four times Minnesota advanced to the big game in the 1970s and four times it lost, no minor frustration for the Vikings' worst loser. But 11 division championships eased Yary's pain, as did seven Pro Bowl invitations and eight straight All-NFC citations. Yary's performance level was remarkably consistent, thanks to his burning desire to be the best offensive tackle in professional football.

That pride and desire also kept him in the line-up. The Chicago-born star missed only five games in 14 Minnesota seasons and played several 1980 contests on a broken foot. Yary ended his 15-year career after playing the 1982 season with the Los Angeles Rams.

Player/Year elected: 2001

JACK YOUNGBLOOD

Born: 1-26-50, Jacksonville, Fla. **Ht/Wt:** 6-4/247 **College:** Florida **Drafted:** 1971, 1st round, Rams **Primary position:** DE
Teams: Rams 1971-84 **Honors:** 1970s All-Decade Team

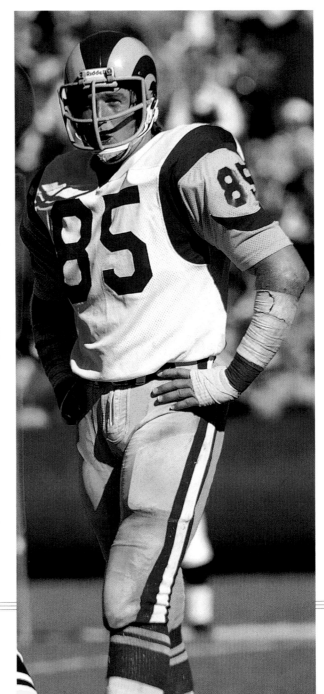

Nobody was more entitled to his football swagger than Jack Youngblood, the so-called "John Wayne of pro football." Not only did the colorful and hard-charging defensive end epitomize one of the stingiest defenses of the 1970s, he inspired it with painful and heroic fervor. NFL legend will forever remind us of a determined Youngblood battling courageously on a broken leg, trying vainly to rally his Los Angeles Rams to victory in Super Bowl XIV.

Youngblood's legacy was sealed by that performance, but it was only half the story. The 6-foot-4, 247-pound ironman actually fractured his fibula in a 1979 divisional playoff game against Dallas, played the following week in the NFC championship game with a plastic brace and never missed a practice leading to the Super Bowl. It was typical Youngblood, who played 201 straight games and 202 of a possible 203 during a remarkable 14-year career.

When healthy, the former University of Florida star was a determined run-stopper and sack specialist who could blow past slow offensive tackles, outsmart quicker ones. Youngblood was so impressive as a 1971 rookie that the Rams traded aging Deacon Jones, a future Hall of Famer. Youngblood was a starter by 1973 and the defensive captain for teams that won an unprecedented seven straight Western Division titles and played in five NFC championship games, winning only one.

The unpredictable and always intense Youngblood unnerved quarterbacks with blood-

"He was the most unique football player I've ever been around. No one worked harder to be great than Jack. People assume that greatness is a gift, that you just have it. It's not true. I think Jack understood how hard and brutal greatness is."

— *John Robinson, former Rams coach*

curdling screeches as he closed in for the sack, prompting flinches that sometimes produced incomplete passes. Off the field, he hung out with teammates who dressed like cowboys and called themselves "The Outlaws," dedicated to searching out saloons in every league city. Youngblood was popular in Los Angeles, an easy target for fan abuse anywhere else he played.

Statistics (sacks were not official until 1982) credit Youngblood with 24 career sacks, but unofficial totals put him in the 150 range. He also recovered 10 fumbles and earned seven Pro Bowl invitations before back problems forced him to retire after the 1984 season.

HALL OF FAME INDEX BY CLASS

Name	Class	Page	Name	Class	Page	Name	Class	Page
Jim Otto	1980	276	Mel Blount	1989	46	Charlie Joiner	1996	170
Red Badgro	1981	28	Terry Bradshaw	1989	48	Mel Renfro	1996	292
George Blanda	1981	44	Art Shell	1989	312	Mike Haynes	1997	142
Willie Davis	1981	82	Willie Wood	1989	392	Wellington Mara	1997	229
Jim Ringo	1981	296	Buck Buchanan	1990	58	Don Shula	1997	314
Doug Atkins	1982	26	Bob Griese	1990	128	Mike Webster	1997	376
Sam Huff	1982	162	Franco Harris	1990	140	Paul Krause	1998	187
George Musso	1982	260	Ted Hendricks	1990	146	Tommy McDonald	1998	239
Merlin Olsen	1982	274	Jack Lambert	1990	190	Anthony Munoz	1998	258
Bobby Bell	1983	36	Tom Landry	1990	192	Mike Singletary	1998	318
Sid Gillman	1983	118	Bob St. Clair	1990	302	Dwight Stephenson	1998	334
Sonny Jurgensen	1983	178	Earl Campbell	1991	64	Eric Dickerson	1999	88
Bobby Mitchell	1983	246	John Hannah	1991	138	Tom Mack	1999	224
Paul Warfield	1983	372	Stan Jones	1991	174	Ozzie Newsome	1999	266
Willie Brown	1984	56	Tex Schramm	1991	308	Billy Shaw	1999	311
Mike McCormack	1984	238	Jan Stenerud	1991	333	Lawrence Taylor	1999	350
Charley Taylor	1984	346	Lem Barney	1992	29	Howie Long	2000	218
Arnie Weinmeister	1984	378	Al Davis	1992	80	Ronnie Lott	2000	220
Frank Gatski	1985	112	John Mackey	1992	226	Joe Montana	2000	250
Joe Namath	1985	262	John Riggins	1992	294	Dan Rooney	2000	299
Pete Rozelle	1985	300	Dan Fouts	1993	110	Dave Wilcox	2000	382
O.J. Simpson	1985	316	Larry Little	1993	212	Nick Buoniconti	2001	60
Roger Staubach	1985	330	Chuck Noll	1993	270	Marv Levy	2001	209
Paul Hornung	1986	156	Walter Payton	1993	284	Mike Munchak	2001	256
Ken Houston	1986	158	Bill Walsh	1993	370	Jackie Slater	2001	320
Willie Lanier	1986	198	Tony Dorsett	1994	96	Lynn Swann	2001	340
Fran Tarkenton	1986	344	Bud Grant	1994	123	Ron Yary	2001	394
Doak Walker	1986	368	Jimmy Johnson	1994	167	Jack Youngblood	2001	396
Larry Csonka	1987	78	Leroy Kelly	1994	184	George Allen	2002	20
Len Dawson	1987	84	Jackie Smith	1994	322	Dave Casper	2002	68
Joe Greene	1987	124	Randy White	1994	380	Dan Hampton	2002	136
John Henry Johnson	1987	168	Jim Finks	1995	104	Jim Kelly	2002	180
Jim Langer	1987	196	Henry Jordan	1995	176	John Stallworth	2002	324
Don Maynard	1987	234	Steve Largent	1995	200	Marcus Allen	2003	21
Gene Upshaw	1987	362	Lee Roy Selmon	1995	309	Elvin Bethea	2003	40
Fred Biletnikoff	1988	42	Kellen Winslow	1995	388	Joe DeLamielleure	2003	86
Mike Ditka	1988	92	Lou Creekmur	1996	77	James Lofton	2003	214
Jack Ham	1988	134	Dan Dierdorf	1996	90	Hank Stram	2003	336
Alan Page	1988	279	Joe Gibbs	1996	114			